Items should be returned to a library by closing
time on or before the date stamped above,
unless a renewal has been granted.

Swindon
BOROUGH COUNCIL

Pink Ice

Pink Ice

Britain and the
South Atlantic Empire

KLAUS DODDS

I.B.Tauris *Publishers*
LONDON • NEW YORK

Published in 2002 by I.B.Tauris & Co Ltd
6 Salem Road, London W2 4BU
175 Fifth Avenue, New York NY 10010
Website: http://www.ibtauris.com

In the United States and Canada distributed by Palgrave Macmillan, a division of
St. Martin's Press, 175 Fifth Avenue, New York NY 10010

ISBN   Hardback 1 86064 769 3
         Paperback 1 86064 770 7

A full CIP record for this book is available from the British Library
A full CIP record for this book is available from the Library of Congress

Library of Congress catalog card: available

Typeset in Stone by Dexter Haven Associates, London
Printed and bound in Great Britain by MPG Books, Bodmin

CONTENTS

ILLUSTRATIONS

1 The author at Pendulum Cove, Deception Island.

2 A 'Las Malvinas son Argentinos' signpost near the Argentine–Brazilian border. These signs are found all over the country and serve as important reminders of Argentina's territorial ambitions.

3 A British surveyor working at Turning Point, Livingston Island, in the summer season 1955–6. Reproduced by permission of Peter Mott.

4 The abandoned Norwegian whaling station at Stromness Bay, South Georgia, showing the large storage tanks used for whale oil.

5 The Governor's residence, Stanley, Falkland Islands.

6 Half Moon Island, South Shetlands. This aerial photograph was taken in January 1956.

7 A view of the northern tip of the Antarctic Peninsula.

8 Liberation Monument, Stanley. The monument was built and funded by Falkland Islanders as a gesture of remembrance to the British servicemen who lost their lives in 1982.

9 A signpost for the local authority in Argentina's southernmost city, Ushuaia, which is also the capital of the province of Tierra del Fuego, Antarctica and the South Atlantic Islands.

10 A spectacular iceberg in the Lemaire Channel, Antarctica.

11 The author first travelled to the Antarctic on board the Russian registered vessel, *Akademik Shuleykin*. The vessel is flying the Union Jack because it was moored in Falkland Islands waters.

12 Tom Smith's famous photograph of a British soldier accepting a cup of tea from a Falkland Islands family in May 1982. Reproduced by permission of the Press Association.

13 Port Lockroy Base in Antarctica. Originally constructed in the 1940s as part of the Falkland Islands Dependencies Survey's activities, it is now a major tourist attraction.

14 The Malvinas Memorial at Ushuaia. The image shows the outline of the two main islands of the Falklands/Malvinas.

15 Whalebone Arch, Stanley. A reminder that the Falkland Islands were a major transit point for Antarctic expeditions and oceanic voyages.

16 A sign for the Colony Bar in the Upland Goose Hotel, Stanley. The Colony Bar used to be the preserve of farm managers and British expatriate employees.

17 A snowcat attached to the 1955–8 Commonwealth Trans-Antarctic Expedition. Unfortunately the rivalry between the two leaders, Sir Vivian Fuchs and Sir Edmund Hillary, overshadowed the success of the Antarctic crossing.

18 Falkland Islands Governor Donald Lamont in full ceremonial uniform during Queen Elizabeth II's birthday celebrations, April 2000.

19 Referee Kreitlin moves in to send off the Argentine captain, Rattin, during the 1966 Argentina–England World Cup quarter-final. By permission of Popperfoto.

20 Liberation Monument, Stanley. Inscribed on the front of the monument are the words: 'For those who liberated us'.

21 A signpost warning of a minefield outside Stanley. It is estimated that about 18,000 mines buried by the Argentine forces remain to be cleared. Under the 1997 Ottawa Convention, Argentina and Britain have agreed to conduct a feasibility study to see whether they can all be cleared in due course.

22 One Falkland Islander's protest at the improving Anglo–Argentine relations, which witnessed Argentine passport-holders being allowed to enter the Falklands from July 1999 onwards – after a 17-year ban. The sign reads: 'Long Island. No access to Argies, 7 Councillors or Argie Supporters. God Save the Queen. Neil Watson.'

23 Lord Chalfont, the then Foreign Office Minister, made an unpopular appeal to the Falkland Islanders in November 1968 to consider a closer political future with Argentina. To the left is his private secretary, M. L. Tait, and to the right is the then Governor of the Falkland Islands, Sir Cosmo Haskard. The photograph was taken by John Leonard on 24 November 1968 and is reproduced with his kind permission.

24 King Edward Point, Grytviken, South Georgia. The buildings in the foreground were home to the British armed forces, who were stationed there in small numbers between 1982 and 2001. The British Antarctic Survey (BAS) now maintains a scientific station at King Edward Point.

25 The RAF air link between RAF Brize Norton (Oxfordshire), Ascension Island and the Falkland Islands has been vital to the post-1982 security of the Falklands.

26 (a) An Argentine stamp released after the 1982 conflict, commemorating the struggle and reminding citizens of the Argentine territorial claim to South Georgia and the South Sandwich Islands;
   (b) An Argentine stamp depicting tri-continental Argentina – mainland, insular and polar territories;
   (c) A British Antarctic territory stamp depicting the HMS *William Scoresby*, a frequent visitor to Antarctica in the 1940s and 1950s;
   (d) A British Antarctic Territory stamp showing HMS *Endurance*, the ice patrol vessel whose uncertain future in the months leading up to the 1982 Argentine invasion provoked a major defence review crisis.

In general terms, Argentine stamps tend to depict the relative geographical proximity of the Falklands and Antarctica, while British stamps focus on the people and ships that have operated in the region.

FIGURES

GLOSSARY OF ACRONYMS

AA	Australian Archives
ATCP	Antarctic Treaty Consultative Parties
ATS	Antarctic Treaty System
BAS	British Antarctic Survey
CCAMLR	Convention for the Conservation of Marine Living Resources
CRAMRA	Convention on the Regulation of Antarctic Mineral Resources Activities
CTAE	Commonwealth Trans-Antarctic Expedition
DEA	Department of External Affairs
DCS	Directorate of Colonial Surveys
FA	Football Association
FIC	Falkland Islands Company
FICZ	Falkland Islands Interim Conservation and Management Zone
FID	Falkland Islands Dependencies
FIDASE	Falkland Islands Dependencies Aerial Survey Expedition
FIDS	Falkland Islands Dependencies Survey
FO/FCO	Foreign Office/Foreign and Commonwealth Office (official title of the Foreign Office after 1968)
ICJ	International Court of Justice
IGM	Military Geography Institute
IGY	International Geophysical Year
NAC	National Archives of Canada
NERC	Natural and Environmental Research Council
NZA	New Zealand Archives
PRO	Public Record Office
RRS	Royal Research Ship
SAA	South African Archives
SATO	South Atlantic Treaty Organisation
SPRI	Scott Polar Research Institute
UKFIC	United Kingdom Falkland Islands Committee

FOREWORD

Peter J. Beck

Reading Klaus Dodds's manuscript was akin to thumbing through a photo album in the sense that it offered a vivid reminder of several events that I had not only lived through but also written about at some time or another. It was interesting – often revealing – to look again at these episodes through the eyes of another person, particularly someone whose vision benefits from, say, access to recent archival openings, interviews with individuals involved in these events and knowing what happened next.

Perhaps the key memory evoked by the manuscript concerned my visit made to the Falkland Islands in the mid-1990s. Standing on the foreshore in Ross Road, Stanley, it was difficult to imagine that this peaceful setting – despite being Stanley's main thoroughfare, only a passing Land Rover or the occasional shriek of a seabird broke the silence – had been a central battleground in the 1982 Anglo–Argentine Falklands War. However, a short walk away, the Liberation Monument provided a sobering reminder of the human costs of war, just as any mention of Argentina in the bar of the nearby Upland Goose Hotel provoked a predictably hostile reaction. As a result, reading the manuscript recalled images combining wartime events at, say, Goose Green and Darwin, with post-war reconstruction and investment in the form of the new airport and military base at Mount Pleasant. References to the perennial controversies about the Argentine cemetery touched upon the most moving experience of any trip to the Islands; that is visits to the modest memorial in honour of Lieutenant Colonel H. Jones, and the Argentine military cemetery. For the latter, the whole scene, bathed in sunlight, struck an unforgettable blend of white crosses and fencing set against green grass, even if the cemetery's remote and isolated location means that it is hidden away to avoid confronting Islanders' sensitivities.

Nor can any British visitor forget the distance and remoteness of the Falklands from Britain. Following a brief transit stop at Ascension Island, the RAF Tristar flew over an empty ocean for what seemed an eternity. And Britain's Antarctic territory is even further south! Even so, the term 'Far South' has not found favour with Dr Dodds, who suggests an alternative term. Admittedly, I saw no pink ice on my visit, but his chosen descriptor focuses our attention upon the imperial dimension, particularly the manner in which the Falkland Islands, South Georgia and British Antarctic territory can be interpreted as making up Britain's South Atlantic Empire. Historically, British Governments attempted to paint many parts of the world red or pink – depending upon the atlas's colour chart – not excluding the southern polar regions. By contrast, in Argentina maps and textbooks described and coloured Britain's South Atlantic Empire as Argentine in what might be regarded as an audacious act of cartographical wish-fulfilment stressing that the Islas Malvinas, far from being a 20-hour flight from RAF Brize Norton in Oxfordshire, are a mere 300 miles away from Argentina.

Reference to the 'pink ice' phrase reminded me of the help given to my research by Nick Barker, who captained HMS *Endurance* at the time of the Argentine invasion of the Islands. In 1986 he published *Red Ice*, a story set in the South Atlantic. The Admiralty's refusal to allow publication of a thesis written as part of a post-war research study forced him to use a novel to articulate his views about South Atlantic geopolitics, a theme omnipresent in Dr Dodds's research, including this publication.

This book is timely given the way in which the ongoing Anglo–Argentine sovereignty disputes over the South Atlantic region were highlighted in December 2001 by speculation about the implications of Argentina's political and financial crises for the Falklands dispute and the survival of democracy. The 1982 war established the continued ability of seemingly marginal and insignificant territories – what James Callaghan called the 'dots on the map' – to give rise to serious international problems. The Falklands dispute has been followed by problems focused upon, say, Grenada, Kuwait and Afghanistan. I often quoted Callaghan's views when looking back on the fate of one of my initial studies of Britain, Argentina and the Falklands dispute. Submitted for publication in early 1982, it was described by the journal's referee as well written and researched but was rejected, principally upon the grounds of apparent irrelevance! A few months later the dispute escalated into war. Certainly, South Atlantic affairs have established the ephemeral nature of relevance and irrelevance alongside the value of critical informed studies on such international friction points. Over the years, Dr Dodds's publications have proved very relevant and helped to fulfil this need for critical informed studies, especially as the short, bitter war failed to resolve the Anglo–Argentine disputes over the sovereignty of South Atlantic territories.

Whether or not the war transformed Britain in the way proclaimed by Margaret Thatcher remains debatable. Was Britain really 'Great' again? However, the event did foster a Falklands renaissance in more ways than one. Selected manifestations of the infamous 'Falklands factor', like the new airfield and military base, have already been mentioned, but another consequence was enhanced academic interest in the region. Dr Dodds uses the acknowledgements section to provide a rationale for his research on the South Atlantic, but some might view him as yet another manifestation of the Falklands factor. We first met when he was doing his doctorate, and for several years he seemed a permanent fixture at conferences and seminars on South Atlantic and Antarctic matters. Having gained his doctorate, he has continued to work on the region; indeed, in Britain he has emerged as the leading and most active researcher on the political, legal, economic, social and cultural perspectives of the Falklands and Antarctic questions. Nor has his research been imprisoned by narrow disciplinary boundaries. On the contrary, he has shown the merits of adopting an interdisciplinary approach to South Atlantic studies. In particular, this book's coverage of footballing and agricultural relations yields illuminating insights into frequently ignored topics, while touching on aspects of contemporary relevance, given the serious foot-and-mouth outbreak in Britain in 2001 and the fact that Argentina and Britain have been drawn in the same group for the 2002 World Cup finals. Readers will also find that this book casts light upon issues of wider relevance. These include the role of science as an instrument of politics and law, the power of maps as politico-legal statements, the gap between perceptions and international realities, the decline of empire, the impact of personality upon events, and particularly the role of the men and – in the case of one Falklands Governor – women.

Peter J. Beck

Kingston upon Thames, December 2001

PREFACE

One of the amateur painters on that [ill-fated Scott] expedition once showed Wilson a snow scene, which he had just painted in which the snow was mostly a dead white. Wilson said, 'Is it what you really saw, white snow? It's very rare, you know.' There was an argument around the table and at last Wilson said, 'Lets go and have a look at it', and took his friend outside. They walked for a while and on going in again, the friend told the others, 'Blow me if Bill isn't right, it's gone pinkish since I painted it'. The amateur was your author.[1]

Beyond 40 degrees there was no law and beyond 50 degrees no God. [Norwegian whaling folklore]

The Antarctic, as Norwegian whalers recognised, was largely beyond the realm of human realisation until the twentieth century. Surrounded by myths, false claims and heroic endeavour, it was coveted by the British in particular, who sent naval officers, scientists and artists to explore the far ends of the earth. The voyages of Captain James Cook during the reign of King George III (1760–1820) initiated a long and largely distinguished scientific and exploratory interest in the Antarctic and the Southern Ocean. By the turn of the twentieth century, the ill-fated Captain Scott and his party even attempted to occupy the South Pole in the name of King George V. While the rival Norwegian party under Roald Amundsen shattered the hopes and dreams of the British establishment, Amundsen's compatriots and their whaling activities provoked the British to claim Antarctica for the Crown. Formally incorporated into the British Empire in 1908 and again in 1917, the Antarctic Peninsula and windblown island chains such as South Shetland became part of a pink-tinted empire. In the 1920s, the then Secretary of State for the Colonies, Leo Amery, entertained a hope that the entire Antarctic continent would be annexed to the British Empire. This aspiration was dashed by the territorial ambitions of France and Norway and by the overlapping claims of Argentina and Chile to the Antarctic Peninsula. Until the Second World War, the regulation of whaling provided a reasonable economic rationale for holding onto a polar empire, and science offered a scholarly excuse for an effective presence.

In the aftermath of the Second World War, continued ownership of polar land became controversial, as the US implicitly and Argentina explicitly challenged the imperial authority of London. No stranger to territorial conflict, Argentina was a persistent thorn in the flesh of the British polar empire, not least because it never accepted that the loss of the Falkland Islands in 1833 should simply be put down to imperial experience. Separated by only 400 miles of South Atlantic Ocean, the Falklands remained an outstanding and frustrating territorial grievance, and post-1945 Argentine Governments recognised that there were new opportunities to pursue these claims with the passing of the European and imperial order. For those British officials charged with managing the British polar empire, including the

Falklands, these territories presented particularly difficult but at the same inviting challenges. On the one hand, remote colonies such as the Falklands were no longer seen to be strategically significant in an era dominated by air travel and missile technology rather than by steam ships and shipping lanes. On the other hand, the Falklands were populated by a small community determined to remind their political masters in London of their loyal, white and British qualities. Following anti-colonial resolutions in the UN, the Falklands became a problem despite being populated by colonial subjects unable and unwilling to clamour for independence. Unlike other parts of the British Empire, the Antarctic offered national prestige safe from any interference by an indigenous population.

Living and working on the edge of the British Empire could also be enjoyable, as successive generations of white men were able to sledge across the polar ice with little to fear from native populations.[2] Scott and his team carried their party outfits and the men attached to the Falkland Islands Dependencies Survey (FIDS) had, by and large, the time of their lives. Governors of the Falkland Islands are still expected to order their colonial uniforms, complete with white feathers for the ceremonial hat, from the London-based outfitters Hogg and Johnstone. Dressing up could be fun and as the former Governor of the Falkland Islands, Sir Rex Hunt recalled in his autobiography:

> As a colonial officer at heart [Hunt served in Uganda and Malaya], I was thrilled at the prospect of the Falkland Islands. It had been the ambition of most young district officers to the Colonial Service, one day to become a Governor; but my generation was too late – or so I thought until now. Although the Falklands enjoys a vigorous democracy, the population of about two thousand is too small to have independence. It has, therefore to be a colony. Today colonialism is a dirty word, but there is no doubt that the British colonial officers always served the people with dedication and devotion, administering British justice with fairness and impartiality.[3]

It is easy to forget that the Falklands, the South Atlantic and Antarctic were not always considered problems, especially in the era before the dissolution of the Colonial Office and the amalgamation of the Commonwealth and Foreign Offices in 1968. With the absence of a 'native' population clamouring for a post-colonial future, colonialism did not have to be a 'dirty' word. As Sir Rex recounted, 'Port Stanley had a Victorian charm' and the Falkland Islands reminded him of 'James Herriot country and I felt immediately at home'.[4] The small numbers of Royal Marines stationed on the Falkland Islands in the 1960s and 1970s also enjoyed themselves, and some even left their mark on the genetic stock of the local community.[5]

Even those who were more at home in the international corridors of power could find opportunities to relieve the tedium of diplomatic negotiations concerning the future of Antarctica. Brian Roberts, the architect of the 1959 Antarctic Treaty and the Foreign Office's polar advisor for over 30 years, revealed how he was able to find time to unwind after a long day at the conference table:

> In the evening I found a bar with a coloured band possessing rhythm and producing ear-splitting noise. Two drummers who performed solo with prodigious gusto gave great satisfaction to the rock 'n' roll dancers whose careless abandon was most stimulating, I found the whole performance a splendid antidote to the conference atmosphere.[6]

This book explores how British officials and political figures maintained a foothold on the apparent edge of the world and how these distant territories were not only administered and mapped in a literal sense but also invested with cultural significance and national importance. Antarctica in particular, although remote from London, became synonymous with British exploratory zeal, ingenuity and pride. Successive post-war British Governments approached the South Atlantic in a fundamentally different manner to their main rival, Argentina. It was argued that ideas attached to 'people and principles' clashed with Argentine concerns over 'territorial integrity and geographical continuity'. For much of the second half of the twentieth century, British officials considered 'Argentina' an enigma. For those with experiences of South America prior to 1945, the situation was an unhappy one, as the old idea of Argentina being part of an 'informal empire' or even the 'sixth dominion' was dashed by claims that Argentine political leaders were hysterical, unreliable and addicted to territorial aggrandisement. Despite the pressing need for meat, Anglo–Argentine relations in the post-1945 period were characterised by public arguments over the Falklands, foot-and-mouth disease and even football. When Foreign Office (FO) officials attempted in the late 1960s to persuade Parliament that Argentine sovereignty should prevail over the Falklands, the Falkland Islands' supporters were able to draw upon the support of popular newspapers such as the *Daily Express* to tell their readers that a 'Falklands sell out' was planned. Unlike most British citizens, when the Falklands were invaded in April 1982 Argentine adults and even children could not only locate the disputed Islands on a map but also draw an outline of their geographical shape.

This account provides further evidence that the post-1945 period was not exclusively characterised by imperial decay and preordained decline of global influence and power.[7] The dissolution of the British Empire did not automatically symbolise weakness. Both Labour and Conservative Governments were anxious to retain the UK as the third 'world power', and the Antarctic provided evidence where necessary of Britain's capacity not only to execute spectacular expeditions but also to influence international affairs. Informal ties and formal alliances did provide opportunities for retaining a presence on the world stage, as did a scattered collection of colonies including Gibraltar, Hong Kong and the Falklands. Victory in the Falklands provoked, predictably enough, the *Daily Star* to lead with 'V for victory' and the *Daily Express* with 'VF Day' in June 1982. The then Conservative Government's interest in national character, national identity and imperialism was widely shared by the national media and readily made connections with older victories over the German and Japanese forces.

Despite its opposition to Mrs Thatcher's policy of strengthening British interests in the Falklands and the South Atlantic, the new Labour Government elected in May 1997 has merely consolidated this basic trend. Renamed 'overseas territories', New Labour's white paper on the remaining imperial portfolio confirmed that the 'wishes' of the Falkland Islands community would be respected, and in doing so Argentina would not receive any concessions on sovereignty. A cross-party consensus in Britain on the Falklands question shows little sign of diminishing.

Four major themes relating to Britain's post-1945 involvement in the Antarctic and South Atlantic deserve closer scrutiny. First, there has been little appreciation in Britain of the fact that Argentine views of the Falklands have been strongly conditioned by their formal educational system, which continues to emphasise the ideological significance of the 'loss' of the Islas Malvinas. The relative geographical proximity of the Falklands and the Antarctic plays a significant role in shaping public and political opinion in Argentina.

Second, the Falklands invasion of April 1982 needs to be situated within a longer historical and wider geographical context. The Falklands were only one element in the South Atlantic Empire and Anglo–Argentine territorial competition, which stretched from the Falklands to the South Sandwich Islands lying over 1200 miles beyond Stanley. Anglo–Argentine disputes over the South Atlantic and Antarctic were also conditioned by the activities of the US and international regimes, notably the Antarctic Treaty System.

Third, I have often felt that the British-based Latin American specialists who comment on the Falkland question have rarely treated the Falkland Islands community with empathy, let alone any form of sympathy. The Falkland Islanders should not be held responsible for the ongoing sovereignty crisis.

Finally, Anglo–Argentine relations surrounding the Falklands and Antarctic tend to be treated in an isolated manner and thus neglect other cultural and economic dimensions such as cinema, football, trade and commerce in the post-1945 period. Even England–Argentine football matches could be most troublesome, as in the case of the then England manager Alf Ramsey's infamous comment about the Argentine players being 'animals', which had, as we shall see, diplomatic consequences for the disputed Falklands in the aftermath of the 1966 World Cup.

NOTES ON PREFACE

1   F. Debenham, *Antarctica* (London, Herbert Jenkins, 1959), p. 200.

2   See L. Bloom, *Gender on Ice: American Ideologies of Polar Exploration* (Minneapolis MN, University of Minnesota Press, 1994), for one attempt to explore these issues further.

3   R. Hunt, *My Falkland Days* (Exeter, David and Charles, 1992), p. ix.

4   Hunt, *My Falklands Days*, p. 7, and author interview with Hunt, 26 January 1991.

5   This observation is based on interviews with retired Royal Marines living in Britain and the Falkland Islands. For an important study on empire and masculinity see G. Dawson, *Soldier Heroes: British Adventure, Empire and the Imagining of Masculinities* (London, Routledge, 1994).

6   Scott Polar Research Institute (SPRI) Archives MS 1308/9;BJ Diary entry of Brian Roberts for 25 October 1959.

7   See, for example, the careful analysis of D. Low in *The Eclipse of Empire* (Cambridge, Cambridge University Press, 1991).

ACKNOWLEDGEMENTS

In 1951–2, at the age of 17, my late Scottish father was chosen together with three other cadets to join the German four-mast sailing ship, the *Passat*, and sail across the South Atlantic ocean to the ports and cities of Argentina, Uruguay and Brazil. He witnessed Evita Perón's funeral in Argentina, and my brother and I remember as children hearing his account of post-war Argentina and the exciting stories of life in the 'roaring forties'. A year later, he rejoined the British Merchant Navy. By 1958, and now a flight lieutenant in the Royal Navy's Fleet Air Arm, his aircraft carrier HMS *Albion* embarked on a world tour which included a visit to the South African port city of Durban. In 1959, at a social reception for the European consular officials on board the HMS *Albion*, my father met my Austrian-born mother, and years later they were married in Edinburgh. After a farewell flypast over Durban, HMS *Albion* continued its 'world tour' via Cape Town to South America where, 60 miles from Buenos Aires in the supposedly dredged channel, the BBC were able to report that she was 'the first British warship to land on Argentine soil'. When I asked my mother about her abiding memories of Durban, she recalled the pungent smell (when a southwesterly wind blew) emanating from the whaling stations responsible for processing whales caught in the immense Southern Ocean. Although my father died in February 1988, I was fortunate enough to be able to study the geopolitics of the South Atlantic at Bristol University, and my younger brother became a captain in the British Merchant Navy.

Throughout my academic career, I have benefited from the support of a number of friends and colleagues. I am still indebted to my doctoral supervisor, Dr Leslie Hepple, for providing me with the opportunity to carry out research at Bristol University in the early 1990s. Thereafter, I was fortunate to have Professors Susan Smith, David Sugden and Mike Summerfield as colleagues at the University of Edinburgh. My colleagues and friends at Royal Holloway, University of London, have been generous in their support: I am very grateful to Dr Justin Champion, Professor Felix Driver, Dr David Gilbert, Professor Rob Imrie, Professor David Simon and Professor Tony Stockwell for their comments on particular chapters of the book. I am also very grateful to Jerry Lee, Justin Jacyno, Nigel Page and Jenny Kynaston for their collective cartographic and technical skills. The research assistance and support of Bridget Robison and Kathryn Yusoff was most helpful. Dr Andrew Cook, Professor Denis Cosgrove, Professor James Dunkerley, Professor Mike Heffernan, Professor Peter Hennessy, Dr Jim McAdam, Professor David Newman, Professor Jeffrey Richards, Dr Beau Riffenburgh, Dr Stephen Royle, Professor Colin Seymour-Ure, Dr John Heap and Dr Bernard Stonehouse also provided invaluable support for this project. I also have the good fortune to be part of a small geopolitical community and have found inspiration in the work of Professor John Agnew, Dr Sanjay Chaturvedi, Dr Simon Dalby, Dr Gerard Toal and Dr James Sidaway. My greatest professional debt lies with Professor Peter Beck, who not only xxii — PINK ICE

reviewed virtually everything I have written on Antarctica and the Falklands, but has also been extraordinarily generous with his time on my account. It is a great honour for me that he has agreed to write a foreword to this book.

I have drawn upon the services of many institutions, including the British Antarctic Survey, the British Film Institute, the British Library, the British Petroleum Archives at the University of Warwick, the Falkland Islands Archives, the Football Association, the Hydrographic Office, the Public Record Office, the Royal Geographical Society and the Scott Polar Research Institute. I owe thanks to all the archivists who have been so generous with their time. My visits to Antarctica New Zealand, National Library of Argentina, the Institute of Geography at the University of Buenos Aires, the Australian Archives, the Australian Antarctic Division, the National Archives of Canada, the South African Archives and the National Archives of New Zealand have been immensely helpful. None of this research work would have been possible without the generous support of the Arts and Humanities Research Board, the British Academy, the Shackleton Scholarship Fund, and in particular the Leverhulme Trust, which allowed me to work with Lara Manovil on related projects concerned with the contemporary situation of the Falklands. As part of that project we had a fascinating series of interviews with the former and now late Argentine foreign minister, Dr Guido Di Tella.

The support from these various research grants enabled me to travel to Argentina and Chile, and on seven occasions to the Falkland Islands, where Mike Rendell of the Malvina House Hotel and Tony Smith of Discovery Tours made my stays comfortable, enjoyable and informative. Sukey Cameron of the Falkland Islands Government Office in London, John Barton, Bob Reid, Phylis Rendell and Councillors John Birmingham, Jan Cheek, Sharon Halford, and Mike Summers were consistently helpful. Successive Governors of the Falkland Islands also agreed to be interviewed and thanks are due to Sir Rex Hunt, Donald Lamont, Jim Parker, Richard Ralph, David Tatham, and especially Sir Cosmo and Lady Haskard. I also owe a great deal to the people of the Falkland Islands who agreed to talk to me, and thank them for their unfailing hospitality and kindness.

I am indebted to all those people – especially current and former civil servants, explorers and politicians – that agreed to be interviewed for this project. These include Dame Margaret Anstee, Lord Chalfont, Lord Carrington, Sir Edmund Hillary, Lord Hurd, Lord Owen, Ted Rowlands MP, the late Lord Shackleton and the late Sir Vivian Fuchs. I had several delightful interviews with Sir Cosmo and Lady Haskard and thank them for their generous hospitality in Ireland. Sir Martin Holdgate and Frank Elliot greatly improved my knowledge of Antarctic science and the pre-1982 commercial life of the Falklands respectively. While many of my interviewees attached to the Foreign and Commonwealth Office and the Ministry of Defence did not want to be publicly acknowledged, I am very grateful to them for their support. None of the aforementioned individuals bears any responsibility for the subsequent analysis, however.

I am also grateful to David Stonestreet and the I. B. Tauris production team for their invaluable support and assistance.

Finally, it is a pleasure to acknowledge the support from my brother who cast a helpful eye over the project. My godparents, Ian and Vivian Ward, have provided me with not only endless support but also generous hospitality in London and west Wales. My wife Carolyn has been wonderfully understanding of my obsession with the Antarctic and the South Atlantic. I am sorry that the dining room in our Kingston home was taken over by my papers for rather longer than she had imagined.

If acknowledgements are the place to recognise your intellectual and personal debts, then my greatest debt lies with my mother. I now understand why it used to be said that there are few certainties in life, but one of these is my mother's love and encouragement. I dedicate this book to her as a small token of a lifelong 'debt'.

Klaus Dodds
Kingston upon Thames
March 2002

1

Limpet Colonies

December [1968] was an absolute watershed. From then on, in my view, in this country the Falkland Islands issue became primarily an issue of domestic politics. Previously, we have regarded it, rightly or wrongly, as largely a foreign-policy issue with, of course, like every foreign-policy issue, some overtones of domestic politics. From then on it was exactly the other way round – a domestic policy with foreign policy overtones.[1]

We have rejected the French system of incorporation, of making them an intrinsic part of the French Department of State with Representatives in the French Assembly…I am going to spend part of next week in Geneva, meeting my opposite Argentine number in another round of negotiations in relation to the Falkland Islands. There you have got the very clear, understandable, fundamental wishes of 1900 people who wish to have nothing whatsoever to do with the Argentine government, except in the form of economic co-operation. Who can blame them? That is their wish.[2]

INTRODUCTION

The Falkland Islands must rank as one of Britain's most persistent 'limpet colonies' which continues openly to defy post-colonial transformation.[3] Located at the northern edge of the Southern Ocean, this colony – equivalent in size to Northern Ireland or the US state of Connecticut but inhabited by just over 2000 people – has steadfastly refused to accept that Argentina should be allowed to exercise sovereignty over these disputed Islands (see figure 1.1).

It would certainly be unfair to accuse the British of being inattentive to the territorial dispute despite the impasse. In the midst of the Cold War, successive British Governments allowed a series of FO ministers and officials to travel to the Falklands in an attempt to cajole the community into accepting a settlement with its South American neighbour. A great deal of time and effort has been expended on defending and negotiating with Argentina over the future of the Islands. Spurred on by the prospect of an agreement and improved commercial relations, the FO

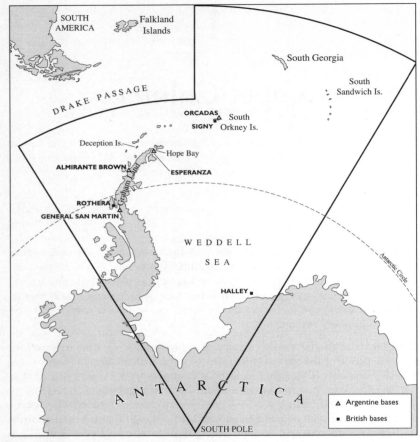

Figure 1.1: The Falkland Islands Dependencies (1917–62)

(later the Foreign and Commonwealth Office, FCO) sought to impose a solution on the Falklands in the late 1960s. Unfortunately for the British negotiators, the seemingly powerless Falkland Islanders now enjoyed support from elements of all the major political parties and the national press, which between them accused the then Wilson Government (1964–70) of abandoning 'loyal' British subjects. By 1968, the Falklands community had become a domestic issue, and the words 'loyal' and 'kith and kin' formed an elaborate code designed to highlight that they were British and white subjects.

British interests in the region were still on the advance in the 1940s and 1950s and remained remarkably resilient despite Latin American specialists in the FO warning of the damage to Anglo–Argentine and wider Anglo–Latin American relations. At times, political leaders and their civil servants have either found their policy options restricted or national prestige enhanced depending on the circumstances. With the ratification of the Antarctic Treaty in 1961, the British territorial claim to the Antarctic was effectively secured, and the diplomatic spotlight once again turned on the Falklands question. Other South Atlantic islands such as St

Helena and Tristan da Cunha were too small and remote to be challenged by any other state. A post-colonial future with Argentina was quite literally unthinkable as the Falklands clung to Britain: when it came to the ultimate test in April 1982, Britain stuck with the Falklands.

GEOPOLITICAL TRANSITION: BRITAIN AND THE END OF EMPIRE

In their influential essay 'The imperialism of decolonization', Louis and Robinson call into question the idea that British enfeeblement was the prime cause of the imperial decline. As they note for the period prior to 1945:

> The difficulty of attributing the fall to British decline is that it leads us into a paradox. Colonial emancipation is not necessarily a sign of metropolitan weakness. Virtual independence was conceded to Canadian, Australasian and South African nationalists before 1914, when Britain was at her strongest. Conversely, when she was much weaker during the inter-war years, the Empire reached its greatest extent, with the addition of the Middle East and more of Africa. By 1940, when there was scarcely strength to defend the home islands, the British were able to crack down on nationalists in India, Egypt and Iran and mobilise the Empire for war.[4]

They neglect to mention the extraordinary twentieth-century expansion of the British Empire in the far south, but they do point to the need for a more refined analytical account of Britain in the aftermath of the Second World War.

These post-war activities did not occur in a geographical vacuum: British officials and political leaders had to reappraise actively a political world greatly changed after six years of global conflict. As Peter Taylor contends, the immediate post-war period led to a reassessment of global politics by the FO and most famously by Winston Churchill in his speech in Fulton in March 1946, which warned of an 'iron curtain' descending over the eastern and central parts of Europe.[5] Maintaining Britain's great-power status was a priority which required officials in the FO to examine how relations with the superpowers could be juggled with British interests in Europe and the Commonwealth. Recent research in geopolitics has drawn attention to the spatial specification of global politics and warned that the meanings attached to place deserve critical attention.[6] Our descriptions of the world are never politically innocent, and geographical descriptions are often critical in facilitating strategic discussion and policy options. These not only occur within policy-making circles as practical forms of geographical reasoning but are reflected in popular culture via cartoons, films, monuments, sport and the formal education system.[7] Geographical expressions do not have to be sophisticated to be effective. Even remote Antarctica, for example, was routinely interpreted by civil servants and national newspapers in the 1940s not only as a token of Anglo–Argentine–Chilean geopolitical rivalry but also as a place of heroism and international scientific co-operation, and a beacon of national prestige.

With the loss of India in 1947 and the debacle of the Suez crisis in 1956, successive post-war British foreign secretaries from Ernest Bevin onwards were eager to retain Britain's place as the third most powerful nation in the world. Whether through the acquisition of nuclear weapons or the consolidation of a 'special relationship' with the US, Britain was anxious to maintain power and influence in the wider world. As the former diplomat Anthony Verrier recalled, the FO saw itself as guiding post-war Britain in a manner which recognised that, despite possessing global interests, attention would have to be focused on the core regions of Europe, the Mediterranean and the Middle East.[8] In other parts of the world, Louis and Robinson suggest that 'the United Kingdom government invested relatively few resources in the imperial upkeep'.[9] Periods of imperial retreat were inevitably followed by episodes of consolidation of influence, such as the period following the initiation of decolonisation in Africa after Ghana's independence in 1957. British officials and ministers sought to extend British power in Antarctica and the South Atlantic, and in order to do so Argentina and Chile were periodically re-imagined as territorial competitors rather than commercial and anti-communist allies.[10] It was also acknowledged that the so-called old Commonwealth states of Australia, Canada, New Zealand and South Africa could assist Britain in retaining influence over a remote region in which Britain, Australia and New Zealand maintained claims to over two-thirds of the entire surface area.

The significance of a place, in this case the Antarctic and South Atlantic, depends almost entirely on the practical geopolitical reasoning of FO ministers and civil servants responsible for defining the national interest. Much of this material is drawn from the released papers of Government departments in the period between the 1940s and 1960s and offers some evidence of Britain's perceived role in the region. Before the Second World War, neither the US nor the Soviet Union had pressed territorial claims; hence their occasional presence did not interfere with British interests in the Antarctic. Anglo–Argentine relations were at that stage overwhelmingly cordial, and few would have imagined the Republic as anything but a reliable friend. After 1945, the situation became tense and the routine depiction of Argentina as a bogeyman unquestionably shaped and constrained policy options. However, the Republic was also seen as a reliable and potentially lucrative source of trade and commerce. Once commercial contact with Argentina improved, it was often argued that the entire Latin American region could be opened up to further British trade.

With British colonial involvement limited to the Falkland Islands, British Guiana and British Honduras, Latin America and even Antarctica assumed considerable significance in the post-1945 period. In the late 1940s, at a time of rationing, the supply of meat from Argentina ensured that the Falklands question retained a policy saliency. The Attlee Government, desperate to initiate economic recovery, was locked in arguments with Argentina over the cost and quantity of meat supplies. This resulted in a hardening of views over the retention of territorial and political interests in the South Atlantic, and was exacerbated by the election of President Juan Domingo Perón in 1946. Undeterred by diplomatic pressure from the US, the new Argentine Government appeared determined to challenge the colonial authority of Britain and the superiority of the US in a region they considered part of their backyard. Under the guise of a 'third position', Argentina was apparently committed to pursuing foreign policies independent of the two superpowers in a manner similar to the Non-Aligned Movement. This show of defiance was costly in the long term, and Argentina found that the Americans were not prepared to force their British allies to relinquish their claims on Antarctica or the Falkland Islands.

Established loyalties in combination with the onset of the Cold War ensured that Argentina was largely isolated from the US plans for greater American hemispheric defence and co-operation.

The determined approach to the Falklands and Antarctic possessions occasionally wavered when doubts over the legal strength of claims were articulated. Britain unsuccessfully proposed on a number of occasions to put these interconnected disputes with Argentina and Chile before international arbitration. From the British point of view, this proposal seemed sensible given the persistent legal challenge of two other states and their vast distance from London. Both South American states rejected these suggestions as inappropriate because they were utterly convinced of the validity of their claims. They doubted whether an international body such as the International Court of Justice would in any case treat their claims in a fair and even-handed manner.

Given the prevailing uncertainties, the creation of the Falkland Islands Dependencies Survey (FIDS) in 1945 signalled a determination to use scientists rather than the regulated activities of Norwegian whalers to consolidate influence in the Antarctic region. As in other parts of the British Empire, the map emerged as a potent and visual symbol of polar sovereignty.[11] Stanley was the major Antarctic gateway and henceforth successive Governors of the Falkland Islands were authorised to use the Royal Navy to patrol and monitor the movements of South American navies. The battleship HMS *Nigeria* was despatched to Antarctic waters in 1948 in order to deter South American vessels from harassing British personnel, and with mission completed proceeded to British Honduras to prevent invasion by Guatemala. At the height of this period of imperial consolidation, Britain under Winston Churchill was prepared to fund the Commonwealth Trans-Antarctic Expedition (CTAE), maintain the FIDS and fund other new expeditions to consolidate territorial claims to a distant part of the empire. The ratification of the Antarctic Treaty in 1961 effectively protected polar claims in the name of international co-operation, but it also forced the advocates of Britain's presence in the far south to persuade the Treasury with scientific rather than political arguments to justify the activities of the FIDS.

The key turning-point was in the late 1960s, when the FO, mindful of a UN resolution calling for negotiations over the Falklands, agreed to transfer the sovereignty of the Falkland Islands once the 'interests' of the small community were secured. Between 1968 and 1982, both Labour and Conservative Governments attempted to secure a settlement with Argentina over the Falklands question. Although aware of mounting opposition in the Falklands and the British Parliament to the plans, the Wilson Government (1964–70), anxious for new commercial opportunities and worried over persistent balance-of-payment crises, sought to consolidate Argentine influence over the Falkland Islands. Under the Heath Government (1970–4), the 1971 Joint Statement on Communications facilitated Argentina's presence in the South Atlantic by ensuring that it was responsible for providing communication, fuel and transport services between the Islands and the South American mainland. The Latin American Department of the FCO hoped that the Falkland Islanders would eventually come to recognise that their long-term interests lay with Argentina and not distant Britain.

Moreover, so it was commonly argued, trade and commerce with Latin America would be unquestionably improved once the Falklands question was settled in favour of Argentina. Unexpectedly, the Falkland Islands community and their lobby in London did not follow the political script and proceeded to call into question the negotiations with Argentina. Successive FO ministers failed to persuade the Falklands community to accept the proposal, despite the parlous state of the local community and inherent dependency on Argentina. Unperturbed, successive Argentine Governments were determined to ensure that the 'wishes' of the Falkland Islanders should not be used as an excuse by British Governments to stall the transfer of sovereignty. Mindful in part of the forthcoming one-hundred-and-fiftieth anniversary of the British permanent settlement (or occupation) of the Falklands, an unpopular military regime invaded the Islands and South Georgia in April 1982.

Faced with arguably one of the most severe foreign-policy disasters since the 1956 Suez crisis, Prime Minister Thatcher decided that the Argentine invasion of the Falklands should not be allowed to go unchallenged. Despite feverish negotiations involving the US and the UN, a task-force was despatched from Portsmouth to engage the Argentine armed forces. After a 74-day occupation, the Falklands were once more restored to the 'British Empire', albeit with the loss of 255 British lives. Given the campaign's relative brevity and successful outcome, Mrs Thatcher was able to claim that the 'Great' had been restored to 'Great Britain'. Her personal determination to maintain influence and sovereignty in the South Atlantic and Antarctic led to the third and decisive phase (1982–present), sometimes called 'Fortress Falklands'. Notwithstanding domestic economic crises, hundreds of million of pounds were found to fund a new airbase in the Falkland Islands and invigorate the British Antarctic Survey (BAS) in order to improve its scientific presence in Antarctica. Mrs Thatcher's efforts and political longevity as Prime Minister consolidated and transformed the economic and political fortunes of the Falkland Islanders. By the time a Labour Government took power in May 1997, the basic Thatcher position of no negotiation over sovereignty had become political orthodoxy, and unlike his predecessors in the 1980s Prime Minister Blair did not embark on sovereignty negotiations with the now democratic Argentina.

NATIONAL PRESTIGE: EXPLORATION, SPORT AND WAR

Victory in the 1982 Falklands War finally erased Dean Acheson's hurtful jibe of 1961 that 'Britain had lost an Empire but not found a role'. The post-war rhetoric of Thatcher and her claim that the 'Great' had been put back into 'Great Britain' became a symbol for British prestige. It also echoed the period after the coronation of Queen Elizabeth II in June 1953, when it was claimed that a new 'Elizabethan era' would be defined by the traditions of gentility, chivalry and soldier-heroes. Great achievements, such as the conquest of the Everest by the New Zealander Sir Edmund Hillary and the Indian-born Norgay Tenzing were taken as symbols of a successful Britain and its Commonwealth.[12] The new Queen spoke of the similarities with her sixteenth-century predecessor when she noted that the country was 'great in spirit and well endowed with men who were ready to encompass the earth'.[13]

Five years later, Hillary and the Anglo-German explorer Sir Vivian Fuchs completed a mechanised crossing of Antarctica. Their achievement seemed to provide further evidence that while earlier British monarchs had presided over an empire, Britain retained a Commonwealth built on 'the highest qualities of the spirit of man: friendship, loyalty, and the desire for freedom and peace'. Notwithstanding the grandiose rhetoric about Commonwealth solidarity and achievement, the endeavours of Fuchs and Hillary were marred by argument over the execution of the continental crossing. Thirty years after Elizabeth II's coronation, Nepalese soldiers serving with the Gurkha regiment successfully clambered over the wind-swept mountains of the Falkland Islands and helped their Commonwealth colleagues repel an unwanted future with Argentina. Both cases illustrate how a multi-national and multi-ethnic dimension combined to achieve a 'Greater' Britain.

Music also defined the nation from aggressive nationalism and self-righteousness to nostalgic patriotism in the period between the despatch of the British task-force in Portsmouth and its return in July 1982. While Argentines were subjected to songs depicting the Islas Malvinas as 'Little lost sisters', the British task-force left with Rod Stewart's 'I am sailing' ringing in their ears. On their return, the veteran Second World War performer Vera Lynn sang, 'We'll meet again' and 'I love this land' in front of flag-waving crowds at Portsmouth harbour.[14] The Falklands victory parade in October 1982 completed this extraordinary outburst of national celebration, when in a manner reminiscent of the VE and VJ Day celebrations of 1945, the 1951 Festival of Britain and the 1953 conquest of Everest state honours were distributed to the deserving participants.

Phrases such as 'island race', 'our boys' and 'rejoice' – used by Thatcher to describe the Falklands Islands community and the achievements of the task-force – were not politically innocent, and their judicious use mobilised support in the face of the threat from Argentina.[15] Since at least 1968, right-wing discourse on immigration and national identity had drawn on a series of biological and cultural metaphors to depict black people as a 'problem' and thus an unwelcome presence in British society. According to Paul Gilroy, images of Argentina as an unwelcome cultural and racial presence were used in 1982 to draw attention not only to the insidious dangers of multicultural life but also to the sad reality of imperial decline. As the conservative commentator Peregrine Worsthorne of the *Sunday Telegraph* noted, 'Most Britons today identify more easily with those of the same stock 8000 miles away than they do with West Indian or Asian immigrants living next door'.[16] The strength of cultural ties not only helped to justify the despatch of the task-force in April 1982 but also articulated an insular rhetoric, which identified Argentina and even elements of British society such as the BBC, students and war critics as opponents.

Although reluctant to explore the more problematic aspects of her political and military victory in the Falklands, Thatcher's evocation of defending another 'island race' from an aggressive continental neighbour drew upon established ideas of masculinity, nationalism, race and patriotism.[17] For many in Parliament, the Falklands were like Britain, a place reluctant to be overwhelmed by unwelcome immigrants. With British troops engaged on the battlefields and in the waters off the Falklands, the Conservative Government and the popular press played their part in legitimising the Falklands campaign. The empire became once again a major jus-tification for the superiority of British national character, and Argentina occupied the place of aggressive competitor previously reserved for European states such as France and Germany. The great imperial polar heroes of the early part of the twentieth century, such as Robert Scott, were replaced by the British armed forces as symbols of imperial pride, manly character and national regeneration. In the wake of the 1980 Iranian Embassy siege, British cinema produced films such as *Who Dares Wins* (1982), which celebrated the military prowess of the Special Air Service (SAS) in overcoming a fictitious bunch of left-wing radicals intent on destroying Britain's nuclear submarine base.

While Argentina was the obvious opponent in the weeks punctuated by fighting, British representations of the enemy between April and June 1982 did not emerge in a cultural vacuum. Among those old enough to remember the 1966 World Cup competition, few failed to remind me of the infamous remark by the English manager Alf Ramsey about the Argentine team playing like 'animals'.[18] Sport and politics became thoroughly intertwined and the FCO recognised that football matches could derail plans to transfer the sovereignty of the Falklands to Argentina. Notwithstanding the elegance of Argentine footballers, polo players and showjumpers, Argentina became identified in the British tabloid media as a country that did not 'play by the rules'. Football now defined Argentina, even if many British football fans welcomed the inclusion of two great Argentine footballers, Ricky Villa and Ossie Ardilles, into English first-division (now premiership) teams in the months preceding the conflict. During the Falklands conflict, newspaper columnists and cartoonists drew parallels with war and football to denigrate Argentina through the persistent stereotypes of the hysterical and cheating nature of Argentines in general. England fans complained of police harassment throughout the 1982 World Cup competition in Spain, and shortly after the conflict some added Argentina to their repertoire of infantile abuse, which was directed even at Ardilles, a respected Tottenham player.[19]

The credibility of national and racial ties reached their limits when the black British sportsman and Olympic champion Daley Thompson refused to carry the Union Jack during the opening of the Commonwealth Games in September 1982. In 1984, despite a general determination to limit the rights of citizenship to immigrants from the new Commonwealth, the white South African runner Zola Budd was granted citizenship in 10 days when it was considered beneficial to British athletics. In 1986, as all English football fans recall, Argentina gained 'revenge' for the Falklands conflict when a controversial display by Diego Maradona sealed England's fate in the Mexico-based World Cup competition. As the *Sun* reflected with its infamous headline, 'Outcha! Argies get their own back on us', the so-called 'hand of God' goal helped 'the South Americans knock us out of the World Cup to get their own back for the hammering they took in the Falklands War four years ago'.[20] After the match English fans were involved in scuffles with Argentine fans wearing T-shirts declaring that 'Las Malvinas son Argentinos'. At the time of writing (summer 2002), the England team has not played a match in Latin America since that fateful 1986 encounter, and the 1998 World Cup match in France with Argentina led to an English loss on penalties and the sending off of one of the team's best players, David Beckham.

THE GEOPOLITICS OF THE SOUTH ATLANTIC

In an intriguing study of Argentine and British primary education, a group of researchers found that Argentine children were far more aware of their nation's geography than their British counterparts.[21] The manner in which Britain and Argentina have mapped their opposing histories on the same terrain is a major concern, given the last 50 years of diplomatic intrigue, political tension and outbreak of war in 1982. For much of the period leading up to the Argentine invasion of the Falklands, public and political understanding of Argentina and Latin America more generally was limited in Britain. Apart from the former British colony of Guyana, the South American continent had been routinely described as a region of low strategic importance. Britain's major geopolitical interests lay in Europe and the Middle East and thus little time and resources were devoted to South American countries, with the exceptions of Argentina, Brazil and Chile. While the FCO sought to promote trade and commercial opportunities, there was scant public consideration of either the strategic importance of the South Atlantic or Argentina's obsession with the 'recovery' of the Falkland Islands and other disputed territories such as South Georgia and Antarctica.

Through the work of the Argentine political scientist Carlos Escudé, we are better able to understand the nature of Argentine nationalism and the significance of a public culture infused with territorial anxieties.[22] Even in the apparently remote areas such as the South Atlantic, Argentina's 'territorial' public culture continues to give excessive emphasis to the defence of national territory and the military production of national maps. Distinctive signposts declaring that 'Las Malvinas son Argentinos' are to be found from the sub-tropical north to the sub-polar south of the Republic. Since the late nineteenth century, the formal curricula of primary and secondary schools have instructed children on the geographical realities of the Republic. Every student is taught that the Falklands belongs to Argentina and that the state has a legitimate right to recover these national territories. Geographical education has a far higher public profile in Argentina compared to Britain, and this perhaps reflects the fact that Argentina's territorial boundaries have often been under dispute from the high-altitude Andes to the frigid waters of the Beagle Channel. The geographical proximity and geological continuity of the Falklands and the Antarctic to Argentina not only consolidates domestic public support but also highlights the unwelcome presence of imperial Britain.

In an important geopolitical study, Leslie Hepple cites the French geopolitical writer Coutau-Begarie's claim that Britain and other NATO countries had been guilty of 'suicidal blindness' vis-à-vis the South Atlantic.[23] During the Cold War, it was suggested that Western strategists were preoccupied with the potential threat of the Soviet blue-water navy and the safety of the oil routes around the Cape of Good Hope. With the exception of British-based studies by Penelope Tremayne and others such as Patrick Wall in the 1970s, the southwest Atlantic was considered marginal.[24] This long-term neglect of the Falklands sector mirrored a wider geopolitical lack of interest in the Anglophone academic and policy-making world. As Jack Child noted astutely, 'If there is one part of the world where geopolitics is flourishing, it is in southern Latin America'.[25] In Argentina and Chile, geopolitics has been an important part of the military and educational curriculum since the 1920s. By drawing attention to the symbolic and strategic value of territory, it has informed and shaped national development strategies, educational programmes and military planning. Under military regimes, geopolitical thinking enjoyed a particular prominence, and military officers produced substantial pieces of work concerning Argentina's territorial and strategic interests.

In complete contrast to British strategic assessments of the southwest Atlantic, therefore, Argentine geopolitical writers and military planners drew public attention to the great importance of the region not only to South American states but also to the West more generally. After the creation of NATO in April 1949, Argentina and Brazil seriously considered the formation of a South Atlantic Treaty Organisation (SATO) in order to defend the region from possible Soviet expansionism. In July 1956, for example, Argentina suggested that naval co-operation in the South Atlantic should form the basis for an organisation dedicated to the defence of Western sea-lanes. While there was limited political progress, the idea of a South Atlantic pact never disappeared from policy debates in Argentina and other potential partners such as South Africa. In 1967, Argentina and South Africa began a series of naval exchanges in the hope of resurrecting a South Atlantic pact in the face of wider diplomatic isolation. Military planning involving other South Atlantic states continued well into the late 1970s, and military-ruled Argentina routinely shared naval intelligence with apartheid South Africa.

On the eve of the Falklands conflict, geopolitical writers urged the military regime to intervene decisively, pointing to the strategic, resource and communication potential of the Falkland Islands to Argentina's future development.[26] The Falklands and the South Atlantic were, in Argentine eyes, not only a place of great mineral and fishing potential but control of the Islands was considered to be an essential stepping stone for overall supremacy of the South Atlantic and access routes to the Pacific. As a consequence, Britain and Chile had to be excluded from this region. These were strategic concerns, not merely flights of fancy, as international legal developments in the form of the long-running UN Law of the Sea Conference (1973–82) added further urgency to new maritime claims. The Falklands, with a 200-mile-wide exclusive economic zone, looked an even more attractive proposition to those geopolitical writers obsessed with resource acquisition and territorial aggrandisement. Unlike their British competitors, the South Atlantic and the Islas Malvinas offered the Argentine military an opportunity to articulate a new sense of mission for the country, and geopolitical writers argued that the oceanic spaces around the Republic offered unprecedented chances for economic, political and even spiritual development. In order to divert attention from the brutal suppression of internal dissent, an opportunistic military regime in April 1982 pursued a long-standing territorial ambition.

SUMMARY

These 'limpet colonies' in the South Atlantic and Antarctica remain part of Britain's overseas portfolio despite attempts in the past to seek a territorial settlement with Argentina and, to a lesser extent, Chile. While the 1959 Antarctic Treaty appeared to put to one side the rival territorial claims in the Antarctic Peninsula, geopolitical attention in Argentina increasingly turned to the outstanding territorial grievances in the region north of the Antarctic Treaty. The Falklands, South Georgia and even the remote South Sandwich Islands became scenes of international discord. Arguably, while the Argentine regime must bear a heavy responsibility for the 1982 invasion and the subsequent conflict, the British administrators responsible for the region failed to appreciate the prevailing strength of feeling over these disputed territories. While international law may not give great emphasis to geographical proximity and geological continuity when it comes to assessing the legal strength of claims, these factors were significant in inspiring Argentine citizens to support a deeply unpopular military regime in April 1982. Thereafter, the geopolitical condition of the Antarctic and South Atlantic was transformed in British strategic thinking as Thatcher ensured that the Falklands would neither be surrendered to a territorial rival nor neglected by longer-term economic and defence planning. But as Mrs Thatcher claimed in October 1982, there was also a cultural factor at work: 'The spirit of the Falklands was the spirit of Britain at its best. It surprised the world that British patriotism was rediscovered in those spring days. But it was never lost.'[27]

NOTES ON CHAPTER 1

1   Cited in M. Charlton, *The Little Platoon: Diplomacy and the Falklands Dispute* (Oxford, Blackwell, 1989), p. 27.

2   T. Rowlands, 'The end of empire', *Journal of the Royal Society of Arts* May (1979): pp. 360–269. The quote is taken from pp. 362 and 365.

3   See, for example, J. Darwin, *Britain and Decolonization* (London, Macmillan, 1988). The author owes the phrase 'limpet colonies' to John Darwin.

4   W. Roger Louis and R. Robinson, 'The imperialism of decolonization', *Journal of Imperial and Commonwealth History* 22 (1994): pp. 462–511. The quote is taken from p. 462.

5   P. Taylor, *Britain and the Cold War: 1945 as Geopolitical Transition* (London, Pinter, 1990).

6   On critical geopolitics see G. O. Tuathail, *Critical Geopolitics* (London, Routledge, 1996) and G. O. Tuathail and S. Dalby (eds), *Rethinking Geopolitics* (London, Routledge, 1998).

7   See K. Dodds and D. Atkinson (eds), *Geopolitical Traditions* (London, Routledge, 2000).

8   A. Verrier, *Through the Looking Glass* (London, Jonathan Cape, 1983). See also A. Adamthwaite, 'Britain and the World 1945–1949: The view from the Foreign Office', *International Affairs* 62 (1985): pp. 223–235.

9   Louis and Robinson, 'The imperialism of decolonization'. The quote is taken from p. 463.

10   See also S. Mawby, 'Britain's last imperial frontier: The Aden protectorates 1952–1959', *Journal of Imperial and Commonwealth History* 29 (2001): pp. 75–100. He explored how British Governments sought to extend their political influence in the region by binding local leaders into a system of British control.

11   On the significance of the map see M. Edney, *Mapping an Empire: The Geographical Construction of British India 1765–1843* (Chicago IL, University of Chicago Press, 1997) and G. Burnett, *Masters of all They Surveyed: Exploration, Geography and a British El Dorado* (Chicago IL, University of Chicago Press, 2000).

12   P. Hansen, 'Confetti of empire: The conquest of Everest in Nepal, India, Britain and New Zealand', *Comparative Study of Society and History* XX (2000): pp. 307–32.

13   Quoted in Hansen, 'Confetti of empire: The conquest of Everest in Nepal, India, Britain and New Zealand', p. 325.

14   Other artists produced anti-war songs, such as Elvis Costello's 'Shipbuilding' in 1983. Thanks to Kathryn Yusoff for reminding me of this point.

15   K.Manzo, *Creating Boundaries: The Politics of Race and Nation* (London, Lynne Rienner, 1996), p.138.

16   Quoted in P.Gilroy, *There ain't no Black in the Union Jack* (London, Hutchinson, 1987) p.52.

17   See, for example, W.Wallace, 'Foreign policy and national identity in the UK', *International Affairs* 67 (1991): pp.65–80.

18   My thanks to Professor David Newman and Dr David Gilbert for reminding me of this remark and for sharing their football knowledge with me.

19   See H.O'Donnell, 'Mapping the mythical: a geopolitics of national sporting stereotypes', *Discourse and Society* 5 (1994): pp.345–80.

20   The *Sun*, 'Outcha! Argies get their own back on us', 23 June 1986. See also the *Daily Mirror*, 'What a way to go!' and 'Diego's a Mexican bandit!', 23 June 1986, and the *Daily Express* 'England are out: Argies' hero Maradona in hand-ball row', 23 June 1986.

21   K.Cutts-Dougherty, M.Eisenhart and P.Webley, 'The role of social representations and national identities in the development of territorial knowledge: A study of political socialisation in Argentina and England', *American Educational Research Journal* 29 (1992): pp.809–32.

22   C.Escudé, 'Argentine territorial nationalism', *Journal of Latin American Studies* 20 (1988): pp.139–65.

23   H.Coutau-Begarie, *Geostrategie de l'Atlantique Sud* (Paris, University of Paris Press, 1985).

24   This does not mean that officials and ministers attached to the FO, for example, were unaware of the resource potential of the Falklands and the Antarctic. By and large, however, it was decided that improving relations with Argentina would not be helped if greater public emphasis was given to the resource question. Author interview with Lord Chalfont, 23 October 2001.

25   J.Child, *Quarrels among Neighbours* (New York, Praeger, 1985), p.110.

26   P.Calvert, 'Argentina turns south: geopolitics triumphant', *Paradigms* 2 (1988–9): pp.76–85.

27   Cited in the *Sunday Express*, 10 October 1982.

2

Mapping British Antarctica

It will be necessary to bring Admiralty charts up to date with all the latest information, and this work will be taken in hand. At the present time, what are undoubtedly secure British claims are somewhat prejudiced by some earlier incorrect information which still remains depicted and which might give rise to powerful arguments in favour of other powers such as America.[1]

INTRODUCTION

Deception Island or Isla Decepción is one of the most coveted areas in Antarctica. Located within the South Shetland archipelago, its distinctive broken ring shape has surprised and intrigued successive generations of scientists, sealers and whalers. Deception was well named because access to its extraordinary natural harbour created by the collapse of a volcanic cone appeared impossible until a narrow opening named Neptune's Bellows was discovered. Originally used by American, British, Chilean and Norwegian sealers and whalers, Deception Island was incorporated into the British Empire in 1908. The Norwegian company Hektor was issued with a 21-year whaling licence by the Colonial Office in 1911, and Deception became a hive of activity as 13 floating stations co-existed with the onshore station processing the whales caught around the South Shetlands and the northern tip of the Antarctic Peninsula. By the 1930s, activity had ceased due to the severe depletion of whaling stocks, and the fuel stocks once so vital to the whaling station were destroyed by British forces in order to deny German sea raiders operating in the region the benefit of these abandoned supplies. Within a year, however, naval personnel landed and claimed Deception for the Argentine Republic. The timber from the abandoned Norwegian whaling station was used to construct their new base. By the end of the Second World War, Britain, Argentina and Chile had established rival bases and ordered their respective personnel to ensure 'effective occupation' on Deception Island.

The subject of this chapter is Britain's response to South American intrusions in Antarctica and outlying islands such as Deception. In the midst of the Second

World War, Britain, under the wartime leadership of Winston Churchill, felt obliged to send the Royal Navy to challenge Argentine and Chilean claims to Antarctic sovereignty. The secret Operation Tabarin was the catalyst for imperial consolidation. Thereafter, a post-war organisation, the FIDS was at the heart of imperial defence through its mapping and surveying activities. Of all those British personnel charged with monitoring Antarctic responsibilities, the scientists attached to the FIDS performed rather better in the field compared to those based in the office. Funding and political crises ensured that the mapping of British Antarctica was never an unproblematic affair. By the end of the 1950s, hundreds of thousands of pounds had been spent on land-based surveying, air photography, logistical support and base maintenance in order to preserve imperial claims to Antarctica and sub-Antarctic islands such as Deception.

OPERATION TABARIN

Named after a Parisian café, Operation Tabarin was the code name for a secret naval operation designed to raise Britain's profile in the South Atlantic and Antarctic in the Antarctic summer season of 1943–4. A handwritten note composed by the FO's chief polar advisor, Dr Brian Roberts, revealed the provenance of the code name:

> This was after the 'Bal Tabarin', a night club in Paris[2] – a code name chosen by John Mossop and myself when this operation started because we had to do a lot of night work and the organisation was always so chaotic just as the club and hence the origin of its name.[3]

An FO paper entitled 'Argentine encroachments in the Dependencies of the Falkland Islands' in October 1942 provided further impetus for a fundamental review of British Antarctic policy. It was noted that Argentina had committed three 'acts of trespass' by creating a post office in the South Orkneys, occupying an abandoned whaling factory in the South Shetlands and establishing a navigation beacon in the Melchior archipelago off the Antarctic Peninsula. Despite the long-standing research voyages of the RRS *Discovery II* in the Southern Ocean and the 1934–7 British Grahamland Expedition, the eruption of World War II created a hiatus in British Antarctic commitments and left the South Atlantic Empire vulnerable.[4] In the absence of British endeavour, Argentine incursions occurred in a region where the British thought they had a special right to occupancy. An FO paper noted that:

> Our legal title to the Antarctic territories in question, is not perhaps, very strong, and the practical value we have hitherto been able to make use of them small, but on strategic and other grounds, both the Admiralty and Colonial Office consider it most important to maintain, and if possible, strengthen it…The consideration of additional practical measures to strengthen our title appears to be desirable. [On the question of the disputed Falklands Islands] HM Representatives in Buenos Aires have consistently warned us that this is the one subject on which the whole Argentine nation feels as one man.[5]

Despite some reluctance from the Admiralty to release ships from active wartime service, a Cabinet-level decision, supported strongly by Churchill, gave credence to the belief that Britain had to retain a 'presence' in the Antarctic and South Atlantic.[6]

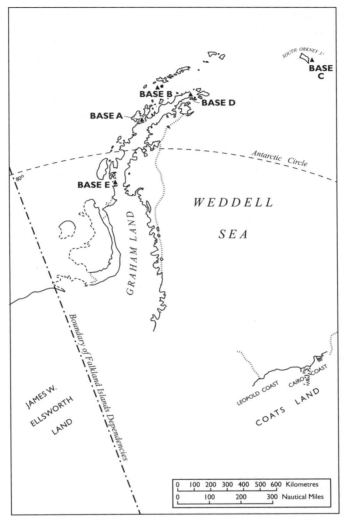

Figure 2.1: Bases of the Falkland Islands Dependencies Survey

Hence, the War Cabinet instructed the Admiralty's M Branch to take charge of the planning and interdepartmental negotiation involving the Dominion, Foreign and Colonial Offices were initiated. After a period of consultation, it was agreed that HMS *Carnarvon Castle* would be despatched to the Falkland Islands Dependencies (FID) and bases on Deception Island (Base B) and Port Lockroy (Base A) were to be established by the end of February 1944 (see figure 2.1). The FO commissioned new stamps for the FID to coincide with the operation in the belief that it might be helpful to post some mail from the newly established post offices to indicate sovereign authority, even if British media were only informed of the mission in April 1944.[7] By the time the first phase of the operation was implemented in the Antarctic summer season of 1943–4, the Tabarin in Paris had been transformed into a cabaret club specialising in French cancan and the owners accused of collaborating with the German occupiers.[8]

Under the leadership of Lieutenant Commander James Marr, a Royal Naval officer well-versed in Antarctic undertakings as a member of both the last Shackleton expedition and the RRS *Discovery II* voyages, Operation Tabarin encountered alarming evidence of Argentine Antarctic occupation.[9] In his report, Marr acknowledged that they found evidence of the earlier visit of the Argentine vessel *Primero de Mayo* in March 1943. Shockingly, they discovered 'Primero de Mayo' painted in red letters in the midst of a penguin rookery on Deception Island, thereby effectively rendering the chinstrap penguins Argentine citizens. Just as disturbingly, brass cylinders containing proclamations and the remains of an Argentine flag confirmed that there was indeed a tangible Argentine claim to the FID. Royal Navy personnel were instructed to destroy all Argentine flags and deliver other Argentine materials to the Governor of the Falkland Islands for safekeeping. On Deception Island, the Royal Navy erected two new flagpoles and hammered into the ground four signposts informing the potential occasional visitor that he or she was entering 'British Crown Lands'. These basic removal procedures were repeated at Port Lockroy and on the island of Signy in the South Orkneys.[10] Despite the fact that the British party had uncovered some uncomfortable reminders of an Argentine presence, Commander Marr remained positive about the achievements of the mission:

> Taking the purely political standpoint, we are firmly established in Antarctica at two widely separated points both of which have been surreptitiously visited and claimed by Argentina...after a break of five years forced on us by war, the active interest displayed by Great Britain...has once again been revived.[11]

At the heart of the 'purely political standpoint' was the FO's polar advisor, Dr Brian Roberts. In a remarkable career stretching from the beginning of the Second World War to his eventual retirement from the FO in 1975, Roberts was also the leading figure in the shaping of the Scott Polar Research Institute (SPRI) at Cambridge University.

After reading geography as part of his degree at Cambridge, Roberts established his polar interests following a university expedition to Iceland in 1932. After another expedition to Greenland in 1933, he accepted an invitation to join the British Grahamland Expedition (1934–7) to pursue geographical and biological research in the Antarctic Peninsula.[12] On his return to England in May 1937, Roberts resumed his studies at Cambridge and completed a doctoral thesis on 'The biology of some Antarctic birds', built on his research accumulated during the expedition.[13] In February 1940, the award of the Polar Medal acknowledged Roberts' polar endeavours and led to his involvement in producing topographical intelligence of the Arctic during the first years of the Second World War. Roberts was not alone in this role: other professional geographers such as Kenneth Mason of Oxford University and Clifford Darby of Cambridge University updated hydrographic charts and Admiralty handbooks.[14] In 1943, after researching the clothing and equipment requirements for the British military operating in the Arctic, Roberts participated in the secret naval operation designed to restore Britain's claims to the FID. Appointed to the FO Research Department in February 1944, he released his first planning paper, entitled 'Territorial claims in the Antarctic', which acknowledged that 'politically, though not legally, Argentine claims to the Falkland Islands

Dependencies are difficult to separate from her claims to the Falkland Islands themselves'. Fittingly for the man widely credited by the British for inspiring the Antarctic Treaty, Roberts argued that 'the time is rapidly approaching when the variety of conflicting claims in the Antarctic must be settled by conference and/or agreement'.[15] He was, by the age of 31, established as the FO's leading polar advisor.

Roberts was subsequently also responsible for encouraging Commonwealth co-ordination with British Antarctic policy. As claimant states, Australia and New Zealand were important partners in the post-war international political arena, and other parties such as South Africa and Canada were also regularly consulted. Underlying this commitment was a belief that Britain's legal position was precarious and thus Commonwealth support was crucial in maintaining the UK's title to the FID. In a memorandum prepared by Roberts but released from the Dominions Office to the Prime Minister's Department in Canberra, a remarkably frank assessment was offered for the legal position of Britain's possessions in the Antarctic and the South Atlantic:

> While our titular claim of the Falkland Islands is comparatively weak, our legal position is becoming increasingly strong owing to our continued possession and use, which we have made of these islands. As regards to the Dependencies, the position is the reverse. While our titular claim is stronger we have made little use of the islands and our legal position is therefore becoming weaker and is in part disputed by Chile as well as the Argentine.[16]

Argentine and Chilean interest in the region had gathered momentum since 1904, when the Argentine authorities first occupied Laurie Island in the South Orkneys. Ironically, given the subsequent turn of events involving Anglo–Argentine friction, the scientific base on the island had been donated to Argentina by the Scottish explorer William Spears Bruce, who led the Scottish National Expedition between 1901–4. Disappointed over his treatment by the English geographical establishment and its apparent lack of interest in civilian polar explorers, Bruce offered his base to Argentina; the occupation of this base became an important element in subsequent Argentine claims to a permanent Argentine Antarctic sector. Roberts, moreover, was aware that previous British administrators had considered ceding parts of the FID: in 1914, for example, the legal title to the South Orkneys was offered to Argentina, provided financial compensation was forthcoming. The deal collapsed when Argentina disputed the final settlement.[17] Argentine interest had been restricted to the annual relief of the Laurie Island station and the fishing activities of the South Georgia-based company, Compania Argentina de Pesca, but in July 1939, Argentina created a permanent interdepartmental National Antarctic Commission to co-ordinate future Argentine expeditions to the Antarctic and surrounding islands.

Under decree number 35,821, the National Antarctic Commission was created on the understanding that:

> The geographical situation of the territory on the most southernmost part of South America assigns to it on scientific and political grounds a natural interest in the questions arising from the study of problems of the Antarctic continent, whose geographical resemblance to our territory is a fact which is of interest to elucidate. The Committee shall make a comprehensive study of the present state of Antarctic problems and shall propose a plan of action to include questions of

oceanography, meteorology, fisheries and any explorations which Argentina might undertake.[18]

As a consequence of this presidential decree, the Argentine Government agreed to fund new expeditions to the Antarctic Peninsula and the South Shetlands in 1942 and 1943. After a period of surveying and limited map-making, the Argentine parties, as the British discovered, created a post office on Laurie Island and the Republic's flag was hoisted over Deception Island.

The basis for this Argentine claim was derived from a mixture of historical precedents, recent polar activity, geographical proximity and geological continuity. Regardless of their international legal merits, successive Argentine Governments have argued with considerable conviction that the Argentine Antarctic sector is a natural geographical extension of the continental Republic. As the Argentine Ministry of Foreign Affairs and Worship reiterated in February 1943:

> The Argentine government reaffirm on this occasion their sovereign rights over all Antarctic lands and dependencies south of 60 degrees latitude South and between meridians 25 degrees and 68 degrees longitude West. The Argentine government regret that the British government have considered it opportune to take such measures as the removal of the national emblem and signs on Deception Island where, previous to the placing of such, there was no effective occupation or possession belonging to the British government.[19]

Unsurprisingly, the rationale for Operation Tabarin was explained retrospectively by a Ministry of Information briefing as an act of colonial resistance: 'A major purpose of the expedition now is to act as a counter-measure to encroachments, which the Argentine government has made in the Falkland Islands Dependencies in recent years'.[20] While Operation Tabarin was considered useful in removing offensive materials from the Antarctic, there was no substitute for a permanent presence, given that Argentina had been in the FID since 1904. Britain was forced to establish a new network of scientific bases and to develop a new *modus operandi* for claim protection.

The major bases were established in Port Lockroy and Deception Island, with additional bases in Hope Bay on the Antarctic Peninsula and in the South Orkneys. Whether Britain was genuinely prepared for such a sustained period of investment is a moot point, as many of the Government papers dealing with Antarctic sovereignty have been withheld beyond the normal 30-year period of restriction. There is evidence to suggest that British advisors such as Roberts believed that if a permanent presence in the FID was re-established, then Argentina and Chile might be persuaded to consider a form of international settlement for the Antarctic and acceptance of international arbitration for the Falkland Islands. Unfortunately for the optimists in the FO, neither South American state had any intention of solving the Antarctic dispute, apart from strengthening their claims in the legal and popular geographical sphere. Within two years of the conclusion of Operation Tabarin, it became apparent that Britain was going to be embroiled in a long and costly struggle over the FID. A revised FO report, 'Territorial claims in the Antarctic', dated 1 May 1945, perversely acknowledged that the Royal Navy's interest in the Falklands and South Atlantic was diminishing at a point when British claims in the region were being strengthened through 'effective occupation'.[21]

THE FALKLAND ISLANDS DEPENDENCIES SURVEY

Dr Bernard Stonehouse, a distinguished polar biologist, made his first visit to the Antarctic in 1946 after a wartime stint as a naval pilot. Over 50 years later, he recalled how an advertisement had fired his geographical imagination and led to his recruitment by the FIDS.[22] The specification for the FIDS position was brusque: 'Candidates, SINGLE, must be keen young men of good education and high physical standard who have a genuine interest in polar research and travel and are willing to spend 18 to 30 months under conditions which are a test of character and resource'.[23] After submitting his application for the post of meteorologist stationed in the Antarctic Peninsula, Stonehouse attended an interview in the Colonial Office's building in central London. Chaired by the then director of the SPRI, Lancelot Fleming, he was questioned by Brian Roberts and a Colonial Office official whose name he can no longer recall.[24] During the short discussion, the unknown civil servant noted that the mission was 'covert' and precluded any discussion as to why Britain was sending men and equipment to a remote part of the British Empire. Thirty minutes later, Stonehouse was offered the post and appointed as a FIDS meteorologist and reserve pilot for two Antarctic summer seasons. Due to inclement weather, he was trapped on the Antarctic ice and the posting was extended for another year. This unscheduled stay enabled him to travel more widely on the Antarctic Peninsula and led to spells at Base E on Stonington Island and Base B on Deception Island.

On completion of Operation Tabarin, the Attlee Government had agreed to the creation of a civilian polar survey service to be administered by the Colonial Office. As manager of the FIDS, the Colonial Office was advised by the FO on the international aspects of the Antarctic and the Dominions Office was responsible for developing links with the claimant states of Australia and New Zealand. The first meeting of the sub-committee of the FIDS was held on 12 July 1945, with Roberts a member of the committee. The aims and objectives of the FIDS were several: 'The promotion of British territorial claims, the administration of the Falkland Islands Dependency, the deterrence of rival claimants and their surveyors and the pursuit of accurate geographical knowledge'.[25] In March 1946, the FIDS Committee was reconstituted as new members were recruited in order to replace – amongst others – Surgeon-Commander Bingham, who had left for Antarctica as field leader of the FIDS. After deliberations within the FIDS Committee, the Colonial Office's instructions to surveyors in 1947 were unequivocal: 'The primary objective of the Survey [the FIDS] is to strengthen His Majesty's title to the sector of Antarctica. The secondary objective of the Survey is to continue the scientific work in the Antarctic.'[26] In the event of encountering Argentine parties in the region, surveyors were reminded that 'you should not enter into any discussion concerning sovereignty with the Argentine party'.[27] In spite of the confident pronouncements by the Colonial Office in the 1940s and 1950s, the FIDS failed to serve as the cornerstone of British administration. As a newly created colonial survey service, FIDS personnel were in danger of being anachronistic in a post-imperial period. Paradoxically, the dismantling of the imperial survey operations of India and Southern Africa were paralleled by imperial endeavours to strengthen the British polar survey.

In order to forestall and counteract any potential threat to British sovereignty in Antarctica, the FIDS was expected to collect and analyse geographical information as well as contribute to the British 'presence' in the region. Roberts, in a letter to the FIDS leader Surgeon-Commander E.W. Bingham, was adamant that the latter should 'always remember that you have entirely fulfilled all the essential political requirements and that everything else achieved is sheer gain. I am not nearly so pleased with our achievements this end.'[28] Despite the quasi mission statement, many of the surveyors and meteorologists despatched to the polar continent were either unclear or ambivalent about the geopolitical and legal objectives of the FIDS. The preposterous nature of the FIDS's strategic mission was evident every summer season, during which some 20–30 men were to map and survey thousands of square miles of ice, rock and water. Fierce winds and the stormy waters of the Southern Ocean made accurate mapping a hazardous undertaking. It was not uncommon to find that the polar landscape had changed markedly from season to season. Despite some extraordinary endeavours in this dangerous landscape, the challenges facing the surveyors were unrelenting, as the eventual leader of the FIDS, Dr (later Sir) Vivian Fuchs acknowledged in the BBC magazine, *The Listener*:

> Imagine a small rocky, snow-covered ridge (about 800 yards by 300 yards) joined at one end to the high ice cliffs of a glacier: that is Stonington Island…In the course of 1948 and 1949, some 700 miles of coastline were surveyed by Brown and Blaiklock [FIDS surveyors]. Though most of this was previously known to exist, many areas were inaccurate. The maps had been compiled by air photographs without the control of accurate fixed points on the ground or rigid flight control.[29]

FIDS personnel were required to negotiate a network of bases with intermittent radio communications, which were in turn further frequently interrupted by severe weather and served by irregular sea and air transport. Once in the field, FIDS surveyors were expected at all times to maintain Britain's political presence in the Antarctic.[30]

Flags, plaques, maps and memoranda played an invaluable part in highlighting sovereignty claims in the Antarctic Peninsula. Given 10 minutes to prepare a 'sovereignty speech', Stonehouse recalled how he had delivered his first 'protest note' to a bemused party of senior Chilean naval officers in the summer season of 1946–7. After politely listening to his address, a junior naval officer reminded the FIDS meteorologist that he was mistaken in his belief that this was Crown territory. After an awkward interlude, the parties eventually agreed to differ and afternoon tea was offered to the Chilean visitors. It is sobering to recall that FIDS personnel never received any formal briefing on the contested sovereignty of Antarctica from the Colonial Office. The task was delegated informally to the Governor of the Falkland Islands and /or the field leader of the FIDS.[31]

Although the spatial remit of the FIDS was substantial, it was not allocated sufficient funds or men to enable the complete mapping of British Antarctica. Administrators and surveyors were faced with difficult political choices, and geographical compromises were necessary throughout the history of the FIDS (1945–62).[32] Annual maps produced by the Research Department of the FO monitored the geographical location of Argentine, Chilean and British bases in the FID. As Roberts noted in 1962, 'This episode of Antarctic history reflects well the difficulties of international co-operation in technical and scientific matters and the dominance of political and personal issues during the decade before the Antarctic Treaty was signed in 1959'.[33]

Initially funded by Colonial Office grants, the FIDS created and maintained five Antarctic and sub-Antarctic research stations stretching in a westerly arc from Stonington Island to the South Orkneys. In terms of surveying and logistical investment, effort was concentrated on and around the Antarctic Peninsula but the FIDS was also expected to perform the duties of postmaster, Justice of the Peace and magistrate. Four bases at Port Lockroy (Base A), Hope Bay (Base D), Deception Island (Base B) and Stonington (Base E) formed the nucleus of the FIDS's year-round operations due to their ease of access and general strategic distribution. South Georgia did not feature in the FIDS's mapping remit, and only the private expeditions organised by Duncan Carse in the 1950s began to redress this lacuna.[34] In the summer season of 1945–6, four men were based at Port Lockroy and Stonington, and later on Laurie Island (Base C) in the South Orkneys. Between 8 and 10 men were stationed at Hope Bay and on Deception, with its sheltered harbour (Port Foster) and relatively benign weather conditions compared to the fierce conditions endemic of Alexander Land. The most southerly base on Stonington Island was significant insofar as it acted as a reference point for existing cartographic knowledge of the Antarctic Peninsula.

Despite the British Grahamland Expedition discovery that the Peninsula was joined to the continental land mass, British maps were still vague on the outline of the coastline surrounding the eastern side of the Weddell Sea. Given the vast distances and dangerous ice condition beneath the Antarctic Circle, the managers of the FIDS encouraged mapping projects closer to the existing network of research stations, not least because they were more likely to deliver results in terms of improved sheet maps and subsequent political kudos.

Further to the north of Britain's South Atlantic Empire, FIDS personnel were also expected to liaise with the Governor of the Falkland Islands and the Norwegian whalers operating in South Georgia. In the immediate post-1945 era, senior figures in the Royal Navy were vociferous in their demands for commitment, even if the strategic significance of the Falklands and the South Atlantic was questionable in the Cold War era. A candid example of this emerged in a letter to the First Sea Lord, Sir John Cunningham, from Vice-Admiral Sir William Tennant, dated 5 May 1948:

> The only British interests that I can discover…appears to be the control of whaling. I can discover no strategic interest in the whole area [the FID] other than a possible 'hide out' for commercial raiders. I would hold onto the Falkland Islands and South Georgia at all costs, even to the extent of going to war. But for the rest, would it not be a good idea to form an Antarctic club of those countries interested…and discuss the question of internationalising the whole of the Antarctic. If the Argentines were too stupid to listen to any of this then I see no alternative to continue the rather childish performance that has gone on between our ships for a number of years.[35]

The Royal Navy's involvement was manifest to the operational history of the FIDS, not only providing logistical and mapping support but also a military presence. While the FIDS concentrated on land-based surveying, the Hydrographic Office of the Admiralty was responsible for updating charts regardless of whether information was supplied by British or other naval parties. Unlike the Argentine and Chilean naval forces, the British never had an icebreaker on South Atlantic duty to facilitate movement further south from the tip of the Antarctic Peninsula. Other ships, such as the RRS *William Scoresby*, travelled thousands of miles for the purpose of 'flying the flag', supporting FIDS personnel and to erect signs proclaiming 'British Crown Lands' along the Antarctic Peninsula, South Orkneys and South Georgia.[36] If British ships confronted Argentine and Chilean personnel, their captains were ordered to despatch 'protest notes' informing the South Americans of their act of trespass.

Noticeably, Vice-Admiral Tennant and others consistently criticised the Argentines for their 'childish' behaviour but failed to extend this condemnation to British behaviour, which involved tearing up flags, throwing rival plaques into the sea and threatening South American 'intruders' with a splashing of cold water. In practice the Royal Navy, while attentive to its geopolitical duties, was also frequently hospitable as, for example, when RRS/HMS *William Scoresby* left 'a thousand cigarettes and half a sheep [from the Falkland Islands of course]' to a short-supplied Argentine party based near Scotia Bay. Successive Governors of the Falkland Islands depended upon the Royal Navy to patrol the FID. Most notably, Governor Sir Miles Clifford was particularly keen to brave the ice-filled seas of British Antarctica in pursuit of this mission.[37] Before the era of mass defence cuts, post-colonial change and domestic financial crises, this geopolitical assessment committed the Royal Navy to despatch ships to the South Atlantic in order to offer protection from South American 'intruders'.

IN AND OUT OF THE OFFICE: ADMINISTERING THE FIDS

In London, the administration of the FIDS was haphazard and therefore largely dependent upon the strategic calculations of Brian Roberts and Sir James Wordie. As a former member of the British Grahamland Expedition, Roberts combined a measure of practical experience of Antarctica with the energy of a zealot determined to protect Britain's territorial claims. Described by one ex-FIDS surveyor as 'devious, pompous and an intellectual bully', Roberts was the FO's chief advisor on Antarctic issues. For others who encountered Roberts, he was a powerful and dedicated advocate of British Antarctic interests and recognised that activities such as surveying and aerial photography were essential in the defence of the FID. As the then secretary of the Royal Geographical Society, Laurence Kirwan astutely recognised in a written reference on behalf of Roberts:

> He is an energetic and capable administrator, though in this and other matters he tends sometimes towards an excessive concentration on minutiae…He is a man of strong character and decided, somewhat rigid, opinions who has some time been the moving spirit in the Institute [the SPRI].[38]

In conjunction with Wordie, a former geologist with the Trans-Antarctic Expedition of 1914–16 and Master of St John's College Cambridge, he shaped the political and scientific framework for Britain's post-1945 involvement in Antarctica and the South Atlantic. In May 1948, the FIDS Scientific Committee, under the chairmanship of Wordie, was charged with considering the scientific aspects of the annual programme of work as prepared by the Governor of the Falkland Islands and the proposals for British occupation of the FID.[39] It was Roberts, in particular, who ordered the FIDS to combine surveying with the despatch of 'protest notes' to neighbouring base camps and their personnel. And when deemed appropriate, Roberts even insisted that FIDS surveyors wear military uniforms in order to convey an administrative manner. The first leader of the FIDS, Fuchs, was instructed to pack his wartime major's uniform in order to lend solemnity, should a sudden change of circumstances require it.[40]

Given the enormous remit of the FIDS, it is perhaps understandable that the organisation and administration of this survey service was for much of the time confused. In 1946, the FIDS Scientific Committee was created under the chairmanship of a Colonial Office official and representatives from the Dominions and Foreign Offices. Within Whitehall, the Colonial Office administered the FIDS and funded it for the first three years of its existence. However, other Government departments such as the Admiralty, the Dominions Office and the FO were also involved in frequent Antarctic consultations. Unlike the FO, the Colonial Office did not have an official to match the commitment of Roberts, who was also a central figure in the emergence of the SPRI in Cambridge as the pre-eminent polar research centre. Roberts was effectively allowed to promote Britain's polar interests with little direct interference from senior managers. By 1946 Roberts, with his appointment as a part-time research fellow at the SPRI, spent two days a week at Cambridge and three days working at the Research Department of the FO. This pattern of work was continued until his retirement from the FCO in 1975. Throughout, he was perhaps fortunate that he could call upon scientists such as Fuchs for support in the field.

While Fuchs was committed to the geopolitical objectives of the post-war British Government, he also applied considerable intellectual energy and administrative vigour to the FIDS. As a natural-sciences student at Cambridge University, Fuchs initiated a lifelong interest in exploration and participated in expeditions initially to the Arctic and East Africa. His first polar journey was undertaken in July 1929, when he left with three other students on board a Norwegian sealer bound for the high Arctic. After returning from this mountaineering expedition, he pursued his doctoral research in East Africa around Lake Rudolf (now called Lake Turkana) and did not return to the polar environments until some 20 years later. During the Second World War, Fuchs served with some distinction in the Cambridge Regiment stationed in North Africa, France and Germany. In 1946, together with other FIDS staff and Stonehouse, he applied for a post with the recently created polar survey service. To his evident surprise, he recalled that he was not only appointed as a geologist but also offered the post of field commander for the 1946–7 season.[41] Given vague instructions on the political and scientific remit of the FIDS, and urged by Roberts to carry out as much geological research and surveying as was possible, Fuchs set off for his first season.[42] After a number of seasons in Antarctica, he was transferred to London and became central to the administration of the FIDS.

With the support of the FIDS Scientific Committee, the Falkland Islands emerged as the major gateway for FIDS operations.[43] Stanley was both the centre for Antarctic operations and the collection point for information generated by meteorologists and surveyors.[44] The FIDS's activities were closely linked to the Directorate of Colonial Surveys (DCS), and it was Roberts who campaigned for the creation of a new map of the FID to 'show everything we at present know and to bring out at successive editions new information as it comes in'. Blank spaces on British sheet maps provided a ready and visually compelling *raison d'être* for sustained investment in cartographic enterprise. The collection of accurate geographical information was essential not only to justify the endeavour but also to legitimate the claim to a very distant territory administered under British law. Maps and surveys provided solid evidence that the taxpayer in ration-hit Britain was not being short-changed. As the Secretary of State for the Colonies, Creech Jones acknowledged to an audience at the Royal Geographical Society in 1948: 'Ladies and Gentleman, as you paid for the expedition, I hope you feel from those words and also from what you have heard and seen tonight that you are getting good value for money.'[45]

In the political setting of 1945–7, confidence was high that, given time and resources, the FIDS could achieve its objectives, namely to contain South American challengers by an elegant and effective display of mapping combined with effective occupancy.

In the first few years of his time at the FIDS, Fuchs was instrumental in establishing a network of research stations with organised programmes of geological, biological and mapping-based investigations. Initial conditions in the field were harsh and at times farcical, as FIDS staff struggled with insufficient equipment and clothing. Some planes proved inadequate, as did many of the wooden ships, which were perilously close to being crushed by the unforgiving Antarctic ice. The personal equipment designed for the staff was not much better. The so-called 'Brian Roberts anorak' was so badly designed that the surveyors could not operate on the ice with the hood up, thereby exposing the face to painful winds and eventual frostbite. Perhaps, therefore, Francis Spufford was right to conclude that the British were for much of the twentieth century uniquely unprepared for polar conditions.[46]

Fittingly for a country that produced the Official Secrets Act, surveyors were expected to conduct operations in a culture of secrecy. FIDS operatives recalled that a vast amount of field time was spent using a five-letter code devised to transmit and receive messages from Stanley in the Falkland Islands. All messages to and from the Antarctic were relayed via the Falklands and then transmitted on to the Colonial Office in London. Occasionally, if the instructions from the Governor's residence in Stanley appeared too outrageous or simply silly, such as issuing further protest notes, FIDS staff would simply pretend that the radio signal was too weak. A common complaint in the field was that officials in the Colonial Office, including 'old hands' such as Roberts, failed to appreciate the unpredictable conditions as well as the logistical challenges facing a small group of surveyors and scientists in the Antarctic Peninsula.

By 1948, the FIDS had established four permanent research stations in addition to a score of summer season only bases. In the same year, funding for polar survey was changed to allow monies collected by the Governor of the Falkland Islands for whaling and sealing to be channelled into the FIDS. As Governor Clifford concluded in September 1950:

> FIDS is financed from the Dependencies' revenue which is derived from an export
> tax on whale and seal oil produced in South Georgia and an obligation rests on

it to serve the interests of the whaling industry... one of its first objectives is the establishment of an efficient meteorological service.[47]

Henceforth, FIDS staff were instructed to devote research time to collecting weather information for the benefit of the taxpayer – in this case the Norwegian whalers and sealers. Described as a rather overbearing individual in some quarters and a pompous ass in others, Sir Miles (nicknamed Ginger George), who had a record of colonial service in Nigeria, was a committed advocate of British claims to the FID. According to some ex-FIDS staff, Sir Miles relished the position of Governor and was a keen advocate of regular Royal Navy patrols to that part of the world. He was determined to derive 'an ultimate view to the economic development of the resources of the Dependencies, and thus particular attention should be paid to the chance of finding minerals'.[48] Following pressure from the Treasury, a mineral resource audit was commissioned together with mapping, in order that the Colonial Office could evaluate the strategic value of maintaining the FID.

Despite the rather 'gung-ho' tones of Clifford, the FIDS was forced to adjust its geopolitical objectives within three years of its creation, thus prompting Roberts, in consultation with the Colonial Office, to issue new instructions to the FIDS in November 1948. In the light of Argentine, Chilean and American polar expeditions, the FIDS's policy of issuing protest notes to so-called 'trespassers' was reviewed. A memorandum prepared by the Colonial Office reflected this change of tack:

> I have taken into account your proposal regarding the possible use of cold water sprayed from hoses to frustrate Argentine attempts to land at Admiralty Bay, but I do not consider that such a measure would be advisable. You should restore any British marks of occupation, which are found obliterated and you should obliterate any foreign emblems or marks of occupation or claims. Obliteration should not, however, be effected while the parties responsible for setting up the emblems are still in the locality.[49]

Mindful of the political circumstances, the FO agreed to the revised instructions and a Cabinet-level discussion confirmed that physical violence on the ice should be avoided at all costs.

However, within two years this change in emphasis was reversed to counteract the fact that Argentina's Antarctic programme was becoming too well-organised and ambitious. It was noted that Argentina was increasing the number of research stations in the Antarctic and planning to launch a series of surveying expeditions in the Antarctic Peninsula and sub-Antarctic islands. Roberts was once again at the centre of these geopolitical concerns when he noted that the Argentines under Perón were determined to bolster claims to the Argentine Antarctic sector. The key turning-point was the so-called Hope Bay incident in February 1952, when British and Argentine personnel clashed over the existence of rival Antarctic stations. Unlike previous incidents, which although official had been cordial, this incident provoked the Argentine party to shoot over the heads of the British team, while they were attempting to restore a burnt-out station in the vicinity. While Clifford demanded 'firm action' from the Royal Navy, the FO and the Admiralty agreed that a British warship would have to be despatched to the region in order to deter future Argentine 'aggression'. Much to the collective outrage of British officials in London and Buenos Aires, Perón personally greeted the Argentine expedition members on their return to Argentina.

In a series of exchanges, Roberts outlined the challenges that lay ahead and noted that, 'although I doubt the scientific value of much of the work or the accuracy of the surveys [carried out by Argentine parties], from a political or legal point of view that is irrelevant'.[50] As such, Britain would have to increase its 'presence' in the South Atlantic: 'examples of Argentine attacks on HMG's sovereignty in the Falklands themselves have been frequent during the past 40 years … if the Argentines behave childishly, then it seems to me no reason for us not to do'.[51] Aware that Argentina enjoyed stronger logistical support in the 'field', Roberts lamented in October 1952 that a basic shortage of Royal Navy ships would:

> Allow no charting or other useful work such as being done by Argentina. The Hydrographer told me last week that he thought it was most unsatisfactory that the Admiralty should now have to correct their charts of the Falkland Islands Dependencies from Argentine and Chilean surveys. We must act now if there is to be any hope of stepping up FIDS activity.[52]

A month later, the Argentine Navy Ministry sent Roberts some copies of their new Antarctic maps. As he ruefully noted, 'all this is presumably part of the documentary evidence they are building to bolster their claim'.[53] In December 1952, Roberts conceded that the Argentine airforce had conducted an aerial survey of the Antarctic Peninsula and the South Shetland Islands, thereby confirming his worst fear – the FIDS was being 'outclassed' by its South American rivals.

PRODUCING MAPS OF 'BRITISH' ANTARCTICA

The Antarctic explorer Francis Ommanney recalled in 1938, 'If you are lucky or clever enough to be there at the right time, you may reach the coast of the continent and plant yet another name on the chart'.[54] With the absence of an indigenous population, Antarctica appeared to offer unprecedented opportunities for place naming. For the surveyor or explorer, naming a new place acted as confirmation (if it was needed) that one's expedition had been useful and possibly heroic. As British officials appreciated, place names such as the 'Falkland Islands Dependencies' not only record previous acts of colonisation and settlement but also serve as a public reminder of territorial sovereignty. Once accepted by others with Antarctic interests, new place names were invested with considerable prestige. Roberts was, according to those who knew him, obsessed with maps, place names and scientific terminology. The appropriately titled Antarctic Place Names Committee operated to a tight remit in order to ensure quality control prevailed over British maps. This sub-committee on names in the Antarctic was created in June 1932 by the interdepartmental Polar Committee, and by 1934 had already issued the first guidelines for naming Antarctic features.

In 1948 Roberts, as secretary to the renamed Antarctic Place Names Committee, was often embroiled in fierce disputes with Wordie over the correct procedures for implementation of place names and the terms to be used for describing features such as sea ice.[55] Far from being trivial, Roberts recognised that the place names were part of the exercise of 'effective occupation' and hence essential in the defence of imperial polar claims. The committee decided that the following list of names would be unacceptable: names already in usage elsewhere in the FID; well-known names of existing territories, towns or islands, names in any foreign language including Scottish, Welsh and Irish, names of sledge dogs, 'names in low taste', and 'names with obscure origins which cannot be easily explained'.[56] The FIDS teams could and did propose new names for geographical features but the decision to incorporate them in British maps of the FID rested with the committee composed of officials from the FO, the Colonial Office and the DCS. Names found on Argentine and Chilean maps of the Antarctic Peninsula were not recognised and omitted from British maps of Antarctica.

Unfortunately, evidence was mounting that the FIDS was squandering precious research materials by failing to 'write up' and convert field data for use by the DCS. With the guidance of the DCS (subsequently the Directorate of Overseas Surveys), the collection of basic geographical information formed the starting point in map creation. FIDS staff knew that meticulous record-keeping and careful analysis of aerial material supported by precise ground-based surveys was vital. As the FIDS geologist, Raymond Adie acknowledged: 'It was a constant problem to encourage field workers to complete their work. Some of them sought places in universities with a view to obtaining a higher degree, but unfortunately much of the fieldwork remained unpublished.'[57]

The reasons for this tardiness lay in a combination of factors, including a desire to seek paid employment on return from Antarctica and a reluctance to commit to writing up research without suitable remuneration. While understandable from the point of view of the young surveyors, this apparent loss of geographical information was unhelpful given the persistent territorial challenges of South American states and the changing international politics of the Antarctic.

The image 'Surveys in the Falkland Islands Dependencies' was completed in 1955 and was intended to provide a public record for administrators of the cartographic achievements of FIDS personnel (see figure 2.2). While most of the northern part of the Antarctic Peninsula had been covered by aerial and land-based survey, knowledge of the southern part of the Peninsula and outlying islands remained fragmentary, reflecting the difficulties encountered by massive areas of polar ice and sea. The map of Scotland in the corner of the diagram was intended to provide a sense of scale for readers and a reminder that work was being carried out in a wild and untamed landscape. It would be unrealistic, as Fuchs frequently argued, to expect the FIDS teams to survey and map such a vast area in a comprehensive manner. Adaptation and concession were often the order of day, as was reflected in the official guidelines from the DCS for polar surveying. As the director of the DCS acknowledged in June 1952:

> The object of this meeting [with FIDS staff] is to suggest that the standard of accuracy required is not so high as has been assumed to be necessary...We recognise that the standard of these surveys cannot compare with that necessary for inhabited British colonial possessions. We wish to emphasise the difference of accuracy that exists between the requirements for non-polar territories and those that would serve areas such as the Falkland Islands Dependencies.[58]

These apparent concessions are obvious in the final production of maps and their scales. The DCS also approved a sliding scale for map projection, with 1:500,000 being judged sufficient for administrative and political purposes and 1:200,000 or even 1:100,000 adequate for practical assistance in developing awareness of the

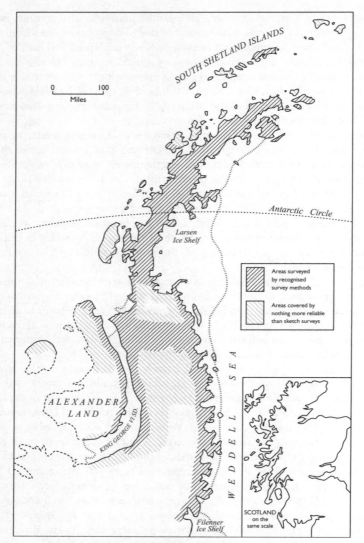

Figure 2.2: Surveys in the Falkland Islands Dependencies

detailed topographies. The more detailed the map, the greater the sense of ownership and control. While British civil servants were inclined to romanticise about
imperial surveying, they also expected results:

> The scientific fieldwork which is carried out in the Dependencies is not research
> for the benefit of colonial peoples. It is done to maintain a UK interest. It is UK,
> not FIDS policy that the activity should be maintained at a sufficient level to
> enable us to compete with our South American rivals, and it is inescapable that
> the receipt, co-ordination, working up, and publication of results of fieldwork at
> the bases must be regarded as integral to these activities.[59]

The relationship with the DCS (the then major producer of all UK maps of Antarctica) was crucial for the FIDS's collective political and scientific legitimacy. Fuchs, the head of the FIDS scientific bureau, acknowledged that the DCS provided invaluable advice and training for FIDS surveyors during and after their spells in Antarctica. However, co-operation and co-ordination between the FIDS and the DCS could be problematic. When Frank Elliot wrote to Colonel Wiggins of the DCS in 1956, he confirmed that the FIDS's London office had amended the polar guidelines. Without the professional input of the DCS, it was not until February 1957 that Elliott could note that 'new instructions' were prepared after noting that 'With the appointment of Sir Raymond Priestly and the reorganisation of FIDS' London Office and the Scientific Bureau under one roof, this impression that we have too many 'cooks' should disappear'.[60]

THE LAST HURRAH: THE 1955–7 FALKLAND ISLANDS DEPENDENCIES AERIAL SURVEY EXPEDITION

In March 1955, Clifford published a five-year plan for the FID advocating further base construction in the region, which was carefully scrutinised by the FIDS Scientific Committee. While Clifford's proposal was premised on the view that 'ground occupation was the only means of maintaining our sovereignty in the area', Roberts was conscious of the escalating costs attached to sustaining these sovereignty claims. In 1955–6, over £150,000 of British taxpayers' money was spent on FIDS-associated logistical costs in the Falkland Islands and the network of bases scattered around the FID. The geopolitical rationale for such a wide-ranging distribution of research bases was undermined by the high transport costs incurred due to the distances separating the stations. After 10 years of FIDS operations, six permanent bases ranged along the Antarctic Peninsula and surrounding islands, and six temporary research stations and a handful of summer-season bases complemented these. The largest permanent station in 1955–6 was at Hope Bay and housed 12 scientists and support staff; the smallest was the five-strong base at Admiralty Bay. The *Gazetteer* of the FID recorded over 1000 place names that were directly attributable to the work of the FIDS.[61] A private expedition (supported by the UK Government) led by Duncan Carse had completed several seasons of surveying work in South Georgia (see figure 2.3). Unsurprisingly, the new Governor of the Falkland Islands, O.R. Arthur, was reminded by an official at the Colonial Office that 'with over 10 manned bases in the Dependencies, the action of demonstrating sovereignty is probably adequately catered for'.[62]

Aware that procurement of additional funding was slim, attention turned from overtly political projects to other scientific projects, which might generate Colonial Office and Treasury support. Since the 1940s, aerial photography had been identified as an area of future investment precisely because the 'view from the air' appeared to hold out the promise of rapid and comprehensive coverage of the Antarctic Peninsula. This was a radical departure from the FIDS's earlier priorities, which advocated 'effective occupation' via base construction and weather collection rather than aerial photography. As a memorandum prepared by the Colonial Office on 'the possibilities of survey with the aid of photography' recognised:

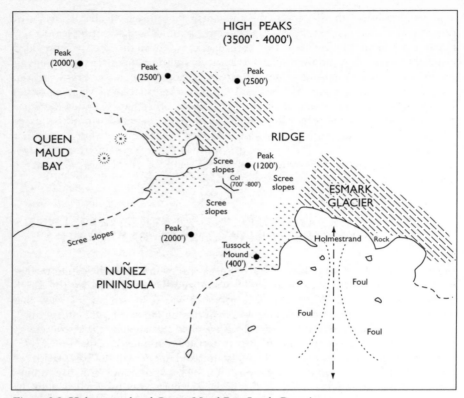

Figure 2.3: Holmestrand and Queen Maud Bay, South Georgia

We can continue indefinitely with ground methods to improve the map of selected areas each year, but this procedure is slow and uneconomical in comparison with the possibilities of survey with the aid of air photography...It is hoped that the results of this complex and hazardous enterprise will consolidate the long and continuous history of British polar exploration and survey endeavour in Grahamland and other areas of the Falkland Islands Dependencies.[63]

Wiggins argued at a meeting of the FIDS Scientific Committee on 25 March 1955 that a programme of air photography should be expanded to improve the FIDS's maps, provided that ground control data so vital for accurate mapping was also accumulated. The aim of any such programme should be to carry out vertical photography of approximately 42,000 square miles of the Antarctic Peninsula, together with detailed land-surveying of the region. After consultation with departmental colleagues, the company Hunter AeroSurvey Limited was awarded the contract to carry out two seasons of aerial photography. The contract for the aerial survey was worth £250,000 and explicitly assumed that the contractor had access to helicopters and fixed-wing aircraft designed to undertake photographic sorties over the Antarctic Peninsula.

Under the directorship of Peter Mott, a former member of the India Military Survey and the DCS, the project was named the Falkland Islands Dependencies

Aerial Survey Expedition (FIDASE). Before its departure to the Antarctic, the Colonial Office went to considerable lengths to brief the leader of the FIDASE on the merits of high altitude photographs of the Antarctic Peninsula. The FIDASE was conducted over two Antarctic summer seasons 1955–6 and 1956–7, and the many hours of flying sorties generated 10,000 aerial photographs of approximately 35,000 square miles of the FID. Progress, however, was not as straightforward as those statistics might imply, as bad weather in the first season and indifferent management hampered the FIDASE. As one FIDASE pilot, John Saffrey, admitted in December 1956:

> These sorties are over appalling country. For most part it is precipitously mountainous, some areas are too steep for ice or snow to cling…Beautiful, spectacular, and vastly interesting it may be to an artist, geologist, or geographer, but to an airman several hundred miles from the only base, an engineer with his senses alert for a false beat in the engines, or a pilot with the possibility of an emergency landing ever at the back of his mind, it is a nightmare landscape.[64]

In the second season, the aircraft flew over the western side of the Antarctic Peninsula and the Falkland Islands and completed coverage of the South Shetlands. The planes would fly over the region with the mounted camera directed towards an opening on the floor of the aircraft. By flying in parallel traverses over the designated area it was hoped each photograph would overlap with the other. To conclude such a task successfully, the pilot was dependent upon not only the skill of the navigator but also the unpredictable weather.

While aerial photography was unquestionably revolutionary in terms of expanding and accelerating the photographic coverage of the Antarctic, ground-based observation and land-based surveying were not made redundant.[65] By employing geometric methods such as triangulation, the surveyors hoped to construct survey diagrams of islands and polar landscapes. The collection of orderly data pertaining to those locations depended upon a network of control points. Even with the concessions from the DCS regarding the eventual accuracy of polar maps, the FIDASE struggled to obtain ground control for the interpretation of the aerial photographs, which provoked widespread recrimination and frustration amongst the British polar community. The terrible weather conditions encountered by the FIDASE led to 'gaps' appearing in ground-based observation. According to some observers, such as the harbour-master of Stanley, John Huckle, the management of the FIDASE was fatally flawed:

> I am further prompted by a personal impression that a most injudicious expenditure of public funds is involved in this matter. The weather conditions appear to have been a shock to the expedition, both here and in the Dependencies why? The British taxpayer will have to wait a very long time before his extra 2d per packet on cigarettes will bring a complete series of Antarctic picture cards in the packet.[66]

These criticisms were unjustified in the sense that Mott's organisational skills were only one part of an increasingly complex political and scientific equation. The plans for an International Geophysical Year (1957–8) changed the context for science and politics, and the mapping interests of the FIDASE were later judged to be inappropriate in an emerging era of co-operation and political compromise.

SUMMARY

Since the creation of the FIDS in 1945, Britain was locked into a political and geographical battle with Argentina and Chile. The surveyors and their struggles over the ice were only one element in a complex battle over the visual imagination of Antarctica. Basic geographical information had to be transported back to the UK for processing and subsequent incorporation into sheet maps of the FID. Indeed in the first years of the FIDS, there was some concern that Argentina actually possessed a superior map collection of the Antarctic. In 1949, the Colonial Office expressed its surprise that Argentine citizens were purchasing papers and maps relating to nineteenth-century British activities. Remarkably, the then FO librarian noted to his Colonial Office counterpart that 'we don't think that, politically, this really matters'.[67] Such complacency was quickly swept aside when British officials recognised that the formal cartography produced by agencies such as the DCS was deemed vital in terms of substantiating British Antarctic claims. Postage stamps, maps and brochures were also employed in this paper battle over the disputed sovereignty of Antarctica and the Falkland Islands. Protests and counter-protests were routinely exchanged and it is little wonder then that Sir Jack Ward, the British ambassador to Argentina, hoped that the Antarctic Treaty would diminish Argentine determination:

> When the Antarctic Treaty of December 1st [1959] has come into force...it is hoped that the Argentine government will give up this ridiculous game although I am by no means sure. No Argentine minister or official dare expose himself to the charge of being lukewarm in this paper battle.[68]

While officials tended to concentrate on ensuring that the legal basis for British claims was properly protected, the geographical dimension of this problem caused persistent irritation and occasional outrage. Due to the inaccessibility of the Antarctic and the Southern Ocean, paper-based representations of the region were always going to assume a greater importance compared to other parts of the British Empire. The extreme and remote FID were thus largely the preserve of an elite group of men who were determined to preserve Britain's imperial interests against South American opportunism. What must have been galling for the administrators of the South Atlantic Empire was not only that their South American rivals were skilled at raising the public profile of their Antarctic claims but also unrelenting in their harassment of British territorial claims.

Maps and stamps depicting the Falklands and Antarctic as 'British' were favoured targets. In a letter to the Foreign Secretary, Selwyn Lloyd, dated 17 December 1958, Ward provides an amusing illustration of the British predicament. Apparently, the Chilean customs service found and then impounded some British diaries at Santiago airport because they contained maps of the Antarctic labelled part of the FID. Until the maps were excised, the customs service would not release the diaries to the intended recipients. While these events had occurred in Chile, Ward was nevertheless attentive to the wider implications for the British South Atlantic Empire: 'What makes the Chilean behaviour particularly absurd was that the map in question was minuscule, and the designation FID scarcely legible to the naked eye. You may consider that some official protest is called to safeguard our legal position.'[69]

After taking advice from the Colonial Office, the Foreign Secretary suggested in March 1959:

> I am advised that a protest should be delivered, not so much to preserve our legal position, which cannot be affected by anything so trivial, but because of the fact that the inclusion in the diaries of references unpalatable to the Chilean government is no valid reason for their arbitrary detention.[70]

Although it is not clear what happened to the diaries, events surrounding the international politics of the Antarctica were changing and the catalytic role of the US was exposing such trivia as increasingly irrelevant in a new era of international scientific co-operation and territorial settlement. However, the Chilean diary saga confirmed that the visual representation of British Antarctica was an essential element in the defence of Britain's South Atlantic Empire. Paradoxically, the rival stations on Deception Island had to be abandoned when a violent volcanic eruption in the late 1960s forced human survival to take priority over flag-waving and map-making.

NOTES ON CHAPTER 2

1   Public Record Office (PRO) CO 532/34/58368. Memorandum from the Admiralty, 'Antarctic regions: territorial claims', 5 December 1919.

2   The club was opened in the second half of the nineteenth century at 58 Rue Pigalle.

3   SPRI Archives MS 1308/22/1. Correspondence and Committee Papers of Tabarin. Brian Roberts' note was written over a telegram from the Governor of the Falkland Islands to the Secretary of State for the Colonies dated 19 November 1943.

4   On the RRS *Discovery II* expeditions, see the review paper by N. Macintosh, 'The fifth commission of the RRS *Discovery II*' *Geographical Journal* XCVII (1941): pp. 201–16. The RRS *Discovery II* undertook five commissions of research in Antarctica and the Southern Ocean. The maps in Macintosh's paper provide a remarkable visual testament to the sea-based movements of the vessel.

5   PRO ADM 116/4670. FO paper, 'Argentine encroachments in the Dependencies of the Falkland Islands', October 1942. Peter Beck has shown, however, that British uncertainty over the legal strength of its claims has a longer history.

6   PRO ADM 116/4670. The head of Military Branch of the Admiralty noted: 'There are better employments for HM ships in wartime than to visit a distant British dependency in order to counter a fictitious claim to that territory by a neutral South American Republic', 27 September 1942.

7   See the *Evening News*, 'Unique stamps for uninhabited islands', 6 May 1944, and an earlier piece by the *Daily Sketch*, 'Surprise stamp issue for British islands', 27 April 1944.

8   I owe thanks to Jean-Louis Tissier and Claire Hancock for their help in tracing the history of café Tabarin. After the Second World War, the name changed to 'La Lune Rousse' in order to avoid the taint of German collaboration.

9   V. Fuchs, *Of Ice and Men* (Oswestry, Anthony Nelson, 1982), pp. 22–3.

10   PRO ADM 116/4670. Report of proceedings of HMS *Carnarvon Castle*, 25 January–11 July 1943. This remarkable file also contains the hand-drawn map of

Argentine activities at Deception Island in the South Orkneys, and located the navigation beacon on the Melchior Islands.

11   SPRI Archives MS 1308/22/1. First Report on the Work of Operation Tabarin Part 1: The Work of Base A 1943–1944, written by Lieutenant Commander James Marr RN.

12   See the official account of the 1934–7 British Grahamland Expedition by J. Rymill, *Southern Lights* (London, Chatto and Windus, 1938).

13   On Roberts' career at the FO and the SPRI, see H. King and A. Savours (eds), *Polar Pundit* (Cambridge, Cambridge University Press, 1995).

14   W. Balchin, 'UK geographers in the Second World War', *Geographical Journal* 153 (1987): pp. 159–80.

15   PRO ADM 116/4670. FO Research Department, 'Territorial claims in the Antarctic', May 1944.

16   Australian Archives (AA) AWM 123 211, Letter from the Secretary of State for the Dominions Office to the Australian Prime Minister's Department, 13 February 1943.

17   PRO ADM 116/4670. This offer of settlement is noted in a letter from the FO to the Secretary of the Admiralty dated 23 October 1943. The letter does not specify the names of the correspondents.

18   Cited in K. Dodds, *Geopolitics in Antarctica: Views from the Southern Oceanic Rim* (Chichester, John Wiley, 1997), p. 50.

19   Cited in Dodds, *Geopolitics in Antarctica*, p. 51. The declaration was published on 20 February 1943.

20   Cited in Dodds, *Geopolitics in Antarctica*, p. 51.

21   A copy of this restricted FO research report, written by Roberts can be read in the Canadian Department of External Affairs' (DEA) files, and was included as part of a background brief on the 'Falkland Islands dispute' prepared by A. Blanchette, 2 March 1948. National Archives of Canada (NAC) RG 25 4765 50070-40 part 1.

22   Author interview with Dr Bernard Stonehouse, 9 October 2000. I am indebted to Dr Stonehouse for sharing with me his extraordinary recollections.

23   The words of the advertisement were reproduced in the *Times*, 12 September 1955. The salary for a FIDS surveyor was approximately £400 per annum.

24   Launcelot Fleming accompanied Roberts on a 1932 Cambridge University expedition to Vatnajokull, Iceland.

25   Fuchs recited these instructions to the FIDS to the author verbatim in an interview, 1 July 1998.

26   PRO CO 537/4010. Political instructions to the Leader of the FIDS dated 4 November 1948. The FO supported the revised instructions, which included recommendations designed to avoid actual physical violence in the Antarctic. Letter from C. Shuckburgh of the FO to P. Carter of the Colonial Office dated 26 October 1948.

27   SPRI Archives MS 1308/22/1 CC. Instructions issued by the Colonial Office to Surgeon Commander E. W. Bingham dated October 1945.

28   British Antarctic Survey (BAS) AD6/15/17/7. Letter from Brian Roberts to E. W. Bingham dated 6 December 1946.

29   V. Fuchs, '2 years in Antarctica', *The Listener*, 8 June 1950: pp. 981–2. See also Fuchs, 'The FIDS 1948–1950', *Journal of the Royal Society of Arts* 4866 (1950): pp. 193–211.

30 E. W. Bingham, 'Recent British activity in the Antarctic', *United Empire* 39 (1948): pp. 31–5; J. Wordie, 'The FIDS 1943–1946', *Polar Record* 32 (1946): pp. 372–84; G. Hattersley-Smith, 'King George Island', *Alpine Journal* 58 (1951): pp. 67–75.

31 M. Clifford, 'FIDS', *Corona* 1/9 (1950). This document can be found in SPRI PAM 91 (08). See also Fuchs, *Scientific Reports Number 1: Organisation and Methods* (London, HMSO, 1953).

32 R. Adie, 'Twenty-five years of Antarctic exploration', *University of Birmingham Gazette* 20 (1968): pp. 127–9.

33 SPRI Archives MS 1278 ER. Brian Roberts correspondence and papers relating to the Ronne Antarctic Research Expedition 1946–1948.

34 BAS AD6/2M/1952/L, 'South Georgia Survey 1951–2, expedition reports', prepared by Duncan Carse. He returned to South Georgia for three further seasons to complete the task, and his account of the expeditions was published in a modified form as 'The Survey of South Georgia 1951–1957', *Geographical Journal* 125 (1959): pp. 20–37. See also BAS AD6/2M/2952/1, 'South Georgia Survey, 1951–1952 expedition reports', prepared by E. W. K. Walton. Previously, Walton had served with the FIDS and the Norwegian, British and Swedish expedition in 1951–2.

35 PRO ADM 1/21126. Letter from Sir William Tennant to the First Sea Lord, Sir John Cunningham, dated 5 May 1948.

36 PRO ADM 1/19509. This file contains details of the voyages made by HMS *William Scoresby* between 1944 and 1946. When not at war, the *William Scoresby* retained its designation as a RRS.

37 Most Governors of the Falkland Islands in the post-1945 era have also admitted that they enjoyed executing their responsibilities for the FID because it provided an opportunity to visit the Antarctic, South Georgia and South Orkneys. The South Sandwich Islands were rarely included on such visits because of their inaccessibility from the other elements of the FID.

38 Royal Geographical Society Archives, Sir Laurence Kirwan Personal Papers File 15. Letter from Kirwan to B. Farmer dated 8 May 1957. Kirwan was asked to comment on Roberts' suitability for the post of Director of the SPRI.

39 The British National Antarctic Committee eventually replaced the FIDS Scientific Committee in 1961 for Antarctic research.

40 PRO CO 537/4010. This directive is contained in correspondence with the Colonial Office and its military staff, dated 13 November 1947.

41 Author interview with Sir Vivian Fuchs, 1 July 1998.

42 Fuchs, *Of Ice and Men.*

43 J. Roberts, 'The FIDS', *British Medical Journal* 15 (1949): pp. 863–4 and D. Dalglish, '2 years in the Antarctic', *St Thomas' Hospital Gazette* 2 (1952): pp. 62–5, 111–17.

44 As the FIDS and then subsequently the BAS became more established in the Antarctic and South Georgia, it is striking how the Falkland Islands declined in significance as the 'gateway' to British Antarctica.

45 D. Mason, 'The FIDS: Explorations of 1947–1948', *Geographical Journal* CXV (1950): pp. 145–60. The quote is taken from p. 155.

46 F. Spufford, '*I May be Some Time': Ice and the English Imagination* (London, Faber and Faber, 1996), p. 5.

47 BAS AD3/1/A5/ 155A (1). Letter from Sir Miles Clifford to the Colonial Office, dated 10 September 1950.

48 BAS AD3/1/A5/164/A. Letter from the Secretary of State for the Colonies to the Governor of the Falkland Islands, dated 12 April 1948.

49 PRO CO 537/4010. Letter from the Colonial Office to the FIDS office in Stanley, which included the memorandum entitled 'Political instructions from the leader of the FIDS', dated 4 November 1948.

50 PRO FO 371 97367. Letter from Roberts to the American Department of the FO, dated 29 May 1952.

51 PRO FO 371 97367. Letter from Roberts to the American Department of the FO, dated 23 July 1952.

52 PRO FO 371 97367. Letter from Roberts to the American Department of the FO, dated 16 October 1952.

53 PRO FO 371 97367. Letter from Roberts to the American Department of the FO, dated 18 November 1952.

54 F. Ommanney, *South Latitude* (London, Longman, 1938), p. 56.

55 King and Savours (eds), *Polar Pundit*, p. 58.

56 SPRI Archives MS 1277/4, Letter from Roberts to W. Wiggins of the DCS, dated 10 August 1956.

57 Adie, 'Twenty-five years of Antarctic exploration'.

58 BAS AD2 /1/34/(1). Comments made by the Director of Overseas Surveys to the FIDS Scientific Committee, 11 June 1952.

59 BAS AD3/1/A5/155/A (1). Letter from the Colonial Office to the Treasury, dated 15 September 1952.

60 BAS AD3/1/A5/155/A (1). Letter from Frank Elliot to Colonel Wiggins of the DCS, dated 14 February 1957.

61 The *Gazetteer* of the FID (London, FO Research Department, 20 September 1955).

62 SPRI Archives MS 1308/22/9. Letter from A. Lennox-Boyd of the Colonial Office to Governor of the Falkland Islands O. R. Arthur, dated 10 December 1956.

63 BAS AD8/1/34 (1). Memorandum on the possibilities of survey with the aid of air photography, dated 14 February 1952.

64 Quoted in P. Mott, *Wings over Ice* (Exeter, Wheaton, 1986), pp. 93–4.

65 See P. Mott, 'Airborne surveying in the Antarctic', *Geographical Journal* CXXIV (1958): pp. 1–17.

66 BAS AD/1/62. Report from J. Huckle to the Governor of the Falkland Islands, dated 10 April 1956.

67 PRO FO 370 1800. Memorandum on 'Buying of manuscripts dealing with the Falkland Islands by persons abroad', dated 10 May 1949.

68 PRO FO 371 138956. Letter from Sir Jack Ward to Henry Hankey, head of the American Department of the FO, dated 17 December 1959.

69 PRO FO 371 138956. Letter from Sir Jack Ward to Foreign Secretary Selwyn Lloyd, dated 17 December 1958.

70 PRO FO 371 138956. Letter from Lloyd to Ward, dated 26 March 1959.

3

Anglo–Argentine Friction:
Education, Meat and Trade

Perón's education ministry had ordered that every school in the land teach children that the Malvinas were an integral part of Argentina's territory, inherited from Spain, and usurped by Britain. Las Malvinas son Argentinas was a sentence that every human being repeated from his or her first day at school.[1]

The uncritical assumption of the Argentine public that the Antarctic sector claimed by their government is rightfully part of their national territory persists. There has been no indication of any change in their policy, which remains to try and establish sovereignty by 'saturating' it and increasing the degree of scientific work.[2]

INTRODUCTION

Such has been the commercial, logistical and cultural influence in Argentina that it was customarily referred to as part of Britain's 'informal empire' or 'sixth dominion'.[3] When the Prince of Wales visited Argentina in 1925, in order to celebrate the 100-year-old Treaty of Friendship, he drew the following endorsement from President Alvear: 'The Prince is the representative of a glorious dynasty...and of a government which is the model of good sense and efficiency'.[4] Such expressions of flattery became scarce following the 1932 Ottawa Conference on Imperial Preference, which stipulated that declining British purchases of Argentine chilled beef and wheat would be compensated for by rising imports from the Dominions of Australia, Canada and New Zealand. Given Argentina's dependence on beef exports to Britain, the reconfiguration of imperial trade patterns was unsettling, and the 1933 Anglo–Argentine Roca–Runciman Pact attempted to restore some semblance of economic order by guaranteeing a greater share of the British meat market for Argentine producers. Sir Nevile Henderson, the then British ambassador to Argentina, astutely recognised that 'Our good or bad relations seem to depend entirely on the import duty which was levied on chilled beef'. By the time World War II ravaged Europe and North Africa, Anglo–Argentine trading relations were undergoing further change as Argentina had to accept sterling balances held at the

Bank of England in lieu of Argentine produce. Anti-British sentiment in Argentina sharpened: according to one commentator, 'the Argentine Republic is an immense fly trapped and immobilised in the network of English economic domination'.[5] When released after 1945, these blocked balances were later used by Colonel – subsequently President – Perón to 'buy out' the British proprietors of the Argentine railways and public utility companies such as the telephone system. Anglo–Argentine relations were strained in the process by commercial tension and geopolitical intrigue, which spilt over into territorial competition in the faraway, windswept islands of South Shetland and South Georgia.

To understand the nature of Anglo–Argentine relations before and after the Second World War, the demise of British influence in Argentina needs to be linked to the corresponding intensification of geopolitical competition in Antarctica and the South Atlantic. The post-1945 transformation in particular owes much to the extraordinary influence of Perón and his reforming economic programme and geographical re-education of Argentine citizens. The new generation of schoolchildren was versed and immersed in the importance of the Argentine Antarctic sector and the Falkland Islands. Inevitably, Britain was represented as an unwelcome colonial presence, while Chile's claims to polar territory were tolerated as 'co-existing' within a South American Antarctic sector. The extent of Britain's colonial influence was further challenged by the 1948 nationalisation of the railways (originally built and mostly financed by the British) and the uncertainty over regular and adequate meat supplies for a Britain hit by rationing.[6] The meat controversy was not to surface again until 1967, when it was linked to a devastating outbreak of foot-and-mouth disease in Britain. Political dissatisfaction with the state of Anglo–Argentine relations convinced British officials to believe that Argentina under Perón was unstable and opportunistic vis-à-vis the question of meat, Antarctica and the Falkland Islands. The Anglo–Argentine connection was no longer characterised by an easy familiarity based on successive Argentine Governments recognising the imperial authority of Britain.

THE ANGLO–ARGENTINE CONNECTION

For the past 200 years, trade, investment, exploration, football and the occasional outbreak of violence typified relations between Britain and Argentina. Despite two failed attempts to invade Buenos Aires in the earliest part of the nineteenth century, this relationship remained cordial: Argentina supplied Britain with meat and grains in return for industrial goods and access to capital resources. By 1889, Argentina absorbed between 40 and 50 per cent of all British investment outside the British Empire. By the end of the nineteenth century, the Anglo–Argentine community numbered 40,000 and was the largest British community outside the imperial dominions. Although dwarfed by Italian- and Spanish-speaking immigrants, they published their own newspaper, the *Buenos Aires Herald*, and commanded a considerable commercial and financial presence in the Republic. It was after all only the British who referred to Argentina as the 'Argentine'. With predominantly British investment (60 per cent out of a total of £400 million by 1914) in the railway and banking sectors, the Republic was transformed into one of the world's richest states with exports of wheat, corn, meat and wool.

The term 'Anglo–Argentine community' fails to distinguish the diversity of the nineteenth-century immigrants from the British and Irish Isles. Irish labour helped to construct the railways, which opened up the pampas to the railways and economic development. Welsh settlers extended and expanded settlements in Patagonia and the most southern area of the continent, while the Scots created schools, managed the railways and helped to create new communities in the north of Argentina.[7] In the process they all left an impact on Argentine culture and society. When Anglo–Argentine relations soured in the aftermath of the Second World War, the English, rather than the 'British' or 'Irish', were frequently identified as the unwelcome colonial presence in the case of disputed territories such as the Falkland Islands. When the Argentine media condemned Britain for its occupation of the Falklands in the 1940s and later in 1982 they referred, amongst other things, to 'English pirates'.

Prior to the decline and eventual collapse of cordial Anglo–Argentine relations in 1945, the Anglo–Argentine community represented the fusion of two communities bounded by trading, sporting and cultural contact and thus seemed to defy the claims of the Falkland Islands community that integration with Argentina was impossible. When the ship carrying the Prince of Wales (later Edward VIII) docked in Buenos Aires on 17 August 1925, the then Argentine President Alvear showered the Prince with praise and organised a 21-gun salute. After the event, even the Spanish-language newspapers commented favourably on the role of British commerce and culture in shaping the Argentine citizen. One newspaper, *La Prensa*, even claimed that Britain was a 'noble nation'. Twenty years later, British royalty had lost its allure and served only as a reminder of imperial economic domination. The 21-gun salute in March 1948 celebrated the nationalisation of the railways and signalled an altogether different relationship between Britain and Argentina.

Although diminishing trade changed the nature of relations, the 1933 Roca–Runciman Agreement was intended nonetheless to secure Argentina favourable access to British trade and investment in return for continued supplies of chilled beef.[8] However, it was designed to protect Britain's influence at a time of economic dislocation and the emergence of the US as a global challenger to the traditional imperial policy of free trade. The agreement, so it was hoped, would consolidate the position of the Anglo–Argentine community and maintain strong links to the political elite, which dominated the production and supply of agricultural commodities. The then British ambassador, Sir Nevile Henderson, before his controversial posting to Berlin, was inclined to point to the reassuring stability of the 1930s, when Argentina still deferred to Britain on matters of economic concern. For those unconnected with the agricultural elite in Argentina, the Roca–Runciman Agreement was further evidence that 'the English will impede spontaneous development, foreclose industrial possibilities and maintain us in a state of agricultural and stock producers'.[9]

According to the diplomatic script written in London and Buenos Aires, Argentina was expected to be grateful for continued British economic support, and it was hoped that potentially divisive issues such as territorial competition in the South Atlantic could be settled. In a letter to the Foreign Secretary, Anthony Eden, dated 28 August 28 1936, Henderson suggested that 'a solution of the Falkland Islands question might be found on the basis of a recognition of Argentina's legal rights to the island in return for Great Britain's undisturbed occupation thereof'. In a reply to this proposal, Eden rejected this plan and reminded Henderson that 'you should be aware that the legal basis of the claim is far less weak than at one time supposed'.[10] Unwilling to contemplate arbitration at this stage, Eden was also concerned that Britain's strategic position in the South Atlantic would be complicated by any proposals to solve the outstanding dispute with Argentina. Despite growing evidence of Argentine agitation on the question of the disputed islands, it was felt inadvisable to tackle the issue, given the importance of commercial and trading contact.

The outbreak of the Second World War challenged Henderson's widely shared interpretation of Argentina as a place filled with a political and economic elite sympathetic to Britain's imperial trading interests. The Argentine Government's agreement not to take advantage of Britain's confrontation with Nazi Germany to pursue its claims to the Falklands did not preclude expeditions to the Antarctic conducted to remind Britain of its southerly claims. Despite widespread irritation with Argentina over its reluctance to declare war on Germany, the ambassador to Argentina, Sir David Kelly, urged restraint – especially if it meant that the 'beef barons' of the country remained in power. As Kelly noted in a letter dated 3 February 1943:

A policy of liberal neutrality or an indication that the people of Argentina, forgetting their past glorious history, have not fully appreciated the true nature of the conflict [the Second World War] now being waged against the forces of tyranny...I was particularly grateful to receive of the importance, which the Argentine government attach to the maintenance of the British Empire...Latin Americans are temperamental creatures, in dealing with them, effects are often produced quite out of proportion. They experience little hesitation in acting contrary to common sense.[11]

Unfortunately for those intent on upholding the political status quo in Argentina, Britain's deepening involvement in the Second World War called into question the capacity to maintain a strong position.[12] Even before the emergence of Perón after the military coup in June 1943, members of landed elite were beginning to question the wisdom of ignoring the possibility of new trading and commercial contacts with North America and Europe for the sake of maintaining sentimental ties with Britain.

PERÓN AND GEOGRAPHICAL EDUCATION

Perón and his political followers were committed to implementing a programme based on social improvement and economic nationalism. This did not augur well for complacent British views, and it has been argued that 'The rise of Perón and the new social and economic forces which he represented was the death knell for the Anglo–Argentine connection'.[13] While a great deal of attention was focused on the implications for trade, the cultural and educational influence of this new order was overlooked. According to the political scientist Carlos Escudé, the unsettled condition of the Argentine frontier and territorial disputes with Britain and Chile were given considerable public precedence under Perón's presidential years between 1946 and 1955.[14]

In a series of analyses of primary and secondary education in the Republic, Escudé argued that the new post-1945 Government was able to draw upon a public culture which remained wedded to the belief that the country had suffered a series of territorial 'losses' since its creation in 1810. Despite the territorial expansion of the Republic in remote areas such as Patagonia and the Andes, attention remained focused on the 'loss' of the Falkland Islands in 1833 and the persistent geopolitical uncertainties regarding South American neighbours. In the late 1920s, geography textbooks began to focus for the first time on the 'Argentine Antarctic territory', which followed a formal memoranda prepared by the director of Argentine post and telegraphs in 1927 outlining Argentine interests in polar territories.

Perón's commitment to pursue these territorial disputes was the culmination of a long-standing grievance. For more than a hundred years, successive Argentine Governments had protested at the illegal British annexation and occupation of the Falkland Islands. Given their inability to 'persuade' an imperial power to reconsider the legal and geographical position, the struggle to regain these Islands was as much a visual as a diplomatic dispute. Maps and stamps contributed to the public education and in March 1937, Argentina issued a new peso stamp depicting the Malvinas as Argentine territory. While no formal protest was offered by the British Embassy in Buenos Aires to the Argentine authorities, rumours and fears abounded that German propaganda in neutral Argentina was responsible for this mischief. It was alleged by the FO that Germany financed a group called the Alianza de la Juventud Nacional, which campaigned for the return of the Falkland Islands and the Antarctic Peninsula. By 1939, the growing media and educational interest in these disputed territories galvanised Argentina to express a public determination to raise the topic at Bergen's forthcoming international conference on Antarctica. Unsurprisingly, the British ambassador in Buenos Aires, Sir Eamond Overy, warned the FO in March 1940 that he suspected German spies in Argentina of attempts to inflame local opinion against British commercial and territorial imperialism. A local 'manifesto' produced by 'Junta de Recuperacion de Las Malvinas' in 1940 was cited as an example of such sedition because it called for the ending of British imperialism in the Falkland Islands.[15]

While stamps and maps can be subtle symbols of nationalism, they nonetheless form part of the daily life of citizens. When the ownership of a place is disputed, the visual representation of territory gains prevalence as each side strives to remind its citizens and the wider international community of the legitimacy of its claim (see figure 3.1). Notwithstanding the British occupation of the Falkland Islands, FCO officials recognised that even stamps could be useful in the pursuit of this aim. A British post office had been maintained at South Georgia since 1909 precisely because it provided evidence of 'effective occupation'. Unlike the Argentine remit, promotional stamps were never distributed widely within the UK, thus limiting the purpose of visual reminders of the South Atlantic Empire. In a British Government file headed 'Argentine claims to the Falkland Islands: Stamp issue of Dependencies', examples were included of Argentine first-day covers showing maps depicting the Argentine Antarctic sector and duly stamped by the Argentine polar post office in the South Orkneys.[16] These geographical depictions of the Argentine polar territory were all the more vexing for the Colonial Office just as it was engaged in plans for Operation Tabarin. British officials were further frustrated in the light of Argentina's continued reluctance to declare war on Nazi Germany, which they considered to be an unforgivable betrayal. Neutrality was equated with at best a form of appeasement, at worst a closet sympathy for Nazism.

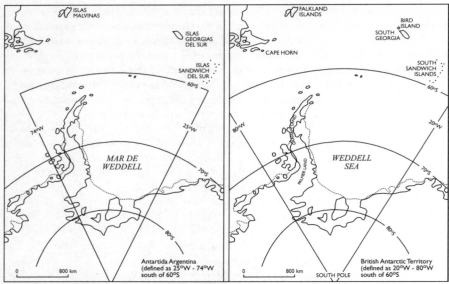

Figure 3.1: Overlapping claims to Antarctica

The democratic election of Perón in March 1946 was greeted with collective dismay and apprehension by British observers in London and Buenos Aires, fearful not only of meat shortages but also of the new developments in economic relations which coincided with the consolidation of Argentine interest in the Antarctic. Fernando Daus, the president of the Argentine Society for Geographical Studies, identified geographical education as an essential element in formal education of primary and secondary schoolchildren.[17] After 1947, the Republic had officially 'expanded' from 2.8 million to 4 million square kilometres as the Antarctic Peninsula was incorporated into the national territory. Geography and geology were marshalled in order to demonstrate that Argentina was connected to the Falklands, South Georgia and Antarctica. The Military Geography Institute (IGM) was ordered to produce new maps of the Republic showing the Malvinas Islands and the Antarctic Peninsula as Argentine possessions. Under a formal presidential decree dating from 1948 all maps of Argentina had to encompass:

> River islands of the Plata, the Malvinas Islands, the Islands of Lennox, Picton and adjacent islands in the Beagle Channel, the South Orkneys, South Georgia, the South Sandwich Islands and the Argentine Antarctic sector which we maintain sovereignty over. The limits of the latter are; meridians 25 and 74 degrees West of Greenwich and from the parallel of 60 degrees South to the South Pole. It is to be called Argentine sovereign territory in the Antarctic sector.[18]

Perón's determination to educate the population and a new generation of schoolchildren, produced geography textbooks in a relatively short period of time (1938–48) to reflect the new mood:

> In 1939, he [L. Dagnino Pastore, a popular textbook writer] wrote that Britain 'possesses' more than eight million square kilometres in Antarctica (to which he applied the British term, the Falkland Islands Dependencies); in 1940 he changed

the word 'possesses' for the expression 'attributes to itself', adding that Argentina might get a part of this if the criterion for the distribution of territories used in the Arctic were applied; in 1944 he stated that Argentina has 'unquestionable' rights and 'legitimate basis for sovereignty over a vast Antarctic sector'; in 1946 he reports that Argentina has made it known to the world that it claims the Antarctic sector over which 'it has rights'; and finally in 1947 he writes matter of factually of an Argentine sector over which Argentina 'exercises authority'.[19]

The use of maps and images in education was essential to promulgate geographical realities, in contrast to British schools and institutions eager to remind their school-children of imperial heroes such as Captain Scott.[20]

The promotion of a new national geographical identity had not yet captured the imagination of his citizens, despite the nationalist rhetoric of Perón.[21] A public vision of a post-war Argentina free from colonial and imperial interference was perhaps opportunistic, given his country's own post-colonial history, involving the occupation of Patagonia at the expense of indigenous populations.[22] However, it did underline a broader ambition to end all forms of European colonialism in the Americas. The determination to recover the Falklands and Antarctica from British colonial rule was reflected in the decision to create a specialist Antarctic and Malvinas Islands Division within the Ministry of Foreign Affairs and Worship in 1948. New post-war treaties, such as the 1947 Treaty of Inter-American Reciprocal Assistance signed in Rio de Janeiro, also aided this anti-colonial aspiration because it pledged that an armed attack by any state against a member state should be considered as an attack on all member states. Article I stated that the geographical jurisdiction of the treaty extended southwards and incorporated the Antarctic continent. Argentina and Chile argued that Britain's frequent despatch of Royal Naval warships such as HMS *Nigeria* constituted a direct threat to these countries which should provoke (at the very least) others such as the US to protest against British 'intrusions' in the American Antarctic.

The direct intervention of Perón in international forums such as the Organisation of American States and the Inter-American Conference generated a growing number of debates on the future of European colonies in the Americas. Between March and April 1948, for example, Argentina had been instrumental in the creation of an American Commission on Dependent Territories at the Inter-American Conference held at Bogota. According to the *Falkland Islands Weekly News*, the commission's remit was 'to study the situation regarding colonies, possessions and occupied American territories'.[23] The commission noted that one of the enduring sources of European colonialism was Britain with its occupation of British Honduras, British Guiana and the Falkland Islands and its dependencies.

The changing international politics of inter-American relations were monitored closely by one of those vestiges of European colonialism. Reverend R.G. Calvert, in a letter to the *Falkland Islands Weekly News* speculated on a possible post-colonial compromise to this territorial dispute:

> Would it satisfy the American nations if these colonies were given complete self-government? And as an interim measure could a solution be found by the UK handing over responsibility for the Crown colonies in or close to the Americas say to the Canadian government? This would still leave the question of French and Dutch possessions but they are hardly our concern.[24]

While some may have dreamt of post-colonial settlement, others in the Falkland Islands were not inclined to compromise on the question of the South Atlantic Empire. In the immediate post-war period, Clifford was instrumental in resisting Argentine geopolitical objectives by organising armed naval tours around the FID in order to maintain British interests in the wake of Operation Tabarin. The Governor of the Falkland Islands was also the administrator of the dependencies and noted in his Governor's broadcast that he had ensured that protest notes were despatched to neighbouring Argentine and Chilean bases. Both sides had found visual reminders vital in the protection of remote territorial interests, and as Clifford concluded:

> The Argentines and Chileans have meanwhile made common cause and ships of both countries have been making free use of our territorial waters. We are at present witnessing a great deal of ostentatious and provocative display by both countries. One does not bore water on one's neighbour's land without asking his consent.[25]

Under Clifford's watchful eye, the remote and virtually unpopulated FID mimicked the private property of the British Crown. Given the absence of traditional indicators of private ownership such as ditches, fences and hedges, Clifford's penchant for Royal Navy ships such as HMS *Snipe* served to ensure that trespassers were evicted. It was ultimately his uncompromising approach that triumphed in the face of the Argentine geopolitical challenge to the Falkland Islands and its dependencies. Within three months of publishing his proposal, Calvert noted, 'It is certainly as well to put out a reminder in some quarters that we are British: We are citizens of British Islands, and in addition we can claim descent from those who actually lived in the UK. We are proud of it, but it is our birthright'.[26] While Britain and Argentina were locked into a diplomatic conflict, the three claimant states (Argentina, Chile and the UK) nonetheless did agree in November 1948 to a naval agreement which stipulated that warships should not be sent below the latitude of 60 degrees south.

Despite these occasional successes in confidence-building, concerns over weak legal claims to the Falkland Islands forced the Colonial and Foreign Offices to concentrate on highlighting the post-1833 occupation of an Anglophone community. For much of the 1940s, the standard and well-established British response to the Argentine counter-claim was to ridicule its territorial competitor while subsequently offering to place the future status under the review of the International Court of Justice (ICJ) rather than engage in bilateral negotiation.[27] The *Falkland Islands Weekly News* carried this view in a trenchant article on the Falkland Islands and its dependencies:

> The Falkland Islands and the Dependencies have been in the news of late, owing to the action of Argentina in advancing yet another claim for their possession. This 'claim' is of true comic opera pattern. The 'argument' is that, because Spain was once in possession of all South American territories, therefore Argentina, having assisted in expelling the Spaniards from the continent, the Falkland Islands are now the property of Argentina! At the present time, the population is mainly British, and our brethren have a rooted objection to being handed over lock, stock and barrel to a power whose ideals, whose religion and whose system of government are diametrically opposed to their own.[28]

Perón had challenged the moral and geographical right of the British to be in those places, and a wide-ranging and expensive battle over territorial claims commenced as the pressure on Britain to despatch the Falkland Islands and the dependencies to a post-colonial future gathered political momentum in South America. As his Foreign Minister Albert Molina grandly concluded in February 1953 after a visit to the Antarctic:

> Argentine sovereignty over the territory is based on deep-rooted historic rights which are spiritually identified with the feelings of the entire people of the nation, on the superior geographical position of the Republic, on the geological continuity of its land with the Antarctic territories, on the climatic influence which the neighbouring polar zones exercise on its territories... and finally on its uninterrupted activities in the Antarctic territory itself.[29]

MEAT AND ARMS: ANGLO–ARGENTINE TRADE AFTER 1945

The continued territorial dispute over the Falkland Islands and its dependencies was all the more remarkable given the reliance on Argentina by austerity-weary and rationed British families after 1945. An agreement that Argentina would be paid for meat through sterling balances secured on British assets in Argentina provided a *modus operandi* for the Second World War. These accumulated resources now allowed the Republic to develop a post-war industrial strategy, which abolished the foreign domination of infrastructure and investment in Argentina. When Perón published his first five-year plan for commercial and industrial development in 1946, he was determined to promote indigenous manufacturing and capitalise on Britain's dependency on meat imports. Apart from the vexed question of meat supplies, British commercial influence was dramatically reduced with the nationalisation of the railways, and confined to limited trade rather than capital investment.

The supply of meat was one of the most controversial factors in post-1945 Anglo–Argentine relations, which led to repeated British accusations of Argentine greed and unrestrained opportunism. The content and assumptions that carried the 1933 Roca–Runicman Agreement was now part of Anglo–Argentine trading history. Britain was weakened by five years of war, and by June 1947 sterling had become a convertible currency under the terms and conditions attached to American and Canadian post-war loans. With further financial pressures mounting on the British currency, Argentina was struggling to supply meat to Britain in a manner acceptable to both parties.[30] Meat, as Colin Lewis has noted, was one of Argentina's major exports to Britain between 1945 and 1952, even if rising domestic consumption and a decline in animal slaughter reduced the value of those exports from 1295 million pesos per year (1940–4) to 1000 million pesos per year (1945–9).[31] The FO was deeply concerned that: 'Since the War, Anglo–Argentine relations have turned upon the price of meat... and the hungry world could be forced to pay whatever Argentina chooses to demand'.[32]

Between 1946 and 1952, the Attlee and Churchill Governments despatched six trade missions to Argentina to discuss the prevailing economic situation. Cabinet-level discussions of the meat question were frequent, and one such minute prepared by the Ministry of Food in November 1950 captured the pessimistic mood:

> In view of the difficulties, which were being experienced in trade negotiations with Argentina, the meat ration should be reduced if settlement [with Argentina]

is delayed. The Argentine government has been endeavouring to take an unfair advantage of this country's dependence on imported supplies. The reduction in the ration was necessary to ensure that these tactics [of arguing over price and supply] should not succeed.[33]

A report by the Ministry of Food dated 11 December 1950 persisted with the allegation that Argentina was exploiting the situation for its own benefit: 'HMG should bring pressure to bear on the Argentine government to adopt a more reasonable attitude on the price of meat'.[34]

The British magazine the *New Statesman* reflected the sombre minutes prepared for British political leaders in 1951 when it published a famous parody of Anglo–Argentine relations entitled 'Frozen Out' on the eve of the British ambassador's departure for Madrid:

Deadlock in the Argentine
No meat upon the plate!
Failure of a mission to a foreign Fascist state!
Buenos Aires beef chief's their frozen shipments stop
Diplomatic temperatures down to zero drop
(Haggling is proceeding on the Foreign Office plane)
But Britain's chilled ambassador is on his way to Spain.[35]

The dispute was humiliating. Having defeated the axis forces in Europe, North Africa and the Far East, British officials schooled in the traditional ways of conducting imperial trade now struggled to accommodate Perón's vision of post-war Argentina. The first meeting of the trade mission in 1946 formally considered the renewal of the 1933 Roca–Runciman Treaty, and the British ambassador to Argentina, Sir Rex Leeper, suggested in September 1946 that 'It is important that these people should be stopped in their present course in order to put them in their proper place in the world and in our interests as a country considered dependent on the purchase of their products during the next two years'.[36]

This inability to understand their 'proper place in the world' caused British officials and the print media to speculate that Perón's Argentina was guilty of commercial opportunism and heartless scheming. A bulk-buying agreement was eventually agreed and continued until the early 1950s when New Zealand finally emerged as the major overseas supplier. The nadir was 1947–8, when Argentina threatened to halt meat supplies until the convertibility of sterling had been restored after the dollar shortage.

In February 1951, fresh meat rations fell to a record low in the wake of further price disputes, which left a legacy of prejudice when the crisis eventually abated in 1952–3. Already regarded as an unreliable trading partner populated with hysterical and opportunistic individuals, Perón and his wife Evita (the former actress Eva Duarte) were now singled out for ridicule. Her proposed visit to London in July 1947, for example, had to be cancelled not only because a stay at Buckingham Place was dubious but also due to the lack of interest by the FO in hosting such an event. As an FO memorandum to the Cabinet concluded:

In view of our dependence on the goodwill of the Argentine government for food supplies, it would be inexpedient not to offer her some government hospitality.

On the other hand, the character of her husband's government would make it extremely embarrassing for the Foreign Office to entertain her'.[37]

British newspapers were deeply embroiled in the controversy surrounding the proposed visit, with the conservative press grudgingly advocating support only if it could be demonstrated that British trade would benefit.[38] The visit was later cancelled but fierce internal political battles between the Labour Government and the Conservative Party over the merits of bulk-buying meat from Buenos Aires further contributed to the widely held view amongst the British that the Argentine Government was not trustworthy. This view endured for the remainder of Perón's presidential term until his ousting in 1955. As Gwyn Howells astutely concludes, for the immediate post-war period 'Argentina was a serious political matter, which involved British national prestige, democratic principle, and the supply of cheap meat'.[39]

Passions, frustrations and harsh words were set aside at the prospect of arms exports to Argentina and other Latin American states. The FO was eager to gain a share in the unregulated arms market, aware that besides earning valuable currency it would also help to consolidate influence in the region. The Americans were determined to exclude others from this potentially lucrative market.[40] When the South American Department of the FO persisted in exploring the commercial opportunities to sell off surplus armaments in the absence of European competitors such as France and Germany it encountered high-level opposition from the British Cabinet, which was anxious not to upset Anglo–American financial negotiations. Between 1945 and 1947, the British reluctantly agreed to these demands even though there was a real concern that the US might assist Argentina in its Falkland Islands claim in return for Perón's involvement in inter-American defence co-operation.

When it suited the FO, representations of Argentina and Perón alternated between a country populated by hysterical figures unable to recognise 'their place in the world' and one whose democratic credentials deserved consideration when opportunities for commercial transactions arose. It should be remembered that, for much of the Second World War, the US was determined to force Argentina to declare war on Nazi Germany, and when it refused punished it with an American boycott, which damaged Argentina's industrial sector.[41] Although the post-war period afforded short-term benefits, Anglo–Argentine–American relations were characterised by uncertainty and instability. A critical point in the reappraisal of Argentina came with the announcement in 1946 that Argentina wished to re-equip its naval forces. A £20 million commercial opportunity was on offer and British companies such as Vickers-Armstrong were anxious to tender for the contract. The South American Department of the FO pushed for the British Government to pursue this matter with the US and ensure that the State Department in Washington did not exclude British firms. By December 1947, Foreign Secretary Bevin concluded that the 'Gentleman's Agreement' with the Americans concerning arms sales was 'inappropriate' and 'harmful to our interests'.[42] British arms manufacturers Vickers-Armstrong and Hawker Siddeley later supplied Argentina with naval vessels and bomber planes, assisted by a British Government able to take political advantage of the fact that the US had become more preoccupied with responding to the ensuing Cold War problems in Europe and East Asia.[43]

While the topic of arms sales perturbed Anglo–American relations, Britain gambled that commercial opportunities and rewards in Argentina and Chile outweighed the risk that those bombers and ships would be used against British personnel in Antarctica and the Falkland Islands. The sale of British warships such as HMS *Orion* and HMS *Ajax* to Argentina and Chile did not alarm the FO, even though it recognised that the 'Antarctic problem' remained undiminished. Bevin informed the Cabinet in March 1949 that 'there was little prospect that the position in the Antarctic would be improved [by the delay of naval sales], since the discussions were not making very satisfactory progress'.[44] Five years later, this policy dilemma returned to dominate discussions within the FO's South American Department as the question of a potential sale of helicopters to Argentina arose. As one memorandum noted, 'Sir Henry Mack [the then British ambassador to Argentina] might be instructed to tell the Argentine that we should like to sell them the helicopters. [However, it] would be very awkward if they were to be subsequently used for adventures in the Antarctic'.[45] After pressure from the Colonial Office, the opportunity for this supply was eventually refused and the Argentines turned to the US to complete the purchase. The Colonial Office feared that the Argentine navy would fly its operatives around the region and thus assist in the effective occupation of existing and even polar bases. Six months later, the FO confirmed its approval of the sale of 10 crop-spraying helicopters to Argentina after being reassured by the British suppliers, Westland, that they could not be used in the Antarctic.

As with meat supplies, it was recognised that Britain could ill afford to reject or neglect any commercial opportunities with Argentina and, provided that the Royal Navy continued to patrol the waters of the South Atlantic, the risks of further Argentine and even Chilean geopolitical opportunism would be reduced.[46] Clifford was instrumental in ensuring that naval patrols were continued, and even pressed the British armed forces to remove persistent Argentine trespassers from Deception Island in 1953–4.[47] Argentina's relative economic advantage over the British vis-à-vis the meat trade proved short-lived, as recession and foreign debt began to undermine any post-war recovery based on expanded trade. Despite worsening relations over Antarctica and the Falkland Islands, Britain and Argentina continued to negotiate arms contracts even when Argentine politics became dominated by military regimes.

SUMMARY

During the presidential years of Perón, British officials repeatedly complained of Argentine ingratitude and opportunism. Imperial Britain was no longer welcome in Perónist Argentina and the Anglo–Argentine connection was under severe pressure. Unsurprisingly, the role of British ambassador to Buenos Aires was no longer in the post-war period deemed a comfortable posting. With the decline of Anglo–Argentine activity in the fields of commerce, culture and trade, Argentina had to be re-imagined. Despite the private outpourings of anger and disbelief, a balance, however difficult, had to be maintained. On the one hand, British officials longed to retain some commercial and political influence in Argentina and Latin America more generally given the state of post-war Britain. As Henry Hankey, a senior FO official responsible for South America concluded, 'Our policy was to build up economic and political relations with Latin American countries...there were definite openings for trade expansion'.[48] On the other hand, Argentina was presented as a geopolitical threat during the 1940s and 1950s, intent on restoring ownership rights over the Falkland Islands and Antarctica, which challenged Britain's role in the South Atlantic and provoked territorial competition.

With the onset of the Cold War and further imperial dissolution in Asia and Africa, the wider strategic significance of Latin America diminished following the ending of meat rationing. A report by the Chancellor to the Duchy of Lancaster following a lengthy visit to South America in 1960 conveyed not only Britain's uncertain and ultimately jaundiced views of the region but also a warning that political neglect carried with it dangers for the longer term:

> I endured prolonged cocktail parties and interminable meals, mostly based on tough hunks of beef. One has been warned about making generalisations about South America...The giant is Brazil, which may become a leading world power. Argentina and Venezuela have high ambitions also. Peru and Chile are important as nations, which are likely to exert an increasing influence in Pan-American affairs. Between them and the nations to the east of the Andes seems to lie a fundamental difference in temper and outlook. On the east you will find all the vigour, speed and brashness traditionally associated with North America. But on the west the tempo is more subdued, more European, and the gracious architecture of the Spanish colonial period is not yet subdued. For our [British] institutions there is admiration and envy. Our people are liked for their character, their steadfastness, and their easy good manners. We need powerful friends in all continents and should not neglect South America. During a period of post-war stringency, our information in Latin America was afforded the lowest priority and suffered the worst of the cuts. I was struck by the degree to which the work of Embassy information sections is being hampered by the lack of staff at junior grades.[49]

NOTES ON CHAPTER 3

1   A. Graham-Yooll, *Goodbye Buenos Aires* (Nottingham, Shoestring Press, 1999), p. 165.

2   PRO CO 1024/295. Memorandum on 1960/1961 Antarctic season by the Military Branch of the Admiralty, dated October 1960.

3   See, for example, H. Ferns, 'Argentina: Part of an informal empire?', in A. Hennessy and J. King (eds), *The Land that England Lost* (London, British Academic Press, 1992), pp. 49–61. Ferns's earlier work included 'Britain's informal empire in Argentina', *Past and Present* 4 (1954): pp. 60–75 and *Argentina* (London, Ernest Benn, 1969).

4   *The Times*, 16 May 1925.

5   Quoted in R. Scalabrini, *Ortiz Historia de los Ferrocarriles Argentina* (Buenos Aires, Reconquista, 1940), p. 6.

6   On the role of the British in the construction and management of the railways see C. Lewis, *British Railways in Argentina 1857–1914* (London, Athlone Press, 1983).

7   On the role of Welsh settlers see G. Williams, *The Desert and the Dream; A Study of Welsh Colonisation of Chubut 1865–1915* (Cardiff, University of Wales Press,

1965) and 'Welsh settler and native Americans in Patagonia', *Journal of Latin American Studies* 11 (1979): pp. 41–66. Also E. Bowen, 'The Welsh colony in Patagonia 1865–1885', *Geographical Journal* 132 (1966): pp. 16–32. On the role of the Irish, see D. Keogh, 'Argentina and the Falklands: The Irish connection', in Hennessy and King (eds), *The Land that England Lost*, pp. 123–42.

8   See the analyses in D. Platt (ed.), *Business Imperialism 1840–1930* (Oxford, Oxford University Press, 1977).

9   Scalabrini, *Ortiz Politica Britanica en el Rio de la Plata*, p. 203.

10 PRO FO 373/7. Letter from Sir Nevile Henderson to Anthony Eden, dated 28 August 1936.

11 PRO FO 371 33518. Letter from Sir David Kelly to the FO, dated 3 February 1943.

12 See R. Gravil, *The Anglo–Argentine Connection 1900–1939* (Boulder CO, Westview, 1985).

13 C. MacDonald, 'End of empire: The decline of the Anglo–Argentine connection 1918–1951' in Hennessy and King (eds), *The Land that England Lost*, pp. 79–92. The quote is taken from pp. 85–6.

14 The mythical role of the frontier in Argentina and Latin American development more generally has been explored by A. Hennessy in *The Frontier in Latin American History* (London, Edward Arnold, 1978).

15 PRO CO 78/213/3. Letter from the British Ambassador in Buenos Aires to Viscount Halifax of the FO, dated 21 March 1940.

16 PRO CO 78/217/11. 'Argentine claims to the Falklands: Stamp issue of the Dependencies'.

17 M. Escolar, S. Quintero Palacios and C. Reboratti, 'Geographical identity and patriotic representation in Argentina', in D. Hooson (ed.), *Geography and National Identity* (Oxford, Blackwell, 1994), pp. 346–66. See also F. Daus, *Geografia y Unidad Argentina* (Buenos Aires, El Ateneo, 1957).

18 Cited in C. Escude, *El Fracaso del Proyecto Argentino* (Buenos Aires, Instituto de Torcuato Di Tella, 1990), p. 174.

19 C. Escude, *Education, public culture and foreign policy: the case of Argentina* (working paper, Latin American Studies Program, Duke University, 1992), p. 10.

20 These issues will be explored further in chapter 4 via a discussion of the 1948 Ealing Studios film *Scott of the Antarctic*.

21 See, for example, G. Blanksten, *Perón's Argentina* (Chicago IL, University of Chicago Press, 1974).

22 See, for example, *Comision Nacional del Antartico Soberania Argentina en la Antartida* (Buenos Aires, Ministerio de Relaciones Exteriores y Culto, 1948). Perón contributed a foreword to this document.

23 *Falkland Islands Weekly News* 6/9, 4 March 1949.

24 *Falkland Islands Weekly News* 5/15, 5 April 1948.

25 *Falkland Islands Weekly News* 5/9, 24 February 1949.

26 *Falkland Islands Weekly News* 5/29, 15 July 1948.

27 *Falkland Islands Weekly News* 5/23, 3 June 1948, carried a paper on 'Notes on the Falkland Islands and Dependencies' published by the Central Office of Information.

28 *Falkland Islands Weekly News* 5/47, 19 November 1948.

29 Quoted in P. Beck, 'Argentina and Britain: The Antarctic dimension', in Hennessy and King (eds), *The Land that England Lost*, p. 260.

30   MacDonald, 'End of empire: The decline of the Anglo–Argentine connection 1918–1951', pp. 86–7.

31   C. Lewis 'Anglo–Argentine trade 1945–1965', in D. Rock (ed.), *Argentina in the Twentieth Century* (London, Duckworth, 1975), pp. 114–34.

32   Quoted in K. Dodds, 'Geopolitics in the Foreign Office: British representations of Argentina 1945–1962', *Transactions of the Institute of British Geographers* 19 (1993): pp. 274–91.

33   PRO CAB 128/17 CM 79 (50). Memorandum prepared by the Ministry of Food, dated 30 November 1950.

34   PRO CAB 128/17 CM 84 (50). Memorandum prepared by the Ministry of Food, dated 11 December 1950.

35   Quoted in MacDonald 'The end of empire: The decline of the Anglo–Argentine connection 1918–1951', p. 80.

36   PRO FO 371 1775. Letter from Sir Rex Leeper to the American Department of the FO, dated 20 September 1946.

37   PRO CAB 128/10 CM 55 (47). Memorandum prepared by the FO, dated 19 June 1947.

38   G. Howells, 'The British press and the Peróns', in Hennessy and King (eds), *The Land that England Lost*, pp. 227–45.

39   Howells, 'The British press and the Peróns', p. 227.

40   J. Knape, 'Anglo–American rivalry in post-war Latin America: The question of arms sales', *Ibero-Amerikanisches Archiv* 15 (1989): pp. 318–50. I am indebted to this paper for background information on the question of arms sales to Argentina in the late 1940s.

41   On the implications of Argentina's neutrality during the Second World War, see G. di Tella and C. Watt (eds), *Argentina Between the Great Powers 1939–1946* (Pittsburgh PA, University of Pittsburgh Press, 1990) and J. Tulchin, *Argentina and the United States: A Conflicted Relationship* (Boston MA, Twayne Publishers, 1990).

42   Cited in Knape, 'Anglo–American rivalry in post-war Latin America: The question of arms sales', p. 338.

43   A. Conil Paz and G. Ferrari, *Argentina's Foreign Policy 1930–1962* (London, University of Notre Dame Press, 1966), p. 160.

44   PRO CAB 124/17 CM 24 (49). Report by Foreign Secretary Ernest Bevin, dated 31 March 1949.

45   PRO FO 371 108815. Memorandum on the potential sale to Argentina of helicopters prepared by Sir Ian Kirkpatrick, dated 8 January 1954. See also the *Times*, 'Helicopters in the Antarctic', 11 January 1954.

46   PRO ADM 1/25082 contains details of plans for the Royal Navy to maintain 12 Royal Marines on Deception Island in order to prevent Argentine and Chilean parties from landing. However, the plan was shelved because of concerns that this might provoke the South American parties to commit their own armed forces in greater numbers.

47   PRO CAB 128/12 CM 8 (48). Memorandum prepared by the Admiralty on the current Antarctic situation, dated 29 January 1948.

48   PRO FO 371 147650. Memorandum prepared by H. Hankey, dated 12 December 1959.

49   PRO CAB 129/102. Memorandum prepared by the Chancellor to the Duchy of Lancaster, dated 7 July 1960.

4

From Scott to Fuchs

It may cause you to like ice cream less but it will make you admire Fuchs and company even more.[1]

Incidentally the film helps to clear up the so-called Fuchs–Hillary controversy. Watching the hazards and heart breaking set backs experienced by Fuchs expedition, we can well understand Hillary's sympathetic suggestion that the team should fly out before the winter just as Fuchs's brave decision to go on to the end.[2]

INTRODUCTION

The zenith of British Antarctic endeavour was the successful culmination of the CTAE under the leadership of Fuchs and Hillary in March 1958. These achievements mirrored the optimism of a Britain recovering from the economic and political dislocation of the Second World War. The popularity of the 1951 Festival of Britain was taken as a sign that the 1950s might promise a great deal for a country which still celebrated Empire Day on 25 May.[3] To general rejoicing on the eve of the Queen's coronation, news broke that the New Zealander Edmund Hillary, with his Indian-Nepalese companion Sherpa Norgay Tenzing, had conquered the highest point on earth. Members of the British Commonwealth stormed the peaks of the Himalayas, set new speed and endurance records on land, sea and air, and up to the eve of the 1956 Suez Crisis, Britain still remained a confident global power with interests that spanned all seven continents.[4] Little wonder, perhaps, that the reign of Elizabeth II was initially promoted as 'the new Elizabethan age', with a particular emphasis on explorers and exploration.

The 'end of empire' in South Asia and the Middle East did not mean therefore that Britain was condemned to an automatic loss of confidence and power. Churchill's celebration of the achievements of the 'English-speaking peoples' seemed to indicate that post-war Britain could, through its 'family' of dominions and colonies and close relationship with the US, maintain its status as a great power.[5] Two events, the screening of *Scott of the Antarctic* (1948) and the planning and execution of the

CTAE, provide evidence of how the remote polar empire was also providing cultural and political solace.[6] As recognised by polar authorities such as Roberts and Frank Debenham, film could play its part in mythologising empire and invoking ideals of service, duty and sacrifice.[7] Ten years later, the short film *Antarctic Crossing* (1958) attempted to convey the heroic endeavour of the CTAE at a time when post-1945 Governments began not only to consolidate political relationships with the Dominions but also when many British citizens were emigrating to Australia, Canada, New Zealand and South Africa. With post-war cinema inclined to reflect on the changing British Empire, any publicity for the CTAE was bound to be confounded by the very real limits of personal and political polar co-operation within the British Commonwealth.[8]

THE FIDS, EALING STUDIOS AND *SCOTT OF THE ANTARCTIC*

'Such a film as *Scott* is welcome at a time when other races speak disparagingly of our "crumbling empire" and our "lack of spirit". It should make those who have listened too closely to such talk believe afresh that ours is the finest breed of men on this earth.'[9] In a review entitled 'The finest breed of men', the *Sunday Dispatch*'s film critic concluded that the Ealing Studios' production *Scott of the Antarctic* was a welcome antidote to stories about imperial decline. In the immediate aftermath of Indian and Pakistani independence, crowds flocked to watch Princess Elizabeth and her husband, the Duke of Edinburgh, attend the premiere of *Scott of the Antarctic* at the appropriately named Empire cinema in London. The star of the film, John Mills (the actor who played Scott and became in 1948 *Daily Mail* National Film Award holder), was reportedly late for the opening performance.[10] As Jeffrey Richards has noted, Mills was 'to incarnate decent Englishness – restrained, good-humoured, determined, honourable and self-deprecating'.[11] The film was released amid great fanfare to cinema houses across the UK, and the screening rights were sold to companies in the US and continental Europe. For many post-war British children, *Scott of the Antarctic* was the first film to be included in voluntary school-based visits to the cinema. Perhaps, therefore, Francis Spufford was right to conclude that, 'as a post-war fable of class integration' it was indeed apt for Britain in an era of ration books, identity cards and a culture of fiscal austerity.[12]

The idea to immortalise Scott and his party in film had already been identified by the Ministry of Information in 1939 as eminently suitable for the purposes of propaganda. The embodiment of the imperial hero in films such as *Clive of India* (1935) and *Stanley and Livingstone* (1939) had proved very popular in both Britain and America. In retrospect, the failure of *Scott of the Antarctic* to take the box offices by storm seems surprising given the popularity of earlier films celebrating imperial heroes, which commanded high cinema attendance.[13] Between 1945 and 1950, 30 million people out of a total population of 51 million flocked to the cinema each week. In 1946, for instance, the average patron watched 28 films a year and it was still obligatory for an audience to stand and sing the national anthem after the last showing.[14] There were no shortages of British cinemas as over 4000 existed; in 1950 over 750,000 children attended the 'children's matinee' at their local cinema every Saturday morning.

Ealing Studios, one of the major producers of British cinema, released about 100 films between 1938 and 1959, and enjoyed a close working relationship with the Ministry of Information.[15] According to Ealing Studios' production chief, Sir Michael Balcon, cinema was likened to church, and he insisted that films should not only be inspirational but also celebratory of British virtues and values:

> The world, in short, must be presented with a complete picture of Britain and not with fragments from the picture: Britain as a leader in Social Reform in the defeat of social injustices and a champion of civil liberties; Britain as a patron and parent of great writing, painting and music; Britain as a questing explorer, adventurer and trader; Britain as the home of great industry and craftmanship; Britain as a mighty power standing alone and undaunted against terrifying aggression.[16]

While Balcon was eager to celebrate British virtues and values through film, the production of *Scott of the Antarctic* cannot be isolated from the geopolitical context of intense territorial rivalries in Antarctica. At the time of its release, Britain was engaged in an expensive and at times dangerous game of territorial occupation, mapping and diplomatic protest.

Debenham, the then director of the SPRI and an Antarctic veteran, resurrected in 1945 the well-established idea of the Ministry of Information of making a film about Scott as an imperial hero. However, some of the survivors were reluctant because they felt 'it was out of date; to film it would be an invasion of privacy, and so on and so forth'.[17] Undeterred by these reservations, representatives of Ealing Studios visited the SPRI in order to seek Debenham's assistance over details relating to dog sledging and the expedition's logistical organisation. The script, which closely followed Scott's diaries and testimony of the survivors and their families, also graphically reproduced the physical hardship of polar exploration, the suffering of Scott and his colleagues and their bravery in the face of unrelenting and appalling climatic conditions in the Antarctic. The script was not intended to 'debunk' the Scott myth but rather to re-enforce a positive assessment of Scott's achievements without contrasting his performance with that of his Norwegian rival, Amundsen. Notwithstanding the subsequent reservations of film critics such as Leonard Mosley of the *Daily Express*, who found the film 'uninspiring', Debenham conceded that 'not even the callous debunker can misinterpret that dying scene in the lonely tent; it is true as it is stark'.[18] Scott's death was widely considered to have been dignified and heroic unlike earlier Victorian stories about the mysterious and unsettling disappearance of Sir John Franklin's expedition in search of the North West Passage.

Charles Frend, the director of the film, was well-known for being an innovative figure in British post-war cinema. Eager to produce a 'semi-documentary' film, Frend aimed to combine a detailed reconstruction of the expedition, filmed where possible on location and in technicolour. In order to achieve a high level of realism, David James, a FIDS surveyor, was engaged as an Antarctic advisor. Without a hint of irony, James noted that Frend had originally conceived the opening scene to portray Scott's final collapse on return from the South Pole but later dropped the idea because the audience might think that Scott's expedition was a preordained failure![19] However, Frend's dilemma was real in the sense that every schoolchild and adult was aware of the Scott saga and therefore conscious that the expedition ended in the death of the five-strong party. His brief was therefore ambitious as he tried to create a film which was realistic in terms of filming locations while simultaneously managing to convey the heroic (and possibly unpredictable) dramas of the Scott expedition. It was not intended to dwell on the questionable choices made by Scott with regards to equipment and personnel.

Frend had to make some important decisions relating to location, filming and scene creation before filming began in January 1947. Ealing Studios' choice of Antarctic locations was dictated not only by logistics but also by finance. As British Government co-operation was vital, the Colonial Office, as the administrator of the FIDS, was approached in order to obtain permission for filming on the proviso that the film shots would be used in publicity material to promote the activities of British surveyors and scientists. FIDS surveyor Bernard Stonehouse remembers having to dress up in replica polar fatigues and pretend to push Scott-era sledges across ice fields close to Hope Bay.[20] Surprisingly, the opening scenes of Hope Bay in Antarctica soon give way to disparate alpine and studio locations, which tend to emphasise the enormity of the landscapes and the unforgiving nature of the katabatic winds rather than the failure of equipment and personalities. The filming process was eventful, as the huskies chewed their way through the leather camera tripods and ripped to pieces a copy of Scott's diaries.[21] Meanwhile, the camera operators grappled with untested Monopack cameras, as the tri-pack Technicolour cameras were considered too cumbersome to travel to Antarctica.[22] After an anxious period of film processing in Hollywood (which revealed yet another form of dependence on the US), the background pictures of Antarctica were ready for eventual incorporation into the film.

The Colonial Office had hoped that co-operation with Ealing Studios would raise the public profile of Britain's Antarctic portfolio. In the event, the partnership with the SPRI and Ealing Studios was not as mutually beneficial as had been first anticipated. Financially, unfortunate misunderstandings undermined this process as a series of letters between Ealing Studios' Andrew Courtauld and the new director of the SPRI, Colin Bertram, revealed.[23] Initially, Ealing Studios made a donation of 100 guineas in 1948 in lieu of professional services rendered by the institute. By October of the same year, Roberts approached Balcon to ask whether there were any other funds likely to be forthcoming from the studios. Roberts received a brief and ultimately disappointing answer from Balcon. In May 1950, the issue of additional funds was raised again, as Bertram wrote to Courtauld reminding the latter that Balcon had offered the possibility of making further financial contributions to the SPRI. According to Bertram's letter, Balcon had indeed offered to consider the matter but Courtauld's reply to Bertram noted that it was unlikely that the company would be making any further donation to the SPRI because entertainment taxes combined with modest audience figures had resulted in lower receipts than anticipated. In later correspondence with his brother S.L. Courtauld, Andrew Courtauld confirmed that Ealing Studios' board had decided that *ex gratia* payments would not be forthcoming unless the film made a profit. According to the records held at the SPRI, this assessment was never re-evaluated and no further monies were forthcoming. The thorny issue of 'possible' fees, initially intended to defray the high spending on research and mapping, was overtaken by political issues. In the late 1940s, Roberts warned the FO that the work of the FIDS was in danger of being eclipsed by rival Argentine and Chilean surveyors. This resulted in the release of large sums of money, which financed the despatch of the warship

HMS *Nigeria* to patrol the ice and underwrote further land- and air-based surveying operations.

The collaboration with Ealing Studios, therefore, was intended to provide the FIDS with a publicity vehicle notwithstanding Scott's well-known tragic failure. Polar authorities such as Debenham hoped that audiences would simply celebrate, with the help of Ealing Studios and the stirring music of Vaughan Williams, the established British polar tradition of bravery and endurance.[24] The hardship endured by and qualities required of the men who ventured onto the ice would be a testament to the FIDS surveyors who battled with the unforgiving elements in order to provide Britain with the basic information so vital to uphold an effective presence in the region. Of course, it had also been hoped when the idea was conceived that the undertaking would be financially beneficial.

THE LIMITS OF FILM AND MAPPING

In February 1949, a Colonial Office document warned that the FIDS faced new dangers – not only from territorial competitors but also from their own scientific inefficiencies. After three summer seasons of endeavour,

> a considerable amount of work was done, the results of which were sent to London in the form of scientific notes, data and collections. This material has accumulated but it has not been until now been possible to make comprehensive arrangements for it to be analysed. It clearly must be done if the fieldwork is not to be wasted and HMG thereby incur justifiable criteria both internationally and in the scientific world.[25]

In response, the memorandum proposed that a scientific bureau for the FIDS should be established in order to help analyse and publicise data and specimens collected from the FID. A new grant from the Colonial Office worth £10,000 was proposed in order to expedite the research process.

Meanwhile, Perón of Argentina ordered the IGM to monitor an Argentine law stipulating that all new maps of the country portray the Islas Malvinas and the Argentine Antarctic sector. The Admiralty warned the Colonial Office in March 1952 that the Argentine authorities had created new tide tables which for the first time included Stanley as a standard Argentine port. There was also new information relating to Port Charcot in the FID. In response the Colonial Office noted that 'There seems to be no reason for Argentines to work out daily times of high water for Port Charcot unless they intend to establish or already have established a base there'.[26] While recognising the significance of this kind of geographical information, the Colonial Office was not aware of any Argentine activities in Port Charcot. Given that they lacked the logistical support to patrol the FID, the FIDS and the Colonial Office were deeply conscious of the need to promote their achievements and to ensure that returning surveyors presented their findings to the widest public audiences.

By their very nature charts and sheet maps failed to convey the sheer amount of effort needed to collect data on the Antarctic Peninsula and surrounding islands such as Deception Island. In the 1947–8 summer season, FIDS staff organised a number of research trips under Fuchs and the geologist Raymond Adie. Starting from Marguerite Bay in the southern portion of the Antarctic Peninsula, dog sledges were used to transport some of the FIDS staff towards Adelaide Island in the north and Palmer Land in the south. Most of the sledges had nine dogs attached to a team and carried around 1200 pounds of supplies and equipment. Armed with only an aircraft compass mounted at the rear of the sledge and the maps generated by previous expeditions, the FIDS staff stopped at regular intervals to carry out base measurements. Most teams had a dedicated dog driver so that the surveyor could carry out his measurements without distraction. The routine involved taking a series of astronomical fixes every 50 miles via the sun or the stars. A light plywood board was used as a plane table to help take compass bearings and to provide a horizon in order to fix the altitudes of the surrounding polar landscapes. Two to three months were spent out in the field and on a good day (but it was often easier to travel at night when the ice was firmer) the teams could cover on average 10–12 miles, although more frequently it was a slow and occasionally dangerous business. On a really bad day, as former FIDS surveyors recounted, movement could be limited to less than a mile.

More disturbingly, however, the upsurge of political and exploratory interest in Antarctica by the US in the post-war period led to further concerns that British activities would be eclipsed. In 1946–7, for example, the US Navy carried out Operation Highjump involving 12 icebreakers, an aircraft carrier and 4000 personnel. The Americans established what was to become a widely emulated model of exploration through the use of aerial flights, overland dog sledging and base camps. Unlike Scott's era, however, US political, economic and cultural power was destined to alter the international politics of the Antarctic (even if the key focus at the time was the Arctic) and to challenge the territorial ambitions of the claimant states.[27] The privately organised expedition, led by Commander Finn Ronne, created difficulties for the Anglo–American entente cordial during the summer season of 1947–8. Roberts was embroiled in a row that was threatening serious damage to co-operation between the two allies. Initially, there was a disagreement over Ronne's decision to use an abandoned US base at Stonington Island for his expedition.[28] The British had established a FIDS base on the same island and Roberts was therefore convinced that there was insufficient seal meat to support the dog parties of both teams. Unable to persuade the Americans to relocate, Roberts then had to deal with the sensitive issue relating to past acts of theft at the abandoned US base.[29]

When Ronne's expedition landed at Stonington Island, the FIDS leader Major Pierce-Butler was instructed to inform the American expedition leader that 'His Excellency [Clifford] deplores the acts of hooliganism against American property by Chilian [sic] gangsters which we did our best to prevent'.[30] Undeterred by the spectre of South American 'hooligans', Ronne proceeded to occupy the old US base and, much to the chagrin of the British, the 'stars and stripes' was hoisted on the flagpole. On further reflection, the British party later confessed that they had 'borrowed' some of the materials at the abandoned American base. The records kept by the FIDS suggested that *inter alia* over 600 gallons of petrol, 12 cases of dog food and 600 feet of salvaged timber was misappropriated by the British party on Stonington Island. Unsurprisingly, Clifford was concerned that if these issues were not handled sensitively then relations with the US would be soured precisely at the time when Argentina and Chile were advancing their political and scientific profiles in the Antarctic region.

Armed with a $500,000 grant from the Truman administration, Ronne had organised a programme of land- and air-based surveying, which generated 14,000 aerial photographs and photographic coverage exceeding 750,000 square miles of the polar continent.[31] While the expedition was supposed to involve British co-operation with the land-based surveys, this was overshadowed by Ronne's failure formally to recognise British sovereignty at the base camp at Stonington. In turn, Ronne was reluctant to agree to British proposals for a division of labour in surveying, and the Colonial Office warned FIDS staff not to share ground control data with the US party. The eventual joint British–American Weddell Coast expedition was not a model of the 'special relationship', as disputes emerged over information exchange, logistical organisation and mutual acknowledgement.[32] More broadly, the local concerns of the FIDS were further replicated in diplomatic exchanges with the State Department concerning US attitudes towards the sovereignty of Antarctica. Once more, surveyors and administrators attached to the FIDS and the Colonial Office were reminded of the importance of maps and photographs in visually representing territorial claims and interests to public audiences. As Brian Beeves, a FIDS surveyor noted in 1948,

> The mass of unco-ordinated scientific data which has been collected has not been fully sifted or worked up as a readable whole … These British achievements have, however, unfortunately received only a fragment of the publicity they deserve, due to the traditional British reticence and to the highly coloured but unfortunately also highly biased reports on the progress of the sledging parties sent out by Commander Finn Ronne.[33]

In modern parlance, Beeves was effectively admitting that the FIDS and the British Government needed to improve its public relations in order to ensure that the work of the survey was duly acknowledged in the wider public domain. In March 1947, the Colonial Office ordered an urgent review of the existing achievements of the FIDS, which were to be publicised in the wake of the Ronne expedition, as the latter had demonstrated that it was possible to keep the media informed via daily radio broadcasts.

Ronne had defied British sensitivities and was not persuaded to inhibit America's pioneering spirit.[34] While Debenham still saw the Ealing Studios' *Scott* as the epitome of British polar spirit, Roberts noted in December 1946 that 'In the long run this has largely been a matter of lobbying in the right quarters and keeping up interest and "educating" civil servants in Antarctic matters'.[35] Perhaps what Roberts and others were less prepared to countenance was that British virtues such as endurance, pluckiness and stoicism were not going to be sufficient in the face of unrelenting territorial competition from South American states and their ally, the US. On the eve of the premiere of *Scott of the Antarctic*, the British Government remained at odds with two South American claimants and uncertain over the future intentions of the US Government.

FUCHS, HILLARY AND THE 1955–8 COMMONWEALTH TRANS-ANTARCTIC EXPEDITION

Ernest Shackleton's dream of crossing the Antarctic was finally accomplished in March 1958 by a high-profile Commonwealth expedition led by Fuchs and Hillary.[36] After two years of intense planning, the British party set off from the Filchner ice shelf and reached the South Pole on 19 January 1958, two weeks after Hillary's team, which had travelled from the Ross Sea. After the meeting at the South Pole, Fuchs's team continued (against the advice of Hillary) the journey across the polar plateau until the Ross Sea was reached.

Sponsored by British Petroleum (BP), the films compiled by George Lowe of the preparations and subsequent implementation of the CTAE were released by Worldwide Pictures in two short films, *Foothold in Antarctica* (1956) and *Antarctic Crossing* (1958).[37] Premiered in London alongside Norman Wisdom's comedy *The Square Peg* on 20 November 1958, the 45-minute film *Antarctic Crossing* provided a spectacular visual rendition of the successful crossing using only a small fraction of the nine miles of film gathered by the CTAE team on both sides of Antarctica.[38] Opening with the spectacle of the supply ship HMS *Theron* cutting through the Antarctic ice, the film blends contemporary colour filming of the CTAE with black-and-white images of the earlier Scott and the Shackleton expeditions. While cautious in its assessment of previous unsuccessful endeavours to traverse Antarctica, the film explained that the CTAE did not depend upon man hauling but instead deployed machines and even huskies to achieve a safe and efficient continental crossing. Standing in front of a map of Antarctica, Fuchs outlined the scientific rationale for the CTAE by focusing on the unknown features of Antarctica, such as the depth of its ice cap and unpredictable weather patterns. The film conveys clearly that Fuchs's traverse of the ice was far more difficult than Hillary's journey from the other side of Antarctica (see figure 4.1). Understandably, it glossed over the ensuing disagreements between Fuchs and Hillary over expedition planning and publicity. After the showing, the critics were generally complimentary and the *Monthly Film Bulletin* in particular praised its

> Skilful editing [which] has resulted in a remarkable picture with moments of honour and despair linked by scenes of grandeur and beauty. This modest and factual film also contained some dramatic sequences from the original films of the Scott and Shackleton expeditions, which provide startling contrasts to the often impressive colour photography of the modern parties.[39]

Despite the undoubted achievement of executing such an expedition, the CTAE was not a shining example of Anglo–New Zealand – let alone wider Commonwealth – co-operation. At the consultation stage, it was evident that some countries – notably Australia and South Africa – were lukewarm in their support of the project, and sceptical of the purported aims of the CTAE. More disturbingly, for British observers the intense media interest surrounding the perceived personality clash between Fuchs and Hillary threatened to undermine Commonwealth polar consolidation.[40]

Given that Australia and New Zealand were also claimant states in the Antarctic, Roberts considered Commonwealth solidarity to be an essential element in the defence of Britain's polar interests. With no disputes amongst the Commonwealth claimants as to their respective 'sectors', and already versed in scientific and

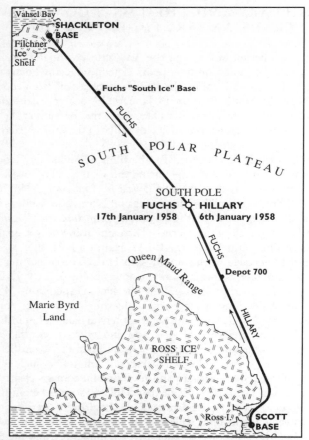

Figure 4.1: The route of the Commonwealth Trans-Antarctic Expedition

exploratory co-operation across Antarctica, a uniform approach to the legal criteria for territorial claims would be significant given the reluctance of others to recognise those claims. Moreover, military co-operation was also possible, as exemplified by a newspaper report that in February 1948 the Australian Navy had offered to send a vessel to support HMS *Nigeria* to deter further Argentine incursions in the South Atlantic.[41] Roberts believed, therefore, that there was safety in numbers, and that if the British co-ordinated the Commonwealth bloc of claimant states then this *tour de force* would surely convince South American rivals and the US of Britain's prowess on the ice.

The planning and execution of the CTAE was a long and tedious affair, given Fuchs's claim that he envisaged such a crossing in the late 1940s. As Director of the FIDS's scientific bureau, he was pivotal to the creation of the managerial infrastructure, which involved representatives from the Royal Geographical Society, the SPRI and various Government departments. The scientific rationale for such a major expedition appeared overwhelming in view of the lack of detailed geographical data available. As the Australian polar expert Philip Law recalls, 'Man's knowledge of the

Antarctic continent before 1954 was fragmentary. There were many stretches of coast that had never been explored and many mountains that had never been sighted. The Antarctic plateau was almost wholly unknown.'[42] The official statement from the Management Committee for the CTAE declared that

> The first aim of the expedition is to accomplish a great journey, important scientific objectives are combined with this and will include topographical and geological survey ... It is hoped that the glaciology programme will throw further light on the two conflicting theories about this great land mass. The first is that the Weddell Sea and the Ross Sea are joined beneath the ice cap and Antarctica is in reality not one continent but two. The second theory is that the Andean Chain continues through South America to the Falklands [a theory that was favoured by South American jurists] ... to re-emerge in the mountains of Grahamland and thence to the polar plateau.[43]

Funding for the enterprise was difficult to secure, as it was by no means guaranteed that the Commonwealth would be sufficiently persuaded by such an undertaking. Britain's Treasury was already committed to maintaining the 35,000 troops stationed in Malaya fighting 8000 Communist guerrillas throughout the 1950s.[44]

With an eye on the continuing territorial and political struggle with Argentina and Chile in the Antarctic region, Clifford emerged as a vocal supporter of the CTAE and proposed in 1953 that the Polar Committee in London endorse the project.[45] Roberts as ever remained concerned that the British were not producing sufficient 'evidence' of 'effective occupation' in the FID so vital to the politics of control. The Polar Committee offered this sobering conclusion in 1954:

> The Committee are acutely aware that the expanding occupational and scientific activities of other powers in the Antarctic threaten to forestall FIDS work in some fields and restrict it in others. Argentine occupational activities are shaped towards eventually restricting FIDS areas of operations. In these circumstances, there is a danger that FIDS may be robbed of the fruits of its work already done at great effort and considerable cost. To prevent this, FIDS must aim to produce within the financial resources available, an expanded programme.[46]

In other words, the Polar Committee acknowledged that Argentina's activities were beginning to cast doubt on the strategic and cartographic mission of the FIDS. Consequently, the FIDS faced a stark choice: either they acknowledged that the British surveying teams were being 'outclassed' by Argentine surveyors and map-makers or they improved operational efficiency and cartographic output.

The eventual decision to support the CTAE owes as much to luck as to good timing. In 1954, despite mounting concern over Argentine polar activities, the inter-government Polar Committee felt confident enough to claim that a polar crossing would 'have little value towards strengthening our claim to sovereignty ... but it would demonstrate leadership in the area'.[47] Within the FO, opinion was divided as to whether the CTAE could not only tackle the burning scientific questions but also further British territorial interests within a wider Commonwealth setting. Roberts and prominent polar experts were critical of the idea, because they felt that the CTAE would draw funds away from the politically vital work of the FIDS. As Fuchs recalls in his autobiography,

I was soon aware that there was a solid body of opinion against my project. This seemed to be headed by Dr Brian Roberts. His views were supported by Dr Colin Bertram, Director of the Institute [SPRI] and Sir Laurence Kirwan, Director and Secretary of the Royal Geographical Society. They were the three big guns with most influence on opinion, and their opposition was based on the possible embarrassment to Britain if the project failed. They preferred to 'leave such a journey to the Americans'.[48]

The persistent lobbying of Fuchs and Clifford neutralised the views of the sceptics such as Roberts, Bertram and Kirwan that the CTAE could not successfully contribute to a variety of cultural, legal, geopolitical and scientific objectives.

If this project was to enhance British Antarctic prestige then it was vital that Fuchs and his team suffered no mishaps either in London or on the ice. One year later and still aggrieved by the plans for the CTAE, Roberts proposed his own five-year plan for the FIDS, arguing passionately for the need to concentrate on specific regions of the Antarctic Peninsula in the event of changes to territorial claims. With the importance of surveys and charts reaffirmed, he then proposed that Government departments support the CTAE in order to demonstrate Britain's leadership in the Antarctic arena. Thus science, national prestige and politics became apparently natural bedfellows.

Fuchs was invited to submit a proposal to the Polar Committee in London, which consisted of representatives from the High Commissions of the old Dominions (Australia, Canada, New Zealand and South Africa). Lord Swinton, the then Secretary of State for Commonwealth Relations, summarised the appeal of such a proposal:

It would enhance the prestige of the nations taking part.
It would have considerable romantic appeal.
It would help justify territorial claims in the Antarctic, in particular by the establishment of bases in Coates Land and the Ross Dependency.
It would increase knowledge of the meteorological conditions of the area of the South Pole.
Knowledge of the area would be gained that would be invaluable if it were ever to be crossed by an established air route.
It would add to our knowledge of the influence of the Antarctic ice-sheet and the biology of the Southern Ocean.
It could be made to provide good training for Service personnel in polar conditions.[49]

Fuchs, with the help of a reluctant Roberts, was shrewd enough to list the proposal in a manner most likely to appeal to political vanity and to proponents of territorial advantage. Implicit was the recognition that the vast empty expanses of the Antarctic served as a blank slate onto which the British and their Commonwealth colleagues could draw claims to national and dominion prestige.[50] Moreover, as with the Scott expeditions, this would involve Commonwealth partners in the planning and execution of the project. At the end of the meeting, Fuchs was instructed to develop a detailed plan for the Antarctic crossing and the Commonwealth Relations Office was directed to gather support from Commonwealth partners. Roberts considered Commonwealth support fundamental, given the estimated costs of more than £500,000. However, while the Treasury welcomed cost-sharing, Roberts was mindful that Commonwealth support was an essential element in the geopolitical strategy of consolidation. Fuchs ensured that the proposed crossing would traverse British, Australian and New Zealand Antarctic territories, and although South Africa was not a claimant state, Roberts advocated inclusion because of its ownership of the Prince Edward Islands in the South Indian Ocean.

With the full support of Churchill, who had been instrumental in approving Operation Tabarin in 1943, the British eagerly began to lobby Commonwealth partners in 1954–5. Previously secret files on the CTAE discussions reveal that none of the Commonwealth states involved was actually persuaded by the British arguments of 'prestige' and 'romantic appeal'. Australia, with the largest Antarctic territorial claim, was decidedly lukewarm – not least because it would only cross 200 miles of Australian Antarctic territory. The Australian external affairs minister, Richard Casey, although aware of the wider strategic rationale, was not persuaded by the British claims 'of scientific and symbolic values' of such a crossing.[51] In a memorandum prepared by the Australian Department of External Affairs (DEA) to the Australian Prime Minister's Department dated 15 August 1955, the geopolitical context for the CTAE was succinctly noted:

> In recent years the UK has been fighting a losing battle with Argentina on the question of UK claims to Antarctica. The UK found the situation a draining one, and in a memorandum sent with the letter of 31st August 1953 the UK proposed 'an orderly reduction of UK political and naval commitments in the area to a scale which the UK is in a position permanently to meet'.[52]

However, the memorandum also noted that a subsequent letter dated 23 August 1954 from the Secretary of State for Commonwealth Relations appeared to reverse British proposals for a reduced commitment in the Antarctic region:

> The Trans Antarctic Expedition will have the effect of attaching British public opinion and prestige to Antarctica and this should induce increased British commitments in the future. Moreover, Antarctica now promises to become a controversial issue following the announcement of Russian interest in the region.[53]

The Churchill Government formally asked Australia for financial support in July 1955; the Australians agreed to offer £25,000 but then pledged only £20,000 after further consultation.[54]

In South Africa and Canada, initial reactions to the CTAE proposal were even less promising. The South African High Commission, in its report to the DEA in Pretoria noted:

> Commonwealth interest appears to be lukewarm. The Canadian government has indicated that they are deeply involved in the Arctic and are anxious not to divert their interests. The Australians consider the project of doubtful scientific value and have referred to the extent to which they are already involved in Antarctic ventures. The New Zealand government has been non-committal thus far but it is known that public opinion in New Zealand is in favour of participation. The CRO [Commonwealth Relations Office] feels that even a symbolic contribution would be of great value in so far as it would demonstrate Commonwealth solidarity.[55]

The above summary in February 1955 was remarkably prescient. Commonwealth support was not readily apparent, and some officials in Commonwealth capitals were cruelly dismissive of Fuchs's master plan. A note by an official attached to the American Division of the Canadian DEA, concluded that 'even for Commonwealth solidarity we would not trudge the wastes of Antarctica! If they wanted to buy some huskies or something of that sort, I am sure we could do what we could!'[56]

British officials endeavoured to persuade their counterparts in Wellington that the CTAE would have substantial geopolitical and legal benefits for New Zealand's claim to the Ross Dependency. Despite New Zealand's status as a claimant, successive Governments had shown little inclination to channel hard-pressed funds into a mapping or scientific programme similar to the FIDS. By the early 1950s, however, this apparent ambivalence was beginning to change as Hillary, the New Zealand Antarctic Society and regional newspapers began to argue that the country had a geographical and political responsibility to take an active interest in Antarctica.[57] When the proposals for a CTAE were first voiced during the Polar Committee in 1953, considerable emphasis was given to the creation of a New Zealand base in the Ross Dependency.[58] Internally, legal advisers to the New Zealand Government had warned that their claim to the Ross Dependency was vulnerable to legal challenge because of an absence of any form of 'effective occupation'. Without a permanent base, therefore, New Zealand was dependent on international goodwill – especially from the US, which planned several major expeditions in the Ross Dependency.[59] In June 1955, the US announced that it would construct a new base at McMurdo Sound while in the Ross Dependency. The New Zealand Government recognised that the substantial presence of US personnel attached to Operation Deep Freeze I and II meant that their claim was compromised, and despatched a protest note. Ironically, the eventual decision to participate in the CTAE was inspired by the decision of the Special Committee for the International Geophysical Year (IGY) requesting the New Zealand Government to create a scientific base in the region in order to assist the Antarctic scientific programme. In January 1956, after months of pressure inside and outside New Zealand, the Ministry of External Affairs publicly agreed to participate in the IGY and the CTAE. In fact, the decision had already been taken earlier in May 1955, when it was agreed to create a Ross Sea Committee to assist CTAE planning and co-ordinate any future logistical plans with the US in the Ross Dependency.

Thankfully for the CTAE Management Committee, Churchill's backing for the project, coupled with the patronage of the Queen, meant that high-level pressure could now be placed on Australia, South Africa and New Zealand to help fund and participate in the polar crossing. The British Government agreed, at a Commonwealth ministerial meeting in February 1956, to pledge £100,000, with support forthcoming from Australia (£20,000), South Africa (£18,000) and New Zealand (£50,000). Within Britain, the Royal Geographical Society and the Everest Foundation were encouraged to launch a mass public appeal in order to raise £175,000 for the remaining costs of the expedition. Sir John Slessor, vice-president of the society, later launched such an appeal and the public were encouraged to participate in fundraising activities as well as donations. The shrewd move to appoint Hillary as co-leader raised the profile of the expedition in Britain and New Zealand and added impetus to CTAE receptions he hosted throughout his native New Zealand.[60] Moreover, Hillary was a household name, whether Fuchs or anyone else in Britain liked it or not. He generated publicity for financial collections and together with the New Zealand Antarctic Society, which organised screenings of *Scott of the Antarctic*, fired the geographical imagination of the public in New Zealand and elsewhere.[61] Three major CTAE appeal committees were created in Auckland, Christchurch and Wellington for the purpose of successfully raising £100,000 in public donations.

Planning the CTAE was a lengthy affair, as fierce arguments occurred between committee members in London over funding, information exchange and personal selection.[62] Disagreements were perhaps inevitable given the different academic, business and political personalities involved in the committee. The final party chosen to cross the Antarctic reflected Commonwealth interests, and the scientific programme was developed after intense discussions with the Royal Geographical Society, the Royal Society and the SPRI. Under Anglo–New Zealand leadership, the team included FIDS surveyors, meteorologists from the South African weather bureau, pilots from the New Zealand airforce and other scientists and support crew from Australia, New Zealand and the UK. The expedition was formally launched in November 1955 and the Ross Sea Committee, headed by Hillary, was responsible for constructing a reception base for the final stage of the journey and for establishing supply depots along the proposed polar route. The British Committee, headed by Fuchs, was responsible for the land crossing starting from the opposite side of the Antarctic continent. In January 1956, an advance party began the construction of Shackleton Base on the Filchner ice shelf and undertook aerial reconnaissance flights over the proposed route. The following year, the CTAE team began the construction of a base in the interior, called 'South Ice'. In November 1957, Fuchs left Shackleton Base near the Weddell Sea and began the crossing of Antarctica. Accompanied by snow cats and specially adapted tractors, the party finally reached its destination, Scott Base, in March 1958 after a 2000-mile journey. Commercial sponsorship by companies such as BP and Kodak provided invaluable practical support for the traverse. During this extraordinary journey, seismic studies were conducted to determine the depth of the polar ice in conjunction with the mapping of the continental interior.

The crossing of Antarctica should have been the high-point of British and Commonwealth polar achievement as men and their machines triumphed against the odds. Polar planners had co-ordinated a multinational project in a difficult and unforgiving environment. Despite some high dramas involving dangerous ice crevasses, the snow cats and tractors were successfully employed to thoroughly 'mechanise' the exploration of the Antarctic. In contrast to earlier expeditions, media relations had been planned carefully and both leaders were contracted to provide reports for the British newspaper the *Times* and radio reports for the BBC. Colour photographs, taken by the New Zealander George Lowe, provided ample visual material for subsequent publicity in the UK, the Commonwealth and the wider world. Unfortunately, the CTAE became immortalised not for its substantial technological and geographical achievements, but for an unfortunate dispute between the two leaders, Fuchs and Hillary. The disagreement came to a head when Hillary disregarded instructions from Fuchs, and rather than wait at the agreed point, called Depot 700, proceeded to the South Pole ahead of Fuchs's party approaching from the opposite direction. The original plan relied on Hillary meeting Fuchs at Depot 700 so as to guide the latter through the Trans-Antarctic mountains and ultimately to Scott Base in the Ross Sea region. Bored with waiting, and anxious to reach the South Pole ahead of the British party, Hillary simply decided to push on to the centre of the continent. He arrived 11 days ahead of Fuchs, who had been delayed by bad weather and treacherous ice. As the *Times* recorded in December 1957, Hillary had covered up to 44 miles in 24 hours while the unfortunate Fuchs had only managed 15 miles in a similar period.[63]

While Fuchs was furious with Hillary for disobeying instructions, the dispute between the two men would not have become the stuff of legends had the newspapers covering the crossing not noticed the rising tension between the two leaders and their support committees.[64] Although the crossing was ultimately successful, everybody attached to the CTAE knew that the public presentation of 'progress' across the ice mattered greatly. If the expedition was to attract positive publicity and prestige, it was essential to secure harmonious media coverage. With a history of British failures to cross the Antarctic continent, it was considered paramount to dispel all notions about an apparent 'race' between Fuchs and Hillary to reach the South Pole.[65] New Zealand could not be allowed to achieve what Norway had managed 47 years earlier. Hillary's decision to 'rush' to the South Pole effectively destroyed earlier aspirations of CTAE managers in London anxious to promote cordiality on British terms.[66] The Management Committee, aware of the dangers surrounding the emerging 'dispute' between the two men, noted:

> Some members of the Committee felt that too much sensationalism was surrounding the reports in the press and that it should be brought to the notice of the public that the expedition was undertaking a serious scientific programme. It is hoped that the first rather sensational reactions to his journey [Hillary's trek to the South Pole] will soon be modified.[67]

Earlier complaints of indifferent media interest in the expedition were soon replaced by accusations of 'sensationalism' and 'exposé' as the press sought to maintain public interest. The planners of the CTAE were hoist with their own petard, and in more modern parlance the well-orchestrated 'media spin' placed on those endeavours had spiralled out of control. The CTAE was no longer a 'scientific journey', it was a battle between two rival personalities who were engaged in a 'race' over the Antarctic continent. Local and national newspapers in the UK were fixated by the rumours of rivalry and intrigue within the British Commonwealth teams.[68] Under their headline 'Dr Fuchs going like a bomb', the *Birmingham Post* reported that Fuchs was entirely happy with Hillary's conduct and that he was retrospectively 'free [to travel to the South Pole] to do so once he had laid the depots required for the completion of the journey'.[69] To compound matters further, the *Daily Express* accidentally coined one of the most famous Antarctic headlines when it led with the immortal 'Dr Fuchs off to the Pole'.

According to the French journalist Raymond Cartier in an article for *Paris-Match*, translated by the New Zealand Embassy in Paris,

> The mortification of the English was complete. Their indignation, however, was still kept within the limits of sportsmanship. It broke all bounds when Sir Edmund Hillary announced he did not intend to wait for Fuchs at the South Pole. He would go back to his base by plane, leave Antarctica and return to New Zealand. The far-off dominion has demanded this honour, pointing out that along the last part of its route, the Commonwealth expedition would travel through a strip of the southern region over which it claims sovereignty... If they

had been free to take their own decisions the English would never have entrusted him with a part in the Commonwealth expedition. One knew he would go to the Pole and that he would be pushed into it by the chauvinistic clamour of his country. [70]

After their meeting at the South Pole, further allegations of a dispute between the two men emerged as Hillary was reported to have advised Fuchs not to continue his journey on to Scott Base. According to press reports, Hillary warned Fuchs that the weather was so unpredictable that it would be dangerous to continue the crossing. After five days at the South Pole, Fuchs did continue the crossing, mindful that further delay would jeopardise the viability of the project. Meanwhile, Hillary had flown to the US base at McMurdo and officially remained there as an emergency backup for the final leg of polar traverse. After 99 days of travel, Fuchs completed his 3472 kilometres journey on 2 March 1958 at an average of 35 kilometres a day.

The animosity stemmed not from the malicious or mendacious press reporting, but from the contrasting styles of their personalities. Hillary's dash to the South Pole was deliberate rather than an unfortunate misinterpretation of instructions. As he recalled to this author in September 1996, he had always intended to travel to the South Pole, and Fuchs had always resented his inclusion in the CTAE.[71] With Fuchs's comparatively slow progress over the ice, Hillary claimed that he was presented with the ideal opportunity to 'dash to the South Pole'. He had, after all, completed the task of setting up the supply route for Fuchs and along the way pioneered an extraordinary new route across Skelton Glacier and the appropriately named Victoria Land. With only 90 litres of fuel remaining in the tank, his modified Massey Ferguson tractor had conquered 1600 kilometres of some of the most demanding landscapes in the world.

Despite his forays into geopolitics, Fuchs was at heart a research scientist, and his desire to lead the CTAE was driven in part by scientific curiosity but to a greater extent by a desire to join the august annals of British Antarctic exploration. In contrast, Hillary was adamant that the CTAE was first and foremost a great adventure and an opportunity to prove to the world that New Zealanders were playing their part in advancing global exploration. Hillary had no interest in the scientific dimensions of the CTAE and remained indifferent to the wider geopolitical objectives. However, he was also astute enough to realise that his arrival at the South Pole was far more likely to excite New Zealand public opinion then the forthcoming IGY. Much to the frustration of Fuchs, it was the high media profile of Hillary which often dominated the media reports of the CTAE. The scientific credentials and apparent character of 'Dr Fuchs' were now a target for public ridicule, as New Zealand newspapers such as the *Southland Evening News* poked fun:

> Team him up with a colourful character like Sir Edmund Hillary and somehow he seems even more incongruous. How many people talk about Fuchs and Hillary in that order? Most of them haven't even heard of Dr V.E. Fuchs at the time they were acclaiming the conqueror of Everest…Hillary makes a cavalier dash for the South Pole behind the wheel of a converted tractor. Fuchs plods across the ice deserts, donnishly [sic] absorbed in his scientific probings.[72]

Other New Zealand newspapers such as the *Auckland Star* also concurred, and argued that Fuchs' successful crossing of the Antarctic in March 1958 had come as a relief as 'the reaction of the British press is: "Thank God we have done something at last"'.[73]

The dispute between Fuchs and Hillary also impacted on diplomatic relations between the Governments of New Zealand and the UK. According to the New Zealand records of the DEA, civil servants were concerned that the British might attempt to humiliate Hillary in revenge for reaching the South Pole ahead of Fuchs. In a memorandum dated 13 January 1958, the DEA noted that it was monitoring closely the 'unbalanced impression given here [in London] that Hillary has merely dashed to the Pole while Fuchs has been held up by careful scientific work'.[74] Moreover, in a subsequent memorandum prepared for the New Zealand Prime Minister, the DEA advised that 'All New Zealand was in Hillary's corner' and that New Zealand should defend Hillary's decision to advise Fuchs not to press on with his journey once he had reached the South Pole. Prime Minister Walter Nash issued several press statements between 8 and 15 January 1958 supporting Hillary's conduct throughout the CTAE. British officials were instructed by the Management Committee of the CTAE to reassure the Ross Sea Committee that Hillary's contribution was welcomed and respected. Unfortunately for both parties, British newspaper reporters such as the *Daily Mail*'s Noel Barber had already published a host of stories concerning the dispute, and no amount of tactful diplomacy was going to dampen public interest in the 'dispute'.[75]

Despite the widespread praise for the achievements of both Fuchs and Hillary, the disagreement between the two men remains part of modern Antarctic legend. Official accounts of the expedition published in 1958 glossed over the disputes, including whether or not to complete the journey in one Antarctic summer season.[76] What mattered to officials such as Roberts was to capitalise on the achievements of Fuchs and the British participants of the CTAE. Hence the UK Information Service was instructed to release a media profile of Fuchs in May 1958 which tried to paint a more exciting and flattering picture:

> This marked the successful completion of one of the great land adventures left to Man, the crossing of the almost unknown Antarctic continent. Sir Vivian looks young for his years, with dark slightly greying hair, busy eyebrows and a humorous mouth. He is an inspiring leader, calm and confident, and at his best in a crisis, for one of his beliefs is that 'nothing is ever as bad as you think it is going to be'.[77]

While not wishing to decry the writing abilities of the staff attached to the UK Information Service, this profile was hardly going to challenge the charge that the Anglo-German Fuchs was actually little different to his predecessor Scott. Understatement, pluckiness and the quiet determination of Fuchs were being up-staged by the confident, brash and 'media-savvy' qualities of Hillary.

Hillary's plans to publish an account of the CTAE in 1960 revealed only too clearly the underlying tensions between the two leaders. In a memorandum prepared by the New Zealand DEA in January 1960, it was noted that Hillary's memoirs were unquestionably harmful to UK–New Zealand relations. Fuchs, who had seen an earlier version of Hillary's recollections, had warned that he would refute the charges against him 'even at the cost of publishing material which in an effort to preserve Sir Edmund's reputation he had deliberately withheld in his own account of the expedition, from the press'.[78] Moreover, according to officials at New Zealand House in London,

Fuchs grew so mad as he got deeper into the book that he began to annotate it. He told the Committee [the thirty-seventh meeting of the CTAE Management Committee] that it was inaccurate, partial and very critical in places of himself, the Committee of Management and the Ross Sea Committee and in general the tone of the book was offensive. Fuchs said he would feel obliged to set the record straight and answer criticisms that Hillary had made if the book was published without amendment.[79]

The Ross Sea Committee and the New Zealand High Commissioner Scott, based in London, agreed to raise the issue with Hillary. To the relief of British and New Zealand diplomats, the expected spat between Fuchs and Hillary did not materialise in their rival accounts of the CTAE.

If the CTAE had been designed to bolster Commonwealth solidarity, the disagreements and rows between the two leaders undermined that premise. For months preceeding the successful crossing, arguments raged over finances and publicity rights attached to the CTAE. While British officials were privately critical of Hillary's adventurism, their New Zealand counterparts despaired of Fuchs' inability to generate sensational reports of the expedition suitable for publicity purposes. Inevitably, far too many people supported the CTAE for conflicting purposes, and commercial sponsors such as BP had their own agenda relating to Antarctica's hydrocarbon potential in addition to developing a close working relationship with the Australian National Antarctic Research Expedition (ANARE) in the Antarctic and Southern Ocean.[80] If Fuchs thought that the CTAE would remain predominantly a scientific enterprise then he was naive, just as Hillary was myopic to imagine that the geopolitical context of the CTAE was a complete irrelevancy. Britain wanted Commonwealth support in order to protect territorial interests and wider political recognition in the Antarctic Peninsula. New Zealand, aware of the importance of the US's build-up of scientific bases in the Ross Dependency, was at pains to improve bilateral relations with Washington and not just with London.[81] The Australian and South African contingents were a token presence to the CTAE once they declared that their concerns lay in the vast expanses of the Australian Antarctic Territory and the Prince Edward Islands respectively.

SUMMARY

If the FIDS expected *Scott of the Antarctic* to generate a boost for their activities then they were to be bitterly disappointed as the film failed at the box offices in Britain and the US, where audiences reportedly found the doomed imperial polar expedition an unattractive viewing option. As the *Daily Telegraph*'s review candidly recorded, 'The story which should have had in dramatic form the power of a Greek tragedy to move pity and terror, has become on the screen just another adventure story, more monotonous than most'.[82] Roberts, who had invested a lot of time and energy in the project, was once again forced to revert to the old ways of lobbying the Treasury for funds. His success continued to depend on the political ambitions of his masters and or the political difficulties of the Government vis-à-vis the territorial claims pressed by South American states.

Critics of the CTAE such as Kirwan, were forced to reassess their views, as Fuchs triumphed where Scott had failed.[83] However, his rivalry with Hillary exposed the real limits of Commonwealth solidarity, heroism and prestige. As if to illustrate the personality clash still further, Fuchs cheerfully recalled in an interview with the author 40 years later that the popular children's book by Gerald Bowman called *From Scott to Fuchs* was originally titled *From Scott to Hillary*.[84] After pressure from Fuchs's associates, Bowman was persuaded to change the book's title even if the last chapter 'Fuchs and Hillary' recognised that Hillary, as the conqueror of Everest, was a household name. Bowman was thus forced to conclude, 'I have mentioned Hillary first here because the ordinary people of any country on this earth would recognise his picture. Also because he is the sort of man who couldn't help becoming an international figure if he had merely beaten a record at flagpole squatting.'[85]

NOTES ON CHAPTER 4

1   *Daily Mail*, 'Antarctic Crossing', 5 December 1958.
2   *Daily Telegraph*, 'Worst journey in the world', 3 December 1958.
3   For a critical examination of the decade see the analysis of P. Vansittart, *In the Fifties* (London, John Murray, 1995).
4   A point made by J. Richards in *Films and British National Identity* (Manchester, Manchester University Press, 1997), p. 135.
5   Sir W. Churchill, *A History of the English Speaking Peoples* (London, Cassell, 1956). Churchill's work was later made into a BBC television series called *Churchill's Peoples* (1974).
6   See M. Girouard, *The Return of Camelot* (London, Yale University Press, 1981), who highlights the revival of mediaeval chivalry in the period leading from the late eighteenth century to the period leading up to the First World War. One popular expression of this interest was the play called *Where the Rainbow Ends*, performed at the Savoy Theatre until the 1950s. The principal character in the play was the naval cadet called Crispin, who has to negotiate encounters with the Dragon King and St George. The play opened in 1912 in the immediate aftermath of Robert Scott's failure to return from the South Pole.
7   See the masterly analysis of cinema and the post-Second World War period by Richards in *Films and British National Identity*.
8   British cinema in the 1950s not only produced films concerned with Edwardian costume drama and imperial nostalgia such as *North West Frontier* (1959), but also productions such as *Simba* (1954), which explored the affects on white settlers following the Mau Mau rebellion in Kenya.
9   *Sunday Dispatch*, 'The finest breed of men', 5 December 1948. For a more detailed analysis of this film, see K. Dodds, 'Screening Antarctica: Britain, the Falkland Islands Dependencies Survey and *Scott of the Antarctic* (1948)', *Polar Record* 38 (2002): pp. 1–10.
10   The story is reported in D. Shipman, *The Story of Cinema Volume 2* (London, Hodder and Stoughton, 1984).
11   Quoted in Richards, *Films and British National Identity*, p. 131.
12   F. Spufford, *'I May be Some Time': Ice and English Imagination* (London, Faber and Faber, 1996), p. xx.

13   See the assessment by A. Vesselo, 'The quarter in Britain', *Sight and Sound* 18 (1949): pp. 49–50.

14   S. Harper and V. Porter, 'Cinema audience tastes in 1950s Britain', *Journal of Popular British Cinema* 2 (1999): pp. 66–82.

15   See T. Shaw, *British Cinema and the Cold War* (London, I. B. Tauris, 2001), pp. 86–7.

16   Quoted in Shaw, *British Cinema and the Cold War*, p. 87. See also M. Balcon, *Michael Balcon Presents...A Lifetime of Films* (London, Hutchinson, 1969).

17   F. Debenham, '*Scott of the Antarctic*: A personal opinion', *Polar Record* 5 (1949): pp. 311–16. The quote is taken from p. 311.

18   Debenham, '*Scott of the Antarctic*: A personal opinion'. The quote is taken from p. 316. See also the *Daily Express*, '*Scott of the Antarctic*', 30 November 1948.

19   D. James, Scott of the Antarctic: *The Film and its Production* (London, Convoy Productions, 1948), p. 141.

20   Author interview with Bernard Stonehouse, 22 October 2000. Fuchs was later critical of the choice of film location and noted that 'neither location could provide the broad sweep of polar scenery needed to give the film an authentic atmosphere'. V. Fuchs, *Ice and Men* (Oswestry, Anthony Nelson, 1982), p. 73.

21   James, Scott of the Antarctic: *The Film and its Production*.

22   M. Balcon, 'The technical problems of *Scott of the Antarctic*', *Sight and Sound* 17 (1948–9): pp. 153–5.

23   SPRI Archives MS 791.44. Letter from A. Courtald to C. Bertram, dated 16 May 1950. See also letter from A. Courtald to S. L. Courtald, dated 20 May 1950.

24   On the role of Ealing Studios in promoting British values see A. Marwick, *A History of the Modern British Isles* (Oxford, Blackwell, 2000), p. 194. On the significance of the music of Vaughan Williams see Richards, *Films and British National Identity* and U. Vaughan-Williams, *RVW* (Oxford, Oxford University Press, 1964), p. 280.

25   BAS AD3/1/A5/155/A (1). Colonial Office memorandum on the FIDS dated 25 February 1949.

26   BAS ADM 1/23561. Report from the Colonial Office to the FO dated 2 March 1952, following receipt of the Admiralty's report on 'The Falkland Islands Dependencies – Argentine activities'.

27   The North Pole was a particularly important geographical point during the Cold War because it provided the shortest route for missiles and submarines to travel between the two superpowers. Both sides created secret bases, such as Drifting Station Alpha (the US) and North Pole 8 (the Soviet Union), which slowly moved on icebergs around the North Pole. The men stationed on the bases used sonar gear to monitor the movement of submarines under the polar ice cap. The 1968 Hollywood film *Ice Station Zebra*, based on the book by British author Alistair MacLean, represented these geopolitical dramas on celluloid.

28   The Stonington Island Base was created as part of the 1939–41 US Antarctic Expedition.

29   *New York Times*, 'US Antarctic base vacated by British', 23 December 1946, claimed that the British had occupied the US base at Stonington Island. The story was denied by the UK Government via its Embassy in Washington DC.

30   SPRI 1278 ER. Letter from Major K. Pierce-Butler to Commander Finn Ronne, dated 16 March 1947.

31   See the account in F. Ronne, *Antarctic Conquest* (New York, G. P. Putnam and Sons, 1949).

32 One interesting illustration of this tension was Finn Ronne's complaint to Brian Roberts in a letter dated 26 June 1951 that a recent paper on FIDS activities in the journal *Polar Record* did not sufficiently acknowledge the surveying achievements of the Ronne expedition. Eight years later, Roberts had dinner with Finn and Jackie Ronne in November 1959 and noted that 'they are both so bitter and anxious to justify themselves that I could do little but listen and sympathise'. The latter is an extract from Roberts' diaries contained within SPRI Archives MS 1278 ER.

33 B. Beeves, 'Work of the FIDS', *The Crown Colonist* 18 (1948): pp. 613–15. The quotes are taken from pp. 613 and 615.

34 The *Times*, 'US flag over base in Antarctica', 22 March 1947.

35 BAS AD6/15/17/7. Letter from Roberts to E. W. Bingham, dated 6 December 1948.

36 The inspiration for the crossing is recorded in Fuchs' handwritten note composed while stuck at Stonington Island Base in 1948. See BAS AD1/D1/S.

37 BP provided all the petroleum fuels and lubricants for the CTAE, and even helpfully provided some BP-embossed windsocks. See 'Trans Antarctic epic', *BP Magazine* 34 (1958): pp. 22–3. BP also created an exhibition of the company's contribution to the CTAE; in 1959 it toured BP company properties in London, Kent, Wales and Scotland.

38 See for example, the *Times*, 'Antarctic crossing', 20 November 1958, which noted that the film 'sensibly concentrated on explaining the practical difficulties of the expedition' rather than focusing on the personalities. The official account was published by Fuchs and Hillary as *The Crossing of Antarctica* (London, Cassell, 1958).

39 *Monthly Film Bulletin*, 'Antarctic Crossing' 26/300, (January 1959). Virtually all the reviews of the film praised it for its factual and visual qualities. See the *Times*, 'Antarctic crossing on the screen', 4 December 1958, *Variety*, 'Antarctic Crossing', 31 December 1958, *Kinematograph Weekly*, 'Antarctic Crossing', 11 December 1958 and *Manchester Guardian*, 'Antarctic crossing', 3 December 1958. The producer of the film was James Carr.

40 Significantly, Fuchs' autobiography, *A Time to Speak* (Oswestry, Anthony Nelson, 1990), makes no mention of the dispute between himself and Sir Edmund Hillary.

41 *Evening Star* 'Attlee declines Aussies' aid in Falkland dispute', 23 February 1948. HMS *Sheffield* was sent to British Honduras in the same period, in response to fears that the Guatemalan Government was intending to invade the colony.

42 P. Law, *Antarctic Odyssey* (Melbourne, Heinemann, 1983), p. 267.

43 Official statement of the CTAE Management Committee, reproduced in South African Archives (SAA) BLO 16/1. Telegram from the South African High Commission in London to the South African DEA, dated 1 September 1955.

44 M. Dockrill, *British Defence Since 1945* (Oxford, Blackwell, 1988), p. 32.

45 This is most evident in the minutes of the meeting of the Polar Committee on 24 March 1953.

46 BAS AD3/1/A5/164B (3) Part 1. FIDS Scientific Committee memorandum, dated June 1954.

47 NAC RG25 4765 50070 Part 3. The conclusion was included in an FO memorandum entitled 'Future UK policy in the Antarctic', dated August 1954.

48 Fuchs, *A Time to Speak*, p. 221.

49 NAC RG25 4765 50070-40 Part 3. Minutes of the meeting between the Commonwealth Relations Office and Commonwealth representatives in London, dated February 1955.

50 This capacity of polar regions to act as a discursive tabula rosa is explored by John McCannon in his investigation of socialist progress in the Soviet Arctic, 'To storm the Arctic: Soviet polar exploration and public visions of nature in the USSR 1932–1939', *Ecumene* 2 (1995): pp. 15–31.

51 AA A1838/1/1495/3/9. Minute by R. G. Casey to DEA official Plimsoll, dated 16 August 1955.

52 AA A4940/1 C1438. DEA memorandum to the Prime Minister's Department, dated 16 August 1955.

53 *Ibid.*

54 AA A4940/1 C1438. Cabinet minute on the CTAE, dated 16 August 1955.

55 SAA BLO 16/1. Letter from the South African High Commissioner in London to the South African DEA, dated 18 February 1955.

56 NAC RG25 4765 50070 40 Part 3. Internal memorandum prepared by the Canadian DEA, dated 4 September 1954.

57 The New Zealand Antarctic Society was created in 1933 when the inaugural meeting was held at the Dominion Farmers' Institute Building in Wellington on 2 November of that year. The aims of the society were described in the minutes of the meeting as raising interest in the Ross Dependency within New Zealand and encouraging scientific research in the region. The minutes of the society are held at the Canterbury Museum in Christchurch.

58 M. Templeton, *A Wise Adventure: New Zealand and the Antarctic 1923–1960* (Wellington, Victoria University Press, 2001).

59 A point that was made in the *Christchurch Press* 'The Ross Sea and you', dated 10 September 1955.

60 In one talk on the expedition given at Wellington Town Hall on 2 June 1956, £630 was raised from the audience of 2000 people.

61 In one public screening of *Scott of the Antarctic* at the Avon Theatre in Christchurch, over £135 was raised for the CTAE; the Christchurch Boys' School raised £50 by organising sponsorship for the accompanying husky dogs. These details are to be found in New Zealand Archives (NZA) CH89 1/1/2/7 TAE Ross Sea Committee Correspondence 15 September 1955–28 May 1958.

62 The personal papers of Sir Laurence Kirwan offer an interesting insight into the ongoing disputes affecting the planning of the CTAE in London. Despite offering a grant to the CTAE, Sir James Marshall-Cornwall, the then President of the Royal Geographical Society, threatened to withdraw his support because he was unhappy with the lack of information provided by the Management Committee. This was deeply embarrassing given the involvement of Sir John Slessor in the running of the Management Committee.

63 The *Times*, 'E. Hillary's progress', 28 December 1957.

64 See for example, *Evening Advertiser*, 'Fuchs refuses to give up – rejects Hillary's advice to stop at Pole', 6 January 1958 and the *Star*, 'Fuchs only a slim chance', 11 January 1958.

65 See for example, the *Daily Mail* 'Hillary races to the Pole', 23 December 1957 and the *Dominion*, 'Hillary dashes for Pole surprises NZ authorities', 27 December 1957. Wordie and Clifford wrote a letter to the *Times* denying that there was a 'race' to the South Pole, dated 1 April 1958.

66 See for example, *Waikato Times*, 'Hillary's dash to Pole', 4 January 1958 and the *Economist*, 'Ice and fire', 11 January 1958.

67   NZA PM 208/71 Part 4. Minutes of the second annual meeting of the Management Committee, dated 20 December 1957.

68   The *Scotsman*, 'Dr Fuchs to continue trek after two days', 20 January 1958, contained details of Fuchs' denial of a rift between himself and Hillary.

69   *Birmingham Post*, 'Dr Fuchs going like a bomb', 3 February 1958.

70   NZA PM 208 7/1. Letter from the New Zealand Legation in Paris to the DEA, dated 30 January 1958. The article in *Paris-Match* was published on 18 January 1958. The New Zealand Legation sent a letter of rebuke to *Paris-Match* on 23 January 1958.

71   Author interview with Sir Edmund Hillary, 3 September 1996.

72   *Southland Daily News*, 'A man of high adventure: Dr Vivian Ernest Fuchs', 1 March 1958.

73   *Auckland Star*, 'Trek hailed as British morale life', 4 March 1958. See also the *Evening Post*, 'Skill, leadership and a polar victory', 3 March 1958 for a similar conclusion.

74   NZA PM 208/7/1. Internal memorandum prepared by the DEA, dated 13 January 1958.

75   N. Barber, *White Desert* (London, 1958). See the *Daily Express* 'This is it: Hello Ed', 22 January 1958, for a diplomatic story on the meeting between Fuchs and Hillary at the South Pole.

76   See, for example, V. Fuchs, 'The Crossing of Antarctica', *National Geographic* CXV (1959): pp. 25–47.

77   UK Information Service, 'Sir Vivian Fuchs' *UKIS Bibliographies* no 640, 12 May 1958.

78   NZA PM 208 7/5 Part 2 CTAE: Publicity and Publications. Letter from the DEA to the New Zealand High Commissioner in London, dated 11 February 1960.

79   NZA PM 208 7/5 Part 2. Letter from the New Zealand High Commission in London to the DEA, dated 8 December 1959.

80   See 'Australia's all-out bid to develop her Antarctic territories', *BP Magazine* New Series 1 (1961): pp. 10–15.

81   See M. Templeton, *A Wise Adventure: New Zealand and the Antarctic 1923-1960*.

82   The *Daily Telegraph*, '*Scott of the Antarctic*', 30 November 1948.

83   See the review in L. Kirwan, 'Polar exploration in the last twenty years', *Geographical Magazine* 32 (1959): pp. 355–64.

84   Author interview with Fuchs, 1 July 1998; G. Bowman, *From Scott to Fuchs*, (London, Cox and Wyman, 1960).

85   Quoted in Bowman, *From Scott to Fuchs*, p. 161.

5

Managing the 'Antarctic Problem'

INTRODUCTION

Conflicting territorial claims in the Antarctic have become somewhat of a fixture after decades of concentrated international exploration there and the recent Argentine and Chilean expeditions, which have served to set off the current dispute, are but the latest symptoms of a malaise which is becoming commonly known as Antarcticitis.[1]

It was the one spot on earth entirely free from Adam and his descendants, a virgin land inspiring man to high endeavour, untrammelled by the lure of profit.[2]

Almost bankrupt by the end of the Second World War, Britain was still prepared to invest in Antarctic science and exploration precisely because it offered solace to those seeking reassuring signs of national heroism and scientific acumen. In retrospect, therefore, the 1959 Antarctic Treaty must be considered not only a diplomatic triumph but also a godsend for hard-pressed British officials charged with preserving territorial claims in Antarctica and preventing conflict from spreading across the FID. Article IV of the treaty was instrumental in this transformation and owes much to scientific co-operation conducted during the IGY.[3] However, the treaty was also the product of a decade of intense diplomatic negotiations and occasional geo-political drama, usually centred on Anglo–Argentine–Chilean tension in the Antarctic Peninsula.[4]

Paradoxically, British officials found that the US Antarctic policy proved to be the most problematic, despite their ongoing disputes with Argentina and Chile. Under the euphemism of the 'Antarctic problem', the political status of the uninhabited Antarctic continent and surrounding seas emerged as a feature of international politics in the period between 1948 and 1959.[5] With the seven claimant states of Argentina, Australia, Britain, Chile, France, New Zealand and Norway already established in the region, the 'Antarctic problem' was inevitably saturated with international overtones (see figure 5.1). The Truman administration's idea for an international trusteeship in the Antarctic was conceived not only to defuse Anglo–Argentine–Chilean tensions but also to reiterate its determination to ensure

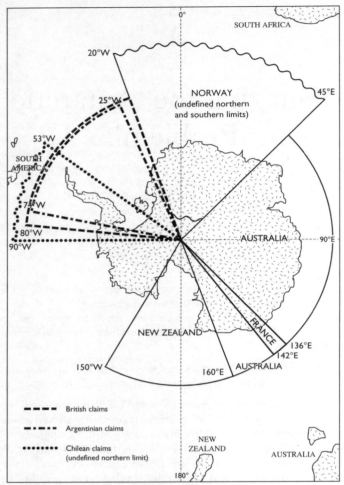

Figure 5.1: National claims in the Antarctic

that US geopolitical and legal interests were protected in these uncertain times. Notwithstanding their best endeavours, Britain and its Commonwealth partners never convinced the US either to press a claim to the unclaimed Pacific sector of the continent or to support actively their collective interests against Latin American and Soviet adversaries. Given the substantial American interests in the British and New Zealand territorial sectors, it was clear that the US under Truman and Eisenhower had no intention of playing the role that Britain secretly hoped it would adopt. As the 1950s unfolded, the divisive politics of the Cold War began to change the geopolitical complexion of Antarctica. While science helped to sustain claims to Antarctica, it also played a powerful role in alleviating tension over this contested continent. The IGY's legacy to Antarctica was the 'enlightened' American and Soviet collective view to forgo a territorial claim in favour of constructing an international regime for peaceful co-operation.

THE US AND THE INTERNATIONALISATION OF ANTARCTICA

For most of the Cold War, the US and Soviet Union confronted each other across the Arctic. As Denis Cosgrove has noted, 'Intercontinental ballistic missiles (ICBMs) routed through the polar skies, nuclear submarines submerged below the icecap, and electronic early-warning systems encircled the tundra desert. This Cold War was aptly named.'[6] When the US first floated the idea of an international trusteeship for the Antarctic in 1948, it did not signify a transition in terms of geopolitical priorities. While the Arctic remained the most significant region within the US strategic imagination at the time, the proposal nonetheless alarmed London and other Commonwealth capitals. Notwithstanding the claims of its Cold War allies, the US was eager to commence diplomatic negotiations over the future territorial status of Antarctica in order to allay discord with the Soviet Union. The proposal and its contents were inopportune for all the Commonwealth parties. Britain was embroiled in local disputes with the Argentines and Chileans in the Antarctic Peninsula, and Commonwealth states such as Australia and New Zealand were in the process of re-examining (privately at least) the legal validity of their territorial claims.[7] Worse still, the US itself was engaged in some high-profile expeditions in the Antarctic with the potential for large-scale exploration and permanent base construction across the entire polar continent. Admiral Richard Byrd, the distinguished American polar explorer, emerged as the greatest individual threat to Commonwealth claims, which led regional newspapers such as the *Des Moines Register* to speculate on a 'formal American claim to strategic areas of the vast Antarctic continent'.[8]

By the time the Department of State proposed a formal review of the international politics of Antarctica, most Antarctic observers recognised that American political and geographical activities were about to create a new post-war polar order. The Australian Antarctic expert, John Cumpston, in a recorded conversation with a colleague from the Canadian Embassy in Santiago de Chile, captured the pessimistic mood of the period:

> One group is to go into the Ross Sea, south of New Zealand, to establish an airfield in Little America. Two other groups will operate to the East and West of the Ross Sea. It is feared by the Australians that the first group operating from Little America will explore the southern portions of the Australian Antarctic Territory. Byrd's eastern party, Mr Cumpston feels, will endeavour, and very likely complete, at least a partial photographic survey of the coastline of the Australian Antarctic Territory as far as Queen Mary Land. Mr Cumpston believes that the Australians must send Catalina flying boats in order to undertake photography so that the Australian map of Antarctica can be updated. It [the map] constitutes, in his opinion, the strongest evidence of the validity of Australian claims over Antarctic territory.[9]

Mindful of the power of maps and their role in consolidating territorial claims, the Dominions Office (replaced by the Commonwealth Relations Office) in London despatched circulars to the Australian and New Zealand Governments in 1946 urging them to support actively their claims to the Antarctic. FO legal advisers had already warned both Governments that 'continuous and effective occupation' was increasingly likely to determine the validity of their claims under international law. As the British had discovered with Operation Tabarin, protecting Antarctic claims was time-consuming and expensive in terms of base construction and maintenance. Given their own difficulties, this was sound geopolitical advice based on their efforts to confront the prospect of routine Argentine and Chilean naval incursions in the FID. To compound matters further, the colony of British Honduras was under threat from neighbouring Guatemala.[10] In an era of financial austerity, it was extraordinary that the British were still prepared to use Royal Navy ships to protect territorial claims in tropical Central America and the frozen wastes of Antarctica at a time when defence commitments in Central Europe, the Middle East and southeast Asia remained significant. Yet Britain's inability to manage commitments closer to home was illustrated only to clearly by US support in the form of Marshall aid and defensive intervention in war-torn Greece in the late 1940s.

When the US Department of State circulated the idea of an international trusteeship for the Antarctic, Australia and New Zealand were unprepared to launch major post-war expeditions to their claimant sectors. As the New Zealand newspaper the *Dominion* later complained in November 1949 'New Zealand has done virtually nothing' with regards to the Ross Dependency.[11] Initially, the US floated the idea for a UN trusteeship of the Antarctic in which existing sovereignty claims to the continent would be suspended indefinitely but after severe criticism from the UK and other Commonwealth claimant states, an eight-power con-dominium was instead proposed as a possible future option. Mindful of Britain's hostility to UN intervention, especially by inexperienced post-colonial states, the US proposed that the seven claimant states in conjunction with the Truman admin-istration should effectively 'pool' sovereignty in an attempt to neutralise potential conflicts between claimant states in the future. At this stage, the US Department of State did not want to raise the Antarctic issue with the Soviets in case it exacerbated an already tense situation. The last time Britain conducted discussions with the US over the future of the polar continent in 1947–8, it had advocated an approach to the ICJ for a formal ruling on the Argentine–Chile–UK territorial dispute only. British officials, particularly Roberts, were certainly not in favour of interfering with the legal and political status of other claimant states. Once the South American parties had deemed that suggestion unacceptable (they rejected the proposal that the ICJ should adjudicate on their domestic territories), Britain reluctantly began discussions with US counterparts in March 1948. The *New York Times* was convinced that this reticence towards the trusteeship proposal was unduly influenced by 'post-war losses of British imperial territory and to recent affronts to British sovereignty [in the Falklands and Belize]'.[12]

Underlying the American proposal was the belief that an International Antarctic Commission could be created to manage the collective territorial interests of all eight parties. Britain was prepared to participate in such a regime if it enjoyed the complete support of all the claimant states and, as an FO memorandum noted, substantial territorial compromise was also possible:

> The United Kingdom has decided, if other Commonwealth countries agree, to negotiate with the other seven governments on the basis of the US proposal. The UK would also hope to retain sovereignty over a limited area in the South

Shetland Islands but, if necessary, to ensure the success of the eight power discussions they would not insist upon this.[13]

In other words, as with the Falkland Islands, British officials were prepared to be flexible over their territorial claims in the region because of the ongoing and ultimately costly struggle with Argentina and Chile.

Despite the negotiations between the US and Commonwealth states, agreement was far from certain for such a proposal. It was known, for example, that the South American and French claimant states were unlikely to agree to such a condominium.[14] All three parties had been stout defendants of their territorial claims and would view any international regime in the Antarctic as an unwelcome intervention. Chile had already rejected Britain's proposal for the involvement of the ICJ precisely because it did not recognise that its sovereignty over the Antarctic was contested by other states. As if to reinforce a long-standing geopolitical strategy of territorial consolidation, President Videla of Chile travelled to the Antarctic Peninsula (renamed Peninsula O'Higgins on Chilean maps) to inaugurate a new base called 'General O'Higgins' (the so-called Founding Father of independent Chile) in February 1948.[15] Moreover, there had been little formal consideration of the likely response of the Soviet Union and other interested parties, such as Japan, to the US proposals. Even within the Commonwealth, opinion was split on the matter, with the New Zealanders displaying considerably greater sympathy for a sovereignty condominium than the Australians or the British. Subsequently, the New Zealanders caused further consternation by advocating formal internationalisation of Antarctica under the control of the UN.[16]

Unwittingly, perhaps, the Washington-based proposal for an international condominium caused a schism within the Commonwealth parties in the northern hemispheric summer of 1948. On the one hand, New Zealand advocated a new international regime under the control of the UN rather than the eight interested parties proposed by the US. This was no gesture of high-minded altruism, the New Zealanders recognised that their claim to the Ross Dependency was weakened not only by limited exploration in the region but also by an active US presence. Some observers were even inclined to conclude that the US could easily maintain a claim given that it enjoyed 'effective occupation' of the Ross Dependency. On the other hand, Australia and Britain [with the support of non-claimant South Africa] were keen to negotiate future options for Antarctic governance with the US. One area for possible concession would have been the invocation of separate treatment of claims to sub-Antarctic islands such as South Shetland, Prince Edward and Heard, in the face of a special legal regime for the Antarctic continent. As the South African Minister of External Affairs noted in 1948:

> The Union government are of the opinion that a clear distinction should be drawn between the Antarctic continent itself and the islands within the Antarctic Circle which lie some distance from it.[17]

Secretly, many Antarctic observers in London, Wellington, Pretoria and Canberra continued to hope that they could persuade the US to consider making a formal territorial claim to the so-called unclaimed Pacific sector in Antarctica, thereby exacting a more sympathetic response to the collective interests of the claimant states. This belief was also shared by their Chilean counterparts, who in August 1948 were sufficiently confident in their beliefs to confess to the Canadians that the

US would 'definitely alter their policy of no claim and will advance claims for Antarctic territory. They will rather claim specific points not sectors on the Antarctic continent as explored by American expeditions.'[18] In other words, Chilean observers believed that if the US did press a claim it would not restrict itself to an unclaimed sector but would concentrate on claiming areas where it had been actively involved in exploration, and this might include parts of the British, Australian and New Zealand sectors. The source of this information appears to have come from a secret briefing the Chileans received from a Department of State official, Green, who had earlier visited Santiago de Chile.

In view of the rumours and counter-rumours surrounding the US proposals for a new international regime and possible new Antarctic claim, Commonwealth states continued to discuss the issue for the remaining months of 1948. It was agreed that no formal response to the Americans and their 'Draft Agreement on Antarctica' could be given until the Commonwealth parties agreed a common course of action. In September 1948, the Polar Committee held a formal meeting with all interested Government departments and represented Commonwealth partners. The Polar Committee was an important mechanism of British Government influence and was used by British civil servants to generate Commonwealth support relating to the Antarctic. Membership was limited to the so-called old Commonwealth states of Australia, Canada, New Zealand and South Africa because of their polar and sub-Antarctic experience and interests. Chaired by a Commonwealth Relations Office official, Syers, in November 1948, official reactions to US plans were presented by British Government departments and the Commonwealth partners. The FO civil servant Peter Stirling reported to the committee that there was 'some divergence of views between Commonwealth governments directly affected by the proposals and until further discussions had taken place, it would be difficult to prepare any formal reply to the United States government'.[19] A month later, a meeting was held between the Commonwealth leaders to consider a formal response to the US. Once again progress was slight, as the Australian Prime Minister Robert Menzies appeared the least inclined to agree to any new international regime for Antarctica because of the implications for Australian sovereignty in the region.[20]

Notwithstanding US willingness to consider future options for the Antarctic, the Commonwealth parties could never agree on a common political strategy, while New Zealand remained ambivalent about its 1933 claim to the Ross Dependency. This inability to secure consent was not the only obstacle in the way of a quasi-international settlement. As Argentina and Chile increased the number of research bases in the Antarctic Peninsula, the mood for geopolitical compromise evaporated and instead most claimant states were determined to concentrate on their position vis-à-vis 'effective occupation'. As if to reiterate this collective determination to resist fundamental change, the Norwegian Government (arguably with New Zealand the least active of all the seven claimant states) sent a formal response to the Department of State in November 1948 formally rejecting the US proposals:

> The Norwegian government considers the establishment of an international administration for Antarctica unnecessary for the carrying out of the desirable scientific tasks and cannot subscribe to an arrangement whereby Norway would waive her exclusive sovereignty over her territories south of 60 degrees south latitude.[21]

Norway had joined Argentina, Chile, and France in formally rejecting the US proposal, thereby isolating New Zealand and its active proposal for a broader and more international regime for Antarctica.

For Britain, the pressure to resolve the conflicting sovereignty claims over the Antarctic Peninsula was eased by the signing in November 1948 of a naval agreement between Britain, Argentina and Chile. Henceforth, the three parties agreed that they would not send warships below 60 degrees south latitude in an effort to avert any possible outbreak of violence in the region. In doing so, they had addressed one of the major concerns raised by the Department of State in March 1948, that this conflict over sovereignty could lead to discord between Cold War allies. Indeed, there was evidence to suggest that by the following year, the 'United States Department of State are treating the Antarctic question as a matter of little importance' in the light of the Anglo–Argentine–Chilean rapprochement. While the question of a possible US claim had not been resolved in 1948, it was apparent that most of the Commonwealth claimant states believed that the US had merely postponed its internationalisation proposals.

Regardless of the lack of agreement over US proposals for a new international regime, 1948 was still a turning-point in the international politics of the region. Most seasoned observers agreed that the culture of territorial claims had been thoroughly dislocated as the US exercised its diplomatic and scientific muscle even though it considered the Arctic to be more significant. Politically, its proposals for a new regime had caused diplomatic panic in all the capitals of the southern hemispheric states of Australia, Argentina, Chile and New Zealand, and the continued uncertainty over a possible US claim to the Antarctic encouraged further speculation and intrigue.[22] Scientifically, US expeditions in the late 1940s and 1950s demonstrated that land-based exploration could be combined with extensive aerial surveys in a manner which was truly breathtaking. More broadly, the long-term implication of the American proposals in 1948 was to reactivate Soviet interest in the Antarctic region after a period of spectacular Arctic navigation and exploration culminating in the establishment of a scientific base on the North Pole in the late 1930s.[23] Whether Britain or the Commonwealth parties approved, the Soviets were robust in their denouncement of any proposals to internationalise the Antarctic, which excluded Moscow from the decision-making processes. By 1950, the military and political language of the Cold War impinged upon the international politics of Antarctica and southern hemispheric states and Britain began to realise that its disputes in the Antarctic were no longer isolated.

In the decade leading up to the 1959 Antarctic Treaty, the British officials charged with managing the Antarctic portfolio devised a strategy which would tie Commonwealth partners into the political and legal defence of the FID. British officials effectively paved the ground for negotiations with the US over the future political status of the polar continent. In 1949, no-one really believed that the idea of international management had been dismissed by the collective unease of the claimant states. The emerging presence of the Soviet Union on the Antarctic scene meant that the US and the claimants would in future have to consider a wider constituency of interested parties. The rationale for the CTAE in 1955 was a direct consequence of this internationalisation process. The IGY was to provoke further vexation when an unprecedented number of scientists converged on the Antarctic ice and new scientific bases were constructed all over the polar continent. Given the military pressures in the Arctic, competitive research was redirected to the Antarctic, much to the irritation of the seven claimant states (especially ones in the southern hemisphere), who demanded reassurances that their claims would not be compromised by this new found scientific freedom.[24] Some of the media reporting in Australia became hysterical as the Sydney *Sun-Herald* warned of a 'Red flag near South Pole', and noted that 'Russia is Australia's neighbour at a huge base being built in the Antarctic'.[25] Other reports sought to convince that the scheming Russians would use science as a cover in order to locate missile stations in the frozen wastes of Antarctica.[26] The final impetus, which ultimately resulted in the Antarctic Treaty, was the growing interest of new Commonwealth states, such as India. The claimant states successfully resisted Indian pressure to place the political and resource management of the polar continent under UN supervision, but failed to anticipate the repercussions of this action some two decades later.

THE INTERNATIONAL GEOPHYSICAL YEAR AND COLD-WAR PARANOIA

The decision to hold an IGY in 1957–8 was taken in 1951 after international scientists agreed that new data was needed in the wake of the last 'collection exercise' during the second International Polar Year in 1932–3. A proposal from the International Council of Scientific Unions (ICSU) was accepted by the Executive Council (of the ICSU), and as a consequence a Special Committee of the IGY was created and later convened in Paris in May 1955 to discuss the format of the intended IGY. It was proposed that a ring of research stations be created in the Antarctic to maximise scientific coverage of the continent. With the aid of new maps under preparation by the British, US and Soviet authorities, it was felt that these bases could be built with some confidence. Despite the Special Committee's commitment to scientific freedom, it was evident that the proposals for the IGY alarmed claimant states. Argentine and Chilean delegations, headed by their ambassadors in Paris, were particularly anxious to secure reassurances over sovereign claims in the Antarctic given the impact that unrestricted freedom for scientific investigation might have on territorial and resource rights in the region. Among the Commonwealth participants, Australia was eager to secure an agreement that the activities of the IGY would not adversely impact on existing territorial claims, especially with regard to the Soviet Union and its plans for the Australian Antarctic territory. As a confidential memorandum prepared by an official attached to the DEA confirmed, 'Australia has never thought that the CTAE would be of much value. The Russian initiative on the Knox Coast makes it even more desirable that we should have done additional work in this area to establish Australia's claims to 2.5 million square miles of Antarctic territory.'[27] Intense debate followed in Australia in 1956 when it became clear that the Soviets decided to establish new bases in the Australian Antarctic territory.

Mindful of growing diplomatic and media speculation, Roberts visited Moscow in May–June 1956 in order to explore what the Soviets intended to achieve during the IGY.[28] In his report to the FO and the Australian DEA, Roberts noted that the Soviets 'are planning the Antarctic work from a purely scientific angle, apparently with only the broadest directive to make a successful contribution to the IGY. It is necessary to look elsewhere for any sinister motives about Soviet intentions in the

Antarctic.' Roberts also took the opportunity to remind his Soviet counterpart, Burkhanov, that Britain had a special geographical relationship with the Antarctic and its outlying islands: 'We regarded places like Deception Island as just as British as the Channel Islands, and would first like to achieve a legal settlement of the dispute with Argentina and Chile before any further change to the political status of the region'.[29]

The cautious appraisal of Soviet intentions in the Antarctic by Roberts was not shared by the Australian Foreign Minister, Richard Casey. Interestingly, Casey wrote to the American Secretary of State, John Foster Dulles to register his concern over Soviet Antarctic plans in July 1956. Dulles, in his reply to Casey assured the latter that 'We are indeed following very closely Soviet activities in the area and are also concerned over the possibility of the Soviets remaining after the conclusion of the IGY'.[30]

Uncertainty over the future governance of Antarctica plagued the build-up to the IGY, and the Australian Government and media became increasingly fearful of the Soviet Union's geopolitical intentions. This point was noted by the *New York Times*: 'The nation most disturbed about the present Soviet activities in the Antarctic, however, appears to be Australia. Its military strategists have a clear picture of what effect on their great island continent would be…should Soviet air bases and operations in Antarctica continue to expand.'[31] Worse still for Casey, he was also being pressurised by eminent Antarctic figures such as Sir Douglas Mawson to encourage the US to recognise Australia's claims in the region.[32] In this climate of uncertainty and fear, India's surprise proposal to place the continent under the control of the UN caused further panic among the Commonwealth parties. After the initial proposal was publicised in February 1956, Britain (which had been given no prior warning) organised a meeting of the Commonwealth claimant states where it was agreed that the Indian representative to the UN, Arthur Lall, should be persuaded to drop this particular line of thought. According to the correspondence between India and Commonwealth partners, Lall argued that it was an appropriate time to consider the matter, given that UNESCO was planning to organise an expedition during the IGY. Moreover, the Indian Government expressed concern that the Antarctic might be used for nuclear testing in the future.[33] The Soviet Union's intentions were also unclear, and the FO was perturbed as to its role and possible involvement in the future governance of the region. As Vincent of the FO told a meeting of Commonwealth partners in August 1956, 'The Americans might usefully be encouraged to claim the vacant part of Antarctica. Such a claim by the Americans would have to be made without prejudice to further claims they might eventually make to other parts of Antarctica.'[34] Unfortunately for the British and their Commonwealth colleagues, the US showed little public inclination to press a claim either before or during the IGY.

In October 1956, a formal proposal entitled the 'Peaceful utilisation of Antarctica' was submitted for inclusion in the 11th Agenda of the UN. A letter from Lall to the Secretary-General of the UN highlighted the future importance of the Antarctic continent for all sections of the world's population. Accordingly, the Indian Government suggested that the UN would be the appropriate mechanism for the governance of the polar continent because of the resource value of the Antarctic, the climatic significance of the region and its global environmental importance. This proposal met with strong opposition from India's Commonwealth partners and other claimant states such as Chile and Argentina. After the UK placed considerable diplomatic pressure on India, it agreed to withdraw its request in November 1956. Nevertheless, this increased pressure on Commonwealth states and challenged the role of the superpowers and the IGY scientific programme. It also served as a timely reminder that British expectations of its old Commonwealth colleagues to operate in unison neglected the abilities of new Commonwealth members such as India to articulate and further the concerns of states not party to IGY discussions.

While scientists were engaged in IGY-approved scientific research programmes during 1957–8, political unease was mounting within the British Government. In a meeting between Commonwealth partners in August 1957, the FO circulated a paper on territorial claims, which contained the following important admissions. First, it was accepted that a satisfactory solution to territorial claims in Antarctica was not possible between the seven claimant states. Second, it was anticipated that the US would press a territorial claim after the IGY. Third, the Soviet Union showed little inclination to leave the Antarctic, so that any future settlement to the governance of the region would have to recognise Moscow as a legitimate participant. In other words, Britain acknowledged that any new international authority would have to include the claimant states and the two superpowers. The Australians, under the leadership of the Casey, were adamant that if the Soviet Union was included then it was essential that 'no publicity be given to these discussions until the future intentions of the Soviet Union were clearer. We do not want the Russians to mount installations in the Antarctic from which they could drop missiles on Melbourne or Sydney.'[35] The Commonwealth parties gathered again in October 1957 to consider new British proposals for an international authority composed of representatives from the seven claimant states, the US, the Soviet Union and possibly South Africa, given its geographically proximate position. The meeting considered in some detail possible funding arrangements and future regulations for the control of whaling, sealing and even mineral rights. At the core of these discussions was the recognition that the Soviet Union could not be excluded, and hence some form of compromise on sovereignty would be necessary to secure international co-operation after the IGY.

The emergence of the Soviet Union as a dominant presence in the Antarctic was the decisive element in the IGY period. Despite Australian misgivings, the British showed a considerable degree of geopolitical pragmatism, resigned to the inevitability that their territorial claims were no longer isolated from the wider currents of world politics. FO officials were determined to ensure that local friction with Argentina and Chile was properly contained within the annual renewal of the 1948 Naval Agreement. Roberts played an important role in persuading the US Government that no settlement on the contested politics of Antarctica would be possible without the Soviet Union. The FO, under some pressure from the Treasury to cut costs and negotiate a political settlement, seized the opportunity to reduce investment in a large number of scientific bases scattered around the FID. Higher research grants, high-profile events designed to supplement the mapping programme of the FIDS and greater Commonwealth co-operation were the last elements in an investment strategy designed to maintain British influence until negotiations over the future of the polar continent commenced. As Harold Macmillan acknowledged to the House of Commons in May 1957,

HMG's policy in regard to Antarctica is to continue the tasks of surveying and exploring the Falkland Islands Dependencies with a particular view to ascertaining their value, particularly from the economic and scientific point of view, and by the establishment of our administration of the necessary bases in our area and in consultation with other Commonwealth governments concerned.[36]

Scientifically, the IGY signalled a sea change in British Antarctic policy as the Royal Society replaced the FIDS as the pre-eminent agent of scientific endeavour. New bodies such as the British National Committee of the IGY were staffed with Royal Society representatives to alleviate concerns that nationalistic endeavours and parochial scientific concerns had tainted the FIDS.

In his review of the Royal Society's contribution to the IGY, Sir David Brunt noted that the construction of Halley Bay in 1956 was the culmination of five years of preparation by British polar scientists and administrators.[37] By December 1952, the British National Committee of the IGY had been established under the chairmanship of Sir James Wordie. In complete contrast to the nationalistic aspirations of the FIDS, Halley Bay was intended to be a showcase for international scientific co-operation. As if to reinforce this new disposition towards collective endeavour, Brunt recorded that even the Union Jack flag fluttering above the roof of the new base had to be taken down because it interfered with solar radiation readings. But despite the rhetoric of international co-operation, the British Government, through the FIDS and the CTAE was still trying to maximise its presence on the ice. Given the activities of the IGY, the nationalistic aspirations of the FIDS were beginning to look at best anachronistic and at worst rendering the FIDS incapable of fulfilling its mandate, which was to produce comprehensive mapping of the FID. Scientific endeavour alone was not going to protect the British from the changing currents of international political life. By the end of the IGY, Britain was being outclassed – not by Argentine and Chilean scientists but by its Cold War allies, the US. The latter had generated 13 tons of information at the end of the IGY Antarctic programme and sponsored countless experiments and activities above and below the ice-sheet.[38] Under the direction of the Special (latterly Scientific) Committee for Antarctic Research (SCAR), significant scientific research was carried out in the fields of meteorology, geology, biology, geophysics and research into the upper atmosphere.[39] As others have shown, however, US scientific ambitions were simply breathtaking as plans for nuclear engineering in the polar world were constructed, which had the potential to radically redefine humankind's relationship to the natural environment.[40]

PRESERVING IMPERIAL CLAIMS: THE WASHINGTON CONFERENCE AND THE 1959 ANTARCTIC TREATY

Throughout the IGY, intense speculation prevailed as the US and Commonwealth allies traded secret position papers over the future governance of Antarctica. Roberts engaged in 'shuttle diplomacy' while co-ordinating British and Commonwealth polar policy. At the heart of British concerns was the cost of defending the FID, which in 1959 was costing the Treasury over £500,000 per annum excluding additional investments such as the FIDASE and the CTAE.[41] Notwithstanding these endeavours designed to bolster British sovereignty, the US continued to vacillate publicly whether it would press a claim to the Antarctic continent. It was abundantly clear that Argentina, Chile and for that matter the Soviet Union would maintain their 'presence' on the Antarctic continent. This prompted a fundamental shift in British geopolitical interests in 1958–9 and henceforth diplomatic energy was expended on influencing US plans regarding a new form of international arrangement which balanced the interests of claimant and non-claimant states.

The problems facing negotiators were formidable, as a briefing paper prepared for Walter Nash in advance of his meeting with Macmillan in January 1958 conceded. The paper noted that 'Since World War II, there have been many suggestions for international regimes for a limited condominium and for practical and technical supervision of scientific and exploratory work by the specialised agencies of the United Nations, to proposals for United Nations trusteeship'.[42] Whatever the final regime for Antarctica, fundamental problems faced all interested parties: which countries would be included in any new regime? What objectives would a new international regime seek to achieve? What links, if any, would the new regime have with the UN? The briefing paper concluded that Britain and Australia remained hostile to the idea of a UN trusteeship because: 'They resent the carping criticism of the Afro-Asian bloc and other anti-colonial powers who, having little interest in the matter, would seek to characterise the activities of western powers in the Antarctic as imperialism'.[43]

Notwithstanding the post-colonial critics, British and New Zealand negotiators were far more concerned with the US and the Soviet Union and their unpredictable attitudes towards territorial claims.

After the meeting in Wellington, Macmillan devised the broad outline of British polar policy in the post-IGY era. The text for a memorandum prepared for the British Cabinet was agreed upon, and confirmed that efforts should be made to find a management strategy for the Antarctic dispute. While a solution might prove elusive, priority would be given to 'the non-militarisation of the Antarctic, the promotion of scientific activities in the region, and the perpetuation of the legal status quo as regards disputes about territorial sovereignty'.[44] International scientific co-operation was underwritten by a temporary 'sovereignty freeze' and it was considered essential that Britain and the Commonwealth allies achieved some kind of consensus over future options for a new international regime. The meeting concluded that co-operation with the US was essential and that any new regime had to secure the Antarctic as a zone of peace with 'free access' to the continent – that is claimant states could not prevent other states from conducting research in 'their' sector. Some legal and political protection for the original claimants had to be secured in return for a regime, which could accommodate non-claimants such as the Soviet Union and Japan. Throughout 1957 and 1958, the Commonwealth bloc conducted secret negotiations with Dulles. The latter, while sympathetic to Australian worries over the future intentions of the Soviet Union, cautioned the allies to concentrate on developing a common policy for the region.

Requested by Macmillan, the review paper 'Future Constitutional Development of the Colonies' set out the strategic, scientific, resource and political issues at stake in the FID in May 1957:

> The strategic value of the Dependencies [FID] depends partly on the possibility of discovering minerals of strategic importance. For the rest, the strategic

importance is largely negative i.e. it is important to the Commonwealth to deny it as a base to a potentially hostile power. Our withdrawal from Antarctica would mean a loss of UK prestige and influence, especially in scientific circles. It might also involve the loss of strategic minerals... Argentina and/or Chile, which have claims to the Dependencies, would probably step in if the UK withdrew.[45]

Despite one-and-a-half decades of financial investment in the region, Britain was secretly considering relinquishing scientific activities in the region and therefore a political presence in Antarctica. The FO's legal adviser, Sir Gerald Fitzmaurice, earlier argued in January 1957 that Britain could withdraw from the region confident in the knowledge that the IGY would have no detrimental consequences for national territorial claims. Symbolically, as the May 1957 report acknowledged, a British withdrawal from the Antarctic would damage national self-prestige and wider Commonwealth solidarity. Following the outbreak of the 1956 Suez crisis and subsequent uncertainties regarding future commitments from 'east of Suez', financial constraints forced ministers to review the defence and foreign-policy options and to reappraise the value of a nuclear deterrent versus conventional armed forces dispersed around the globe.[46] Scientific endeavour was not immune from these fiscal policies, especially as the Royal Navy not only patrolled distant polar waters but also transported scientists and surveyors throughout the South Atlantic and Antarctic. However, the Secretary of State for Commonwealth Relations warned Commonwealth colleagues that a British withdrawal would mean that 'Australia and New Zealand would find themselves without the prospect of British co-operation in any future negotiations about the future of Antarctica since we would have no longer have any *locus standi* in the area'.[47] The US proposed to host a conference in May 1958 and approached the 11 other participants in the IGY Antarctic programme in order to solicit their views. Despite protestations from India over the limited definition of 'interested' parties, there was little formal objection in the UN to this US diplomatic intervention. The Indian proposal for an item on Antarctica to be included on the agenda of the 13th session of the General Assembly reflected the changing circumstances of the international politics of the polar continent. The Nash Government in New Zealand played a key role in reassuring Indian Prime Minister Nehru of the benign political intentions of the Antarctic participants, whereupon the Indian representative to the UN was instructed by the Minister of External Affairs, Krishna Menon, not to press the issue further. By June 1958, the 11 IGY Antarctic participants agreed to join the US at a conference to negotiate the future politics of the Antarctic.

The Washington Conference convened between October and December 1959. Paul Daniels, an official at the US Department of State was instrumental in bringing the interested parties together. The course of international polar politics was now defined by officials based in Washington DC, as Roberts reluctantly conceded 'the Americans were in a stronger position than ourselves to convene a conference'.[48] What made matters tricky, however, was, as Roberts's diary entries for the Washington Conference clearly reveal, his profound dislike for Daniels and his (misplaced) sense of superiority:

> It was unfortunate that he [Daniels] should be drunk on the occasion of this first encounter [cocktail party at the British Embassy in Washington DC] with so many people with whom he will be working... I formed a growing dislike for this

arrogant man, who clearly considers that any success the conference may have will be entirely due to his own efforts. He has very little self-control.[49]

For much of the period leading up to the meeting, the 12 participants were locked into a series of detailed, ill-tempered and often tedious preparatory meetings designed to negotiate a series of troublesome obstacles to international agreement. Some issues, such as territorial claims and the zone of application for any new regime, proved painfully time-consuming, as claimant states such as Australia, Argentina and France were particularly wary of surrendering their 'sovereign rights'. Other concerns, such as the support of scientific freedom and the status of the Antarctic as a zone of peace, were equally fraught, as the Soviet Union was eager to ensure complete freedom of movement within the region. Despite the diplomatic turmoil provoked by allegations and counter-allegations of intransigence and intrigue, Commonwealth and American delegates knew that failure was not an option. Success was vital to ensure that the UN would not be compelled to intervene in the proceedings. Moreover, it might have provoked the US and Soviet Union to press territorial claims in the absence of a political settlement. As the New Zealand delegation concluded, 'Several of the participants in the conference were very unhappy about the whole idea of a treaty and the possibility of complete failure was never far removed. [However the] Chileans, Argentines and French never pressed their objections to the point of breakdown.'[50] For much of the formal conference proceedings, few negotiators would have envisaged that a *modus operandi* for the new international regime could be established.

The conference formally opened on the 15th October 1959 and the British delegation led by Sir Esler Dening found itself between the Soviets and the Americans at the conference table. Brain Roberts, as a member of the British delegation, recorded the opening event: 'With gay tea-time music, bright lights and a background of potted palm trees and the flags of 12 nations, it seemed more like a prelude to a theatre than an opening of an international conference. Sir Esler's entry was accompanied by Henry VIII's dances.'[51]

Thirteen topics were considered via a series of committees and informal meetings under the chairmanship of Herman Phleger. Two formal committees were created to consider the zone of application and freedom of scientific investigation (Committee I) and the provisions of the treaty, including territorial claims and jurisdiction (Committee II). The most controversial topics, such as the future of territorial claims, the geographical extent of the treaty region and access to the polar continent presented harsh geopolitical realities. To the collective surprise of Commonwealth delegates, given the comparatively small size of their Antarctic claim, the French delegation proved to be the most hostile to any compromise on territorial claims. In their review of the Washington conference, the Australians noted how some claimant states responded to the new agreement:

In spite of the considerable degree of agreement reached among officials in the working group, it became apparent that some governments had not really grasped the issues involved. This was particularly true of Argentina, Chile and France. The UK's main objective was clearly to secure a treaty, which would relieve them of their historical obligations and embarrassments in the Antarctic without prejudicing their national prestige.[52]

The inclusion of Article IV of the Antarctic Treaty owes a great deal to the endeavour of the British and US delegations, which sought to protect the interests of claimant and non-claimant states alike (a point identified by the Chilean Escudero Declaration in 1950). In essence, it was agreed that in order to secure international agreement, all signatories would have to 'suspend' existing and/or future claims to sovereignty for the duration of the treaty. While it did not solve the territorial disputes within the region, Article IV managed to find a compromise between intransigent claimant states and the Soviet delegation, which at one stage threatened to leave the negotiations. According to the Australian and New Zealand delegate reports, the superpowers in alliance with Britain eventually overcame diplomatic resistance from the 'ultra-conservative' group of claimant states comprising Australia, France, Argentina and Chile.

The geographical extent of the Antarctic Treaty region was also deeply controversial because of the implications for territorial ownership in the Antarctic and the Southern Ocean. Two fundamental issues had to be resolved; the first involved the formal jurisdiction area of the Antarctic Treaty. While there was general agreement that the entire polar continent should be included, it was unclear where the northern limits of the treaty lay. The FO did not want the Falklands and South Georgia to be included in the Antarctic Treaty discussions, because of fears of further conflict with Argentina.[53] Compounding this issue was the lack of an agreed definition for the Southern Ocean hitherto defined by British authorities as terminating along an imaginary line drawn along the bottom of South America, Africa and Australia with the southern limit provided by the presence of the Antarctic continent. Other authorities argued that the Southern Ocean was defined by the Antarctic convergence, an area situated between 52 and 55 degrees south latitude, where the polar waters converge with the warmer waters of the South Atlantic, Indian and Pacific Oceans. This was later resolved by selecting 60 degrees south latitude because it covered the entire Antarctic continent and part of the surrounding Southern Ocean. The treaty's provisions did not therefore include islands such as South Georgia and Prince Edward, which lie to the north of 60 degrees south. This proved to be significant in terms of the military action in South Georgia in 1982 and also in the long-term conservation of living resources in the Southern Ocean.

The second area of major controversy was the legal status of 'high seas' within the treaty region, where the Eisenhower Government in particular was adamant that, in the words of Phleger, 'strategic freedom in the high seas below the 60th parallel' was maintained.[54] According to Commonwealth observers, the US delegations argued that 'security of free nations' would be imperilled if there were restrictions on military exercises being carried out within the high seas of the treaty region. The Soviet Union was in favour of the high seas being excluded from the treaty's provisions, but hostile to the US proposal to permit military activities within those zones. Southern hemispheric states such as Australia and Argentina were anxious to ban all forms of military activity regardless of whether they occurred in the high seas or the Antarctic continent.[55] Irrespective of whether all forms of military activity were banned from the treaty region, all the negotiating parties recognised that the treatment of the high seas was significant in terms of international legal precedent. After some heated discussions in October and November 1959, a compromise (favoured by Britain) was reached, which declared that

> The provisions of the present Treaty shall apply south of 60 degrees South Latitude, including all ice shelves, but nothing in the present Treaty shall prejudice or in any way affect the rights, or the exercise of rights, of any state under international law with regard to the high seas within that area.[56]

Elements of the Washington treaty proved highly significant in terms of Britain's Antarctic profile, as Article II stipulated scientific freedom in the Treaty region and Article V reiterated that Antarctica was a zone of peace where military activities, including nuclear testing and armed-forces training, were banned. The Argentine proposal for a complete ban on nuclear testing, storage and dumping was strongly supported by the British delegation. Both superpowers recognised that it was not in their collective interests to transform the Antarctic into a zone of discord, given existing tensions in central Europe and in the high latitudes of the Arctic. Despite some initial reluctance, the Americans agreed that the Antarctic should be the first continental nuclear free zone in the world, thereby ensuring not only that the Cold War did not descend onto Antarctica but also safeguarding the sovereign claims of Britain and the six other claimant states. Unsurprisingly, given the costs and uncertainties of maintaining a polar empire, Britain was first to ratify the Antarctic Treaty in June 1960 and, to Roberts's relief, Argentina and Chile's ratification followed later in June 1961.[57]

SUMMARY

The Washington Conference was undoubtedly a remarkable diplomatic achievement. While it did not solve the territorial disputes over the Antarctic, it did result in a legal and political framework for future international collaboration and co-operation in the region. All the delegates appreciated that issues such as ownership and access to resources were not going to be solved at the conference. Claimant states had to accept some unpalatable compromises including the suspension of territorial claims and unhindered access to their sectors in Antarctica. In other words, Argentine, Chilean and Australian delegates had to accept that the Soviet Union was not going to abandon its bases after the treaty negotiations. Ironically, it was the British Foreign Secretary, Selwyn Lloyd, who played a part in persuading the Argentines that all the interested parties would have to learn to compromise in the post-treaty era.[58] Non-claimant states such as the US acknowledged the existence but not the legal validity of seven territorial claims and the presence of the Soviet Union. The Antarctic Treaty was judged to be sufficiently flexible in preserving the interests of all the participants. By July 1961, all 12 participants in the Washington Conference had ratified the Antarctic Treaty.

Arguably the treaty was a geopolitical and legal success for the British delegation, as territorial claims were preserved for the duration of the treaty. It was a welcome relief in an era dominated by post-colonial change and occasional anti-colonial violence in Africa, Asia and elsewhere. The neutralised status of the Antarctic eased Britain's relationship with Argentina and Chile, and the work of the FIDS could be considered complete by evidence that an agreement had been found on the governance of the polar continent.[59] Polar science contributed to geopolitical advantage and fostered national prestige. The network of contacts between academics, civil servants and the armed forces had been remarkably successful in persuading the Treasury to spend thousands of pounds on surveying, aerial photography and naval movements in order to protect distant territorial claims. Evidently, if this money had not been expended, Britain's role in securing the 1959 Antarctic Treaty would have been lessened, notwithstanding the strong historical ties to the region and wider Commonwealth involvement (even if South Africa was to leave in 1962). Moreover, the mere existence of these sovereignty claims in the Antarctic provided a considerable incentive to secure an agreement for the future management of the polar continent. While British officials might understandably indulge in some nostalgic reflection on their achievement, the Antarctic Treaty offers only a temporary refuge from the contested geopolitics of Anglo–Argentine relations. The geopolitical profile of the Falkland Islands and South Georgia increased as Argentine diplomatic attention turned towards another outstanding territorial dispute not covered by the provisions of the Antarctic Treaty.[60] As Ward concluded in January 1960:

> There is now some evidence that there are some people in Argentine officialdom who may be working up a little campaign on this issue [the Falkland Islands]. The Malvinas are quite a separate issue from Antarctica [as recognised by the 1959 Antarctic Treaty]…in the light of all this I judge that with claims and counter claims to the Antarctic territory satisfactory [sic] sealed up by the Washington Treaty, the Argentines are thinking of raising the issue with us. There is undoubtedly a general impression in this part of the world that the general objective of British policy these days is to divest ourselves of colonial responsibilities.[61]

Judging by his letter, Ward had failed to recognise that British foreign and defence policy since 1945 was in favour of reducing imperial commitments in order to concentrate additional resources in key regions such as Western Europe and the Middle East. The following decade, however, proved that the Falklands and the Antarctic were not immune from financial and post-colonial pressures.

NOTES ON CHAPTER 5

1   NAC RG25 4765 50070-40 Part 1. Memorandum prepared by A. Blanchette of the DEA entitled 'A summary of recent developments in the Antarctic and in the Falkland Islands Dependencies', dated 23 April 1948. An important contemporary source on the so-called Antarctic problem was W. Hunter Christie, *The Antarctic Problem* (London, George Unwin, 1951). Christie served in the British Embassy at Buenos Aires and was later to become a central figure in the emergence of the Falklands lobby after 1968.

2   F. Debenham, *Antarctica* (London, Herbert Jenkins, 1959), p. 238.

3   See W. Sullivan, *Quest for a Continent* (New York, McGraw-Hill, 1957). More generally, P. Beck, *The International Politics of Antarctica* (London, Croom Helm, 1986), J. Myhre, *The Antarctic Treaty System: Politics, Law and Diplomacy* (Boulder CO, Westview, 1986) and S. Chaturvedi, *The Polar Regions: A Political Geography* (Chichester, John Wiley, 1996).

4   For an early Argentine interpretation of this trilateral dispute, see C. Alzerreca, *Historia de la Antartida* (Buenos Aires, Editorial Hemisferio, 1949).

5   For reviews of US Antarctic policy after 1948, see F. Klotz, *America on the Ice: American Policy Issues* (Washington DC, National Defence University Press, 1990).

6   D. Cosgrove, *Apollo's Eye: A Cartographic Genealogy of the Earth in the Western Imagination* (Baltimore MD, John Hopkins University Press, 2001), pp. 218–19.

7   In the New Zealand case, public pressure was also mounting as witnessed by the revival of the New Zealand Antarctic Society and their publication Antarctic News Bulletin in 1949. In Australia, the DEA created an Antarctic Division in 1947 as part of its fundamental review of Australian polar policy.

8   *Des Moines Register*, 'US planning expedition to the Antarctic', 17 April 1949.

9   NAC RG25 4765 50070-40 Part 1. Letter from P. Tremblay of the Canadian Embassy in Santiago de Chile to K. Kitrkwood of the Latin American Division, DEA in Ottawa, dated 19 December 1946.

10   For an interesting American analysis of the issue, see the *New York Times*, 'Britain orders cruiser to Belize as Guatemala revives old claim', 27 February 1948.

11   *The Dominion (Wellington)*, 'New Zealand and Antarctica', 7 November 1949.

12   *New York Times*, 'US proposes joint rule to end Antarctic disputes', 29 August 1948.

13   NAC RG25 4765 50070-40 Part 1. Memorandum prepared by the DEA in Ottawa entitled 'Canadian policy concerning Antarctic questions', 30 July 1948.

14   *New York Times*, 'Chile is said to reject South Polar plan of US', 5 August 1948.

15   On Chilean geopolitical strategy in the Antarctic, see O. Labra, *Chilenos en la Antartida* (Santiago, Direccion General de Informaciones y Cultura, 1947).

16   See M. Templeton, *A Wise Adventure: New Zealand and the Antarctic 1923–1960* (Wellington, Victoria University Press, 2001), for a recent assessment of New Zealand's attitudes towards the 1948 American proposals.

17   NAC RG 25 4765 50070-40 Part 1. Telegram from the South African Minister of External Affairs to the Canadian Secretary of State for External Affairs in Ottawa, dated 9 March 1948.

18   NAC RG 25 4765 50070-40 Part 2. Letter from the Canadian Embassy in Santiago to the Secretary of State for External Affairs, dated 6 August 1948.

19   Polar Committee meeting held at the Commonwealth Relations Office on 28 September 1948. A record of the meeting can be found in NAC RG 25 4765 50070-40 Part 2.

20   For further details on the Australian concerns, see K. Dodds, *Geopolitics in Antarctica: Views from the Southern Oceanic Rim* (Chichester, John Wiley, 1997), especially the chapter 'Australia and the Australian Antarctic Territory'. See also R. Casey, *Friends and Neighbours* (Sydney, Cheshire, 1954).

21   A copy of this memorandum from the Norwegian Embassy in Washington to the US Department of State, 15 November 1948, can be found in NAC RG 25 4765 50070-40 Part 2.

22   I discuss this issue in more detail in Dodds, *Geopolitics in Antarctica: Views from the Southern Oceanic Rim*.

23   See J. McCannon, 'To storm the Arctic: Soviet polar exploration and public visions of nature in the USSR 1932–1939', *Ecumene* 2 (1995): pp. 15–31.

24   See W. Sullivan, *Quest for a Continent* (New York, McGraw-Hill, 1957).

25   Sydney *Sun-Herald*, 'Red flag near South Pole', 5 August 1956.

26   The *Canberra Times*, 'Danger from Russian base in Antarctica', 26 September 1956.

27   AA A4940/1 C 1438. Confidential memorandum from the DEA to the Prime Minister's Department, dated 16 August 1955.

28   See, for example, F. Illingworth, 'Scramble for Antarctica', *New Commonwealth*, 23 November 1953; R. Cromley, 'We're losing the Antarctic', *American Mercury* 87 (1958): pp. 5–11.

29   A report by Roberts on his visit to the USSR in May–June 1956 and found in an Australian file of correspondence between the Australian High Commissioner in London and the DEA. AA A1838/283/ 1495/1/9/1 Part 4, 'IGY–Russian participation'.

30   AA A1838/2 1495/3/2/1 Part 3. Letter from J. Dulles to R. Casey, dated 12 July 1956.

31   The *New York Times*, 'Air power in Antarctica', 31 July 1956.

32   AA A1838/2 1495/3/2/1 Part 3. Letter from Sir Douglas Mawson to Richard Casey, dated 2 August 1956.

33   An important element in the release of the proposal was unquestionably linked to developing India's sense of international presence and perceived geographical proximity to the Antarctic and the Southern Ocean. See Dodds, *Geopolitics in Antarctica: Views from the Southern Oceanic Rim*, especially the chapter 'India in the Antarctic'.

34   AA A1838/2 1495/3/2/1 Part 3. Minutes of a meeting held between British Government departments and Commonwealth representatives in London on 12 March 1956.

35   NAC RG 25 4765 50070-40 Part 4. Minutes of a meeting hosted by the Commonwealth Relations Office held in London on 23 August 1957.

36   *House of Commons Hansard*, 14 May 1957, col 213.

37   D. Brunt, 'The Halley Bay expedition and the IGY', in *The Royal Society IGY Antarctic Expedition Halley Bay, Coats Land, Falkland Islands Dependencies 1955-1959* (London, Royal Society, 1960), pp. 1–7.

38   See S. Pyne, *The Ice: A Journey to Antarctica* (Seattle WA, University of Washington Press, 1992).

39   See the review in D. Walton (ed.), *Antarctic Science* (Cambridge, Cambridge University Press, 1987) and C. Fogg, *A History of Antarctic Science* (Cambridge, Cambridge University Press, 1992).

40   See special issue edited by Denis Cosgrove on 'Nuclear engineering and geography', *Ecumene* 5 (1998): pp. 263–322.

41   These figures were quoted in the *Daily Telegraph* on 10 December 1958.

42   NZA PM 208 5/1 Part 6. Memorandum prepared by the New Zealand DEA, dated 23 January 1958.

43   NZA PM 208 5/1 Part 6. Memorandum prepared by the New Zealand DEA, dated 23 January 1958.

44   PRO CAB 128/32. Joint memorandum prepared by the FO, Commonwealth Relations Office and the Ministry of Defence, dated 13 May 1958.

45   PRO CAB 134/1551. Colonial Office paper on the Future Constitutional Development in the Colonies, dated May 1957.

46   In February 1958, the Campaign for Nuclear Disarmament (CND) was created and the first CND protest march directed at the nuclear weapons establishment in Aldermaston was held in March of that year.

47   NZA PM 208 5/1 Part 7. Telegram from the Secretary of State for Commonwealth Relations to the UK High Commission in Australia, New Zealand and South Africa, dated 25 January 1958.

48   SPRI Archives MS 1308/9. BJ Brian Roberts' diaries of the Washington Conference between October and December 1959, p. 6.

49   SPRI Archives MS 1308/9. BJ Diary of Brian Roberts and the entries relate to 13 and 14 October 1959.

50   NAC RG25 4766 50070-40 Part 8. New Zealand Delegate Report on the Antarctic Conference included in a letter from the Canadian High Commission in Wellington to the DEA in January 1960.

51   SPRI Archives MS 1308/9. BJ Brian Roberts' diaries of the Washington Conference between October and December 1959, p. 9.

52   AA A1838/283/1495/3/2/9. Memorandum prepared by the Australian DEA on the Conference of Antarctica, dated 11 January 1960.

53   PRO FO 371 138955. Letter from H. Brain to Ward, dated 12 February 1959.

54   AA A3092/2 221/16/1/2/ Part 3. Telegram from the Australian Embassy in Washington DC to the DEA in Canberra, dated 5 November 1959.

55   See Dodds, *Geopolitics in Antarctica: Views from the Southern Oceanic Rim*, for more details on the southern hemispheric states and their attitudes towards the 1959 Antarctic Treaty.

56   Article I of the 1959 Antarctic Treaty.

57   See PRO FO 371 147732, for detailed evidence of how nervous civil servants were that the Antarctic Treaty might not be ratified by Argentina.

58   NAC RG25 4766 50070-40 Part 8. Record of a conversation between Selwyn Lloyd and the Argentine head of delegation Ambassador Scilingo, dated 16 November 1959.

59   After the ratification of the Antarctic Treaty, the FIDS was renamed the BAS and the FID was separated into the British Antarctic Territory and the Falkland Islands Dependencies, which only included South Georgia and South Sandwich Islands.

60   PRO FO 371 147755. Annual Review of Argentina prepared by Ward in January 1960.

61   PRO FO 371 147713. Letter from Ward to Brain of the American Department of the FO, dated 21 January 1960.

6

Football, Foot and Mouth and the Falklands

Football will join the Falklands and foot and mouth as part of the trio, which stands in the way of improved Anglo–Argentine relations.[1]

It seems a pity that so much Argentinian talent is wasted. Our best football will come against the team who come out to play football and not act as animals.[2]

The British embassy [in Buenos Aires] was under special guard from hostile crowds today as all the Argentine – knocked out of the World Cup on Saturday – protested.[3]

INTRODUCTION

Football matches between England and Argentina continue to generate considerable passions amongst supporters, journalists and political figures. One game remains a *leitmotif* of Anglo–Argentine sporting and political angst. On 23 July 1966, England and Argentina took to the field for the quarter-final of the 1966 World Cup. Argentina had qualified easily for the final stages and was confident of upsetting the host nation's team at the Empire Stadium in Wembley. Right from the start, the game was dominated by robust challenges on both sides, and an early appeal for an England penalty was dismissed by the West German referee, Rudolf Kreitlein.[4] With just minutes remaining before the end of the first half, the referee controversially dismissed the tall and imposing Argentine captain, Antonio Rattin, for persistent dissent and foul play. Instead of leaving the pitch, Rattin and the Argentine team became embroiled in a bitter dispute with the referee and FIFA (football's world governing body) officials over the decision. After eight frantic minutes of suspended play, Rattin eventually left the field and the game resumed. He had earned the dubious distinction of being the first player to be sent off from a Wembley match. Despite being reduced to 10 players for the entire second half, a solitary goal by Geoff Hurst eventually settled the game in England's favour. When the players began to swap shirts at the end of the game, England's manager became embroiled in an unseemly tug-of-war between George Cohen and an Argentine player. Cohen later recalled that Ramsey had shouted at him, 'You're not changing shirts with these people'.[5]

In the aftermath, Argentine players reportedly kicked the door of the England dressing room and harassed the referee, and one Argentine player even urinated in a corridor leading to the changing rooms. FIFA later fined the Argentine team 1000 Swiss francs (the maximum penalty at the time) for dissent and unprofessional conduct. The Argentine captain was suspended for four games and two other players were banned for three games. When asked to comment on the game in a television interview, Ramsey retorted that

> England played to win, and win we did, which was important. We are afraid of no one. We still have to produce our best football. It is not possible until we meet the right type of opposition, a team which comes out to play football, not as animals, as we have seen in the World Cup.[6]

His comment regarding 'animals' immediately elevated the football match to an 'international incident' involving Britain, Argentina and the wider football community. While British newspapers such as the *Daily Mirror* reflected on 'Latin lunacy', FIFA later demanded that Ramsey issue an apology and the England manager grudgingly obliged.[7] Geoff Hurst captured the seriousness of the situation when he noted that 'On reflection I'm sure he'd like to withdraw the "animals" remark because it's ill advised, it's almost a diplomatic incident at that level!'[8]

The match is still remembered by both sets of fans as controversial and a turning-point in Anglo–Argentine football competition. The timing of the controversy was unfortunate in the sense that Anglo–Argentine relations were already strained by the Falklands question. Before the 1966 World Cup game, popular representations of Argentina had been relatively muted. Suddenly Argentina became synonymous with the word 'animals', and FO diplomats engaged to resolve the Falklands question (in eventual favour of Argentina) were alarmed by the fusion of sport and nationalism. Argentina, the critics of British foreign policy vis-à-vis the South Atlantic contended, could not be trusted because, as their football style demonstrated, it did not respect the 'rules of the game'. In the context of wider Anglo–Latin American relations, the result of a football game seriously undermined diplomatic relations.

Football was not the only *bête noire* of Anglo–Argentine relations. Argentine beef was held responsible for the 1967 outbreak of foot-and-mouth disease, which devastated large numbers of British herds just when a series of balance-of-payments crises forced Britain to increase trade with established and new markets. The Anglo–Argentine rivalry was so entrenched that even Antarctic science was not immune despite the ratification of the Antarctic Treaty. Nonetheless, British officials continued to negotiate with Argentina on prospective trade, including arms sales and the 'Falklands question', although concerns over Argentina's intentions towards the Falklands were intensifying.

ANGLO–ARGENTINE FOOTBALL MATCHES

Anglo–Argentine football encounters seem to invite controversy, and the game played at the Estadio Antonio Vespucio Liberti 'Monumental' de Nunez in Buenos

Aires on 17 May 1953 was no exception, when the referee was forced to abandon play because of excessive rain. Although the 1953 game was officially recorded as a draw, the first game played two years earlier at Wembley had resulted in a 2–1 victory for an English team celebrating the Festival of Britain. According to Dave Bowler, Ramsey's biographer, there was 'a clash of cultures…In South America, their conduct was part of the drama, football was bullfighting. This would act to England's advantage if they kept their shape and discipline.'[9] While Bowler is perhaps right to draw attention to the different styles of play, he underestimates not only the powerful relationship between Argentine territorial nationalism and football but also the influence of English players in the development of the Argentine game.

In his definitive study of Latin American football, Tony Mason argues that British sailors who came ashore at the ports of Buenos Aires, Montevideo and Rio de Janeiro in the late nineteenth century were instrumental in promulgating the game.[10] The large Anglo–Argentine community, working in the public utilities and numbering some 40,000 by 1890, brought with them their favourite sports of football, rugby, polo, cricket and tennis. Under the guidance of Alexander Watson Hutton, a British teacher at St Andrew's Scottish school, an Argentine Association Football League (AAFL) was created in 1893. Famous clubs such as River Plate (1901), Racing Club (1903) and Boca Juniors (1905) emerged and were invested with a strong British sense of 'fair play' and 'to play well without passion'.[11] Within 10 years, the British influence on Argentine football waned and the AAFL, by now renamed the Argentine Football Association (AFA) became known as the Asociación Argentina de Football in 1912. English professional teams such as Tottenham Hotspur, Nottingham Forest and Southampton enjoyed successful tours to Argentina before the First World War, and Argentine teams too embarked on international tours. As football became more professionally based, AFA managed the national championship largely for the benefit of the 'big five' clubs (Racing, Boca, San Lorenzo, Independiente and River Plate) located in and or close to Buenos Aires, rather than for the lower division clubs scattered across the Republic.

While Argentina was isolated from world competition for much of the period prior to the 1957 South American tournament, successive leaders – especially Perón – encouraged a view that Argentine football actively contributed to national pride. The reasons behind the reluctance to participate in the 1949 South American championships and the 1950 World Cup is unknown, as new slogans such as 'Perón sponsors sport' and 'Perón, the first sportsman' were designed to draw attention to the way in which sport could contribute to a politically confident Argentina. Perón's wife hosted the 'Evita Championships', intended to encourage children's football, which resulted in the participation of over 200,000 children in 1950.[12] When Argentina beat a Football Association (FA) eleven 3–1 during England's tour of Argentina, Chile, Uruguay and the US, Perón declared that the day of the match (14 May) should be celebrated as 'Footballers' Day'.[13] Their self-confidence was abruptly shattered by the 1958 World Cup defeat by Czechoslovakia (6–1). The so-called 'Disaster in Malmo' provoked an intense period of introspection and review not only of Argentine football but also of society at large. New methods of training and tactics were combined with the import of overseas players in an attempt to change the style and pace of Argentine football. The desire to succeed intensified following Brazilian victories at the 1958 and 1962 World Cups.

Argentina's controversial defeat during the 1966 World Cup competition not only soured Anglo–Argentine relations but also affected international football, as divisions between European and South American administrators became apparent. Indeed, Sir Stanley Rous, the British president of FIFA, had already suggested that Argentina's performance during the quarter-final might lead to their disqualification from the 1970 World Cup finals. The Argentine FIFA delegate, Juan Santiago allegedly retorted that 'If we are refused entry in the 1970 World Cup, Sir Stanley Rous is something of a moron'.[14] Accusations of 'moronic' behaviour and Ramsey's reference to 'animals'[15] tainted the otherwise undeniable achievements of England's subsequent victory over West Germany in the final.

Politically, the timing was unfortunate, given that Foreign Secretary Michael Stewart's visit to Buenos Aires in January 1966 hailed a new era of Anglo–Latin American rapprochement. The visit was intended to promote British exports, but as Stewart records in his memoirs the Falklands question dominated all his discussions with Argentine counterparts:

> The problem, as with Gibraltar, was to discover whether there were any measures we could take, short of surrendering sovereignty, which would satisfy Argentinian national feeling. We could make no progress, but I was to hear much more on this question when I returned to the Foreign Office in 1968.[16]

Shortly after Stewart's visit to Latin America, the political complexion of Argentina changed when General Juan Carlos Ongania seized power from the civilian Government of President Arturo Illia during the 1966 World Cup championship. On its return to Argentina, Ongania acclaimed the football team the 'moral champions' of the world. The popular newspaper *Crónica* printed the now famous headline, 'First they [the English] stole the Malvinas from us, and now the World Cup'.[17] Notwithstanding Stewart's attempts to promote British business interests in Argentina, English football authorities and the wider British public remained fixated on the on-field behaviour of the Argentine team. The FA's Report of the 1966 World Cup was uncompromising in its criticism of the Argentines: 'One could almost sympathise with a depleted Argentina, were it not for the total cynicism of their disregard for the rules of the game [and the Argentine captain, Rattin] also shares the Argentine habit of fouling the man who beats him, almost as a reflex action'.[18]

In response, England and FIFA were accused not only of cultural insensitivity but also of rigging the World Cup in favour of European teams including England and West Germany. British commentators such as Lord Lovat while deploring Ramsey's crassness nonetheless argued that one had to understand the 'Latin temperament and the different way a game is played in South America'.[19] When the organisers of the World Cup allowed the host nation, England to play all their games at Wembley and allocated exclusively European referees, these decisions were retrospectively condemned by Latin American participants as unfair.[20]

The diplomatic ramifications of the 1966 Argentine–England game became evident as the FO began to receive reports from British embassies scattered across Latin America. The British ambassador to Argentina, Sir Michael Cresswell, noted in one telegram that 'The favourite joke in local football circles, following the notorious game at Wembley, was that FIFA was run by three people, Sir, Stanley and Rous'.[21] However, in the aftermath of the match, angry Argentine supporters besieged the British Embassy in Buenos Aires and embassy staff felt obliged to intercept abusive phone calls to the ambassador. Later, the British trade stand in Palermo in Argentina was reportedly vandalised by 'gangs of youths' who pinned an unfortunate receptionist to the ground and asked her whether any referees might be for sale.[22] In La Paz, the British Embassy reported to the Information Policy Department of the FO that

> We have a lot of evidence that a great many people do believe all that they have read about British dirty play and the Anglo–German 'conspiracy' against the South Americans. What should have constituted a big boost to our reputation in Bolivia, which like most South American countries is football mad, has had the reverse effect.[23]

The only British Embassy to report any positive press coverage of England's World Cup victory appeared in San Salvador, the capital city of El Salvador.

At the British Embassy in Rio de Janeiro, the despatches to London and the British Embassy in Buenos Aires became increasingly frantic as officials endeavoured to minimise the damage of the 1966 World Cup to Anglo–Latin American relations. By September 1966, it was commonplace to note that the Brazilian sporting media were alleging that England had 'fixed' the World Cup with the assistance of Rous. The most alarming aspect of this reporting was the condemnation by the president of the Brazilian Football Federation (Havelange, who later took the Presidency of FIFA from Rous in the election of 1974) of the entire World Cup proceedings. According to the staff at the British Embassy in Rio de Janeiro, the president's 'ravings' were based on:

> His assertion that the results of the final, and even semi-final matches were all part of a devious political plot by the British government, is so absurd that, as it stands, it invites ridicule…Having lost his reputation as a result of his team's debacle in the World Cup, and in danger of losing his job, he has been looking for a scapegoat.[24]

In order to mitigate further diplomatic damage, the FO urged the FA in London to look favourably on a strange request by the Guanabara Metal Workers Trade Union of Brazil to acquire an England World Cup shirt for their official football collection. As an official from the Joint Information Policy and Guidance Department noted to the FA on 14 October 1966, 'I cannot truthfully say that I expect the gesture to improve Britain's image in Latin America but I hope at least [that] the metal workers of Guanabara will think more kindly of us as a consequence'.[25] Despite its misgivings, the FA duly despatched an England shirt to the FO, which was then flown to the British Embassy at Rio de Janeiro in the diplomatic bag. The shirt was later sent to the metal workers who acknowledged the kindness of the gesture.

The Joint Information Policy and Guidance Department of the FO had the dubious pleasure of co-ordinating angry reactions from Latin American political and sporting figures. A memorandum prepared by one official in London drew a sobering conclusion from this football-cum-diplomatic debacle:

> With hindsight it is easy to see that there ought to have been care exercised over the choice of referees and venues i.e. England not playing all the time at Wembley. However, this whole storm has only blown up because Argentines, Brazilians et al are bad losers and no doubt other reasons would have been found as an excuse

for losing if it had not been these. Senor Havelange's rantings really reached rock bottom... the only reason Brazil was knocked out of the World Cup was that, on the day, at any rate, Portugal, who beat them, were a better side.[26]

By October 1966, the 'football crisis' in Latin America had reached a climax with the Argentine Government's hosting of the Congreso Sudamericano de Futbol. Despite fears for the worst, the Brazilian and Argentine delegates decided not to press for 'root and branch' reform of FIFA. Ramsey's 'animals' television interview haunted the collective memories of Latin American observers and FO officials in London and Buenos Aires as they battled to improve relations over the Falklands problem.[27]

Two years after England's controversial quarter-final victory over Argentina in the 1966 World Cup, the Intercontinental Cup final between Manchester United and Estudiantes de la Plata exerted renewed pressure on Anglo–Argentine relations. Estudiantes, in the first leg of the final, won by a 'solitary goal' after a controversial equaliser by Manchester United was ruled offside. Incited by recriminations, an angry Argentine press accused the English team of being 'bad losers' and lacking a sense of 'fair play'. The second leg, played in Manchester, produced a 1–1 draw and Estudiantes were duly crowned the world club champions. George Best, the footballer of the year, had been sent off during the second leg and the game was widely condemned by the British press as a travesty of fair play and sportsmanship. The *Sun* condemned the game as 'gutter soccer' and contended that 'They [Manchester United] surely must be bold enough to ask themselves this morning – are they the Animals or are we? Or should it be both?...More than 60,000 fans roared [at the Argentine team] Animals, animals, animals.'[28] A small club from the city of La Plata had not only succeeded on the global stage but also revolutionised Argentine football. Estudiantes had broken the hegemonic grip of the 'big five' Argentine clubs.[29] Predictably enough, a section of the British media retorted by publishing unflattering profiles of the Argentine football champions and condemned the championship as 'shoddy' and 'phoney'.[30]

Despite the traditional rhetoric of separation between sport and politics in Britain, football had affected not only Anglo–Argentine relations but also tentative attempts to pursue stronger trading and political relationships with Latin America. In Buenos Aires, Cresswell was once again confronted by football-related developments with the potential to wreck diplomatic intercourse. Due to renewed Argentine pressure over the Falklands, plans were afoot to raise the lack of diplomatic progress at the General Assembly and the C24 Committee in the UN. In an informal meeting with the Argentine Foreign Minister, Dr Costa Mendez, Cresswell reflected on the controversy raised by the 1968 interclub final:

> Footballers were inclined to wreck with their feet, all we had tried to do with our heads. In this case however it was the press rather than the footballers who were to blame as the match (which we had both seen) had been far less open to criticism than those last year. [Despite reassuring the ambassador that the football controversy would pass] Costa Mendez reaffirmed 'We will assert our right, our firm claim and the necessity for the return of the Islands to us'.[31]

While Cresswell may have been referring to expressions of anti-British sentiment in Buenos Aires following the match, the representation of Argentina within the popular British media as 'cheats' also had implications for the Falklands question.[32]

For Cresswell and the British Embassy in Buenos Aires, the football game in October 1968 was the final episode of a difficult period. Local agitation in the Falklands was mounting over Anglo–Argentine sovereignty talks, and the visit of the FO Minister of State Lord Chalfont, had provoked a defiant reaction from the Islanders. To compound these matters still further, Argentina and Chile were embroiled in a long-standing dispute over the remote Beagle Channel close to the icy seas of the Southern Ocean.

Interestingly, the unexpected triumph of the obscure Argentine football club Estudiantes at the Intercontinental Cup final was later deemed by General Ongania to justify his dictatorship as a progressive intervention in Argentine society. As Pablo Alabarces argues, 'the values praised for Esutidantes were the same ones that the dictatorship in power claimed for all Argentine citizens'.[33] According to Argentine sporting journals such as *El Gráfico*, the small club from La Plata demonstrated a strong defensive style coupled with tactical discipline. This extraordinary claim is understandable given that the regime was an 'alliance between conservative and ultra-catholic sectors, with fascist temptations, and militantly anticommunist, framed by the Cold War and the Doctrine of National Security'.[34] Argentine militaries have tended to argue that internal order and security was the *leitmotif* of good governance even if the Ongania regime was comparatively short-lived. Moreover, as with the 1978 World Cup, military regimes remained adept at extracting political legitimacy from international football successes.[35] With football so deeply implicated in the politics of Argentine nationalism, it crystallised the British press's collective view of 'Argentina' in terms of adjectives such as irrational, hysterical and temperamental. As one critic of the English game, Brian Glanville of the *Sunday Times*, noted in the aftermath of the 1968 Intercontinental Cup final,

> Tactical fouls as practised tonight by Estudiantes, by Racing last year and by Argentina in 1966 at Wembley, simply make it impossible to practice the game. If a man dodges another and the other fouls him coldly then it is better to leave the game and to enter with a bomb in the pocket and a stick in the hand.[36]

For most people in Britain, Argentina by the late 1960s had become identified as a place filled with people who reflected their footballers (as England was later to experience itself) and thus incapable of respecting rules of the game. Subsequent Anglo–Argentine football matches in 1974 and 1977 both resulted in hard-fought draws.[37]

BEEF AND ARMS: TRADING WITH ARGENTINA

The outbreak of foot-and-mouth disease in 1967 not only brought the commercial dimension of Anglo–Argentine relations into disrepute but also provided a further reminder as to the parlous state of the British economy. The timing was un-fortunate, as the Foreign Secretary, Michael Stewart, had visited Argentina, Chile and Peru for the explicit purpose of improving trading and commercial relations. The Queen's visit to Chile, the first by a reigning monarch, offered the opportunity to use the Royal Yacht *Britannia*, which had sailed ahead, for trade purposes. Controversially, the Queen was advised not to visit Argentina and the Falkland Islands because of the ongoing sovereignty dispute. There was, as Calvert has noted, a widespread hope in Whitehall that the Wilson Government would initiate a closer relationship with South America – in particular Argentina, Brazil and Chile.[38] Although Argentina was no longer a strategic food supplier, beef imports from the River Plate region continued, albeit on a more modest scale, until the suspension on environmental health grounds – which unfortunately came too late to prevent a massive crisis in the British rural sector.

The first case of the disease was recorded in October 1967, and within six months over 2300 farms were infected and over 400,000 animals slaughtered and incinerated. British public life was greatly affected by movement restrictions, and the Conservative Party was forced to cancel its annual conference in November 1967. By February 1968, Parliament debated the issue of infected meat supplies, and on advice from the Board of Trade interdepartment conference recommended a complete ban on meat imports from Argentina. One amusing story to emerge involved the Foreign Secretary, George Brown, who had replaced Stewart after an economic crisis embroiled the Wilson Government in 1966. The following year, Brown was invited to a dinner at the Argentine Embassy in London and caused a diplomatic stir when he refused to touch the main course of Argentine beef. The outbreak was officially declared at an end in June 1968 and estimated to have cost £150 million in lost revenue to the farming sector. Another £27 million was paid to farmers by the Labour Government in the form of compensation. A subsequent Government enquiry, the Northumberland Committee, traced the source of infection to the importation of carcass meat from the River Plate.

The FO had already instructed Cresswell to seek assurances from the Argentine authorities that British trading contracts would not be adversely affected, aware that the foot-and-mouth crisis would impact on Anglo–Argentine relations. In January 1968, Cresswell met Costa Mendez and asked for reassurance that eight contracts ranging from road building to the supply of 2 submarines, 15 Canberra supersonic aircraft, 8 Avro 748 aircraft and missile launchers would not be compromised.[39] In return for his guarantee that commercial orders would not be delayed for retaliatory reasons, Costa Mendez requested a relaxation of the British meat ban. British officials, aware that the meat ban was deeply resented in Argentina, conducted tense negotiations between the Ministry of Agriculture, Fisheries and Food (MAFF) and the Argentine Director General of Animal Health, Dr Jorge Borsella. During the period between 1968 and 1970, Argentina endeavoured to reassure Britain that new animal hygiene conditions had been implemented in the meat packaging plants. However, the newly devised British restrictions on the beef market (in terms of import restrictions and minimum price scheme) were perceived to sabotage further the restoration of Argentine meat imports. In February 1970, Argentine and British negotiators met in London in an attempt to resolve the dispute over beef and lamb imports. An FO letter to MAFF officials reflected on the broader nature of the controversy, 'It is not only about beef and commodities…Argentines are jittery at present. We are having a variety of difficulties with them over the Falkland Islands, which may or may not erupt into a serious row.'[40] By the early 1970s, restrictions were eventually lifted on Argentine imports, but British farmers were ordered to continue to scrub their farms twice a day with special disinfectants.

The promotion of arms sales in Argentina and Latin America reflected a long-standing conflict between commerce and geopolitical priorities. When in 1964 the

Wilson Government began to commercialise the arms export drive, it rapidly became an important facet of British foreign policy. With the creation of new inter-governmental bodies such as the Defence Sales Organisation (DSO), Government ministers were determined to promote a commercial area in which the British were major market leaders. Denis Healey, the then defence secretary, declared in 1966 that 'We must also take what practical steps we can to ensure that this country does not fail to secure its rightful share of this valuable commercial market'.[41] For much of the post-1945 period, Latin America had been a small but stable market for British naval arms trade and military aircraft. These sales included the ex-Royal Navy aircraft carrier HMS *Colossus* in 1958 and Short Sea Cat missiles in 1965 to Latin American countries such as Argentina and Chile.[42] However, discussions surrounding the export of arms to Argentina also provoked remarkably frank reflections on both the strategic importance and the military security of the Falkland Islands. In May 1970, for example, the proposed sale of two Type 42 destroyers to Argentina prompted the FCO to conclude that 'this order could not, of course, affect the Argentine capability to seize the Falkland Islands if so minded since this is already super abundant'.[43] The prospect of Argentina using these ships against the British interest was simply discounted, because Argentina was seen as committed to settling disputes peacefully. While there was some evidence of this based on Britain's recent role in arbitrating between Argentina and Chile over the disputed Beagle Channel, the Falkland Islands were judged to be impossible to defend because of distance and the limited resources available for this purpose. After a further review of the destroyer order, the £35 million order was confirmed and delivery of the ship, HMS *Hercules*, occurred. At the same time, another Type 42 destroyer was built under licence by the Rio Santiago shipyard in Argentina.

It is clear from the exchanges within British Government departments that officials were predominantly concerned with a possible 'arms race' in Latin America, because British naval vessels were also sold to the Chilean navy by the British firm Vickers-Armstrong. When the prospect of supplying Argentina with Harrier aircraft was initially raised in January 1970, Chalfont noted:

> I have an ineradicable distaste for a policy that involves selling weapons of an advanced type in an area like Latin America – especially to two countries involved in territorial disputes with each other. However, the interests of exports and balance of payments are presumably overwhelming.[44]

Five days later, the FCO discussed the implications for the Falklands Islands and Anglo–American relations with the Ministry of Technology in the event of Latin American geopolitical tension. In a pattern that was to be replicated on numerous occasions, the Treasury later authorised credit terms for approval of the sale not-withstanding residual concerns over regional arms escalation. As with past episodes of Anglo–Argentine relations, geopolitical and commercial priorities co-existed uneasily in a prevailing climate of balance-of-payments crises, which brought to the fore difficult choices.

ANTARCTIC SCIENCE AND ANGLO–ARGENTINE TERRITORIAL COMPETITION

Although the Antarctic Treaty suspended all territorial claims, Antarctica remained a contested territory and British hopes of a reduced scientific presence were dashed. Argentina and Chile were not going to mollify their determined claims and, unlike Britain, geographical proximity meant that their operations required a less resource-intensive enterprise. In the light of these circumstances, it was recognised that even the name 'Falkland Islands Dependencies' was unnecessarily provocative to Argentine observers. As Roberts confided in his dairy during the Washington Conference,

> This Treaty [the Antarctic Treaty] holds out the possibility of ending our quarrel about the Antarctic, there is no hope at all of ending the Falkland Islands dispute within a measurable time. Why then link the two together and daily rub salt into the wounds? We have discussed it at intervals in the Foreign Office for years but there has always been a very natural reluctance in the Colonial Office to take any action. If the Treaty is signed and ratified, the most immediate and practical result will be to remove (or at least substantially reduce) the political arguments for financial aid to FIDS from the Treasury.[45]

As if to reinforce Roberts' concerns relating to the future of the FIDS and British territories south of the Antarctic Treaty region, funding was cut by £50,000 to £650,000 in response to the improvement in overt geopolitical disputes with Argentina and Chile.[46] FIDS bases in the Antarctic such as those located on Anvers Island and Danco Island were closed in the months leading up to the Washington Conference. After the ratification of the treaty, the base at Admirality Bay was closed in 1961 as the old geopolitical reasoning for the FIDS based on countering Argentine territorial nationalism was no longer, excusing the pun, cutting ice with the Treasury.

Mindful of Argentine sensitivities, and in the wake of a high-profile visit to Deception Island by President Frondizi in 1961, the FO insisted that the 'FID' be renamed. The rationale for such a move was made clear in correspondence between Robert Saner of the British Embassy in Buenos Aires and Robin Edmonds, the head of the American Department of the FO. As Saner noted in March 1961, 'So long as our Antarctic territories are known as the Falkland Islands Dependencies any incident in the Antarctic automatically brings up the much more deeply felt and explosive dispute over the Falklands themselves'.[47] Later that year, the recommendation Roberts put forward in October 1959 to rename the territories south of the Antarctic Treaty region 'British Antarctic Territory' was implemented in order to defuse the Falkland Islands question. Interestingly, the announcement of the name change was not made public until 1962, by which time the Argentines and Chileans had already ratified the Antarctic Treaty within their domestic parliaments. The FIDS was also renamed the British Antarctic Survey (BAS), the major British stakeholder in the British Antarctic territory.

These geopolitical upheavals in the Antarctic and the South Atlantic were not divorced from a broader transformation in British defence and foreign policy. In the aftermath of the Suez Crisis, it became evident that a fundamental review of Britain's overseas interests was required. The withdrawal from Suez, just two months after the launch of an operation to recover control of the canal from the Egyptian regime headed by Colonel Nasser, was dictated by a financial crisis. US disapproval

1. ABOVE. The author at Pendulum Cove, Deception Island.

2. RIGHT. A 'Las Malvinas son Argentinas' signpost near the Argentine-Brazilian border. These signs are found all over the country and serve as important reminders of Argentina's territorial ambitions.

3. ABOVE. A British surveyor working at Turning Point, Livingston Island, in the summer season 1955-6. Reproduced by permission of Peter Mott.

4. BELOW. The abandoned Norwegian whaling station at Stromness Bay, South Georgia, showing the large storage tanks used for whale oil.

5. ABOVE. The Governor's residence, Stanley, Falkland Islands.

6. BELOW. Half Moon Island, South Shetlands. This aerial photograph was taken in January 1956.

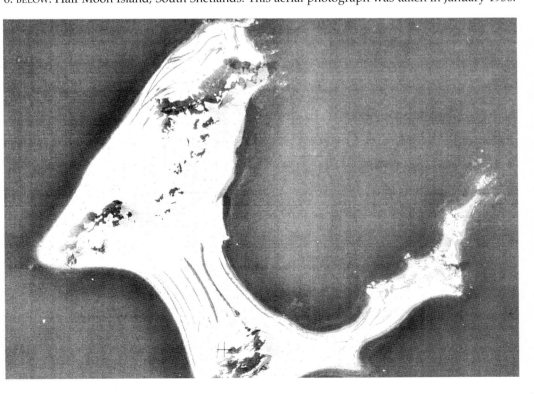

7. FACING PAGE. A view of the northern tip of the Antarctic Peninsula.

8. ABOVE. Liberation Monument, Stanley. The monument was built and funded by Falkland Islanders as a gesture of remembrance to the British servicemen who lost their lives in 1982.

9. BELOW. A signpost for the local authority in Argentina's southernmost city, Ushuaia, which is also the capital of the province of Tierra del Fuego, Antarctica and the South Atlantic Islands.

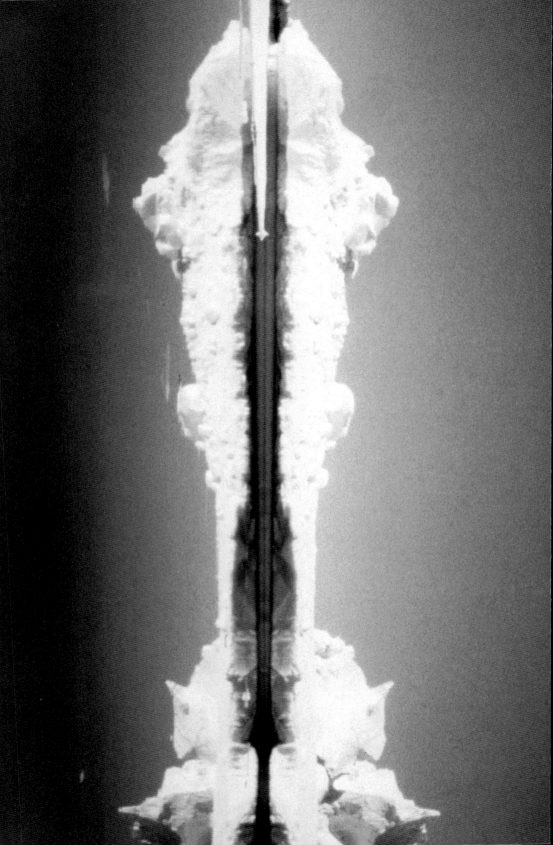

11. ABOVE. The author first travelled to the Antarctic on board the Russian registered vessel, *Akademik Shuleykin*. The vessel is flying the Union Jack because it was moored in Falkland Islands waters.

10. FACING PAGE. A spectacular iceberg in the Lemaire Channel, Antarctica.

12. ABOVE. Tom Smith's famous photograph of a British soldier accepting a cup of tea from a Falkland Islands family in May 1982. Reproduced by permission of the Press Association.

13. BELOW. Port Lockroy base in Antarctica. Originally constructed in the 1940s as part of the Falkland Islands Dependencies Survey's activities, it is now a major tourist attraction.

of the military operation and refusal to sanction an international loan until troops were withdrawn severely dented British political and financial confidence. Eden resigned as Prime Minister a month later and was succeeded by Macmillan. With rapidly declining gold reserves, the white paper prepared by Defence Secretary Duncan Sandys in 1957 effectively paved the way for a substantial reduction in the size of Britain's conventional forces.[48] The UK's possession of nuclear weapons provided a strategic rationale for the reduction because, so it was argued, there was no need for land forces in particular to defend key interests. The revised white paper also argued that the armed forces should 'defend British colonies...against local attack and undertake limited operations in overseas emergencies'.[49] Defence expenditure was to be reduced from 10 to 7 per cent of GNP by 1962, but overseas commitments in the Middle East and southeast Asia were preserved despite the dramatic decline in the numbers serving in the armed forces (from 690,000 in 1957 to 375,000 by 1962).[50] As Michael Dockrill has rightly concluded, 'Britain was faced with a number of colonial and post-colonial crises after 1957 and she was hard put at times to find the manpower and equipment to deal with them: if they had all occurred at the same time, she would have faced a very serious situation'.[51]

Despite Cabinet approval in 1958, and then again in 1960, to maintain British activities in the Antarctic, the future of the BAS and its scientific research was inevitably precarious. With British territorial claims suspended under Article IV of the Antarctic Treaty, Government departments, led by the Treasury, were instructed to review all forms of overseas expenditure. The uncertainties over the Antarctic and the South Atlantic mirrored Britain's changing defence commitments in an era of post-colonial change in Africa and Asia. Despite the intent of the white paper, Britain's overseas commitments continued to be punctuated by skirmishes in Indonesia and the Middle East. As with the Falklands and Antarctic, these territorial disputes would not be solved by the nuclear deterrent. It was also apparent that Argentine interest in the South Atlantic and the Antarctic was not going to diminish, despite the termination of direct communications between the Falklands and Argentina. Inevitably, the isolation of the Islands from Argentina had profound implications, as Islanders came to rely upon the sea link with Montevideo for their only point of contact with the wider world.

The subsequent debate within Whitehall revealed only too clearly how the Colonial and Foreign Offices tried to justify their claims that withdrawing funding for the BAS would jeopardise British interests in the Falklands and the South Atlantic. With intense budgetary pressures on the armed forces and overseas commitments, including the despatch of British troops to post-colonial crises in Aden, Kenya, Kuwait and Malaysia competition for resources was intense. In a letter dated December 1964 from the Colonial Office to the Treasury, territorial competition with Argentina (rather than Chile) was held to be the *raison d'être* for the BAS: 'The active resuscitation of the Argentine claim to the Falkland Islands in the United Nations Committee of 24 (in September) underlines, if anything, the case for maintaining the British position against the Argentine in the Antarctic'.[52]

The FO reiterated this line of geopolitical thought at ministerial level in December 1964:

> The Foreign Office would be strongly opposed to any decision to reduce the scope of the British Antarctic Survey's activities. We have taken a leading part in

the activities of the Antarctic Treaty and any suggestion of withdrawal would be greeted...with delight by others, notably Argentina, who would regard this as a surrender of our claims to the Antarctic and probably also to our sovereignty over the Falklands themselves.[53]

In response, the Minister of State at the Treasury called into question the significance of British territorial claims and asked whether there was any value in these possessions apart from 'prestige'? Treasury ministers and civil servants alike argued that the BAS budget of £750,000 (a slight improvement on the 1960 budget) was over-inflated, and questioned whether the BAS should not be phased out in the next two or three years. As John Diamond, Minister of State at the Treasury concluded, 'We cannot afford to be spending money on maintaining claims to the icy wastes of the Antarctic'.[54] If Britain's presence in the Antarctic was worth maintaining, then the Treasury was minded that territorial and geopolitical ambitions should not be used to justify future investment.[55]

Given the hostility of the Treasury to further funding for the BAS, the FO urgently revised its views on British policy towards Antarctica and Argentina in 1965. A new review paper was ordered to take account of this rebuke. Previous FO review papers had assumed that 'maintenance of our claim to British Antarctic Territory was desirable. This assumption has now been called into question, and I think a fresh approach is called for.'[56] Attached to the letter was a file (which remains restricted by the FO because of the ongoing sovereignty dispute) which clearly considered the connections between Britain's territorial claims in the Falklands and the Antarctic. Internal discussions between the Foreign and Colonial Offices revealed that Britain's claim to the Falkland Islands would be 'weakened' by Britain 'pulling out' of the Antarctic. But as the Colonial Office warned the FO, the review of the BAS should avoid sensational geopolitical arguments and 'over-simplifying the Falklands problem by appearing to assimilate too closely to the Antarctic'.[57] The apparent danger that could have followed from such a connection was the issue of whether or not the Falkland Islands should contribute to the cost of the BAS.

Differences of opinion over the future importance of the BAS came to a head in July 1965 when the FO released a paper entitled 'UK policy in the Antarctic'. While the FO argued that all scientific research in the Antarctic was for academic reasons, it was abundantly clear that the Treasury review of expenditure was not going to be sympathetic to this quasi-geopolitical remit of the BAS. The rising diplomatic and geopolitical profile of the Falkland Islands placed further pressure on the British Government to decide the strategic and political importance of the wider South Atlantic region. By urging Argentina and Britain to negotiate a peaceful resolution (UN Resolution 2065) to these disputed islands in the South Atlantic, the Falklands became a 'global' problem intimately linked to the uncertain and at times traumatic post-colonial condition. For those administering the South Atlantic portion of the British Empire, the post-colonial impulse was minimal, given the unpopulated wastelands of Antarctica and the micro-community of the Falkland Islands. Arguably, it was the perfect colonial fantasy, a 2000-strong white Falklands community determined to resist a post-colonial future with the Argentine Republic. In the main, however, the Falklands left ministers and civil servants with a policy headache, as they complained that commercial opportunities were being squandered.

The mounting balance-of-payments crisis throughout the 1960s necessitated all forms of overseas Government expenditure to be subjected to critical scrutiny. By the time Wilson had been elected Prime Minister in 1964, Britain was on the eve of a major reassessment of its defence and geopolitical priorities. Under the leadership of Healey, the 1965 White Paper on Defence acknowledged that there would be further reductions in the size of the armed forces. Mindful of Cabinet spending limits, it was proposed that the Royal Navy should bear the brunt of the reformation. Within two years, however, the geopolitical situation in the Middle East and Africa worsened and the Wilson Government was faced with escalating crises in Aden and Rhodesia. The 1967 supplementary White Paper on Defence signalled a sea change in British foreign and defence policy when it was confirmed that British troops stationed in southeast Asia would be reduced and Aden was evacuated. The shift from 'east of Suez', initiated by the financial crisis of November 1967, meant that further cuts in conventional defence appeared inevitable. Britain was no longer in the financial position to support military commitments in the fragmenting tropical and temperate parts of the British Empire. Despite the radical change in Britain's global commitments, the garrisons in Gibraltar and Hong Kong were secure due to the ongoing sovereignty disputes. In the case of the Falkland Islands, no major military garrison had been maintained since the Second World War. For much of the year, the Islands were left with a small British military presence (usually Royal Marines), which was supported by volunteers attached to the Falkland Islands Defence Force.

ARMING AND DETERRING ARGENTINA

Ignoring occasional misgivings in the post-1968 period, successive British Governments – especially under Callaghan (1976–9) – attempted to develop a dual strategy of containing Argentine ambitions while at the same seeking to promote trade and co-operation. Mark Phythian has argued that Argentina throughout the period remained a regular and reliable customer of British naval vessels and jet aircraft. In contrast to Chile, ministers with the Labour Government under Wilson and Callaghan remained willing to explore defence contracts with Argentina despite the 1976 military coup.[58] It is salutary to recall that during this period of violent repression the FO continued to promote and was involved in detailed negotiations over the sale of additional naval vessels. The contract was ultimately awarded to the German firm Blohm and Voss but it is now known that a senior Argentine naval officer, Admiral Massera made a 'private' visit to London in July 1978 to discuss future arms purchases. During his stay in London, Massera held a meeting with the First Sea Lord, Admiral Sir Terence Lewin, and representatives from the FO and Department of Trade. In December 1978, Foreign Secretary David Owen invited General Orlando Agosti, the Argentine Air Force chief, to London for a further 'private visit'.[59] However, Owen, in his recollections of the period, argues that he was never involved in any arms negotiations but felt that contact should be continued with Argentine high-ranking officers, some of whom had been trained by the British military at Sandhurst.[60]

Unbelievable as it may seem that senior officials encouraged 'private visits' from senior military officers attached to the Argentine military regime, the rationale for such contact was understandable. FO officials were keen to continue negotiations with the Argentine military regime in the hope that a territorial settlement over the Falkland Islands could be reached. In order to do so, incidents such as the Argentine occupation of Southern Thule were deliberately represented as exceptional episodes of geopolitical opportunism. British military officials privately conceded that the Falkland Islands were indefensible and hence were unwilling to divert ships to the remote South Atlantic.[61] The Royal Marine detachment in the Falklands was a token presence. It was a risky strategy, and Callaghan acknowledged that it depended not only on watchful diplomacy but also on the capacity and availability of the Royal Navy.[62] Ensuring the provision of reliable military intelligence from the British Embassy in Buenos Aires was critical because under the Wilson Government (1974–6) defence spending fell in real terms as resources were concentrated on social security and welfare investment after several reviews of expenditure and commitment.

Although the Callaghan Government reversed this decline in defence spending, investment was earmarked for the British Army on the Rhine (BAOR) and the worsening security situation in Northern Ireland. The Royal Navy was already under severe pressure following reductions in the surface fleet and the termination of the Simonstown Naval Agreement with South Africa in 1974 emphasised the remoteness of the South Atlantic. The so-called 'Cod War' with Iceland further diverted precious resources – this time to Europe and the North Atlantic. The closure of the Gan air staging post in the Indian Ocean in 1974–5 reiterated concerns that Britain's non-NATO commitments would be confined to worrisome enclaves and islands such as Gibraltar, Cyprus, Hong Kong, Belize and the Falkland Islands.[63]

No wonder, then, that the Latin American arms markets proved a necessary and reliable source of revenue, one which was considered important enough to protect and maintain – especially the existing contacts with Argentina, Brazil and Chile. With another mounting balance-of-payments crisis looming, risks were being taken, even though it was known that Argentina's defence spending increased in tandem with its determination to recover a number of strategic islands in the Beagle Channel, whose ownership was contested by Chile. According to a recent study on British arms sales, the Argentine military regime earmarked £450 million for arms procurement in the wake of rising tension with Chile. Meanwhile, British officials in the FCO and Ministry of Defence were keen to promote sales of Type 42 destroyers and other naval equipment such as Lynx helicopters, not least because extra funds were urgently needed for the modernisation of the British armed forces. In 1979, a further eight Lynx helicopters were added to the earlier orders in 1977 together with military communications equipment from British firms such as Decca, Plessy and Ferranti.

This Anglo–Argentine defence co-operation appeared to contribute to a restoration of diplomatic relations in March 1979 after a period of tension in the South Atlantic. While Callaghan, in his capacity as Foreign Secretary, was keen to promote co-operation in hydrocarbon and communication development, he was also acutely aware of the potential naval threat posed by Argentina. In May 1975, he submitted a detailed report to Wilson on the Falkland Islands question and the British attitude towards the Argentine claim. Callaghan reiterated to Wilson that even if the possibility of a 'territorial settlement' arose (in the form of a con-dominium) the British Government must make it clear that any Argentine aggression against the Falkland Islands would be resisted. As a former naval man, Callaghan was conscious of the symbolic and practical importance of HMS *Endurance* and was instrumental in persuading the Defence Secretary, Roy Mason, not to withdraw the ice patrol ship.[64] Callaghan had the reputation of demanding regular updates on what he called 'the dots on the map'. The academic and journalist Peter Hennessy recalled that Callaghan had explained his approach to international affairs for a 1986 Channel 4 television programme called *All the Prime Ministers' Men*:

> Because of my background, I asked the Admiralty every week to send me a map of the world, about the size of this blotter in front of us here, which set out the position and disposition of every ship in the British Navy, including all the auxiliaries, so that I could know exactly what we could do and how long it would take us to get to the Falklands and where we needed to be. That is the kind of thing I think a Prime Minister must do. There are small things that he must do and large things. That's one of the small things he must do that can save a very large catastrophe.[65]

In conjunction with this attention to geopolitical detail, Callaghan – according to his biographer – developed an insurance strategy, which may well have prevented an Argentine invasion in 1977:

> He also took steps to have an up-to-date assessment of Argentine military and naval deployment, and to have information on possible harassment of British or other shipping or tampering with Falklands air communications. In reply to threatening noises made by Vignes, the Argentine Foreign Minister, it was made transparently clear that no Argentine occupation of any part of the Falklands or surrounding areas such as South Georgia would be tolerated.[66]

In November 1977, in a move widely seen as substantiating this strategy, Callaghan ordered the despatch of the British nuclear submarine HMS *Dreadnought* and the two frigates HMS *Phoebe* and HMS *Alacrity* to the South Atlantic. The decision was taken after intelligence reports from the British Embassy in Buenos Aires in combination with first-hand reports from the polar vessel HMS *Endurance*, confirmed that an Argentine scientific party continued to occupy the remote island of Southern Thule.[67] As with the Falkland Islands and South Georgia, Southern Thule lies outside the Antarctic Treaty region and thus there were no formal restrictions on the movement of armed forces. According to an official with direct involvement in collecting Latin American intelligence, the wording of the report on the Southern Thule occupation was critical in persuading the Cabinet that there was a 'higher risk' of Argentina taking military action against the Falklands.[68] The then Governor of the Falkland Islands, Jim Parker, was sufficiently concerned to ask for urgent reinforcement of the Islands' small contingent of Royal Marines.[69]

On hearing the report, Callaghan asked Sir Maurice Oldfield, the then head of MI6, to transmit a message to Argentine naval intelligence informing them of the despatch of a British task-force.[70] Owen, however, is adamant that no such instruction was given, because the whole point of the exercise was that it should be conducted in complete secrecy.[71] The small task-force was ordered to steer well clear of the Argentine coastline and even the Americans were not informed of the deployment. A former Royal Marine stationed on the Falkland Islands at the time further confirmed that he received instructions to remain with the Governor of the Falkland Islands in case of an invasion in December 1977.[72] Callaghan later suggested that this expression of British naval power was crucial in hardening ministerial determination that any Argentine aggression against the Falkland Islands would not be tolerated.[73]

According to Owen, the despatch of this task-force in November 1977 occurred after some tense months of internal debate over the future of the Falkland Islands and HMS *Endurance*. In April 1977 Owen noted that he wrote to Defence Secretary Fred Mulley warning of the dangers of withdrawing the ship because it 'would be an indication [to Argentina] that the Government's withdrawal from the Falkland Islands and the South West Atlantic was already under way'.[74] In response, Mulley confirmed that the withdrawal of HMS *Endurance* would be revisited after the 1977–8 southern hemispheric summer season. This issue was critical because FCO officials had secretly met their Argentine counterparts in Rome in June 1977 for the sole purpose of reviewing the Falklands problem. According to one official who was present at the time, the Argentine delegation demanded the return of the Falklands and South Georgia.[75] In turn, the British delegation reiterated its determination to retain sovereignty over all its South Atlantic islands and the meeting ended in dead-lock. A possible area for discussion (from the FCO's perspective) that was not explored in any detail was whether Argentina would have been prepared drop its claim to the Falkland Islands in return for sovereignty over South Georgia or even the South Orkneys. As all these islands lie to the north of the Antarctic Treaty region, they were not subject to the sovereignty freeze embodied in Article IV of the Antarctic Treaty. However, according to the same official, this was considered too dangerous to discuss at the Rome meeting because the British delegation was mindful not to escalate the dispute. Setting aside the well-grounded fears over Argentina's appalling human-rights records, the Callaghan Government agreed to continue negotiations against this backdrop of persistent uncertainties.

In December 1977, after the secret despatch of the task-force, talks with the Argentine military *junta* resumed once more to establish the possibility of further diplomatic progress. Despite the high level intervention of Owen, a former Navy Minister under the first Wilson Government, unease surrounded the future of HMS *Endurance*. In view of the additional strain on defence commitments, it was agreed to maintain diplomatic contact and seek to develop co-operation in the field of communications and economic development. A report on the ongoing sovereignty negotiations was also prepared for the UN C24 Decolonisation Committee. Callaghan's strategy vis-à-vis Argentina and the Falkland Islands was, as Kenneth Morgan has noted, a

> dual one…He sought co-operation where possible with the Argentine though well aware of the volatility of the military *junta* in Buenos Aires. More provocative [and expensive] measures such as building a runway for RAF fighters in Port Stanley were not adopted. At the same time, Britain's willingness to defend the Falklands was made transparently plain.[76]

In retrospect, what is remarkable about this period leading up to the 1978 World Cup is how the Argentine authorities reduced the diplomatic pressure on the Falkland Islands question. Mindful of the need to cultivate good publicity in an era of widespread human-rights abuses, Ted Rowlands recalled that the period was unusually quiet in terms of diplomatic contact, given the earlier rounds of meetings in New York and elsewhere. General Videla's regime inherited the preparations for the World Cup and was determined to use the event to boost his own credibility amongst a population brutalised by the 'dirty war'. A total of $700 million, 10 per cent of Argentina's total budget for 1978, was spent on the modernisation of stadiums and transport facilities. Labelled the 'World Cup of Peace' by Videla, the 1978 World Cup not only diverted attention away from the violence of the anti-subversion campaigns but also afforded the opportunity for creating a better international sporting image of Argentina following the 1966 World Cup performance in England.[77]

Due to the ineptitude of the previous Governments, the programme of stadium renovation was severely delayed and resulted in endless allegations of corruption and mismanagement surrounding the administration of the entire World Cup tournament. After a month of football matches watched by only 10,000 overseas visitors, the Argentine team was duly crowned world champion after a 3–1 victory over Holland. The prevailing oppressive political culture ensured that many Argentines were reluctant to criticise the military *junta* publicly at a moment of their national team's success. As one Argentine commentator noted,

> The military men wanted to utilise the Mundial, but they also wanted us to come out champions. Many Argentines who celebrated did not like the military, but we also wanted to be champions. What could we do? Not dance? Boycott the Mundial? Do dictatorships pass away, do Cups remain? We went, we won, and we danced.[78]

The World Cup victory bolstered the political and cultural legitimacy of the military regime and helped to deflect international criticism over the human-rights abuses. Under the Governments of Wilson and Callaghan, the Labour Party remained obsessed with the conduct of the Chilean regime of General Pinochet but tolerated the Argentine Generals' dirty war. In part this political selectivity stemmed from the violent manner employed by Pinochet to overwhelm the socialist Government of President Allende in September 1973. Many on the political left were not only horrified by the overthrow of an elected left-wing Government but also outraged by the covert involvement of the CIA in favour of the General.

Callaghan in particular was anxious that the high-profile human-rights cases in Chile should be weighed very carefully against existing Anglo–Chilean commercial contracts. Many MPs believed that arms sales to the Pinochet regime should not only be reviewed but also cancelled, given that Dr Sheila Cassidy, a British citizen, was subjected to brutal treatment by the Chilean secret police because of her medical ministrations to the left-wing guerrilla-movement leader Nelson Gutierrez. The Wilson Government demanded her immediate release and, as Mark Phythian notes, 'Initially, the Government had no success in attempting to secure Cassidy's release from detention, but succeeded after suggesting that delivery of the remaining naval vessels – the two submarines – and the aero-engines could be linked with it'.[79]

Subsequently, ambassadorial relations with Chile were suspended for four years, even though the Callaghan Government later controversially approved the export of aero-engines for the Chilean airforce in July 1978. After a tense stand-off involving MPs and even the workers constructing the aero-engines in East Kilbride in Scotland, they were despatched in August and eventually arrived in Chile in October 1978. This minor diplomatic incident split the Labour Party over arms sales and concentrated parliamentary attention on Chile rather than on the military regime in Buenos Aires.

Remarkably, Owen wrote a short book on human-rights abuses which significantly failed to mention Argentina in his analysis, even though the death toll in Buenos Aires was far greater than that in Santiago de Chile.[80] The Labour Party's crisis over arms-for-Chile occurred at a time when Argentina had just rejected the arbitration decision of the Vatican on the ownership of the Beagle Channel Islands. While they may have been barren and uninhabited, ownership would determine subsequent claims to exclusive economic zones and strategic influence in the south-west Atlantic. Had it not been for the World Cup tournament, the Argentine regime might well have invaded Chile in retaliation. Unintentionally, Argentine–Chilean geopolitical rivalry was being further encouraged by British commercial ambition in the Southern Cone. Again, as Phythian astutely recognises, 'The fundamental flaw in the Government's position – a consequence of trying to move far enough to appease the left while attempting to minimise the negative impact on Britain's reputation as an arms supplier across the region – surfaced repeatedly. The issue refused to go away.'[81]

With the incoming Conservative Government of Thatcher in May 1979, these ambiguities were removed from the arms sales/human rights equation. Rather than attempt to differentiate between these issues, Thatcher simply restored diplomatic relations with Chile despite Carter's condemnation of the Pinochet regime and his cessation of all forms of military deliveries and economic aid. In contrast to the US policy of an embargo on arms sales coupled with diplomatic isolation, the Thatcher Government restored ambassadorial relations and formally lifted the arms embargo in July 1980. Nicholas Ridley, the junior FCO minister responsible for Latin American affairs and the Falkland Islands, was later to be involved in new negotiations with Argentina and Chile. The Thatcher Government's policy represented a tectonic change in attitudes towards the military regimes of the Southern Cone. As Ridley explains,

> The reason the arms embargo was lifted was that we do not place embargoes against any country except when there are special reasons for doing so connected with our security or matters like that. After careful thought and consideration, we decided to do the same as most other countries and trade with Chile, whatever we might think about their political system. We have, of course, strong reservations about much that goes on of a political nature in Chile, but we don't mix up the two questions of trade and views of the political situation. Nobody does in Chile, and we don't see why we should be the odd man out.[82]

This shocking complacency was to haunt Ridley when he visited the Falkland Islands in an attempt to persuade the Islanders to accept a lease-back agreement with Argentina, whereby sovereignty would be formally transferred and the Islands leased back for an agreed period of time. The apparent cavalier approach to human-rights protection left many Falkland Islanders justifiably worried that they should be asked to join a republic which had killed thousands of its own citizens and, worse still, that the British Government was prepared to sell arms to both the Argentine and Chilean regimes. Many Islanders recalled that his style and demeanour were unconvincing and that sounds of 'Fuck off Ridley' accompanied by those of 'Rule Britannia' played on an old record player greeted his arrival at Stanley in November 1980. Like former ministers such as Rowlands and Chalfont, he had come to inform the Falkland Islanders about negotiations with Argentina, and, as on those previous occasions, was left in little doubt as to the Islanders' determination to resist a sovereignty transfer to Argentina. They came, they talked, but they did not win hearts and minds.

SUMMARY

Football, first introduced by British sailors on shore leave in South America in the late nineteenth century and so enthusiastically embraced by the Argentines, was to haunt Anglo–Argentine relations in the post-1945 period. Ugly scenes and endless recriminations over playing styles marred most encounters between England and Argentina on and off the field and provoked numerous diplomatic incidents. Arms sales to Argentina, however, provided one source of commercial continuity, as the Wilson Government was anxious to secure valuable export earnings in the face of continued balance-of-payment crises. Unbelievably, successive Labour Governments were more concerned with the human-rights abuses in Chile than in Argentina. Despite the dramas, both sides wished to maintain the dialogue even though mounting opposition from the Falklands lobby was unquestionably complicating the possibility of a political settlement for the Islands. British officials and ministers were anxious not to provoke Argentina into military action against the Falkland Islands. The earlier recommendation in April 1969 to develop the transport infrastructure of the Islands was later suppressed by the Overseas Policy and Defence Committee.[83] Later plans to construct an airfield in Stanley were cancelled, despite the recognition that the Falklands remained indefensible given the small size of the British military contingent on the Islands. The Falklands were left vulnerable to impulsive action.

NOTES ON CHAPTER 6

1   PRO FO 7/137. Report from the British Embassy in Buenos Aires to the American Department of the FO, dated 11 October 1968.

2   Alf Ramsey, quoted in *News of the World*, 'Animals! That's how Argentines acted, says Ramsey', 24 July 1966.

3   Quoted in *Daily Express*, 'World Cup ban threatens Argentine', 25 July 1966.

4   See press reports for the referee's reflections on the game such as *Daily Express*, 'Rattin's "look" was enough, says ref', 25 July 1966.

5   Quoted in D. Bowler, *Winning isn't Everything Thing: A Biography of Sir Alf Ramsey* (London, Victor Gollancz, 1998), p. 210.

6   The quote is taken from Bowler, *Winning isn't Everything*, p. 213.

7   *Daily Mirror*, 'Latin lunacy plunges', 25 July 1966.

8   The quote is taken from Bowler, *Winning isn't Everything*, p. 214.

9   Bowler, *Winning isn't Everything*, p. 209.

10 Quoted in T. Mason, *Passion of the People? Football in Latin America* (London, Verso 1995), p. 1. I am indebted to Mason for his account of the earliest development of Argentine football.

11 Quoted in Mason, *Passion of the People?*, p. 4.

12   Quoted in Mason, *Passion of the People?*, p. 67.

13   Quoted in Mason, *Passion of the People?*, p. 69.

14   The quote is taken from H. McIlvanney (ed.), *World Cup '66* (London, Eyre and Spottiswoode, 1966), p. 118.

15   M. Marquis, *Anatomy of a Football Manager: Sir Alf Ramsey* (London, Arthur Barker, 1970).

16   M. Stewart, *Life and Labour* (London, Sidgwick and Jackson, 1980), p. 174. Stewart's tour of Latin America included Chile and Peru as well as Argentina. Post-colonial transformation in Latin America was nonetheless on the diplomatic agenda because much to Venezuela's displeasure, British Guiana had become an independent Guyana in 1966.

17   Quoted in Mason, *Passion of the People?*, p. 70. The newspaper later financed an expedition which landed a small plane on the Falkland Islands.

18   H. Mayes, *The Football Association's World Cup Report 1966* (London, William Heinemann, 1967). The quote is taken from p. 160.

19   Letter to the *Times*, 26 July 1966. See also W. Murray, *Football: A History of the World Game* (Aldershot, Scolar Press, 1994).

20   R. Hutchinson, *It is Now! The Real Story of England's 1966 World Cup Triumph* (London, Mainstream Publishing, 1993).

21   PRO FO 953/2334. Telegram from Sir Michael Cresswell to the FO, dated 9 September 1966.

22   PRO FO 371/184669. Telegram from the British Embassy in Buenos Aires to the American Department of the FO, dated 5 August 1966.

23   PRO FO 953/2334. Telegram from Head of Chancery, British Embassy in La Paz to Information Policy Department of the FO, dated 4 August 1966.

24   PRO FO 953/2334. Letter from J Shakespeare of the British Embassy in Rio de Janeiro to C. Petrie of the FO, dated 26 August 1966.

25   PRO FO 953/2334. Letter from P. Young of the FO to D. Follows of the FA, dated 14 October 1966.

26   PRO FO 953/2334. Memorandum prepared by P. Young, dated 13 October 1966.

27   Little wonder, perhaps, that Argentina's controversial victory over England in the 1986 World Cup quarter-final elicited little Latin American sympathy for an English team beaten by Diego Maradona and the 'hand of God'.

28   The *Sun*, 'United fail, Best sent off in gutter-soccer', 17 October 1968.

29   I am very grateful to Dr Pablo Alabarces for sharing with me his careful analysis of the 1968 Estudiantes–Manchester United games. See his paper, 'The epic of the poor: The Estudiantes de La Plata–Manchester United matches', paper presented to the 19th Annual Conference of the British Society for Sports History, 29 and 30 April 2000.

30   *Daily Mirror*, 'It's time the FA banned our clubs from this shoddy championship', 17 October 1968; *Daily Express*, 'United lose: Best sent off', 17 October 1968.

31   PRO FO 7/137. Telegram from Sir Michael Cresswell to the American Department of the FO, dated 1 October 1968. Peter Beck has demonstrated that concern over the behaviour of a football club has a longer historical tradition. See P. Beck, *Scoring for Britain: International Football and International Politics 1900–1939* (London, Frank Cass, 1999), pp. 225–7. The team in question was Chelsea, on their tour of Poland in 1936.

32   Public protest later erupted in the city of Cordoba in April 1969.

33   Alabarces, 'The epic of the poor: The Estudiantes de La Plata–Manchester United matches'.

34   For a critical review of the National Security Doctrine see D. Pion-Berlin, *The Ideology of State Terror* (Boulder CO, Lynne Rienner, 1989).

35   E. Archetti, *Masculinities: Football, Polo and Tango in Argentina* (London, Berg, 1999).

36   Cited in Alabarces 'The epic of the poor: The Estudiantes de La Plata–Manchester United matches', p. 11.

37   E. Archetti, 'Argentinian football: A ritual of violence?' *The International Journal of the History of Sport* 9 (1992): pp. 209–35.

38   P. Calvert, 'British relations with Southern Cone states', in M. Morris (ed.), *Great Power Relations in Argentina, Chile and Antarctica* (New York, St Martins Press, 1990), pp. 41–58.

39   PRO FO 7/137. Telegram from British Embassy at Buenos Aires to American Department of the FO, dated 22 January 1968. The meeting took place on 18 January 1968 at the British Embassy.

40   PRO FCO 7/1492. Letter from Henry Hankey of the FO to Michael Franklin of MAFF, dated 14 December 1970.

41   Quoted in M. Phythian, *The Politics of British Arms Sales Since 1964* (Manchester, Manchester University Press, 2000), p. 1.

42   This information is derived from Phythian, *The Politics of British Arms Sales Since 1964*, pp. 123–4.

43   PRO FCO 7/1493. Telegram from the FCO to the British Embassy in Rio de Janeiro, dated 5 May 1970.

44   PRO FCO 7/1492. Memorandum from Lord Chalfont to C. Wiggin of the American Department of the FO, dated 7 January 1970. Lord Chalfont was a former defence correspondent of the *Times*.

45   SPRI Archives MS 1308/9; BJ Brian Roberts' diary relating to the 1959 Washington Conference, p. 109. Initially Roberts favoured the term 'Weddell Territory', but later championed the title 'British Antarctic Territory' to refer to all those territories contained within the geographical remit of the 1959 Antarctic Treaty.

46   The *Daily Telegraph*, 'Parsimony in polar grants', 8 September 1960. The grant from the British Government to the FIDS in the financial year 1960–1 was approximately £650,000.

47   SPRI Archives MS 1308/22/11. Letter from R. Saner of the British Embassy in Buenos Aires to R. Edmonds of the American Department of the FO, dated 29 March 1961.

48   *Defence: Outline of Future Policy* (London, HMSO, Cmd 124, April 1957).

49   *Report on Defence: Britain's Contribution to Peace and Security* (London, HMSO, Cmd 363, February 1958). The extract is quoted from M. Dockrill, *British Defence Since 1945* (Oxford, Blackwell, 1989), p. 67.

50   These figures are taken from Dockrill, *British Defence Since 1945*, p. 68.

51   Cited in Dockrill, *British Defence Since 1945*, p. 69.

52   PRO CAB 124/1795. Letter from J. Bennett of the Colonial Office to R. Sharp of the Treasury, dated 11 December 1964.

53   PRO CAB 124/1795. Letter from W. Padley, Minister of State at the FO to J. Diamond, Minister of State at the Treasury, dated 30 December 1964.

54   PRO CAB 124/1795. Letter from J. Diamond of the Treasury to W. Padley of the FO, dated 20 January 1965.

55 A point recognised by Roberts in October 1959 during the Washington Conference. See SPRI Archives MS 1308/9. BJ Brian Roberts' diaries relating to the Washington Conference October–December 1959, p. 110.

56 PRO CAB 124/1795. Letter from R. Slater of the FO to J. Bennett of the Colonial Office, dated 25 February 1965.

57 PRO CAB 124/1795 Letter from J. Bennett to R. Slater, dated 4 May 1965.

58 Author interview with a retired FO official, 15 February 2001.

59 This information is derived from M. Phythian, *The Politics of British Arms Sales Since 1964* (Manchester, Manchester University Press, 2000).

60 Author interview with Lord Owen, 15 May 2001.

61 Private information.

62 J. Callaghan, *Time and Chance* (London, HarperCollins, 1987), p. 372.

63 Dockrill, *British Defence Since 1945*, p. 107.

64 See Callaghan, *Time and Chance*, p. 373. When HMS *Endurance* travelled south into the Antarctic Treaty region, the limited armaments carried by the vessel were covered in recognition of the Antarctic's status as a zone of peace.

65 P. Hennessy, *The Prime Minister: The Office and its Holders Since 1945* (London, Allen Lane, 2000), p. 390.

66 K. Morgan, *Callaghan: A Life* (Oxford, Oxford University Press, 1997), p. 461.

67 Author interview with Lord Owen, 15 May 2001.

68 Author interview with a retired FCO official, 15 February 2001.

69 Telephone interview with Jim Parker, 21 November 2001.

70 My thanks to Professor Peter Hennessy for reminding me that Callaghan had spoken publicly about the incident. It is also important to recall that Callaghan was also aware that there were reports coming in from British Honduras that Guatemala was planning military action against the colony.

71 Author interview with Lord Owen, 15 May 2001.

72 Author interview with a former Royal Marine now living in the Falkland Islands, 2 July 2000.

73 As a member of the opposition, Callaghan, both in Parliament and before the 1982 Franks Committee, reiterated the point that his flexible diplomatic and naval strategy had prevented an Argentine invasion of the Falkland Islands. See, for example, his contribution in the aftermath of the 1982 Falklands crisis: *Parliamentary Debates*, vol. 27, 482 (8 July 1982). Peter Hennessy has argued that there can be no doubt that the relevant Argentine authorities received the message about the task-force. See Hennessy, *The Prime Minister and its Holders Since 1945*, p. 390.

74 D. Owen, *Time to Declare* (London, Michael Joseph, 1991), p. 356.

75 Private information from a retired FO official who did not wish to be identified.

76 Morgan, *Callaghan: A Life*, p. 462. In a letter to the author, Callaghan also noted that the aforementioned work correctly summarised his South Atlantic strategy.

77 J. Arbena, 'Generals and goals: Assessing the connection between the military and soccer in Argentina', *International Journal of the History of Sport* 7 (1990): pp. 120–30. More generally, Arbena, 'Nationalism and sport in Latin America, 1850–1990: The paradox of promoting and performing', *International Journal of the History of Sport* 12 (1995): pp. 220–38 and Mason, *Passion of the People?* pp. 70–3.

78 Arbena, 'Generals and goals: Assessing the connection between the military and soccer in Argentina', *International Journal of the History of Sport* 7 (1990): p. 123.

79   Phythian, *The Politics of Arms Sales Since 1964*, p. 110.
80   D. Owen, *Human Rights* (London, Jonathan Cape, 1977).
81   Phythian, *The Politics of Arms Sales Since 1964*, p. 113.
82   Quoted in Phythian, *The Politics of Arms Sales Since 1964*, p. 120.
83   See the useful summary in G. Drower, *Britain's Dependent Territories: A Fistful of Islands* (Aldershot, Dartmouth, 1992).

7

Kith and Kin: Race, Nationalism and the Falkland Islands

If the Falkland Islanders were British citizens with black or brown skins, spoke with strange accents or worshipped different Gods it is doubtful whether the Royal Navy or Marines would today be fighting for their liberation.[1]

Thank God we are not black.[2]

INTRODUCTION

On 22 June 1948, the *Empire Windrush* arrived at London's Tilbury docks with 492 Jamaicans on board and so initiated a post-war movement of people from the West Indies to a Britain suffering from labour shortages. It has been argued retrospectively that the arrival of the *Empire Windrush* was a catalytic event for a predominantly white community coming to terms not only with the loss of empire in south Asia and the Middle East but also with the prospect of a multiracial nation-state. In the same month, a petition was despatched from one of the remotest outposts of empire to the Secretary of State for the Colonies calling for the removal of the Governor of the Falkland Islands. The petition was signed by 740 residents of Stanley and made direct references to the 'deplorable behaviour' of Clifford and his wife. At the heart of the petition, dated 4 June 1948 was a profound cultural and political claim:

> This British community, 100% white, and noted for its loyalty to the crown in the past, has lost confidence in the administration. In our opinion the policy and bearing of the administration is dictatorial in manner. It is significant that after 115 years the Colony is still without representative government and it is evident that under the present administration elected representation on the Executive Council is a necessary preliminary to self-administration.[3]

Written in the aftermath of south Asian independence, it was unashamedly robust in evoking 'loyalty' and '100% white' to stress the special, if remote, position of the Falkland Islands within the British imperial imagination. Unlike in other parts of the empire, the Falkland Islanders were white and determined to cling to the 'motherland'. The choice of words was, therefore, not innocent.

While the 1948 Falklands petition was never made public in Britain, it occurred at a moment when the discourses of race and nation were about to explode into popular politics and culture. As Paul Gilroy has contended, the 1982 Falklands campaign was not the only moment in post-war British history when race, patriotism, xenophobia and national belonging were powerfully intermingled.[4] While there have been important studies on the political influence of the 'Falklands lobby', scant consideration has been given to the methods deployed in order to infiltrate the British domestic political scene. Falkland Islanders found themselves subject not only to hostile international anti-colonial resolutions but also found themselves excluded by post-1945 fluctuations in British citizenship policy. The then Labour Government's attempts to settle the Falklands question in the 1960s in favour of Argentina inevitably provoked concern that Argentina and its supporters in the UN were a threat to the English-speaking Falklands community. To understand this transformation of the Falklands within British political discourse, the origins of the 1948 petition need to be scrutinised.

THE 1948 PETITION, CONSTITUTIONAL REVIEW AND THE 'LOYAL FALKLANDS'

The position of the Falklands as a 'loyal' if remote colony in the southwest Atlantic was a central theme in the June 1948 petition to the Secretary of State for the Colonies. Notwithstanding the vast distance between London and Stanley, the durability of national ties was being celebrated as testimony to Britain's enduring networks despite the crumbling empire and obvious post-war economic dislocation affecting the country. However, all was not well in the Falklands. The colony was facing difficult issues regarding democratic politics and long-term economic planning. Since the signing of the 1941 Atlantic Charter, British officials were forced to consider the nature and significance of Article III, which stated that all peoples should have the right to choose their own form of government. In a colony where the Governor in combination with the board of the Falkland Islands Company (FIC) largely ignored all forms of direct political consultation with the local populace, this was problematic. In September 1941, the Colonial Office recognised that the Falklands should have some form of local elections without precipitating self-government. After a modicum of local debate involving the Falkland Islands Reform League, Governor Cardinall proposed that a Legislative Council be created which would be composed of four government-appointed officials, two members nominated by the Governor and four members elected by the local voters. Due to tardiness on the part of the Colonial Office, these proposals for a limited form of direct representation were postponed until after the Second World War. Then in 1945, the political status of the Falklands was again subjected to interdepartmental discussion and in an interesting letter dated September 1945, Cardinall reflected on the special status of the Islands:

> This colony is so hopelessly unlike any other Crown Colony in that it is entirely peopled by the British, most of whom look to retire to the motherland, that I am even toying with the idea, now that air traffic is so speedy and certain, to put forward a suggestion that the Island [sic] is incorporated in the United Kingdom.[5]

Condemned by Colonial Office officials for wishful thinking, Cardinall's proposal (which had parallels with later debates over the future of Malta), had it been accepted in 1945, would have radically transformed the cultural, geographical and constitutional relationship between Britain and the Falklands.[6] If an alternative structure might have been constructed before the emergence of Perón, then the Falklands question might have been settled in a different manner. However, in contrast to the French integrationist model of colonisation, the geographical location of the Falklands was considered to be ultimately prejudicial to political representation in Westminster. Moreover, Britain could never consider the Falklands in isolation, as other small territories such as British Honduras, Gibraltar, Hong Kong and British Guiana were also subject to territorial challenge from neighbouring states.

Despite expressions of 'loyalty', Colonial Office officials feared that an angry reaction in Argentina to such a proposal might in turn place pressure on other colonies which were actively contested by a neighbouring state, such as the Spanish claim over Gibraltar. Instead, the Governor was asked to reconsider the proposals for limited representation and to submit a new economic plan for the Islands under the provisions of the 1945 Colonial Development and Welfare Act. While the act committed the Attlee Government to investing over £120 million in the remaining colonies, the allocation to each colony depended upon population size and degree of need. The Falkland Islands allocation was assessed at £150,000 for development related spending. By 1946, Clifford had replaced Cardinall, who returned to Britain and retired into a life of relative obscurity.

According to the 1946 Falkland Islands census, 2339 people inhabited an area equivalent to the size of Northern Ireland, together with 619,000 sheep producing a wool clip valued at £189,000. Under Clifford's tutelage, the Falkland Islands underwent a period of economic and political change. The new Governor proposed social-service reform and sought to maximise revenues from taxation, wool exports and Government assistance from the Colonial Economic Development Council, which was minded to advise the Colonial Office on future development plans. Clifford proposed that a new road across East Falkland be constructed in order to help the movement of goods and people, and that sheep farming should be supplemented by fishing, weaving and other forms of agriculture. A new inter-island air service was introduced in 1948 and a new ship, the MV *Philomel*, was purchased by the Government in order to improve inter-island communication and transport. While the sums of money may have been modest, the Falkland Islands were not neglected, and the council approved a proposal to create a meat freezer plant at Ajax Bay in 1949 in order to utilise the annual surplus of 40,000 sheep carcasses which could not be consumed locally. Unfortunately, through a combination of poor location due to a lack of local consultation and sloppy workmanship, the freezer plant proved to be one of the greatest disasters of the post-war Colonial Office's development programmes. Within three years of opening, the freezer plant closed in 1956 with the loss of £500,000 in investment costs and with only 30,000 carcasses ever processed by the industrial unit. To compound matters further, the South Atlantic Sealing Company, created in 1949 in order to stimulate a local sealing industry, collapsed in 1952. Incompetence rather than neglect resulted in a fiasco rivalled only by the Tanganyika groundnut scheme of the same era. The Ajax Bay plant was never used again for meat processing but proved useful as a military hospital during the 1982 Falklands crisis.

Accusations of economic mismanagement in the late 1940s coincided with a period of intense scrutiny of Government in the Falkland Islands and other small colonies. Former wartime Secretary of State Lord Cranborne approved in principle that the Legislative Council, the major decision-making body of the Falkland Islands administration, should be reconstituted as a democratically elected 'state council'. Since the British occupation in the 1830s, the colony had been under the control of the London-appointed Governor, supported by a pliant legislative council composed of appointed officials. Instead there was now the possibility of local people standing for election to their major decision-making body in the Falklands. Despite Cranborne's approval for this transition, the Colonial Office was concerned that Islanders might not support the democratic transformation and that there would be difficulties in finding 'suitable' candidates. After several months of internal discussion, the Colonial Office approved the Governor's suggestion for a consultative exercise designed to establish local opinion and to address the claim that it was highly anachronistic for nominated members to serve on the Legislative Council in a 'purely European colony like the Falkland Islands'.[7]

In June 1948, after three years of prevarication, the Colonial Office acknowledged that the Governor of the Falkland Islands should address the issue of democratic reform with the local population. This reflected the stated policy of the Secretary of States for the Colonies, Arthur Creech Jones who noted that 'the central purpose of British colonial policy is simple. It is to guide the colonial territories to responsible self-government [not integration with the UK] within the Commonwealth.'[8] As part of this desire to plan for future colonial development, the Labour Government created a 'Committee of enquiry into constitutional development in the small colonial territories' under the chairmanship of Sir Frederick Rees, the then Principal of University College, Cardiff. The committee's remit was to explore a variety of constitutional models for colonial territories considered too small for independence. While some thought was given to incorporating the Falklands and Gibraltar into the UK, Clifford had proposed that the Legislative Council be reformed so that there was a fair balance between nominated and elected Councillors. In due course, it was recommended that there should be a majority of directly elected Councillors, including a representative for Stanley Town Council. In his report to the Legislative Council in October 1948, Clifford proposed that this new body should for the moment be composed of three ex-officio members, four elected members, two nominated (that is selected by the Governor) members and three nominated unofficial (that is selected by elected members) members. Overall, after direct elections, there would for the first time in the history of Britain's occupation of the Falklands be a reasonable mixture of official and unofficial Councillors. At the closing stage of the council's meeting, Clifford nonetheless took the opportunity to thunder against recent Argentine statements on the future of the Falklands at the 1948 Bogota Conference: 'I take the opportunity, therefore, of nailing this monstrous if not indeed seditious, piece of self-slander to the table of this house well aware as I am that no where within the Empire is there any more loyal community than this.'[9] While Clifford's outrage against Argentina's geopolitical opportunism appeared heartfelt, the proposals to reform the Government of the Falkland Islands were in part stimulated by a growing Argentine interest in the sovereignty of the Islands. Mindful of the accusation that the Falkland Islands Government had weak democratic credentials, the Colonial and Foreign Offices were intent on exploring the possibility of a greater measure of self-government. The proposed reforms, therefore, were intended not only to address the issue of democratic representation but also to deny Argentina the opportunity to portray the Falklands as an oppressed colony.

Just as the Legislative Council was considering reconstituting its membership, a fresh crisis appeared over Clifford's leadership in the Falkland Islands. A petition signed by 740 Stanley residents, while proclaiming their loyalty to the British Crown, alleged that the Governor was presiding over an administration composed of highly paid British civil servants and inefficient Government departments staffed by people who were incapable of long-term economic planning. And, just for good measure, the signatories complained that new rises in income and company taxation planned for January 1949 were unwarranted and unjustified in the circumstances. Instead they proposed that a royal commission be created in order to investigate the governance of the Falkland Islands. Notwithstanding a natural reluctance to pay higher rates of taxation, the Falkland Islands Government had nonetheless a short-fall of £15,000 to contend with in the financial year 1947–8.

Clifford's response to the Colonial Office was unrepentant and typically uncompromising. In a letter to a civil servant in London dated 17 May 1948, Clifford argued that the demands for his resignation were 'a plain reaction to unpopular, but necessary, measures to bridge the gap between revenue and expenditure and it leaves me entirely cold'.[10] Moreover, Clifford complained that unlike his experience of colonial service in Nigeria, the Governor's office in the Falkland Islands was far too exposed to direct and highly personal criticism from this small community of 2000 people. He accused the petitioners of 'ill-informed agitation' and noted that 'the root of the present discontent, which I am reliably informed has been brewing for many years, is the absence of popular representation and, as such, I must say at once that it has my entire sympathy'.[11] Under his guardianship, Clifford had approved the appointment of two unofficial members of the Legislative Council and proposed a new constitution that would pave the way for direct elections and improved popular representation.

In a candid review of the colony, claims to 'loyalty' and 'whiteness' appeared to cut no ice with Clifford as he identified the major issues affecting the economic and political condition of the Falkland Islands.[12] The geographical remoteness of the colony in combination with the over-reliance on wool exports made the Islands extremely vulnerable to socio-economic changes in the clothing markets. The lack of communications with the wider world compounded the geographical isolation of the Falklands.[13] Apart from occasional shipping services from Uruguay and Chile, the Falklands had no direct communications with its near neighbour Argentina and no air service to South America. There was a declining population on the Islands and a widespread fear that the younger members of the community would leave for the UK or other Commonwealth countries such as New Zealand. Finally, Clifford argued that the poor educational facilities on the Islands meant that a new generation of Islanders lacked the opportunities to embark on careers other than farming and skilled manual labour. As a consequence, the Islands would continue to depend upon expatriate civil servants and professionals for governance and service provision such as education and medicine.

However, any sympathy Clifford may have had for democratic reform began to evaporate when it became apparent that his wife was also the subject of some stern personal criticism. At the heart of this social crisis lay the simple fact that for much of the twentieth century the Governor, expatriate civil servants and farm managers dominated public life in the Falkland Islands. Native-born Islanders frequently complained (in private and regardless of age and gender) that this stratification of local society encouraged a culture of limited political participation and social deference. Racial difference did not appear to have an obvious role in a community composed of the descendants of white British settlers, but variations in class and social position did contribute to social schisms. One such example emerged when Clifford's wife was accused of improper behaviour in securing the presidency of the local branch of the Red Cross. Coupled with this allegation was another accusing the Clifford family of spending considerable sums of money on renovating Government House.[14] Over the following months, further accusations were to emerge which led to some tense exchanges between the Governor, the Colonial Office and the Falkland Islands community.

Unhappy with the response of the Colonial Office to their petition, several Islanders, including the chairman of Stanley Town Council, L. Hardy, sought to utilise the Government radio station to further their campaign against the condition of the Falkland Islands Government. Clifford had refused permission for such a broadcast, arguing that their intent was to call the Government of the Falkland Islands into question. In their letter to Jones, the Islanders noted

> that while constitutional reform is welcome, under the present Governor it cannot be anything but unpalatable. The immediate course of the crisis is, without doubt, the personalities of His Excellency and Mrs Clifford. There is no need to call for a public meeting to discover the local opinion of Mrs Clifford, her behaviour has disgusted and embarrassed all sections of the community. It is distressing for loyal subjects to hear spoken openly, what was once whispered by a few in public places, 'Would we not be better off under the Argentines?'[15]

In his response to these fresh allegations, Clifford concluded that the inhabitants were 'a notably vindictive and malicious people, easily worked upon and I quite anticipate some further move'.[16] The idea of a 'loyal' community appeared to be in disrepute.

In an attempt to justify his own position, Clifford began to detail a series of 'incidents' that he believed had been instrumental in turning local opinion against his administration. The key figure in these dramas appeared to be his wife. Clifford alleged that local people disliked the fact that his wife had ordered the redecoration of Government House and had displaced the housekeeper, Mrs Williams as the 'Queen Bee here during the long years in which Government House had no lady in residence'. Moreover, Mrs Clifford had earned the wrath of the community by refusing to reform the Girl Guides movement in 1948 because it had been led by a 'troublesome teacher, Page Grey' who was, according to the Governor, 'certifiable'. In his second lengthy reply to the Secretary of State for the Colonies, Clifford combined pomposity and belligerence:

> I have not been a political officer for 27 years without acquiring a nose for atmosphere and had there been any genuine animosity towards me I could not have failed to detect it. This sense of grievance and self-pity, which is deeply implanted in the minds of the less thoughtful members of the community, alas, predominates.
>
> Others have resented her [Mrs Clifford] decided views on public duty and social responsibility which is something not yet understood here.

> I am convinced that nothing but better education, education in civic responsibility
> and the introduction of new ideas will bring about an improvement.[17]

He concluded that some Islanders felt that he and Mrs Clifford should have hosted
a greater number of functions in the renovated Government House.

While the Secretary of State for the Colonies later issued a public message of
support for Clifford and his reform package in January 1949, officials attached to
the Colonial Office were secretly hoping that Clifford and his wife would leave the
Islands. In October 1948, one official concluded that

> His [Clifford's] methods of dealing with the Falkland Islanders is much too
> autocratic and quite out of keeping with these times…There is a very wide gulf
> between Government House and the rest of the colony. Mr Clifford has a
> thankless job of governing this lonely, bad-weathered and bad tempered colony,
> and even if he is perhaps not the ideal Governor for that community, I think we
> owe it to him not to expose him to further needless belly-aching.

Moreover, the Colonial Office also recognised significantly that 'The people are
virtually of UK stock, and it is easy to understand their desire for that measure of
control over their own affairs which they would enjoy in the UK itself through urban
district councils or county councils'.[18] In May 1949, after weathering months of
complaints and agitation, Clifford announced that his wife was leaving the Falkland
Islands on the grounds of ill health.

The repercussions of this constitutional crisis were several and included new
provisions for universal suffrage on the Falkland Islands. In March 1949, the new
Legislative Council gathered for the opening address by the Governor of the
Falkland Islands. Under the new constitution, three senior officials, the Colonial
Secretary, the Senior Medical Officer and the Agricultural Officer, were ex-officio
members of the council. There were four directly elected Councillors, and the remaining members of the 12-strong council were composed of two nominated unofficial
members and three official members. The Governor, as the presiding officer, had
the casting vote in the event of a split vote in the council.[19] More significantly, in
the longer term, the 1948 petition to the Secretary of State for the Colonies from
Stanley residents was instrumental in shaping the racial politics of the Falklands.
Arguments relating to 'kith and kin' fed a political imagination based on identifying
the Falklands community as quite different from other parts of the empire but also
distinct from neighbouring Argentina.

In a minute dated 3 January 1948, prepared in response to a speech by a Colombian
representative at the UN, Bennett of the Colonial Office appeared confident that
the Falklands question could be isolated from a wider discussion on the ending
of colonialism:

> If Senor Sourdis's [the Colombian representative] argument is to be applied to
> 'that which is a colony in the sea of the South', it (the Falklands) should be
> incorporated in Scotland, with particular reference to the counties of Ross and
> Cromarty and Inverness-shire, which 'by virtue of their common language,
> history, customs, and tradition (etc)'. For that reason I don't think we need to take
> the Argentinean claim to the Falklands seriously or fear any international debate
> on it. The Falkland Islands Dependencies are different as they are uninhabited

(or virtually so) and their claim is founded on strategic requirements. Consequently, I think we can only keep the Dependencies [that is territories such as South Georgia rather than the Falklands], in the long run, with the United States' goodwill.[20]

The impact of the crisis over the leadership of Clifford revealed the capacity of the Islanders to challenge the administration of their colonial masters in Government House in Stanley and London. Clifford learnt that while leaders of the petition were swift to point to the 'loyal' and 'white' qualities of the community, they also were vociferous campaigners for a greater measure of self-determination. Unlike other parts of the temperate and tropical British Empire, the emphasis placed on 'loyalty' was imperative given the widespread desire of the Falkland Islands community to resist a post-colonial future involving Argentina.

When Macmillan asked the Lord President of the Council in January 1957 for a 'profit and loss account for each of our colonial possessions', the subsequent report prepared by the Cabinet Committee on Colonial Policy, focused on the future constitutional development of the remaining colonies.[21] Chaired by the Cabinet Secretary Sir Norman Brook, the committee's report carried out a cost–benefit analysis of each colony under four headings relating to political, constitutional, strategic, economic dimensions as well as 'obligations and repercussions'.[22] While Cyprus, Malta and Nigeria warranted a more detailed overview, the brief entry for the Falkland Islands is nonetheless instructive:

> External political pressures are of a minor character but a claim to the Falklands is sometimes voiced in Argentina. Local politics are entirely concerned with domestic issues. There is no demand for constitutional change … [The strategic value of the Falklands is based on its function as] a base from which to support Commonwealth interests in the Antarctic … the main product is wool. [Under obligations and responsibilities the] population is almost entirely of UK origin with a high percentage of persons born in the UK. An independent government would be entirely British and would involve no loss of UK prestige or influence. If, however, protection was also withdrawn [as well as formal UK jurisdiction] the Falkland Islands would be in danger of occupation by Argentina, and the abandonment of a racially British population to such a fate would be discreditable and severely damaging to prestige.[23]

The report concluded that while the British Government would not have been unduly worried by an independent Falkland Islands Government, it had to be understood that the rival Argentine claim also extended to the Antarctic Peninsula and other South Atlantic islands such as South Georgia.

A decade later, the prevailing mood had changed when plans were afoot for the FO to amalgamate with the Colonial and Commonwealth Relations Offices. The new political orthodoxy suggested that Britain's commercial and diplomatic relations in Argentina and Latin America were being hindered by the unresolved status of the Falkland Islands. As Michael Stewart reflects in his memoirs,

> Some day, historians may argue that Britain was short sighted to maintain a running dispute with two important countries [Argentina over the Falklands and Spain over Gibraltar] for the sake of tiny territories with few inhabitants, the more

so as there were no strategic or economic issues involved. (The recent discovery of oil in the South Atlantic may alter the character of the Falklands dispute).[24]

Thus, with the dissolution of the Colonial Office, less overt attention was given to the local needs of colonies such as the Falklands and the 'wishes' of this 'racially British population'. Their grievances were to surface again but in a British domestic context where words like 'loyalty' and 'white' were now politically explosive. Many believed, with good reason, that the newly amalgamated FCO was intent on transferring the sovereignty of the Falklands to Argentina against the direct 'wishes' of the Islanders. The emergence of a 'Falklands lobby' in the Falklands and Britain recalled arguments first articulated in 1948–9 about the 'loyal' nature of the community, which sought to resist the unwelcome presence of a continental neighbour.

THE EMERGENCE OF THE FALKLANDS LOBBY

By the early 1960s, post-war British Governments witnessed post-colonial violence in Kenya, Aden, Malaysia and Cyprus, and immigration from the so-called new Commonwealth was shaping a new politics of race and nationalism. In the decade after the arrival of the *Empire Windrush*, an estimated 125,000 West Indians entered the UK alongside other immigrants from Africa and Asia. This influx of immigrants from the former colonies was accompanied by widely reported fears that the immigrants were 'dirty' and engaged in crime and other forms of immoral behaviour. In 1962 the Commonwealth Immigrants Act restricted immigration because of fears that the strength and cohesion of 'British' society was imperilled. It introduced new divisions between potential immigrants on the basis of their skills and experience. Additional powers were given to the Home Office to restrict entry in the face of the apparent evidence that the resident population was unwilling to accept greater numbers of immigrants. However, as Kathleen Paul has noted, successive post-war Governments justified their increasingly restrictive measures on immigration and citizenship on the basis of alleged 'race riots' in London's Notting Hill and Nottingham in the summer of 1958.[25] While the 1965 Race Relations Act sought to outlaw racial hatred, the White Paper on Immigration from the Commonwealth released in August 1965 outlined the need for further controls on immigration and warned of rising hostility to immigrant communities.[26] The then Minister for Housing, Richard Crossman, astutely recognised that immigration was 'the hottest potato in politics'.[27]

Besides grappling with the contested politics of race and immigration, Labour and Conservative Governments also had to respond to events in the aftermath of UN activity, which called for the British Government to negotiate a settlement with Argentina over the Falkland Islands. Britain had by and large resisted Argentine diplomatic pressure over the disputed colony but in November 1965, the fourth Committee of the UN debated the issue and a resolution (2065) sponsored by 15 Latin American states was adopted by 87 votes to 0, with 13 abstentions. The terms of the resolution were explicit and called on Britain and Argentina to negotiate a solution, which respected the 'interests' of the Falkland Islanders. Accordingly, successive Argentine Foreign Ministers (notably Costa Mendez) argued that the 'interests' of the Falkland Islands community could be secured by bilateral negotiation without direct reference to Islanders themselves. British foreign ministers, after being attacked by the British media and the Falklands lobby, were later inclined to argue that the 'wishes' of the Island community were of critical importance to defining the 'interests' of the Falkland Islands.

Under pressure from the UN and the US, Government departments such as the Colonial, Commonwealth and Foreign Offices initiated an extensive inter-departmental review of the Falklands Islands question. In the aftermath of UN resolution 2065, officials began to devise a geopolitical strategy for dealing with Argentina and the UN. At the heart of this approach was a belief that Britain could not surrender sovereignty over the Falklands because the community did not 'wish' to adopt Argentine citizenship. However, within Government departments some officials believed that if communications could be improved between the Falklands and Argentina then the Islanders' attitude might change towards the South American Republic. Others within Whitehall reassured themselves that even if the Falkland Islanders could not be persuaded, Parliament might approve such a transition in the face of unrelenting post-colonial change. Negotiations with Argentina began in earnest in 1966–7 as a series of high-level exchanges occurred in Buenos Aires, London and New York at the UN.

The purpose of these negotiations was to create a *modus operandi* for improved contact between the Falkland Islands and Argentina. Although many Islanders were not desirous of closer contact with Argentina and hoped that 400 miles of rough seas would be natural protection, the so-called 'Condor incident' in 1966 shattered that illusion. During a domestic flight south from Buenos Aires, a group of about 20 young people hijacked a DC-4 aircraft and forced it to land on the racecourse at Stanley. On board the flight was Admiral Guzman, the Governor of Tierra del Fuego – a territory which, in Argentine eyes, included the Islas Malvinas. Given the passenger list, the hijackers were eager that the unfortunate Argentine Governor should exercise *de facto* authority over the entire administrative region.

The hijackers, including a woman (who appeared to be one of the leaders), were all armed and took 20 hostages from amongst the people who approached the plane under the impression that it had made an emergency landing.[28] Once the reality of the situation became apparent, members of the Falkland Islands Defence Force, the police and a small detachment of Royal Marines training team established a cordon. After prolonged negotiations with the hijackers, the hostages were released together with the innocent Argentine passengers. With temperatures falling rapidly towards freezing, the hijackers eventually surrendered and there were no casualties. Apparently while being driven past Government House on Ross Road, Admiral Guzman turned to Councillor Barton and jokingly gestured 'Mia casa!'[29] There remained the problem of releasing the embedded aircraft from the muddied racecourse, but after a painstaking operation, the pilot, Captain Ernesto Fernandez Garcia, was even-tually able to return the plane to Argentina.[30] An Argentine naval vessel evacuated the hijackers and the other passengers from the Falkland Islands. Faced with such a limited British military presence in the Falkland Islands, Foreign Secretary Brown argued that 'There was every advantage in seeking a quick and amicable settlement since this might assist our longer term objective of resolving the dispute with the Argentine'.[31] After the incident, the Royal Marine detachment was increased from a training team of six soldiers to a complete platoon accompanied by several hover-crafts designed to facilitate coastal survey.

The ensuing talks revealed the profound difficulties surrounding the possible transfer of sovereignty to Argentina. The US State Department was soon made aware of the fundamental problem:

As the British Embassy officer sees it, the most difficult problem in transferring the Islands to Argentina still remains gaining the acquiescence of the Islanders themselves. The Argentines have always tended to think this was relatively unimportant, apparently believing that the British were using this problem simply as a device to avoid coming to terms with the sovereignty issue. However, even though the British are willing to accept Argentine sovereignty over the Islands, they cannot transfer Island administration to the Argentines against the will of the Falkland Islanders themselves without creating serious political problems in the United Kingdom. Consequently, there is still a long sensitive way to go. But an announcement [by Argentina on a possible settlement] would harden Islanders' resistance.[32]

By December 1967, the draft version of the memorandum of understanding caused considerable consternation in the Falkland Islands. Paragraph 4 of the draft produced angry reactions as it cited the 'interests' of the Falkland Islanders and failed (from the widely shared Falkland Islands perspective) to give sufficient weight to the 'wish' of the community to resist a sovereignty transfer.[33] While some officials hoped that attitudes might change once the Argentines had established communications with the Falkland Islanders, Governor Haskard (1964–70), more in tune with the Islanders and their reservations, composed a series of passionate outbursts to Commonwealth and FO officials.[34] By bolstering the 'British' identity of the Islanders, he reminded Bennett of the Commonwealth Office that

We have a strong emotional feeling for the Queen, the flag (flying every day over Stanley) and the national anthem (sung vigorously once a week in the Cathedral and played last thing at night over the wireless). Our links, sentimental and economic, bind us firmly to England. Argentina, seen through Falkland eyes is unknown, foreign, aloof, disdainful, corrupt, feared, a place where taxation is high...perhaps a change of heart is not possible until the price of wool and the drift of population may in the long run decide the issue.[35]

Unintentionally, Haskard had given credence to a widely held view within the British Embassy in Buenos Aires that Falkland Islander views on Argentina were based on cultural ignorance and geographical isolation. His use of the word 'we' suggested that he also identified himself with the plight of the Islanders. However, it should be recalled that Haskard was appointed Governor in 1964 at a time when the Argentine claim to sovereignty had been relatively low key in the post-Perón years. He was also the last Governor to be appointed under the Colonial Office before it merged with the Commonwealth Relations Office and subsequently the FO in 1968. He received no specific briefing from the Colonial Office, and went to the Islands expecting to carry out three fundamental tasks: representative of the sovereign, conveyor of UK policy to the people of the Falkland Islands and conveyor of these people's views to the FO.

It was only during Haskard's term of office that events occurred which led the FO to develop a geopolitical strategy based on the idea that if the Falkland Islands' isolation could be ended then this might transform Islander intransigence towards

Argentina and an eventual transfer of sovereignty. According to this logic, 'wishes' and 'interests' could be made to coincide with one another, once the Islanders understood the benefits to be gained by closer co-operation with Argentina. Haskard's willingness to become an advocate of Islanders' views arose in part from the lack, until February 1968, of any vocal spokesperson for Islander opinion.[36]

By January 1968, Haskard had come to feel strongly that what he described to the author as the 'human problem' of the Falkland Islands was being overlooked by Whitehall, and requested permission to visit London in February 1968.[37] Even before his visit, other officials attached to the British Government were beginning to doubt that a sovereignty transfer would be likely. In one report to Cresswell, an official concluded after a visit to the Falklands in January 1968 that the prospects for a transition would be bleak because of two differing attitudes. On the one hand Argentina would seek a swift sovereignty transfer, on the other hand the Falkland Islanders would seek a slow or non-existent change on sovereignty. He concluded that

> Falkland Islanders profess a strong loyalty towards Britain...and in this and other ways their outlook and social life is much more akin to the 1920s than the 1960s. So far the community is almost completely in the dark about the political discussions going on with Argentina but the intelligent ones see the writing on the wall and are already considerably disturbed by it. [He concluded that the] gap between these two attitudes will be in my view virtually unbridgeable at the present time.[38]

The Governor had noted earlier that 'The future of these Islands has to be looked at against the background of the resolution which was passed in the UN [2065] and this leads us to realise that sooner or later some solution will have to be found. That solution must respect the interest of the people of the Falkland Islands.'[39] He recalled that his London trip was intended to

> do my best to ensure that the views of the Falkland Islanders are fully appreciated at the present time. Those views have been impressed upon me in the past three years and in conversations in many parts of the colony. I think I can confidently say that those in positions of authority are fully informed on Falkland Islands affairs and, in particular, on the feelings of the people of these Islands'.[40]

The Governor consulted with Brown and the Commonwealth Secretary, George Thompson, on the subject of the Falklands.

On his return to the Islands, he expressed confidence that officials and ministers appreciated their concerns with regard to the vexed possibility of a transfer of sovereignty, but failed to reassure the Executive Council of the Falkland Islands anxious to hear further news of his London visit.[41] Unofficial members of the council were unhappy with the secrecy surrounding the visit and on 27 February 1968 sent a statement to all Members of Parliament as well as to the 12 national newspapers in the UK, detailing their concerns over the future sovereignty of the Falklands:

> ARE YOU AWARE THAT –
> Negotiations are now proceeding between the British and Argentine governments which may result at any moment in the handing-over of the Falkland Islands to the Argentine.

TAKE NOTE THAT –
The inhabitants of the Islands have never been consulted regarding their future –
they do NOT want to become Argentines – they are as British as you are, mostly
of English and Scottish ancestry – even to the 6th generation – five out of six
were born in the Islands – many elderly people have never been elsewhere – there
is no racial problem – no unemployment – no poverty AND WE ARE NOT
IN DEBT.
   They have happily pursued their very own peaceful way of life, a very British
way of life, unique in fact, when you consider that the Islands are 8,000 miles from
the country, which they still call 'Home' in spite of the Immigration Act. Is our tiny
community to be used as a pawn in Power Politics? WE NEED YOUR HELP.[42]

In order to ensure that this melodramatic appeal did not fall on 'collective deaf
ears', the four unofficial members of the Falkland Islands Executive Council began to
define resistance to a sovereignty transfer. The four, A.G. Barton, R.V. Goss, S. Miller
and G.R. Bonner, were instrumental in creating the Falkland Islands Emergency
Committee (FIEC) and in mobilising a vision of the Falkland Islands as an imperilled
'British' micro-society.[43] As before in 1948, the identity of the Falklands as a place
populated by a British community was to emerge as the persistent theme in their
campaign to prevent the transfer of the Islands to Argentina.[44]
   It is interesting to note that the petition made reference to the fact that there
was 'no racial problem' in the Falklands. According to Haskard, 'Discussions of race
is a feature of modern Britain but in the sixties in the Falklands 'whiteness' received
little thought'.[45] Unbeknown to Haskard, the petition to the Secretary of State for
the Colonies dated 3 June 1948 had already referred to the '100% white' quality of
the community. Moreover, if the racial characteristics of the Falkland Islands
'received little thought' and thus was simply taken for granted, why did the four
Falkland Islands Councillors mention the phrase 'no racial problem'? By 1968,
British discussions of race and nationalism were imbued with references to national
belonging and the character of British society. Four years earlier, the racist
Conservative politician Peter Griffith, armed with the slogan 'If you want a Nigger
for a neighbour, vote Labour', had defeated his Labour rival in the 1964 election for
Smethwick.[46] The right wing of the Conservative Party, championed by politicians
such as Enoch Powell, MP for Wolverhampton, represented black and Asian immigrants as a 'problem' which threatened to undermine the cultural and political fabric
of British society. Unlike Britain, the Councillors were arguing that the Falkland
Islands did not have a 'racial problem' because 'race' was something that applied to
other people. However, the Falkland Islands community could not afford to be
complacent because, as the Condor incident had demonstrated, the sea did not
always provide a natural defence against unwelcome cultural and racial influences.
   Ironically, the 1962 Immigration Act had restricted the settlement rights of
these 'loyal' British citizens, and the deployment of neo-right discourse on race
and nationalism was aimed to represent Argentina rather than black people as an
unwelcome presence. In Parliament, the campaigning resulted in a decisive
intervention from the Minister of State at the FO, Goronwy Roberts, who
motioned that any negotiations between Britain and Argentina over the Falklands
would proceed only on the basis of consultation and consent.[47] Foreign Secretary
Stewart reiterated this position on 27 March 1968, when he noted that 'Our object

in conducting those talks is to secure a lasting and satisfactory modus vivendi between the islands and Argentina because we believe this is a long term aim of policy'.[48] Seizing upon such a concession from an FO minister, Councillor Barton noted on 31 March 1968 that

> The Falkland Islands will remain British unless the day comes when the Islanders, of their free will, declare they wish to become Argentines; and I cannot see that day ever coming. But we must never slacken our efforts to impress on whatever government is in power in Britain that we are British and want to remain so'.[49]

Barton, who left for London after Haskard had returned from Britain, was anxious to impress upon the Minister of State for Commonwealth Affairs, Lord Shepherd, that the Islanders' 'wishes' had to be respected. Later, Barton recorded that the minister was reassuring and

> He said that any government which sold [sic] even a tiny part of the Commonwealth to a foreign country would be turned out within 24 hours. I got very cross and said we had every reason to fear, and after an hour and a quarter I felt that he and members of the Commonwealth Office were doing some quick rethinking.'[50]

Unbelievably, neither the minister nor Barton appeared to have grasped the cruel irony that the Wilson Government had already evicted the brown-skinned inhabitants of Diego Garcia in order to make way for an American naval base in the Indian Ocean.[51]

Nevertheless, Barton's short visit to London had been highly effective by raising the issue within Parliament and the media by his appearance on the BBC television programme '24 hours' to campaign for the rights of the Falkland Islands people. With mounting interest in the fate of the Falklands, Michael Stewart acknowledged that the British had begun some exploratory conversations with their Argentine counterparts over future sovereignty. In an apparent concession to the FIEC, the Wilson Government (in the wake of four recent by-election defeats) conceded that the Islanders would need to be directly consulted on Britain's response to UN Resolution 2065.[52] The negotiating climate was changing, as Wilson later conceded in private to Stewart in December 1968:

> Opposition to anything that looks like yielding to Argentine pressure has now built up to such an extent that we are bound to have very real difficulty in holding our present course. There is mounting opposition in Cabinet to what was agreed before: feeling in the House is very strong and cuts right across the parties: and Heath [leader of the Conservative opposition] is already beginning to make a big public issue of it.[53]

Following on from the statement by the FIEC, the Falklands was hence actively represented as a 'loyal' colony by Falkland Islands Councillors, the Governor and supporters in Britain. In the same month that Powell made his notorious 'rivers of blood' speech in the House of Commons, warning of the dangers of unregulated immigration into the UK, Falkland Islands Councillors were debating their 'desire to remain British'. In a meeting of the Legislative Council on 20 May 1968, Haskard acknowledged that 'every part of their [Falkland Islanders'] lives are bound up closely to the mother country. But it is as well to remember that outside the colony's borders the world is not static, and the certainties of yesterday are not necessarily the certainties of today.'[54] Whether these 'certainties' related to Anglo–Argentine negotiations over sovereignty or British society in general was never made clear in the minutes of the Legislative Council.

By September 1968, several newspapers, in particular the *Daily Express*, accused the Wilson Government of contemplating concessions to Argentine territorial demands. Accusing the administration of a 'sell out', the paper thundered that 'the Government is to hand over the Falkland Islands to the Argentine. It has now decided in principle, after a tremendous tussle between Ministers, that the colony must eventually pass under the sovereignty of the Argentine.'[55] The FO was later forced into making a statement denying the story but the *Daily Express* reminded readers of the irony that Stewart had told the House of Commons on April Fools' Day in 1968 that the 'wishes of the Islanders are an absolute condition'.

Scepticism over the future intentions of the Wilson Government by the Falkland Islands community and the British Parliament appeared justified given that the British ambassador in Argentina reassured Costa Mendez that:

> He thought that any proposal of this kind [Argentina providing a limited air service to the Falklands] would be welcome as a means of bringing the Islanders in closer touch with Argentina. The process of enlightening the Islanders about this country and gradually improving their attitude towards Argentina was fundamental to the solution of the whole problem... [but] the Argentines themselves must take action to improve their relationship with the Islanders.[56]

In October 1968, the *Daily Express* sent a photographer Aubrey Matthews to the Islands.[57] The now famous photograph depicted local residents in front of Stanley cathedral holding placards (with titles such as 'British and proud of it'), demanding that the Falklands should remain British. This photographic expedition afforded a platform for successive Councillors anxious to reiterate their British identity, not only in the face of post-colonial uncertainty but also in the wake of further defence cuts following the decision to retreat from 'east of Suez'. At a meeting held in October 1968, Goss complained to the Legislative Council that he believed the Queen had been advised against visiting the Falkland Islands in the light of the sovereignty dispute (she later visited Brazil), whereupon Councillor Miller blamed the British Government for 'equivocal and weak attitude' and noted that 'fundamental British staunchness and way of thinking just does not betray its own people. In our own small way we need help from Britain. Remember the cheerful buoyant optimism when Britain was finally threatened with invasion by the Nazi hordes in July 1940.' Councillor Clement, a nominated member, argued that

> In the United Nations, and outside it, words like 'imperialism' and 'colonialism' have been hurled at Britain. How can this apply to us? We have asked to remain under the British flag. How then, can they in our respect level the accusation of imperialism and colonialism? Perhaps in Russian it is translated in a different way. The only indigenous mammal that I know of was the fox.[58]

In other words, the Falklands community was, according to Clement, indigenous rather than imposed, and thus the charges of colonialism and the 1833 annexation were literally misplaced.

Confronted by repeated accusations in the popular media that the Falklands were going to be transferred to Argentina, Chalfont was despatched to the Falklands. In a letter to her parents dated 14 November 1968, Lady Haskard, wife of the

Governor wrote that she sincerely hoped that 'Lord Chalfont's visit will settle all doubts about the future of the colony once and for all. He is supposed to explain HMG's policy with regard to the Islands...I have no doubt that Lord Chalfont will be told quite a few home truths while he is here.'[59] The minister sailed to the Islands in HMS *Endurance*, arriving at Port Howard on 23 November 1968, where the Governor and Miller (the elected member for West Falkland) greeted him; they later accompanied him on a tour of four farms in the remote and sparsely populated West Falkland. The minister then sailed to the capital Stanley, from where he visited the Islanders of East Falkland.

The *Falkland Islands Monthly Review* noted that Chalfont reported to the Islanders that Britain and Argentina had reached an 'agreed position' on the Islands, and that any change would only be sanctioned providing there was widespread consent amongst the Falklands community. Accordingly, there was no question of 'bargaining away' the sovereignty of the Islands and 'Mr Barton pointed out that a number of people here would welcome the opening of communications with Argentina but he would not agree to this if it meant changing the Union Jack for the Argentine flag'.[60] After several rounds of meetings, Chalfont presented the Government's policy on the Falkland Islands to a packed audience at Stanley town hall. According to Lady Haskard, who was present at the time, the meeting was tense, even as

> He confirmed that sovereignty would not be transferred against the wishes of the Islanders. Asked by someone what guarantees we had that HMG would not change its mind on this point (the devaluation of the pound being quoted as an example of what can happen); he said that while the devaluation of the pound was something that the government could do off its own bat, a question of going back on its pledges to the people of the Falkland Islands would be impossible as Parliament would be involved not just the government and he thought that was our best guarantee.[61]

In his recollections of the meeting, Chalfont agreed that many Islanders were extremely worried about the future, especially when they reflected on the domestic financial crises in Britain.[62] Chalfont's subsequent secret report to the FCO in December 1968 attested to the difficulty of the visit and his dismay at the passionate attacks of the Falkland Islands Councillors and other Islanders on Argentina and the possible sovereignty transfer. While Barton was branded 'able but irredeemably reactionary' and Miller was 'more volatile, less intelligent and carries much less weight locally', Chalfont concluded that 'violent parliamentary opposition' would follow any proposal to change the sovereignty of the Falkland Islands.[63] However, his report did hold out the possibility for change if the economy of the Islands declined further.[64]

DIVIDED LOYALTIES AND THE FALKLANDS LOBBY

For much of the 1970s, the FIEC, under the chairmanship of Sir John Barlow (a director of the FIC) sought to strengthen support in London for the Falkland Islands community. Frank Mitchell, secretary to the renamed United Kingdom Falkland Islands Committee (UKFIC) in London, recalled to this author that this period was extremely busy with non-stop lobbying of Parliament.[65] By 1974, the UKFIC had been successful in recruiting support from the three major political parties in Parliament and, as Clive Ellerby demonstrated conclusively, the success of the Falklands lobby owed a great deal to this patronage and active representation.[66] Mitchell recalled, for example, one meeting in the House of Commons which was attended by scores of Conservative MPs including senior figures such as Enoch Powell and Reginald Maudling. In July 1974, for instance, the UKFIC hosted a third reception at Lincoln's Inn in London attended by 50 MPs, 10 members of the House of Lords, 20 media reporters and other interested parties. The presence of Earl Mountbatten of Burma as the special guest demonstrated that the Falklands lobby was cementing important relations with a member of the British royal family.

Earlier in the year, the UKFIC agreed to create a sister organisation in Stanley and the former Buenos Aires-based FO diplomat, Bill Hunter Christie, succeeded in developing stronger ties with the Falkland Islands community. In October 1974, a 10-member Falkland Islands Committee (local branch) was established in Stanley under the leadership of British expatriate Jack Abbott, with former Executive Councillor Sydney Miller acting as secretary. It was agreed that the FIC would liaise closely with the UKFIC and the Executive and Legislative Councillors would be disbarred from the committees. In other words, the Falklands lobby would be effectively independent of the Falkland Islands Government and thus it was hoped better able to represent the views of the community without fear of British Government pressure.[67]

While the Falklands lobby had generated a network of political and diplomatic support, it had also succeeded in strengthening the view of the Falklands as a 'loyal' colony within the popular news media. Christie, as chair of the UKFIC in London, frequently referred to the 'British stock' of the Falkland Islanders in a way designed to separate the racial characteristics of the Islands from mainstream debates about immigration and race relations. Some controversial football games and Alf Ramsey's attack on the Argentine football team reinforced the Falklands campaign. The fundamental objective of the Falklands lobby was to ensure that the Islanders' 'wishes' were treated as a decisive factor by both Argentine and British Governments. However, the UKFIC was also aware that the low strategic priority of the Falklands within British defence policy meant that the Islands were inadequately protected. The 1974 defence review witnessed the decision to withdraw HMS *Endurance* from active service in the South Atlantic and Antarctic.[68] As was to become apparent in 1981–2, the polar vessel not only played a vital role in supporting the small detachment of Royal Marines in the Falklands but also functioned as an active symbol of Britain's determination to hold on to the South Atlantic possessions. In an era of Argentine politics dominated by the navy, HMS *Endurance* was seen as the litmus test of Britain's commitment to the region. After the confrontation between the Argentine navy and the research ship RRS *Shackleton*, Defence Minister Roy Mason announced a temporary reprieve for HMS *Endurance*, which was extended by Labour's Defence Secretary Fred Mulley until the end of the Callaghan Government in 1978–9. With Callaghan aware of the importance of the ice patrol ship, the Falklands lobby, which campaigned vigorously for the retention of HMS *Endurance*, lost no opportunity to publicise the infringements of the Joint Communications Agreement by Argentina throughout the second half of the 1970s. As has been noted, the personal determination of Callaghan first as Foreign Secretary and then as Prime Minister (with David Owen as Foreign Secretary) was instrumental in winning that particular battle against the general constraints of defence resources and logistics.

The political astuteness that Callaghan and Owen attributed to their decision to despatch Royal Naval vessels in November 1977 might well have deterred a possible Argentine invasion, but it did not solve the Falklands problem.[69] The Callaghan Government continued to pursue a leaseback settlement with Argentina, but with one minor modification: the term of the leaseback would now span 75 years rather than 50 years. In order to counteract these proposals the Falklands lobby once again launched a public awareness campaign in the House of Commons and the national media. As one sympathetic reviewer noted, the lobby was determined to remind the British public that the Falklands were not going to be handed over 'to a country unable to govern itself and ruled by successive regimes distinguished by mounting intensity of torture and bloody violations of human rights'.[70]

According to an important study of the Falklands lobby, the period between 1977 and 1980 witnessed intense lobbying of Parliament as well as the creation of a new group called the Falkland Islands Research and Development Association (FIRDA). Determined to see the major recommendations of the Shackleton Report implemented, the UKFIC underwent an organisational transformation so that in future attention would be firmly concentrated on influencing policy-makers in Whitehall and Parliament. Sections of the new lobby, such as the FIRDA, devoted their efforts to developing cultural, commercial and social opportunities for Islanders. This institutional strengthening of the Falklands lobby paved the way for the Falkland Islands office, created in January 1977. The office was intended to act as an information centre and point of contact with interested parties engaged in high-profile campaigns such as the South Atlantic Fisheries proposal designed to encourage British firms to fish in the region. This initiative received some support from MPs and the media but the Callaghan Government was divided between on the one hand supporting declining fishing communities in Scotland due to the Cod War, while on the other hand developing a new industry in the remote Falklands.

The historic moment for the Falklands lobby came with the emergence of a new Conservative Government, headed by Margaret Thatcher, in May 1979. It has been argued that initially there was very little evidence of sustained interest in the Falklands and South Atlantic, as her administration was embroiled in other long-standing colonial disputes. The first two years in office witnessed a post-colonial settlement for Rhodesia/Zimbabwe, and Belize coupled with improved relations over Gibraltar under the 1980 Lisbon Agreement. As during the previous Labour Governments, perceptions of domestic economic vulnerability meant that commercial opportunities in Latin America were considered to be too significant vis-à-vis the Falklands problem. British exports to Argentina amounted to £172 million in 1980 and exports to Latin America had risen to over £1 billion by 1979. While the major export markets remained in continental Europe and the US, Thatcher was keen to promote further trade links with the South American continent.

When Nicholas Ridley, as the FCO minister responsible for the Americas, was instructed to hold talks with Argentine counterparts in 1979 and 1980, he took the opportunity to visit the Falkland Islands for the first time in July 1979 in order to ascertain the views of the community. In July 1980, after further talks in New York with an Argentine delegation, the Cabinet's Overseas Policy and Defence Committee recommended that the dispute should be settled on the basis of leaseback. Ridley returned to the Falklands in November 1980 in order to present the Islanders with three basic options: a joint administration of the Islands, a sovereignty freeze or a leaseback scheme. Under the leaseback scheme, Britain would formally transfer the sovereignty of the Falklands to Argentina and then 'lease' the Islands back for a period of possibly 50 years. According to some Islanders, the community was divided over the issue of leaseback but united in anger over the political and economic treatment of the community. Ridley returned to London and was promptly accused in the House of Commons of 'betraying' the Islanders and their 'way of life' by Conservative MPs such as Bernard Braine and Julian Amery, who championed the Falklands cause. They were not alone: the Liberal MP Russell Johnston, for example, also condemned the 'shameful schemes for getting rid of these Islands which have been festering in the Foreign Office for years'. Within days of Ridley's return, the leaseback proposal was in grave political danger of failing to convince members of the Thatcher Government that this was the solution to the Falklands dispute with Argentina.

Ironically, as Clive Ellerby has contended, the UKFIC was divided on leaseback and actually decided in late December 1980 to demand further information on the various options for resolving the territorial dispute.[71] Within the Falkland Islands too there was, according to the then editor of the local newspaper the *Penguin News*, racial prejudice accompanied by uncertainty as to whether leaseback represented the way forward in terms of long-term security and conflict resolution. As the newspaper noted in December 1979,

> Racist feelings also exist in the public. At a recent public meeting in Stanley the possibility of offering a home to several families of the Vietnamese 'boat people' was discussed and a large portion of speakers felt that 'we do not want to lumber ourselves with the same racial problems that are prevalent in the UK'. By maintaining our population of British origin, we are making a grave mistake and are developing a sense of bigoted racial superiority in our people. We desperately need people![72]

Some Islanders argued that those on the economically depressed West Falkland as well as farm managers in East Falkland were in favour of such a settlement recognising the need for new economic investment. The *Penguin News* provoked further debate when it published a 'provocative' editorial in February 1980:

> We can trust the British government as little as we trust the Argentine government and feeble cries of 'Keep the Falklands British' and other cliches will win us no support. Instead we should look to ourselves and proclaim the Falklands belong to us and not to Britain, Argentina or any other foreign country. We could set ourselves the greatest goal that a people could have – independence.[73]

However, in interviews with the author, many native-born Islanders recalled an influential radio broadcast by Councillor Adrian Monk on 31 December 1980 when he announced that 'I think the whole campaign [leaseback] stinks…Don't be misled. Don't be worried about the consequences of saying "We are British". Our country [sic] will remain British.'[74] Monk, with his long experience of local government, proved to be a powerful source of inspiration for the anti-leaseback contingent within the Falkland Islands. In a small community, an articulate and passionate individual such as Monk can be enormously influential. By January 1981, the executive and legislative councils had rejected the leaseback proposal but concurred that talks should be held with Argentina. After further discussion within the British

Cabinet in January 1981, it was agreed that the aim of the talks should be to prevent any Argentine aggression towards the Falkland Islands while at the same time encouraging the Islanders to reconsider their opposition to leaseback. The FCO appeared to have developed a 'policy' based on appeasing Argentina, in combination with attempting to persuade sceptical MPs that leaseback could serve as the basis for an eventual settlement by ending the costly dispute with Argentina and improving trading and political opportunities in Latin America.

The 1981 local elections in the Falklands revealed that opinions had hardened against any sovereignty negotiations at the same time as Argentina announced a rejection of the sovereignty freeze proposal. With support of MPs in London, the Stanley branch of the FIC demanded the complete rejection of leaseback. As a consequence, the Falklands lobby effectively derailed Anglo–Argentine negotiations not only by lobbying but also by exposing the substantial inadequacies of British policy towards the South Atlantic and the Falkland Islands. According to the Falklands lobby, successive British Governments were neither inclined to enforce a post-colonial settlement nor willing to invest in the future development of a remote colony. The Islanders were left vulnerable to aggressive military reaction, as the Argentine military regime became ever more conscious of high-profile anniversaries such as the one-hundred-and-fiftieth year of British permanent settlement (or 'occupation', in Argentine terms) in the Falkland Islands due in 1983.

SUMMARY

The link between patriotism, nationalism, xenophobia, race and British identity was made well before the 1982 military campaign. Anti-colonial resolutions combined with changing definitions of British citizenship played their part in contributing to a siege mentality in the Falkland Islands. The Falklands lobby used short-hand references such as 'loyal' and 'kith and kin' to signify the 'white' identity of the community not only to rail against Argentina but protest against its systematic exclusion as British subjects. It is doubly ironic, therefore, that Thatcher should have described the Falkland Islanders as a loyal 'island race' in April 1982 because, as Paul Gilroy has argued: 'Phrases like the "island race" and "the bulldog breed" vividly convey the manner in which this nation is represented in terms, which are simultaneously biological and cultural'.[75] Islands can and do provide the perfect conditions for invoking cultural difference because of their apparently distinct territory, which could be easily defined and defended from unwelcome external influences. However, unlike the case presented by the political right in the UK, this racial imagination was complicated by the fact that the predominantly European settler population of Argentina had to be represented as a cultural and political rather than racial threat. Armed with military metaphors, the Falklands lobby used the language of war and invasion to warn of the dangers posed by a near neighbour to the geographical and cultural boundaries of the small community. And as members of the Falklands lobby reflected to this author, if Argentina's footballers were in any way representative of the Argentine polity, British observers should have been more sympathetic to the plight of the Falkland Islanders.

NOTES ON CHAPTER 7

1   Peregrine Worsthorne, writing in the *Sunday Telegraph*, 23 May 1982 and quoted in P. Gilroy, *There ain't no Black in the Union Jack* (London, Hutchinson, 1987), p. 51.

2   Interview with a Falkland Islander, 20 April 2000.

3   PRO CO 78/241/1. Letter to the Secretary of State for the Colonies from Falkland Islands residents, dated 4 June 1948.

4   Gilroy, *There ain't no Black in the Union Jack*, p. 55.

5   PRO CO 78/241/1. Letter from Governor Cardinall to the Colonial Office, dated 25 September 1945.

6   This idea was not unique to the Falklands, as political representatives in Malta also proposed a similar course of action before its independence in the 1960s. I owe this point to Leslie Hepple.

7   PRO CO 78/221/2. Report on the Legislative Council Reconstitution, dated 2 March 1945.

8   Cited in G. Drower, *Britain's Dependent Territories: A Fistful of Islands* (Aldershot, Dartmouth, 1992), p. 20.

9   PRO CO 78/213/3. Report of the Legislative Council meeting, dated 20 October 1948.

10   PRO CO 78 241/1. Letter from Miles Clifford to J. Bennett of the Colonial Office, dated 17 May 1948.

11   PRO CO 78 241/1. Telegram from Miles Clifford to the Colonial Office, dated 3 July 1948.

12   PRO CO 78 241/1. Letter from Miles Clifford to the Secretary of State for the Colonies, dated 17 June 1948.

13   But as one author has claimed, this is a problem common to many small islands: see S. Royle, *A Geography of Islands* (London, Routledge 2001).

14   *Daily Express*, 'Islanders say: Sack Governor', 26 July 1948.

15   PRO CO 78 241/1. Letter from Falkland Islands Petition Committee to the Secretary of State for the Colonies, dated 30 September 1948.

16   PRO CO 78 241/1. Letter from Miles Clifford to J. Martin of the Colonial Office, dated 1 October 1948.

17   PRO CO 78 241/1. Letter from Miles Clifford to the Secretary of State for the Colonies, dated 26 October 1948.

18   PRO CO 78 241/1. Minute prepared by J. Bennett, dated 19 June 1948.

19   *Falkland Islands Weekly News* vol. 6 no 10, dated 11 March 1949.

20   PRO CO 936/30/3. Minute prepared by J. Bennett. Emphasis has been added to this extract.

21   PRO CAB 134/1555. Letter from Harold Macmillan to the Lord President of the Council, dated 28 January 1957.

22   PRO PREM 11/2617. Letter from Norman Brook to Macmillan, dated 31 July 1957. The papers generated by the review were, according to Brook, intended 'primarily as reference material, to give ministers a factual background against which any particular problem can be considered'. Brook had proposed the creation of a Cabinet Committee on Colonial Policy in August 1955 in order to help ministers prepare for post-colonial development. The committee was composed of senior officials from the Colonial Office, the Commonwealth Relations Office and

the FO, and eventually dissolved in December 1961. For further analysis, see D. McIntyre, 'The admission of small states to the Commonwealth', *Journal of Imperial and Commonwealth History* 24 (1996): pp. 244–77.

23 PRO CAB 134/1551. Colonial Office paper on Future Constitutional Development in the Colonies, dated May 1957. The 76-page report divided the British Empire into geographical sectors such as the 'South Atlantic'. It was noted that the Falkland Islands received £50,000 in colonial and development welfare investment for the 1957 financial year.

24 M. Stewart, *Life and Labour* (London, Sidgwick and Jackson, 1980), pp. 174–5.

25 K. Paul, *Whitewashing Britain: Race and Citizenship in the Post-war Era* (London, Cornell University Press, 1994). See also A. M. Smith, *New Right Discourse on Race and Sexuality 1968–1990* (Minneapolis MN, University of Minnesota Press, 1994).

26 J. Solomos, *Race and Racism in Contemporary Britain* (London, Macmillan, 1989).

27 Cited in Paul, *Whitewashing Britain: Race and Citizenship in the Post-war Era*, p. 55.

28 I owe these details to the recollections of Lady Haskard, who was present on the Falkland Islands at the time of the Condor incident.

29 The story was told to me by Lady Haskard, part of a detailed interview with her and the former Governor of the Falkland Islands, Sir Cosmo Haskard, held on 3 April 2001.

30 I am grateful to Lady Haskard for sharing with me her memories of the 1966 Condor incident. Governor Haskard was away on official business in London at the time of the incident.

31 PRO CAB 128/41. Record of the minutes of the Cabinet meeting held on 29 September 1966.

32 US Archives Telegram from the US Embassy in Buenos Aires to the Department of State, dated 18 November 1967.

33 PRO FO 7/154. Letter from Haskard to J. Bennett, dated 15 December 1967. Haskard noted his 'stupefaction, dismay and anger' over the proposed memorandum of understanding.

34 I am grateful to Sir Cosmo Haskard for sharing with me his recollections of his time in office. He was appointed Governor in 1964 after a lengthy spell with the Colonial Service based in Malawi (formerly Nyasaland).

35 PRO FO 7/154. Letter from Haskard to J. Bennett, dated 21 October 1967.

36 Private information from a former FO official who does not wish to be identified.

37 PRO FCO 42/42. Telegram from Haskard to Galsworthy of the Commonwealth Relations Office, dated 19 January 1968.

38 PRO FCO 42/94. Report by D. M. Summerhayes to Sir Michael Cresswell on his visit to the Falkland Islands, 16–24 January 1968.

39 *Falkland Islands Monthly Review*, June 1967.

40 *Falkland Islands Monthly Review*, March 1968. Radio Statement by Haskard via Falkland Islands Broadcasting Service, 22 February 1968.

41 PRO FCO 42/42. Telegram from Haskard to the Commonwealth Office, dated 21 February 1968 expressed the dismay of Councillors over the lack of consultation by Government departments.

42 This 'manifesto or plea for help' was published by the *Times* on 12 March 1968. See also the *Times*, 'Doubts felt in the Falklands', 29 March 1968. Barton was the former manager of the FIC until his retirement in 1964, Goss was the leader of the Falkland Islands Trade Union, Miller and Bonner were both farm managers.

43 The definitive study of the Falklands lobby remains C. Ellerby, *British Interests in the Falkland Islands: Economic Development, the Falklands Lobby and the Sovereignty Dispute 1945–1989* (unpublished DPhil thesis, University of Oxford, 1990). See also C. Ellerby, 'The role of the Falklands lobby 1968–1990', in A. Danchev (ed.), *A Matter of Life and Death* (Oxford, Oxford University Press, 1992), pp. 85–108.

44 K. Dodds, 'Enframing the Falklands: identity, landscape and the 1982 South Atlantic War', *Environment and Planning D: Society and Space* 16 (1998): pp. 733–56.

45 Letter from Haskard to the author, dated 23rd May 2001.

46 Quoted in Gilroy, *There ain't no Black in the Union Jack*, p. 82.

47 *Falkland Islands Monthly Review*, April 1968.

48 *Falkland Islands Monthly Review*, May 1968.

49 *Falkland Islands Monthly Review*, May 1968. Radio Statement by Councillor Barton via Falkland Islands Broadcasting Service, 31 March 1968.

50 *Falkland Islands Monthly Review*, May 1968 and *Falkland Islands Gazette Supplement*, July 1968.

51 J. Madeley, *Diego Garcia: A Contrast to the Falklands* (London, Minority Rights Group, 1985). There is some evidence that senior Labour-party figures such as Callaghan were in 1968 dismissive of the strategic and political significance of the Falkland Islands. See K. Morgan, *Callaghan: A Life* (Oxford, Oxford University Press, 1997), p. 460.

52 It is important to remember that Labour Governments in the 1960s and 1970s did not enjoy substantial majorities in the House of Commons, and the Falklands and Gibraltar questions could and did generate substantial cross-party alliances.

53 P. Ziegler, *Wilson* (London, Weidenfeld and Nicholson, 1993). The quote is taken from p. 343.

54 *Falkland Islands Monthly Review*, June 1968. Recorded minutes of the meeting of the Legislative Council, 20 May 1968.

55 *Daily Express*, 'Britain gives in to Argentine demands – Falklands sell out', 20 September 1968.

56 PRO FCO 7/186. Letter from P. Mansfield of the British Embassy in Buenos Aires to C. Wallace of the American Department of the FO, dated 23 July 1968.

57 The photograph was published in the *Daily Express* on 9 October 1968. The photograph was of a protest rally against the negotiations with Argentina. The rally was held on 2 October 1968.

58 *Falkland Islands Monthly Review*, October 1968. Minutes of meeting of the Legislative Council, 16 and 18 October 1968.

59 Letter from Lady Haskard to her parents, Sir Robert and Lady Stanley, dated 14 November 1968. I am grateful to Lady Haskard for access to her private letters.

60 *Falkland Islands Monthly Review*, December 1968 and *Falkland Islands Gazette Supplement*, November 1968.

61 Letter from Lady Haskard to her parents, dated 28 November 1968.

62 Author interview with Lord Chalfont, 23 October 2001.

63 PRO FCO 42/94. 'Report by Lord Chalfont on the Visit to the Falkland Islands, 23–28 November 1968', 5 December 1968.

64 The Guillebaud Report (1967) on the Falkland Islands economy had already warned that the sheep-based economy was in long-term decline, and was critical of the paternalistic approach of the FIC. Guillebaud was a Professor of Economics at the University of Cambridge, and he also prepared another report for the FO

entitled 'The Falklands and Argentina'. Significantly, he advocated subsidised immigration from the UK and downplayed links with Argentina.

65 Author interview with F. Mitchell, 4 July 2001.

66 Ellerby, *British Interests in the Falkland Islands: Economic Development, the Falklands Lobby and the Sovereignty Dispute 1945-1989*. I owe the basic details of the Falklands lobby to this detailed account, which is based on the archives of various groups concerned with the fate of the Falkland Islands.

67 The FIEC was not funded by the FIC, relying instead on private donations.

68 The Defence Review was carried out in December 1974 and cited in Dockrill, *British Defence Policy Since 1945*.

69 Parliament was not officially informed of the deployment until Callaghan acknowledged the policy decision in March 1982.

70 J. Hickey, 'Keep the Falklands British? The principle of self-determination of dependent territories', *Inter-American Economic Affairs* 31 (1977): pp. 77–88.

71 Ellerby, 'The role of the Falklands Lobby, 1968–1990', A *Matter of Life and Death*, pp. 85–108.

72 *Penguin News*, 'Racial prejudice is disturbingly common in the Falklands', 24 December 1979.

73 *Penguin News*, 'Editorial', 7 February 1980.

74 Quoted in Ellerby 'The role of the Falklands Lobby 1968–1990', p. 93.

75 Gilroy, *There ain't no Black in the Union Jack*, p. 45.

8

Dots on the Map

I do not believe that the Falkland Islands can continue to exist for very many years, as they are presently constituted. I believe one day that the Falkland Islands may be prepared to choose Argentine sovereignty. We must at all costs avoid giving the impression that we want to get rid of them, since that would set up precisely the reaction we would want to avoid.[1]

My purpose was to develop trade links, joint exploration, improvement of communications, as well as educational and social links. One problem was the government [in Argentina] seemed to change rather frequently, and the agreements we thought we had made with one administration were obliterated when the next took over. This policy of creating closer links was of course allied to a firm determination not to promote any incursion on the sovereignty of the Falkland Islands, and as my autobiography recounts, this was made clear to successive Argentine foreign ministers.[2]

INTRODUCTION

That a scattered group of islands and enclaves could induce major foreign-policy issues was recognised over 20 years ago by Ted Rowlands, a junior minister at the FCO under the Callaghan administration:

Jim Callaghan was very clear about my role...he wanted me to watch the 'dots on the map', as he called them. He said that the big issues of foreign policy very rarely bring governments down, but there are 'dots on the map' that create enormous embarrassments...if not bring governments down...I was responsible for the relationship between Belize and Guatemala – we nearly went to war twice in four-and-a-half years – and, of course, for the Falkland Islands. If you read the history of ministerial involvement over the Falklands, it has one recurring pattern. On the whole it blew up, and sometimes blew down ministers.[3]

Regardless of whether Rowlands or FCO officials maintained a vigilant eye on the South Atlantic, distance, logistics and limited resources would dictate their response.

The Royal Navy's HMS *Protector* and HMS *Endurance* were indispensable for the defence of the South Atlantic Empire because they patrolled not only to the inhabited Falklands but also to the remote and uninhabited South Sandwich Islands.[4] Having undertaken several journeys across the South Atlantic by ship, the author experienced at first hand the conditions and distances separating the islands. It takes at least two days to sail from the Falklands to South Georgia.

Successive British Governments sought to exercise cost savings and imperial reform in the period between 1968 and 1982. The prospects for South Georgia evoked debate within Whitehall in 1968 after the demise of the Norwegian whaling operations. The question of the Falklands continued unabated but was complicated by Anglo–Argentine negotiations intent on establishing closer reliance between the Islanders and Argentina. It was widely believed that the Falklands were economically moribund when the Wilson Government commissioned the Labour peer Lord Shackleton, to produce a report on the future prospects of the South Atlantic region. The Shackleton Report (1976) subsequently did not endorse this pessimistic view but recommended a host of new initiatives, including the construction of a major runway in Stanley. But, as Callaghan recognised, any initiative relating to the Falklands also had to contend with Argentine–Chilean territorial competition:

> At one stage during the period of the Labour government it seemed quite possible that the Argentine junta would use force to occupy the Chilean territory of Tierra del Fuego and the islands in the Beagle Channel. The constant manoeuvring among the leaders of Argentina's armed forces heightened the possibility that an ambitious service chief might lash out at the Falklands in frustration at Argentina's lack of success over the Beagle Channel dispute.[5]

Ultimately, British indecision and procrastination was overtaken by the emergence of an Argentine military regime committed to a programme of territorial aggrandisement and resource nationalism. The timing was unfortunate for the Falkland Islands community, which bore the brunt of Britain's indecision and perhaps understandable reluctance to invest in maintaining the South Atlantic Empire.

MAINTAINING SOUTH GEORGIA

When the South Shetland Islands, the South Orkney Islands and the Antarctic Peninsula were incorporated into British Antarctic territory in 1962, the remaining elements of the FID, South Georgia and South Sandwich Islands, were excluded. Located over 800 miles southeast of the Falklands, Norwegian whaling companies operating in the waters around South Georgia created the main settlement of Grytviken in 1904. The revenue generated from whaling licences even helped to fund the activities of the FIDS in other parts of the far south. Unlike the South Sandwich Islands, a permanent Norwegian and British population was stationed on the island, but with the decline in whaling Treasury officials viewed the administration of South Georgia as a financial burden.

The future of South Georgia came to the fore in 1967 when the Commonwealth Office became embroiled in a dispute with the Treasury over the political and scientific rationale. The terms of the debate were set out in a letter from John Sugg of the Commonwealth Office to Haskard, dated 5 January 1967: 'It has since been accepted by the Treasury that it would be premature to withdraw the administration from South Georgia while Anglo–Argentine discussions on the Falkland Islands continue, since to do so would, we believe weaken our position in these discussions.[6]

As a dependency of the Falkland Islands, the FCO argued that South Georgia could not be abandoned in the wake of uncertainties over the Falkland Islands. This line of reasoning was not universally accepted within Whitehall and a crisis over staff replacement provoked further dissent on the geopolitical importance of South Georgia. Unable to find a replacement doctor for the 35-strong British community on the island, an official attached to the Ministry of Overseas Development questioned in a rather exotic manner the need for this remote dependency in a letter to the Commonwealth Office:

> It may seem ludicrous to suggest that my very small medical tail should wave your imperial dog (which may, I believe, be apprehensive of a take-over of this particular kennel by an Argentine breed), but I cannot but think it is a waste of the services of even one man – who just scraped through the Licentiate of the Apothecaries' Hall of Dublin and has since taken to the bottle, to send him to this station, and anyway we can't get him. What are they governing? And are we likely to want to sustain South Georgia as one of Her Majesty's Dominions for much longer?[7]

Stung by this expression of dissent, the Commonwealth Office reminded the official saddled with the troublesome task of finding a new doctor for South Georgia that: 'Argentina also claims South Georgia and might well occupy that island if we left it. This would obviously weaken our position over the Falklands.[8] Roberts and Fuchs were instrumental in eventually securing agreement that South Georgia would not be abandoned in the wake of Norwegian whaling. John Heap, who joined Roberts in the FO Research Department, further assisted them. Over long lunches at Roberts's favourite Italian restaurant in central London, a rear-guard action was fought in order to resist Treasury pressure for financial savings in the South Atlantic and Antarctic.[9] In his recollections of the period 1964–77, Heap recalled the many debates and negotiations between the FCO, the Treasury and the BAS over Britain's future role in the Antarctic and Southern Ocean.[10] While attention centred on the Falkland Islands, there existed even in 1968–9 still a real danger that Britain might withdraw from South Georgia due to persistent balance-of-payment crises. The BAS's incorporation into the National Environment Research Council (NERC) in 1967 was no guarantee that funding would be preserved, and some scientists were privately sceptical of the scientific value of a research station on South Georgia, especially if located close to former whaling stations.[11] Persistent pressure from the Treasury ensured that scientific productivity in combination with managerial efficiency featured strongly in the BAS's strategic remit. The administrative and financial transfer of South Georgia to the BAS in 1969 was actively challenged in a letter from Kennedy of the Treasury to Sugg of the Commonwealth Office dated 2 January 1968:

> There is also surely some merit in the thought that if we removed our administration we should not only avoid the possibility of conflict with Argentina but could quietly ignore the event should they seek to take physical possession of the Island [South Georgia] ... All the economic arguments are in favour of giving

up this administration…We ought to make a more realistic appreciation of the need to maintain our uneconomic foothold on this territory.[12]

Whitehall officials too were anxious to address the financial and political costs of maintaining a British presence in the wider South Atlantic. While Antarctic Treaty consultative parties had agreed to extend the living resource management of the Antarctic, there were no plans to enlargen the Antarctic Treaty north to include South Georgia. In other words, the British administration of South Georgia was not going to be protected by Article IV. The Antarctic Committee of the NERC agreed in October 1967 to support the creation of a new research base in South Georgia to accommodate these geopolitical and legal conditions.[13] After months of interdepartmental negotiation, the Treasury agreed to contribute an additional £45,000 to facilitate the transfer of administration of South Georgia, in the form of a new BAS base. It was recognised by the Commonwealth Office that 'a scientific base would I believe suit the UK's purposes very well and provided we are committed and believe we are, to maintaining our presence on South Georgia for the next few years.'[14] The reference to the 'next few years' was critical because the debates over South Georgia were unfolding at the same time as Anglo–Argentine negotiations were seeking to transfer sovereignty over the Falkland Islands. In the event of such a sovereignty transfer in favour of Argentina, it was proposed that the claim to South Georgia would be dropped. While there are declassified files of the FCO to confirm this point, it was mooted by Roberts that Britain's Antarctic operations could have used South Georgia as a new polar gateway.

COMMUNICATING WITH THE FALKLAND ISLANDS

If there was one event which helped to set in motion events that were to lead to the Argentine invasion of the Falklands in April 1982, it was the negotiations culminating in the 1971 Joint Communications Agreement. Some British and American commentators have pointed to the Argentine military takeover in 1976 and the proposed withdrawal of HMS *Endurance* in 1981 as trigger events, but it was the impact of the agreement which was the precursor.[15] Interdepartmental records for the late 1960s recognised that greater communication links with Argentina might galvanise further discussions over sovereignty.[16] Prior to 1971, there were no direct air or sea links between the Islands and Argentina, besides which the Islanders were often reluctant to enter the Republic because of fears that they would be liable for military service and taxation. Argentine citizens could travel on the RMS *Darwin* to the Islands providing they held a visa, approved by the Governor of the Falkland Islands. Contact with the South American mainland was sustained by a regular monthly shipping service from Stanley to Montevideo in Uruguay and an occasional shipping service from the Chilean port of Punta Arenas. In December 1970, the FIC (as the managers of the shipping service) gave notice of its intention to withdraw the RMS *Darwin* at the end of 1971 because of mounting financial costs.[17] Once this withdrawal was implemented, the Falkland Islands would be faced with the prospect of almost total isolation.[18]

By November 1969, the British Government had approached its Argentine counterpart, and it was agreed that talks would be held in July 1970 to discuss possible communication services between the Islands and the Argentine mainland. In the Legislative Council of the Falklands, Haskard noted, 'The announcement on the 21st November that special talks are to take place in 1970 with a view to reaching agreement on practical measures for promoting free communications and movement in both directions between the Falkland Islands and the coast'. In a helpful comment he also stressed that the 'Communications talks are to be about communications [rather than about formal sovereignty]'.[19] However, in spite of the official remit, the subsequent negotiations were symptomatic of the persistent British indecisiveness and the equally determined attempts of the Falkland Islands community to retain assurances that Britain would not settle the sovereignty dispute with Argentina. This desire to stall sovereignty negotiations was fuelled by fears that due to falling reserves, from £464,000 to £359,000, as a consequence of a declining wool clip, Britain might be willing to 'sacrifice' the Islanders.

On the eve of the communication negotiations with Argentina, the Executive Council nominated two Councillors, Goss and Pitaluga (who was already in the UK at the time) to represent the interests of the Falkland Islands at the official meetings. The condition of the Falkland Islands economy remained weak with a budget deficit of over £100,000 predicted for financial year 1970/1 and the continued uncertainties over the future of RMS *Darwin*. Haskard argued in the Legislative Council that 'by our own exertions we can grasp advantage from the environment in which geography and indeed history have together placed us'.[20] Calling for the development of a fishing industry and tourism, this agenda appeared out of kilter with the negotiations which were leading to an agreement which would make the Falklands dependent upon Argentina for basic services rather than encouraging greater Government or private-sector initiative. After six years as one of the most proactive Governors of the Falkland Islands, Haskard retired from the post in September 1970, much to the relief of the Latin American Department of the FCO. In February 1971, the FCO asked the firm Peat, Marwick and Mitchell to survey the state of Falkland Islands communications in order to generate some clear recommendations based on the needs of the community.[21] According to the new Governor, Toby Lewis, the proposed communications agreement would address the key issue of sovereignty:

> HMG is insisting that any Agreement with the Argentines on communications shall be conditional upon an arrangement such as the 'sovereignty umbrella'. Equally the Argentines are maintaining the stand that an agreement on a 'sovereignty umbrella' basis should be conditional on agreement upon comm-unications. HMG sees the whole communications exercise as a way of defusing the sovereignty issue and helping the Islands without any concessions on sovereignty or their Britishness. I was not appointed Governor and Commander in Chief of these Islands with a view to assisting in disposing of part of the Queen's realm.[22]

Lewis's statement to the Legislative Council was highly pertinent in the sense that he identified succinctly the roots of British complacency. The so-called 'sovereignty umbrella' was a diplomatic fiction used by British and Argentine negotiators to make progress on the communication talks. The sovereignty umbrella, which preserved the legal positions of both sides, did nothing to facilitate the outstanding sovereignty dispute.

In July 1971, after opening discussions in London, the second round of negotiations moved to Buenos Aires, where both Governments addressed in detail the external communication arrangements and supplementary issues such as the travel documentation required by Islanders and Argentines moving between the two places. This was an extremely sensitive geopolitical issue because the sovereignty of the Falkland Islands formed a backdrop to the communication negotiations. According to successive post-war Argentine Governments, 'commuting' between Argentina and the Falklands was a domestic matter. Therefore, there would be no need for Islanders travelling to Argentina to carry their passports either. Moreover, the Argentine Post Office routinely defaced any mail 'wrongly' labelled 'Falkland Islands', and Islanders frequently received mail with tampered address labels.[23] Under the sovereignty umbrella, all flights between the Islands and the mainland would be insulated from formal sovereignty considerations.

After several weeks of tense negotiations, the Joint Communications Agreement was settled in August 1971 and the Argentine Government agreed to establish a regular weekly air service for passengers, mail and freight. Moreover, it was agreed that an airfield in Stanley would be adapted in order to allow a regular air service. In return the British Government was to create a regular shipping service between the Falkland Islands and Argentina to compensate for the withdrawal of the RMS *Darwin*. With regard to the movement of Falkland Islanders, the Argentine authorities agreed to create travel documents (the 'white card') to allow free movement within Argentina and guarantee exemption from military service. A similar arrangement was created for the circulation of Argentine passengers between the mainland and Falklands. In a further attempt to improve relations between the two parties, Argentina promised to provide assistance to the Falkland Islands community in the fields of health, agriculture and education, in combination with technical co-operation. Both Britain and Argentina agreed that a Buenos Aires-based consultative committee should be created in order to ensure that all the interested parties (including the Falkland Islanders) implemented the provisions.

Notwithstanding the wide-ranging nature of the agreement, the implementation of its provisions proved highly controversial in the Falkland Islands.[24] One area of contention was the LADE (Linea Argentina del Estado) air service, which permitted the Argentines to operate from a temporary airfield in the Falklands under a separate agreement signed in May 1972. By November 1972, LADE had introduced a new air link to replace the amphibian service which had operated since the agreement. The Argentine airline also established a sales office in Stanley to co-ordinate the service between the airfield in Stanley and the Patagonian town of Comodoro Rivadavia. Over the next decade, the LADE service attracted considerable criticism in the Falkland Islands, because fares, cargo availability and flight frequency altered as the crisis worsened between Britain and Argentina. In 1976, for instance, the return fare between Stanley and Comodoro Rivadavia was suddenly increased to £200, from a previous high of £118. While the British Government later successfully pressurised the Argentine authorities to reduce this increase, LADE in turn reduced the flight schedule from a twice-weekly to a weekly service in April 1981. While some Islanders made good use of the air service, accusations abounded in the Islands that these 'irregularities' were being deliberately implemented in order to expose Islanders to the realities of their relationship with Argentina.

Despite the vagaries of the LADE air service, a growing number of Islanders were able to have direct contact with Argentina for educational, health, recreational and commercial purposes. Between 1972 and 1975, some 30 Falkland Islands children attended schools in Argentina, but by 1978 the numbers had declined due to the deterioration of the political and security situation of Argentina. Aware that their dependence on Argentina had grown since the Joint Communications Agreement, many Islanders still resented the white-card system. In Stanley, LADE was responsible for issuing the white cards to Falkland Islanders wishing to travel to Argentina, and the Malvinas Department of the Ministry of Foreign Affairs in Buenos Aires was charged with arrangements in the Republic. While the white card was supposed to remove any restrictions on travel within Argentina, many Islanders reported that they had been subjected to considerable delays by the Argentine immigration service. This irritation with the white card system was later to be recorded by Shackleton and his team in their economic survey of the Falkland Islands (1976). In contrast, the number of Argentine visitors increased markedly in the 1970s especially on cruise ships attracted to Stanley because of a favourable peso/sterling exchange rate. In 1976, over 6000 tourists (mainly Argentine) visited the Falkland Islands, often on one-day excursions, and took the opportunity, according to Islanders, to purchase the entire stock of consumer goods from the FIC store in Stanley.

This increased contact with the Republic resulted in a growing presence of Argentines in Stanley, where LADE provided housing for its representatives. As the 1980 Falkland Islands census revealed, 30 Argentines (mainly representatives of LADE, Yacimientos Petroliferos Fiscales [YPF] and the armed forces) were living in the Islands at the time. The Argentine navy regularly visited to deliver oil drums to Stanley. While the agreement stipulated that Argentina had the right to station personnel to manage its installations, it was vague as to how many individuals should be involved. Increasing dependency on Argentina intensified suspicions of the intent and purpose of the Argentines stationed on the Islands rather than fostering tolerance and goodwill. The Joint Communications Agreement was a political disaster, as it had raised Argentine expectations that the sovereignty question would be solved rather than simply managed through co-operation in transport and energy provision.

THE 1976 SHACKLETON REPORT AND THE FUTURE OF THE FALKLAND ISLANDS

In an interview with the author, the late Lord Edward Shackleton admitted that he had never been very interested in the Antarctic and the Falkland Islands.[25] As a Labour minister under the first Wilson Government, he recalled an amusing incident in the Cabinet when Wilson asked 'Does anyone live in South Georgia?' Shackleton was the only one to respond to the question and offered a succinct if incorrect answer: 'No but my father is buried there'. Wilson's question had been posed in 1965 when the future of the BAS was undergoing negotiations in the aftermath of the ratification of the 1959 Antarctic Treaty. The second Wilson Government confronted a situation in the South Atlantic and Antarctic much changed by the legacy of the outgoing Conservative Government's Joint Communications Agreement with Argentina. While successive Governments were eager to explore closer links with the Falkland Islands and Argentina, no-one in Whitehall was able to persuade that community to transfer its political allegiance. A political settlement with Argentina would have suited not only the FCO, as the Islands were consistently viewed as a low strategic priority, but also the Treasury, which was eager to seek financial savings. Despite Argentine claims to the contrary, there were few endeavours to assess the resource and strategic potential of the South Atlantic region.

Significantly, after the merger of the Foreign and Commonwealth Offices in 1968, the Falklands was transferred from the Gibraltar and South Atlantic Department to the Latin American Department after a short spell with the West Indian and Atlantic Department (1972–5). Therefore, the Falklands were now not only administratively isolated from other contested small colonies such as Gibraltar, but also being monitored by Latin American specialists who, as the Falklands lobby believed, had little political sympathy for them and their desire to resist a transfer of sovereignty to Argentina. As Penelope Tremayne suggested in the *Sunday Times* on 25 September 1977:

> The Falklands have undoubtedly suffered from the amalgamation of the Commonwealth Office with the Foreign Office; passing under the control of the Latin American department whose main care is to foster easy relations with those states, not to defend a handful of people's rights to self-determination. Perhaps too, against what were thought larger trade interests, a couple of thousand remote and dour intransigents [sic] were rated expendable.[26]

Frank Mitchell, a former director of the FIC, noted to this author that this shift was more than simply an administrative reform. Before the dissolution of the Colonial Office, he and his fellow directors enjoyed regular and sympathetic contact with the Secretary of State for the Colonies. After 1968, the mood changed and it became apparent that the Falklands were now considered to be a 'burden' that had to be disposed of quickly so that Anglo–Argentine and Anglo–Latin American diplomatic and commercial relations did not suffer unduly.[27]

Despite the apparent improvement in relations with Argentina (following the 1971 Joint Communications Agreement), the co-operative spirit was prejudiced with the return of Perón as President in October 1973. In a manner reminiscent of his first Government in the late 1940s and early 1950s, Perón wasted little opportunity in reminding the British and the wider international community of Argentina's grievance. Armed with UN Resolution 2065, the Argentine Foreign Minister, Vignes, reported to the UN in October 1973 that the Falklands were an 'intolerable anachronism'. Perón's unexpected death in July 1974 did not dampen speculation in Argentina that radical action over the disputed Islands was forthcoming. In November 1974, the Argentine congress witnessed calls to the new Government to suspend Argentina's provision of transport and fuel supplies to the Islands.

The Joint Communications Agreement was beginning to unravel by the mid-1970s as Argentina sought to exploit the political advantage over a vulnerable and isolated Falkland Islands community. As Foreign Secretary under Wilson, Callaghan was compelled to inform Vignes in September 1974 that Britain would counter any military aggression against the Islands. Throughout this period of tentative and sometimes fraught negotiations, Callaghan – as Foreign Secretary and later as Prime Minister – had, according to his biographer, repeatedly 'affirmed the Falklands' sovereign desire to remain British … and had taken the precaution to obtain Kissinger's goodwill on the Falklands issue. On 13 December 1975, the US Secretary of State assured him, 'We shall do nothing to embarrass you.'[28] Despite political pressure from Buenos Aires, it was clear that successive US administrations were not prepared to jeopardise Anglo–American relations for the sake of Argentina and an eventual solution of the Falklands question.

In an attempt to explore the future potential of the Falkland Islands and Anglo–Argentine collaboration, the British Government approached Shackleton, who was then employed as deputy chairman of Rio Tinto Zinc, in order to commission an economic survey of the Islands. As with those earlier economic surveys commissioned by the Central Economic Planning Staff in the late 1940s, emphasis was to be placed on past performances and future aspirations.[29] The timing of the request (October 1975) was significant, given Argentina's continued disruption of the Joint Communications Agreement coupled with a series of ownership changes to the FIC. Allegations of 'asset-stripping' were rife in the Falklands as Charringtons Industrial Holdings acquired control from Slater Walker Securities in 1973. The Falkland Islands wool-based economy was in decline and the budget surplus of £116,000 (1973–4) had been reduced to £68,000 in the financial year 1974/5. Shackleton was under no illusions as to why he had been approached by the FCO. It was hoped that, as the son of the distinguished polar explorer Sir Ernest Shackleton, his eventual report would be invested with considerable prestige and significance. While Shackleton admitted to the author that the 'Falkland Islands were pretty blank to me', he was also aware that the FCO hoped that his study would conclude that there was 'no economic future' for the Falkland Islands unless they collaborated closely with Argentina.

After an offer of £5000 by the Wilson Government to Rio Tinto Zinc in lieu of absence from his post, Shackleton gathered a team of experts, including an oil economist alongside animal husbandry and fisheries specialists. Bob Storey, a research and development officer for the Highlands and Islands Development Board, was appointed to conduct a study of social research. Before travelling to the Falklands, the team visited the Shetland Islands in order to explore how another remote British community negotiated not only geographical isolation but also apparent economic decline.[30] While the Shetlands were not a political analogue in the sense that their ownership was not disputed, the visit was deemed an essential part of the research preparations.

Just before the planned departure to the Falkland Islands, Lord Shackleton was asked by the FCO whether he would be prepared to include an Argentine team member for the duration of the research visit in order to secure political goodwill.[31] His refusal to co-operate provoked the Argentine Government to retaliate by refusing his team entry into Argentina.[32] As a consequence, Lord Shackleton and his team (which included a representative from the FCO) travelled via a co-operative Brazil and then had to be airlifted on to HMS *Endurance* for the final leg of the journey to the Falkland Islands.[33]

On arrival in January 1976, the party spent four weeks researching the community and its economic and social potential. The sovereignty dispute was recognised as central and the report, when published in July 1976, noted that 'the absence of a settlement could well inhibit the full development of the Islands'.[34] Major recommendations ranged from the development of South Atlantic fisheries to the contention that the runway then being constructed at Stanley should be extended to allow for long-haul flights from the South American mainland and even Ascension Island in the mid-Atlantic. British media coverage of the report tended to concentrate either on the living and non-living resources around the Falkland Islands or on the future role of Argentina in any development of the Islands. Shackleton was clear in his own mind that his priority was strategic: 'I was anxious to give a military capability to the Islands' and deliberately placed the latter recommendation in the earliest stages of the report.[35] While this element was rejected emphatically by the Cabinet's Defence and Overseas Policy Committee in December 1976, co-operation with Argentina was accepted as vital for future development.

It was also recognised that diverting defence resources away from core NATO concerns such as Western and Central Europe might provoke American anger given the low strategic priority of the South Atlantic. As the former Foreign Secretary, David Owen, recalled: 'Yet the Fortress Falklands option was ruled out, not just on the grounds of expense but because to be seen to be abandoning a negotiated solution would exacerbate ill feeling in an already fractious region and alienate the United States as well as countries in Latin America'.[36]

Despite advocating logistical and political co-operation with Argentina, Lord Shackleton also recognised that the military regime 'saw the Falklands as the key to the Antarctic and they were also locked into argument with Chile as well'.[37] Controversially, the report also considered the economic potential of oil and fisheries in the waters surrounding the Falkland Islands which confirmed a long-held Argentine belief that the British Government was determined to retain sovereignty for reasons that were not merely political but also resource-based.[38] But as Leslie Hepple has argued, this is a fundamental misunderstanding of the report: 'the interest in development was an attempt to help the Islanders find a future, not a desire to retain the Falklands for Britain for their resource and geopolitical value'.[39] In complete contrast to the Argentine geopolitical and military-based literature, there were remarkably few public assessments of the South Atlantic and the Falkland Islands during the Labour Governments of Wilson and Callaghan.

Chapter 5 of the report was prepared by Bob Storey and included his research on the social condition of the Falkland Islands community. Significantly, the report reflected not only on the cultural identity but also the economic conditions of the Islands:

> Thus, the Islanders came with relatively little in common and have had scant opportunity to establish a distinct Falkland Islands culture. Such cultural features as are readily apparent reflect a strong, even fierce, awareness of their British origins.
>
> There are several important groups among the Islands' population. One is the land owning and managerial class, another is the body of farm workers in the Camp and another is composed of the inhabitants of Stanley. Each of these groups may be further divided into indigenous population on the one hand, and, on the other, those who have come in their lifetime from outside (almost exclusively from the UK and usually on contract). These distinctions are often invoked within the Islands. Common cause is frequently made between native-born people in Stanley and in the Camp.
>
> These locally born people possess a number of important qualities... which include honesty, versatility, physical hardiness and a capacity for sustained effort.

Yet there appear to be other less encouraging features, such as a lack of confidence and enterprise at the individual and community level, and a degree of acceptance of their situation which verges on apathy.[40]

Shackleton and his team had drawn attention to an important if neglected dimension, by exposing the dependency of the native-born Islanders not only on Argentina but also on the UK expatriate community in the Falklands and British-based shareholders.[41]

Many Islanders interviewed by the author recalled that Storey's research provided a pretext to express their anger in the aftermath of the Joint Communications Agreement. Given that the last high profile visit was by Lord Chalfont in 1968, the opportunity was seized to voice their collective dissatisfaction with Argentina and their dependent economic condition vis-à-vis the FIC. The social and economic dominance of the FIC was acknowledged by the report, which advocated rural change so that more native-born Islanders could be encouraged to participate in the ownership of land.[42] Some Islanders have argued in private that the greatest problem facing the Islands in the 1970s was not Argentina but farm managers and the paternalistic culture identified by the report.[43] The then Governor of the Falkland Islands, Jim Parker, also recognised that there had to be some basic changes to the feudal nature of the community.[44] A minimum-wage structure was introduced and educational opportunities in the camp (the areas outside Stanley) were improved. However, Islanders nonetheless recognised that hostility to Argentina provided the 'social glue' to a community deeply divided by ownership and lack of resource access.

In his recollections of the report's political impact, Ted Rowlands recalled that no-one should have been 'surprised' by the recommendations and overall tenor of the report.[45] Shackleton had, in private, been adamant that the Falkland Islanders should not be handed over to Argentina against the 'wishes' of the community.[46] Moreover, given the Argentine authorities' attitude towards his team's visit, confidence-building between Argentina and the Falkland Islanders had already been compromised. It could be argued that the report was a political own goal for the FCO because, far from elucidating the merits of co-operation with Argentina, it had the opposite effect.

In subsequent negotiations with the Argentines in 1976–7, Rowlands spent a great deal of time reassuring his counterparts that the Shackleton report was not the prelude to oil prospecting around the Falkland Islands. Armed with charts and maps, Rowlands recalled one meeting in New York, in February 1976, in which he attempted to persuade his Argentine colleague that the report was about investigating alternative routes for economic development rather than to preordain a hydrocarbon future for the Falklands. The earlier Griffith Report (1975) on oil evaluation in the Falkland Islands region obscured his task, even though it stressed that much of the discussion concerning oil reserves was based on speculation rather than careful geological research. He explained that the Falklands were in economic decline and that steps had to be taken to try and secure the future of the southwest Atlantic islands. However, the British discovery of the Argentine occupation of the uninhabited island of Southern Thule in December 1976 complicated these discussions because it was feared that the Shackleton Report had actually encouraged the Argentines to increase their 'presence' in the wider South Atlantic and Antarctic.[47] Amazingly, senior Labour ministers such as David Owen were not informed of the

Southern Thule occupation until June 1977, which Owen believed was deliberate, as FCO officials were keen to promote further negotiation with Argentina.[48]

In February 1977, Foreign Secretary Anthony Crosland asked Rowlands to visit Argentina and the Falkland Islands in an attempt to recover the political momentum. At the time there had been some debate within Whitehall as to whether a Royal Navy task-force should be sent to the South Atlantic to repel any attempts by the Argentine military to invade the Falklands.[49] On his arrival in the Falklands, Rowlands was 'shocked' to discover the intense isolation endured by the community, especially those inhabitants living outside the only 'town'.[50] Camp settlements such as Darwin and Goose Green were at least several days by horse away from Stanley and many residents living in the camp had never even been to Stanley, let alone outside the Falkland Islands. Living conditions were basic and many families in the camp shared facilities such as telephone lines. Access to television was very limited and the visiting detachments of Royal Marines found to their surprise that their nickname for Falkland Islanders, 'Bennies' found no cultural purchase in the Islands.[51] While their ignorance of the British soap opera *Crossroads* might be considered a blessing in disguise, it gave rise to a veritable industry in Bennie-type jokes. One former marine, who has lived on the Islands since the 1970s, recounted one such variant: 'A squaddie [British soldier] is looking under the bonnet of his car inspecting the engine and a Falkland islander approaches to have a look. The squaddie turns to the islander and says "Are you a mechanic?" Whereupon the islander replies "No, I'm a Mackenzie".'[52] The wider significance of this story should not be underestimated, as according to the Falklands lobby it contributed to a UK expatriate culture of patronising indifference to the Falkland Islands.[53]

On his return from the Falklands and Argentina, Rowlands was adamant that the Falkland Islands should, in his words, have 'the right to decline' large-scale commercial development and increased contact with Argentina. Many Islanders old enough to recall the 1970s noted that the visit of the FCO minister coincided with a period of tense relations with Argentina, culminating in allegations that the Argentine navy was carrying out military operations in Berkley Sound. A mysterious Argentine plane-crash near Johnson's Island in 1976 and frequent Argentine over-flights contributed to a sense of insecurity. Other Islanders recalled being detained at Argentine airports by over-zealous immigration officials in the aftermath of the 1976 military coup in Argentina. Even within the Islands, some Falkland-born Islanders alleged that successive British Governors such as Neville French ordered the local police force to monitor the behaviour of Islanders in case anti-Argentine feelings led to direct violence against the resident Argentine community. As one Falkland-born Islander noted to the author, 'This was the dirty years of the Falklands, it was quite traumatic to see what was happening to the Islands and nobody seemed to care'.[54]

British indifference to the Falkland Islands appeared to be confirmed when the Callaghan Government announced that the major recommendations of the Shackleton report would not be funded because of cost and an attendant fear of antagonising Argentina and the wider UN community.[55] Some former officials have also alleged that the report was sidelined because Shackleton had gone, in FCO terms, 'native' and displayed an overt sympathy for the plight of the Islanders.

The report highlighted four areas that the FCO did not wish to address. The first was the social schisms within the isolated Falklands community and the resultant effect on local political and economic life. The report astutely noted that the local community was fundamentally shaped by the social and economic activities of large farm owners and UK expatriate skilled labour. Native-born Islanders were either in low-wage-earning employment in Stanley or were entirely dependent on the paternalistic benefits of the farm-owning families and managers.[56] The more fortunate Islanders were either farm owners or worked for the Falkland Islands Government. For those living on the remote farms in the camp, employees were entirely dependent on amenities and housing provided by their employer, the FIC.

Second, internal communications were so poorly developed that many native-born Islanders had very little contact with anyone beyond the neighbouring farms. For much of the 1970s, for example, there were very few direct phone lines and many people in the camp still travelled on horseback. Given the mode of transport, journey times could extend into days, especially during winter, as tracks became temporarily impassable. Little wonder perhaps that the radio service provided by the Falkland Islands Broadcasting Service (FIBS) played an important part in maintaining an 'imagined community'.

Third, the Falkland Islands community did not want to increase its dependency on Argentina, not least because many felt that the military regime could not be trusted. Radio also brought 'foreign news' and alerted the Islanders to the rising incidence of human-rights abuse in Argentina as the 'dirty war' began to take a grip on Argentine society. Thousands of Argentine citizens were being abducted, murdered and tortured and, as David Owen later acknowledged:

> Both sides of the House were rightly very angry about the military regime in Buenos Aires; people were just disappearing off the streets of Argentine cities. They were certainly no respecters of human rights at home and no one trusted them, even with joint administration, to be involved in any way with the Falkland Islands.[57]

Finally, the report advocated a runway extension so that jet planes could land in the Islands but British ministers were reluctant to advocate the investment on financial grounds and for fear of antagonising an Argentine military regime determined to resolve the dispute.

UNTAPPED RESOURCES AND THE ISLANDS OF THE SOUTH ATLANTIC

In the region below 60 degrees south, the Antarctic Treaty Consultative Parties (ATCP) had established a mode of contact in the aftermath of the 1959 Antarctic Treaty. With the territorial disputes in the Antarctic Peninsula suspended under the provisions of Article IV, issues such as mineral resources and environmental protection remained outstanding. This was not the result of a collective diplomatic oversight; rather it was recognised that 'the most explosive issue facing the Treaty, and the one without which it probably could not manage, was anything to do with minerals...the thing likely to tear the Antarctic Treaty apart'.[58] Both Roberts and Heap recognised that the question of mineral resources was highly controversial because it touched upon sovereignty and access to the continent. However, the ATCP had to consider how they might approach this dilemma of Antarctic resources and conservation because if they failed to tackle this concern there remained the danger that unilateral action by one party might destroy the Antarctic Treaty. Roberts and Heap were well aware that there would be no political support for increased funding for the BAS in the event of Britain seeking to consolidate its 'presence' on the polar continent. The Treasury had won that particular battle in 1964–5, and Roberts knew that funding increases would only be secured on scientific rather than political grounds, even though this did not rate highly in terms of Britain's scientific priorities. While the distinction was often hard to maintain, the regime was deemed a vital backdrop for the endeavours of the BAS and to weaken the institution was not in the best interest of Britain's South Atlantic Empire.

Viewed retrospectively, the Argentine geopolitical literature provides an invaluable insight into the escalating strategic prominence of the Falklands and the South Atlantic because of the long association between the military and many of the proponents who had been senior officers under a succession of military regimes. In the late 1960s, General Juan Guglialmelli created the Argentine Institute of Strategic Studies and International Relations (INSAR) and established a new geopolitical journal called *Estrategia*.[59] The General was hugely influential in shaping Argentine geopolitical consciousness, not only because of his writings but also due to his position as chief of the Escuela Superior de Guerra and head of the Fifth Army Corps. Furthermore, under the Ongania Military Government, he was secretary to the National Council of Development.

One of the earliest papers published in *Estrategia* was by an Argentine armed-forces officer called Cosentino, who argued, in complete contrast to British strategists, that the 'local' and 'global' strategic value of the Falkland Islands was considerable.[60] Locally, he argued that Argentina needed to control the Falklands in order to protect its own harbours as well as reclaim its rightful possession. Globally, Cosentino argued that the Falklands and the Drake's Passage were important in the event of the closure of the Panama Canal, because shipping would then be diverted south. Significantly, as Hepple recognised, Cosentino did not mention the resource potential surrounding the Falklands and wider South Atlantic.[61]

Within five years, and in the aftermath of the 1973 oil crisis, the Argentine geopolitical literature was transformed, as new assessments appeared extolling the resource potential of the Falklands and South Atlantic. The most striking example of this metamorphic shift in the evaluation of the region was by Hernandez and Chitarroni, who argued that Argentina should recover the Falklands not only because of the outstanding legal claim but also because the South Atlantic was a new 'Kuwait' waiting to be exploited.[62] In 1974, the Institute for Geopolitical Studies (IDEG) launched a new Argentine geopolitical journal called *Geopolitica*, which pursued similar regional and resource themes to *Estrategia*. A growing number of naval officers developed terms such as 'Atlantartida' to describe a broader regional space encompassing the Falklands, South Georgia and Antarctica, and argued that Argentina should consolidate its resource and strategic interests.[63]

New conventions such as the Convention for the Conservation of Marine Living Resources, or CCAMLR (1980), were intended to develop sustainable mechanisms for the management of fisheries in the Southern Ocean, but they also revealed that distant islands such as South Georgia were intimately linked to the political and environmental management of Antarctica (see figure 8.1). Article IV of the polar regime and the provisions of CCAMLR offered some diplomatic and political protection for Britain's South Atlantic possessions. However, it was recognised that the

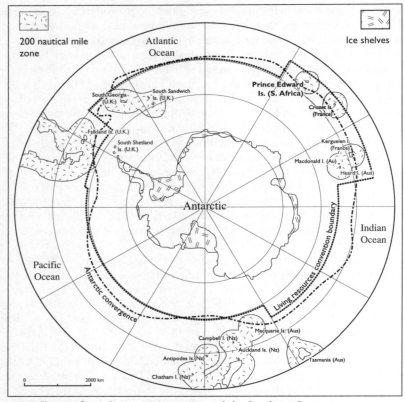

Figure 8.1: Zones of jurisdiction in Antarctica and the Southern Ocean

management of non-living resources was the most divisive issue facing the ATCP. Notwithstanding the voluntary constraint on the part of the ATCP, speculation regarding mineral resources had been heightened by an infamous 1974 report compiled by the US Geological Survey on the seas of Southern Argentina and the Falklands, which reaffirmed the potential of hydrocarbon potential. The report estimated that there was the potential for 40 to 200 billion barrels of oil, and this appeared to be cautiously vindicated by the Griffith Report (1975), which claimed that commercial exploitation might be feasible. During the first Wilson Government, speculation over oil resources in the South Atlantic had pre-dated the report by Professor Griffith of the University of Birmingham.

The *Daily Express*, with headline stories such as 'There is oil off Falklands says experts', contributed to this culture of ill-informed speculation.[64] These speculations prompted an internal Whitehall inquiry in order to verify whether the 'story' was leaked by a civil servant in a Government department.[65] Despite these headlines, a pattern emerged from the position papers, and one claimed that:

> Although there have been no economic or strategic reasons to cling to the Islands, HMG must in accordance with pledges made to Parliament ensure that any future arrangements take into account the wishes of the 2,100 odd Islanders.

Argentina is showing more patience and goodwill then most claimants do. Argentina is our best export market in Latin America. There is a large British community in Argentina and the Islands are indefensible militarily.[66]

Further commentary on the possibility of oil around the Falkland Islands surfaced throughout 1969–71 but the Overseas Policy and Defence Committee concluded, in a position paper entitled 'Falkland Islands: oil exploration', that it was not commercially attractive to companies such as BP. Moreover, it was recognised that resource exploitation would only serve to deepen the crisis over Falklands sovereignty because it might provoke Argentina to take military action against the Islands. The paper recommended that if surveys were conducted of the Falkland Islands basin then the Argentine Government would have to be informed before any such surveys were carried out. It also suggested that the UK Government might consider joint exploration with Argentina 'in an area or areas where sovereignty was not in dispute … [and significantly] it might help persuade the Islanders of the advantages of closer connections with Argentina'.[67]

Speculation that the Falklands was awash with oil coincided with research by the US National Science Foundation of the distribution of Antarctic krill around South Georgia, which further heightened global interest in the region. Despite the appeal of untapped hydrocarbon resources in the southwest Atlantic, the Wilson and Heath Governments realised that to give credence to these speculations could seriously undermine relations with Argentina. Geopolitical and military writers in Argentina already advocated the need to claim these untapped resources at a time when international lawyers were also debating a new UN-sponsored Law of the Sea convention. It would have been highly provocative to authorise the sale of oil exploration licences to companies such as Ashland Oil of Canada, which had expressed a prior interest. Moreover, the 1971 Joint Communications Agreement created on the part of Britain a negotiating culture in favour of cautious co-operation with Argentina in tandem with attempts to persuade the Falkland Islanders of the need to consider their future. Wilson consistently sought to balance these competing demands in a manner which gave 'the Argentine government some of the facts of sovereignty without giving up the legalities'.[68] Contrary to some of the wilder claims surrounding the 1982 South Atlantic war, there is little evidence on the British side, of anyone in London advocating the maintenance of the Falkland Islands on the basis of its untapped resource potential. If anything, the mounting interest in the resources of South Atlantic placed greater pressure on Anglo–Argentine negotiations and Labour ministers recognised that any attempt to exploit these resources would effectively derail the bilateral negotiations.[69]

It is also pertinent to appreciate that Argentina enjoyed the political and military support of South Africa, a nuclear power involved with a number of other southern-hemispheric states in high-level discussions intent on creating a South Atlantic Treaty Organisation (SATO).[70] Stung by the British withdrawal from the Simonstown naval base in Cape Province, the South African navy was determined to strengthen ties with the Argentine and Chilean armed forces for the purpose of ensuring the defence of Western shipping lanes in the South Atlantic, especially the oil supply routes.[71] While many of the strategic arguments in favour of a SATO were self-serving, Admiral Biermann, the then commander of the South African Defence Force, argued that such an arrangement would nonetheless ensure that 'a regional treaty or alliance is an excellent goal which should be pursued with vigour'.[72] Both the South African and Argentine regimes initiated substantial increases in their defence budgets and, unlike Britain, could afford to concentrate on developing regional resources in the South Atlantic.[73] It has now been revealed that South Africa (officially neutral during the conflict) collected military intelligence on the Falklands for Argentina in the months prior to the 1982 invasion. Faced with these complicated cross-oceanic connections, it is little wonder that South African and Argentine naval officers interpreted Britain's limited naval presence as a symbol of official disinterest.

The enduring theme to emerge from the South Atlantic and Antarctic in the late 1970s is that the preservation of the Antarctic Treaty was essential, and Roberts certainly believed that geopolitical bedlam would follow if it ever collapsed. Despite its interests in the South Atlantic, the BAS, unlike its predecessor the FIDS never used the Falklands as a major staging post for its polar activities. Although a research station was based on South Georgia, most of the scientific activity was focused on the Antarctic Peninsula. Aware of the wider connections, officials were occasionally inclined to consider unorthodox solutions in the face of the unrelenting opposition by the Falklands community, to either leaseback or another form of settlement with Argentina. With the failure to secure a negotiated settlement in 1981, Britain's South Atlantic Empire was to face its greatest challenge in the southern hemispheric winter months of the following year.

SUMMARY

With a political crisis looming, Britain was unable to reverse a well-established strategy of consolidation and selective withdrawal in the face of financial stringency. The debates over the future funding of the BAS and the administration of South Georgia exposed how uneasily scientific, financial, political and geographical factors co-existed. Some officials argued that the administrative transfer of the BAS from the Colonial Office to the Department of Education and Science was 'in a way, a piece of decolonisation, and we are now at the last stage'.[74] The last stage in this case was not the renunciation of British territorial claims in the Antarctic and the South Atlantic but an administrative transfer. This was a very limited post-colonial revolution and despite the presence of the Antarctic Treaty, the Falklands and the dependencies of South Georgia and South Sandwich remained embroiled in a territorial dispute between Britain and Argentina. British officials attached to the FCO recognised that the administrative fate of South Georgia and the Antarctic Treaty region had direct implications for the Falkland Islands question.

Notwithstanding the establishment of the sovereignty umbrella, the mechanism for improving communication between Argentina and the Falkland Islands simply raised Argentine expectations for a political settlement. By 1968, it was extremely unlikely that British policy-makers could ignore the 'wishes' of the small community and the implementation of the 1971 Joint Communications Agreement cemented Falkland Islander opinion firmly against any transfer of sovereignty in favour of Argentina. Although the scientific and political lobby attached to the BAS won a series of battles regarding future funding and base creation, the Falklands lobby was unable to persuade successive British Governments to implement the major recommendations of the Shackleton report. The 'South Georgia lobby' was eager to emphasise that the BAS base ensured a wider geographical British presence, but as events were later to prove a small party of BAS scientists and Royal Marines were not sufficient to deter an Argentine military regime determined to end British colonialisation. The Argentines, unlike the British, wanted to resolve rather than manage the territorial dispute.

NOTES ON CHAPTER 8

1   PRO FO 42/94. 'Report by Lord Chalfont on the visit to the Falkland Islands 23–28 November 1968', 5 December 1968.
2   Letter from Rt Hon. Lord Callaghan of Cardiff KG to the author, dated 6 March 2001.
3   Quoted in M. Charlton, *The Little Platoon: Diplomacy and the Falklands Dispute* (Oxford, Blackwell, 1989), p. 45.
4   These ships also played their part in collecting geographical information on the remote islands of South Orkneys and South Sandwich. It was found, for example, in 1964 that Admiralty maps of the South Sandwich Islands were incorrect because of basic cartographic errors.
5   J. Callaghan, *Time and Chance* (London, HarperCollins, 1987), p. 371.
6   PRO FCO 42/34. Letter from John Sugg of the Commonwealth Office to the Governor of the Falkland Islands, dated 5 January 1967.
7   PRO FCO 42/34. Letter from M. Lynch of the Ministry of Overseas Development to J. Stackpole of the Commonwealth Office, dated 2 March 1967.
8   PRO FCO 42/34. Letter from J. Bennett of the Commonwealth Office to M. Lynch of the Ministry of Overseas Development, dated 23 March 1967.
9   J. Heap, 'Dr Brian Roberts CMG', in H. King and A. Savours (eds), *Polar Pundit: Reminiscences about Brian Birley Roberts* (Cambridge, Cambridge University Press, 1995), pp. 3–8.
10 Interview with Dr John Heap, 23 November 2000. Before joining the FCO's polar regions section, Heap was a scientist based at the University of Michigan. He had been a member of the FIDS, and his doctoral research was on the distribution of sea ice in the Antarctic Peninsula. He took over from Roberts in 1975 and retained this post until 1992.
11 Author interview with Sir Martin Holdgate, 4 July 2001.
12 PRO FCO 42/34. Letter from J. Kennedy of the Treasury to J. Sugg of the Commonwealth Office, dated 2 January 1968.
13 PRO FCO 42/34. Letter from Fuchs to the Governor of the Falkland Islands, dated 31 October 1967. The letter noted the support of the Antarctic Committee of NERC and also argued that the Commonwealth Office must offer additional support to the BAS because the base was being created for scientific and political reasons. The idea of the BAS creating a base in South Georgia had been raised in 1962. PRO FO 371/162068. Letter from Fuchs to R. Pettitt of the Colonial Office dated 9 July 1962.
14 PRO FCO 42/34. Letter from J. Sugg of the Commonwealth Office to A. Kennedy of the Treasury, dated 5 January 1968.

15   See, for example, the reviews in P. Beck, *The Falkland Islands as an International Problem* (London, Routledge, 1988) and L. Freedman, *Britain and the Falklands War* (Oxford, Blackwell, 1988). For an Anglo–Argentine collaborative analysis see L. Freedman and V. Gamba-Stonehouse, *Signals of War* (London, Faber and Faber, 1990).

16   FCO 42/94. 'Report by Lord Chalfont on the visit to the Falkland Islands, 23–28 November 1968', dated 5 December 1968 is one of the most obvious examples of this line of thought within the FCO.

17   The Darwin sailing schedules were largely monthly (that is 12 in total from Stanley to Montevideo), but during the winter months (June–August) there were occasionally no voyages and hence the islands were totally isolated.

18   It is important to recall that 90 per cent of the imports to the Falkland Islands came from Britain, and the Montevideo (called Monty by the Falkland Islanders) shipping service was vital for transportation of these goods. By the late 1960s, the FIC was complaining that costs were steadily rising as there were real problems of theft of goods at Montevideo docks, in combination with delays caused by weather. The ships could also be quite empty in the summer months because Falkland Islanders were working on farms.

19   *Falkland Islands Gazette Supplement*, January 1970. Minutes of the Legislative Council, 17 December 1969.

20   *Falkland Islands Gazette Supplement*, August 1970. Minutes of the Legislative Council, 3 June 1970.

21   It is important to remember that even by 1967 it was only just becoming possible to make overseas calls from the Falkland Islands. The service was started by Cable and Wireless on 4 December 1967, and initially the service operated for only one hour a day. Subsequently it became five hours daily. My thanks to Sir Cosmo and Lady Haskard for confirming this issue in a letter to the author dated 23 May 2001. Government House would have continued to use cypher telegram because of the secret and or confidential nature of communication between Stanley and the FO in London.

22   *Falkland Islands Gazette Supplement*, June 1971. Minutes of the Legislative Council, 17 May 1971.

23   *Falkland Islands Monthly Review*, May 1971.

24   The material relating to the Falkland Islands is based on over fifty interviews with Falkland Islanders who had direct experience of the Joint Communications Agreement. All interviews were carried out on a confidential basis in May 1997, November 1998, December 1999, April 2000 and July 2000.

25   Author interview with Lord Shackleton, 26 February 1991.

26   P. Tremayne in the *Sunday Times*, 'Falkland Islands: Why do the British want to quit', 25 September 1977.

27   Author interview with F. Mitchell, 7 June 2001.

28   K. Morgan, *Callaghan: A Life* (Oxford, Oxford University Press, 1997), p. 461.

29   See the important review by C. Ellerby, 'British interests in the Falkland Islands: Economic development, the Falklands lobby and the sovereignty dispute, 1945–1989' (unpublished DPhil thesis, University of Oxford, 1990).

30   It is important to recall that the Wilson Government had approved the creation of the Highlands and Islands Development Board in 1965 in an attempt to revive remote islands such as Shetland. By 1970, population decline had been reversed and the Shetland Islands were establishing new industries such as tourism.

31 In his autobiography, Callaghan noted that the Argentine Foreign Ministry proposed to send two or three scientific experts to accompany the Shackleton team but Perón vetoed this proposal. Despite Lord Shackleton's opposition, Callaghan was prepared to accept their presence within the mission. See Callaghan, *Time and Chance*, p. 374.

32 During the period between the despatch of the team and subsequent publication of the 1976 Shackleton report, the Argentine military regime introduced a compulsory course on geopolitics in secondary schools and included instruction on 'Argentina and the Southern Atlantic: Argentine National Sovereignty, National Priority'. According to one educational directive, teachers were expected to ensure that schoolchildren were instructed on the South Atlantic region. Argentine maps were still expected by law to show the Malvinas and Argentine Antarctic Sector. See, for example, the writing of A. Assef, *Proyeccion Continental de la Argentina* (Buenos Aires, Editorial Pleamar, 1980), p. 232, on the spiritual importance of the recovery of the Falkland Islands for all Argentines.

33 Author interview with Lord Shackleton, 26 January 1991. This is not widely known, and it raised the sensitive issue of Brazilian co-operation with the Shackleton mission to the Falkland Islands.

34 *Economic Survey of the Falkland Islands* (London, Economist Intelligence Unit, 1976), p. iii.

35 Author interview with Lord Shackleton, 26 February 1991.

36 D. Owen, *Time to Declare* (London, Michael Joseph, 1991), p. 354.

37 Author interview with Lord Shackleton, 26 February 1991.

38 The Shackleton report not only caused alarm in the FCO because of its focus on possible oil resources but also upset the directors of the FIC when analysing the role of the company and its investment in the RMS *Darwin* service.

39 L. Hepple, 'The geopolitics of the Falklands/Malvinas and the South Atlantic: British and Argentine perceptions, misperceptions and rivalries', in P. Kelly and J. Child (eds), *Geopolitics of the Southern Cone and Antarctica* (Boulder CO, Lynne Rienner, 1988), p. 228.

40 *Economic Survey of the Falkland Islands*, pp. 73–4. Emphasis has been added.

41 It also should be remembered that the Anglo–Argentine community in Argentina had little political sympathy for the Falkland Islands community – especially in the 1970s.

42 At the time of the Shackleton visit, the FIC owned 4 per cent of land acreage and produced over 50 per cent of the colony's wool output. It also employed about one-third of the total workforce. The FIC also dominated retail distribution, sea freight and local shipping services.

43 The Colony Club provides one example of social apartheid in the Falklands prior to 1982, as only farm managers and UK-born expatriates were allowed to use its facilities.

44 Telephone interview with Jim Parker, 21 November 2001.

45 Author interview with Ted Rowlands MP, 13 March 2001.

46 There is good evidence for believing that Lord Shackleton was in contact with members of the Falklands lobby, and the report's final recommendations mirrored those proposed by the UKFIC in April 1975. See Ellerby 'British interests in the Falkland Islands: Economic development, the Falklands lobby and the sovereignty dispute, 1945–1989', pp. 200–1.

47   There were concerns that, had the British sought to evict the Argentine party from Southern Thule, the Argentines might retaliate by evicting the BAS staff stationed in South Georgia. Britain had re-established a base in South Georgia in November 1969 after an absence of any major expedition since Duncan Carse in the 1950s.

48   Author interview with Lord Owen, 15 May 2001.

49   Owen, *Time to Declare*, p. 355.

50   Author interview with Ted Rowlands MP, 23 March 2001.

51   'Benny' was a character (who was depicted as a bit of a simpleton with a penchant for woollen hats) in a popular television drama called *Crossroads*, based on the everyday dramas of a Birmingham-based motel.

52   Author interview with a British-born Falkland Islander, 21 April 2000. The interviewee was a former Royal Marine stationed in the Falkland Islands.

53   Arguably the greatest legacy left by the Royal Marine presence in the 1970s is genetic in nature, as it has been alleged that quite a few Falklands children born during this period had Royal Marines for fathers.

54   Author interview with a Falklands-born Islander, 28 April 2000.

55   Author interview with a retired FCO official, 15 February 2001.

56   The paternalistic culture of the farm manager continues today with farm managers being addressed for example as 'Mr Bill', and sheep farms are still known by abbreviating the names of former managers, such as 'CB' for Chris Bonner, who was responsible for San Carlos.

57   Owen, *Time to Declare*, p. 354. Emphasis added.

58   J. Heap, 'The Treaty and the Protocol', in G. Mudge (ed.), *Antarctica: The Environment and Future* (Geneva, International Academy of the Environment and International Peace Research Institute, 1992), pp. 35–40. The quote is taken from p. 37.

59   See, for example, J. Guglialmelli, *Geopolitica del Cono Sur* (Buenos Aires, El Cid 1983, 3rd ed.), and one of his last pieces before his death, 'La crisis Argentina: una perspectiva geopolitica' *Estrategia* 73/74 (1983): pp. 9–30.

60   B. Cosentino, 'El valor estrategico de las Islas Malvinas', *Estrategia* 6 (1970): pp. 76–87.

61   L. Hepple, 'The geopolitics of the Falklands/Malvinas and the South Atlantic: British and Argentine perceptions, misperceptions and rivalries', in P. Kelly and J. Child (eds), *Geopolitics of the Southern Cone and Antarctica* (Boulder CO, Lynne Rienner, 1988), pp. 223–36.

62   P. Hernandez and H. Chitarroni, *Malvinas: Clave Geopolitica* (Buenos Aires, Castaneda, 1977).

63   See, for example, F. Milia (ed.), *La Atlantartida: Un Espacio Geopolitico* (Buenos Aires, Editorial Pleamar, 1978).

64   *Daily Express*, 'There is oil off Falklands says experts', 27 November 1969.

65   PRO PREM 13/3179. 'The Falkland Islands, 1969–1970'.

66   PRO FCO 7/1721. Position paper 'Anglo–Argentine talks about the Falkland Islands', July 1970.

67   PRO PREM 13/3178. 'Oil exploration in the Falkland Islands, 1969–1970'. The paper entitled 'Falkland Islands: oil exploration' was prepared by the OPD Committee for Cabinet discussion (OPD [70] 4).

68   P. Ziegler, *Wilson* (London, Weidenfeld and Nicholson, 1993), p. 464.

69   See P. Wall (ed.), *The Indian Ocean and the Threat to the West* (London, Stacey International, 1975), for a rare British analysis of the wider implications of the Cold War on the South Atlantic.

70   On African–Latin American discussions concerning the defence of the South Atlantic, see *Africa Confidential* 17/22 (5 November 1976); T. Forrest, 'Brazil and Africa: Geopolitics, trade and technology in the South Atlantic', *African Affairs* 81 (1982): pp. 3–21.

71   The *Star (Johannesburg)*, 'Latin American navies study SA inclusion', 1 December 1976.

72   H. Biermann, 'The Republic of South Africa and the Southern Hemisphere', *Occasional Paper*, Centre for International Politics, University of Potchefstroom (1973), p. 37.

73   It is also widely suspected that the South African authorities, in co-operation with Israel, were responsible for an unexplained nuclear explosion in the South Atlantic in 1979. Even the *Penguin News* carried a story of the explosion entitled 'Things that go bang in the middle of the night', 3 November 1979.

74   PRO FCO 42/12. Memorandum prepared by J. Bennett, dated 18 January 1967.

9

Fighting for the Falklands

By a funny twist of fate, they [the Falkland Islands] occupied precisely the same latitude in their southern hemisphere as the British Isles did theirs: at 51, 46 S, Port Stanley was the Hemel Hempstead of the southern world. More than that, the Falklands stood off the coast of South America very much as Britain stood anchored off the coast of Europe. You only had to look at an atlas to see that the identity of the Falklanders, like that of the British, was bound up in an endless aggressive assertion of their differences from the continental giant across the water. The Falkland Islanders were us, but they were in a looking-glass reverse...The Falklands held up to our islands, and it reflected, in brilliant sharp focus, all our injured belittlement, our sense of being beleaguered, neglected and misunderstood.[1]

INTRODUCTION

The enduring irony of the 1982 Falklands conflict will be the failure of most people in the UK to recall accurately the exact geographical location of the Falkland Islands. Prior to the event, according to some opinion polls carried out at the time, the majority of respondents thought that the Islands were either off the northwest coast of Scotland or located somewhere in the Atlantic Ocean, possibly close to the Caribbean basin.[2] In complete contrast to this geographical ignorance, virtually every Argentine citizen would have been able not only to locate the Islands in the southwest sector of the Atlantic Ocean but also draw an outline of the major constituents of the Malvinas archipelago.[3] More disturbingly, given the relentless cartographic endeavour of the FIDS and the BAS, the Ministry of Defence (MOD), on hearing the news of an invasion, found to its horror that it had few detailed maps of the Falkland Islands' complex topography.[4]

In an interview with the author, David Sugden, professor of geography at the University of Edinburgh (in 1982 he was based at the University of Aberdeen) recalled the appalling state of ignorance.[5] He remembered seeing a television interview with a MOD official talking about the Falklands and claiming incorrectly that sea ice would be a major impediment to any task-force attempting to land on the Falkland Islands. Alarmed, he contacted a former student of his who worked at the MOD map library and offered his services. As an experienced researcher, he was only too aware that sea ice was not prevalent around the Falklands, and to correct this calamitous lack of knowledge he sent 1000 copies of a pamphlet he and a colleague had prepared in the 1970s on the Falklands and the far south.[6] Moreover, several of his doctoral students worked in the region at the time, and one of them, travelling on HMS *Endurance*, had sent him a postcard from Argentina informing him that he had seen a large Argentine naval task-force in the southern port of Ushuaia.

Another student, David Roberts, engaged in detailed research of the coastal environments of the Falklands, had photographed a great deal of the coastline and noted that the area close to San Carlos in East Falkland consisted of deep waters commensurate with Royal Navy task-force requirements. Without a precise understanding of the Islands' coastline and terrain, no task-force strategy could be devised with any confidence. After the decision had been taken to assemble such a force, MOD officials raced off to Scotland to requisition maps and photographs from geographers who had worked in the Falklands and South Georgia.[7] Sadly the MOD, although alerted to the extremes of South Atlantic islands, did not always follow the advice proffered, as the SAS, convinced that it could land its helicopters on South Georgia's Fortuna glacier and then traverse to Fortuna Bay, found to its cost, when two helicopters were lost. The invasion of the Falkland Islands in April 1982, therefore, provoked not only an administrative panic but also a massive geographical crisis.

British diplomatic representatives in Argentina and the FCO in London failed to appreciate the mounting frustration at the apparent rejection of any form of political settlement, which incited the military regime in Argentina to launch an opportunistic invasion of the Falkland Islands. In response, the British Government launched (and public opinion largely supported) a task-force to retrieve a part of the British South Atlantic Empire which had for some time been judged to be transferable even though it was the only colony to have a permanent British population. An absence of detailed geographical knowledge of the Falklands greatly contributed to and affected the British Government's response to the ensuing crisis. This apparent geographical vacuum was exacerbated by the strict censorship of the war correspondents and the difficulties of despatching information back from the South Atlantic to news managers in London and elsewhere. The 'Falklands factor' was to become a byword for political determination, national prowess and a resurgence of British national identity. As with Argentina, the Falklands now occupy for many in Britain a similar mythical position within the collective imagination. It demonstrated that although Britain was living in post-colonial times, a 'new era of colonial permanence has already begun, its arrival heralded by Britain's victory in the 1982 Falklands War'.[8] With Thatcher at the helm, no-one in the FCO dared to voice any change to the status of the Falkland Islands. The conflict continues to be commemorated in the Falklands and Britain, and with the passing of time some of the controversies relating to the burial of the British fallen and the initial reactions of the relatives to the bleak and inhospitable landscapes of the Falkland Islands have receded.

THE FALKLANDS FACTOR: TRANSFORMING ISLANDS

On 3 April 1982, the first Saturday sitting of Parliament since the 1956 Suez Crisis, MPs gathered to hear the news that Argentine forces had indeed occupied the Falkland Islands and South Georgia. The Governor of the Falkland Islands, Rex Hunt, had been deposed and Argentine forces now occupied Government House in Stanley. As Thatcher noted,

> I must tell the House that the Falkland Islands and their dependencies remain British territory. No aggression and no invasion can alter that simple fact. It is the Government's objective to see that the Islands are freed from occupation and are returned to British administration at the earliest possible moment.
>
> The people of the Falkland Islands, like the people of the United Kingdom are an island race... They are few in number, but they have a right to live in peace, to choose their own way of life and to determine their own allegiance. Their way of life is British: their allegiance is to the Crown. It is the wish of the British people and the duty of Her Majesty's Government to do everything that we can to uphold that right. That will be our hope and our endeavour and, I believe, the resolve of every Member of the House.[9]

The day before, 2 April 1982, the British Cabinet had decided to send an advanced guard of a task-force in the hope that it might lead to an Argentine withdrawal from the Falkland Islands. According to the then Foreign Secretary, Peter Carrington, the Cabinet was adamant that the Government might have been seriously weakened if the decision had not been taken to despatch a task-force, even if it was hoped that conflict could be avoided (for details, see Appendix: A basic chronology of the 1982 Falklands conflict).[10]

Despite later Argentine allegations that the British response was motivated by the resource potential or a desire to maintain strategic control of the South Atlantic, most assessments were consistently in favour of maintaining a British presence in the Antarctic rather than exhibiting a slavish determination to retain the Falklands. As has been noted by other British commentators, recrimination and uncertainty punctuated emergency Government meetings convened to resolve the Argentine occupation. Reportedly, Thatcher sought advice from experienced officials such as Sir Frank Cooper of the MOD and the former Prime Minister Harold Macmillan on the 'art of war'.[11] Cooper, in particular, advised her to create a small 'War Cabinet' to assist in the planning and execution of the campaign. The Treasury had to be excluded in order to ensure that fiscal considerations (especially at a time of domestic recession) did not interfere with military strategy. In terms of planning, First Sea Lord Henry Leach was instrumental in assuring the Prime Minister that the undertaking was feasible.[12] Armed with that strategic reassurance, the Prime Minister secured Cabinet and later parliamentary approval for the despatch of the task-force.

Once the decision had been taken to recover the Falklands, the symbolic qualities of the crisis for Britain rather than the Islands' geographical proximity to Antarctica and possible role as a naval base for the South Atlantic were extolled. Parliamentary debates were punctuated with references to the need to confront evil and maintain major tenets of international law, such as resisting an illegal invasion. Both sides of the House of Commons rose to condemn Argentina for its dictatorship and the invasion. Over the forthcoming weeks, however, the depiction of the

Falkland Islands as a village-like community composed of a rural and quintessentially 'English' character permeated political discourse and media coverage. The fate of Britain became transposed with that of the Falkland Islands, as MPs on both sides of the House of Commons warned of threats faced over the centuries from hostile continental neighbours such as sixteenth century Spain, nineteenth-century France and twentieth-century Germany. Michael English in the House of Commons argued that 'We are defending civilisation against barbarism as our ancestors did centuries ago elsewhere'.[13]

Despite the centuries separating these conflicts, a simple geopolitical message was articulated: near neighbours could not be trusted and aggression against British people had to be resisted. Senior figures in the Conservative Party reiterated this basic theme throughout the campaign. As John Nott, the then Defence Secretary, noted on 20th April 1982, 'When one stops a dictator, there are always and, as my Right Hon. Friend the Prime Minister said the other day, greater risks in not stopping a dictator – a lesson this nation has learnt before'.[14] Francis Pym, the Foreign Secretary who replaced Peter Carrington during the crisis, repeated the basic point 'The Falkland Islanders, victims of unprovoked invasion by a powerful and covetous neighbour...have reacted with courage and dignity to the rape of their islands'.[15]

To dismiss these utterances as simple war rhetoric would have deprived the British Government of a useful reference point for a historical and geographical framework in which to interpret subsequent events. The link with World War II was made explicitly by Thatcher on 3 April 1982 when she reminded the House of Commons that 'We are here, because for the first time in many years, British sovereign territory has been invaded by a foreign power'.[16] The German occupation of the Channel Islands in the 1940s was held up as an example of how important it was not to 'appease' dictators in order to protect British subjects from the terrible consequences.[17] However, the coded references to World War II was not an innocent observation, as some have noted; rather it alludes to the last unambiguously 'good war' in British social memory. As Paul Fussell has argued, 'it served a generation of Britons and Americans as a myth which enshrined purity, a parable of good and evil'.[18] As such the social memories of World War II assisted in the construction of cultural identities, which could be defined by their relation to, and differentiation from, other cultural identities. Thus Buenos Aires became like Berlin, full of grandiose architecture, mindlessly large crowds and a pompous and pretentious atmosphere, the modern-day equivalent of fascist Germany or Italy, displaying the bankruptcy of spatial expansionism and the domination of place. As the Conservative MP Sir Hector Munro noted in the House of Commons on 3 April 1982, 'Never, at any time since the last war [that is World War II], has there been a more important period during which the nation should stand together'.[19]

To dispel the great geographical distances between the Falkland Islands and the UK, the recycling of wartime rhetoric was essential to creating a sense of social and political proximity. The Times' famous headline on 5 April 1982 'We are all Falkland Islanders now' consolidated a collective identity and contributed to a national desire to repel the Argentine threat.[20] Former FCO minister Richard Luce, who, together with his FCO colleagues Peter Carrington and Humphrey Atkins, resigned in April 1982 for failing to prevent the crisis, argued that 'I believe that it matters not whether the invasion took place 80 or 8,000 miles away. It matters not whether it is 1800 or 18 million citizens who have been invaded'.[21] While social distance could be couched in these terms, physical distance had and would continue to confound successive governments. Unable to defend themselves and with many denied the opportunity to claim British citizenship under the 1981 Nationality Act (thereby losing the right of abode in the UK), Falkland Islanders were left in an unenviable position.

The Prime Minister conducted feverish diplomatic negotiations with the US against a backdrop of a dissatisfied home front. Mass unemployment, social dislocation and urban riots in London, Liverpool and Bristol had punctuated the first two years of the Thatcher administration. Post-colonial change in Zimbabwe and Belize provided another reminder that Britain's overseas responsibilities remained in turmoil. The former Foreign Secretary, Peter Carrington, recalled to this author that the right wing of the Conservative Party were absolutely furious with him for negotiating the independence of Zimbabwe in 1980 and how many MPs were eager to prevent a similar act of post-colonial retreat.[22] The Falklands crisis, therefore, provided Thatcher with an opportunity to address her claim made in a campaign speech in 1979 that she would preserve Britain's 'greatness' from being relegated to a 'distant memory of an offshore island'. As the crisis mounted in April 1982, the Irish Government proved to be one of the most unco-operative post-colonial states by its reluctance to restrict trading and commercial relations with Argentina in retaliation for the invasion of the Falkland Islands. As Mrs Thatcher recorded some years after the Falklands crisis, 'We were able to rely on some strange allies [in the UN] – and not on some of those who should have been our friends'.[23]

The unreliability of political 'friends' initially included the US, leaving many within the Conservative Government to question how any form of military action against Argentina would be possible without the political support of President Ronald Reagan. Underlying this political concern was a long-standing fear that the US could, as they had done during the 1956 Suez Crisis, fatally undermine British foreign policy. David Owen also warned the House of Commons to 'Let us not make it like Suez. Let us not have what happened in 1956, when service men went into Suez against a bitter party political debate.'[24] Reagan's Secretary of State, Alexander Haig, was appointed mediator, and for three weeks sought agreement on a plan which would have resulted in the immediate withdrawal of military forces, a tripartite commission and a commitment to negotiate the long term legal and political future of the Falklands/Malvinas. Thatcher was reluctant to agree to any such political accommodation because of persistent concerns that the 'wishes' of the Falkland Islanders would not be respected under a long-term agreement. As Peter Carrington recalled, it was apparent that Thatcher was adamant that there were wider issues at stake, namely Britain's reputation in the world. The Falklands acted once more as a referent for Britain and British Mrs Thatcher later noted in her autobiography, *The Downing Street Years*:

> Since the Suez fiasco in 1956, British foreign policy has been one long retreat. The tacit assumption made by British and foreign governments alike was that our world role was doomed steadily to diminish. We had come to be seen by friends and enemies as a nation which lacked the will and capability to defend its interests in peace, let alone in war.[25]

Having retaken South Georgia in late April 1982 after some fierce fighting, the British Government at last secured American political and military support, so crucial in the final stages of the Falklands campaign.[26]

14. ABOVE. The Malvinas Memorial at Ushuaia. The image shows the outline of the two main islands of the Falklands/Malvinas.

15. RIGHT. Whalebone Arch, Stanley. A reminder that the Falkland Islands were a major transit point for Antarctic expeditions and oceanic voyages.

16. LEFT. A sign for the Colony Bar in the Upland Goose Hotel, Stanley. The Colony Bar used to be the preserve of farm managers and British expatriate employees.

17. BELOW. A snowcat attached to the 1955-8 Commonwealth Trans-Antarctic Expedition. Unfortunately the rivalry between the two leaders, Sir Vivian Fuchs and Sir Edmund Hillary, overshadowed the success of the Antarctic crossing.

18. RIGHT. Falkland Islands Governor Donald Lamont in full ceremonial uniform during Queen Elizabeth II's birthday celebrations, April 2000.

19. BELOW. Referee Kreitlin moves in to send off the Argentine captain, Rattin, during the 1966 Argentina-England World Cup quarter-final. By permission of Popperfoto.

20. Liberation Monument, Stanley. Inscribed on the front of the monument are the words: 'For those who liberated us'.

21. A signpost warning of a minefield outside Stanley. It is estimated that about 18,000 mines buried by the Argentine forces remain to be cleared. Under the 1997 Ottawa Convention, Argentina and Britain have agreed to conduct a feasibility study to see whether they can all be cleared in due course.

22. One Falkland Islander's protest at the improving Anglo-Argentine relations, which witnessed Argentine passport-holders being allowed to enter the Falklands from July 1999 onwards – after a 17-year ban. The sign reads: 'Long Island. No access to Argies, 7 Councillors or Argie Supporters. God Save the Queen. Neil Watson'.

23. Lord Chalfont, the then Foreign Office Minister, made an unpopular appeal to the Falkland Islanders in November 1968 to consider a closer political future with Argentina. To the left is his private secretary, M. I. Tait, and to the right is the then Governor of the Falkland Islands, Sir Cosmo Haskard. The photograph was taken by John Leonard on 24 November 1968 and is reproduced with his kind permission.

24. King Edward Point, Grytviken, South Georgia. The buildings in the foreground were home to the British armed forces, who were stationed there in small numbers between 1982 and 2001. The British Antarctic Survey (BAS) now maintains a scientific station at King Edward Point.

25. ABOVE. The RAF air link between RAF Brize Norton (Oxfordshire), Ascension Island and the Falkland Islands has been vital to the post-1982 security of the Falklands.

(a)

(b)

26. a) An Argentine stamp released after the 1982 conflict, commemorating the struggle and reminding citizens of the Argentine territorial claim to South Georgia and the South Sandwich Islands;

b) An Argentine stamp depicting tri-continental Argentina-mainland, insular and polar territories;

(c)

c) A British Antarctic territory stamp depicting the HMS *William Scoresby*, a frequent visitor to Antarctica in the 1940s and 1950s;

d) A British Antarctic Territory stamp showing HMS *Endurance*, the ice patrol vessel whose uncertain future in the months leading up to the 1982 Argentine invasion provoked a major defence review crisis.

In general terms, Argentine stamps tend to depict the relative geographical proximity of the Falklands and Antarctica, while British stamps focus on the people and ships that have operated in the region.

(d)

In early May 1982, fighting intensified after the controversial and high-profile sinking of the Argentine cruiser *General Belgrano* and the British frigate HMS *Sheffield*. The British task-force, together with 29 journalists despatched from Portsmouth several weeks earlier, had arrived in the Falklands, and plans were afoot for a landing on the western edge of East Falkland.[27] In contrast to later campaigns such as Operation Desert Storm in 1991 and NATO's bombing campaign in Serbia, the Falklands conflict was not characterised by regular television coverage from the battle zone. Immense distances, difficult technology and official censorship combined to prevent the free and regular exchange of information.[28] Censorship, together with outright hostility from the Royal Navy to journalists accompanying the task-force meant that this was the worst-reported war since the Crimea in the nineteenth century.[29] Moreover, it was quite apparent that the military, especially the Royal Navy, was very reluctant to have any member of the press as part of the task-force. Bernard Ingham, the Prime Minister's press secretary, recalled that after a fierce struggle it was eventually agreed that only British journalists would accompany the task-force and the man from Reuters would have to serve international news agencies.[30] As Ingham recalled, 'Nothing I did as a government information officer was more difficult, more nerve-wracking, and ultimately more rewarding than trying to maintain relations between the Government and the press, radio and television, during the Falklands campaign'.[31] Journalists who accompanied the task-force confirmed that the British military made little attempt to accommodate news reporting and the average gap between filming and transmission was 17 days, an extraordinary time lapse in the modern world of media news networks. As the war photographer Martin Cleaver famously noted, 'It wasn't a news war, it's as simple as that. It was in the wrong place'.[32]

The paucity of television pictures from the front line and the distance of the conflict meant that the MOD was able to control the news of the conflict. As Philip Knightley recalled, 'The MOD were brilliant – censoring, suppressing, and delaying dangerous news, releasing bad news in dribs and drabs so as to nullify its impact, and projecting their own image as the only real source of accurate information about what was happening'.[33] Without independent access, television, newspaper and radio reports were thus largely dependent on the regular if haltingly formal briefings provided by the MOD spokesman Ian McDonald and the irregular and frequently delayed footage from the Falkland Islands. Although criticised in some quarters, his slow and halting style was designed to help non-Anglophone audiences and convey a sense of gravitas. However, political debates occurred in a geographical vacuum, as photography, let alone detailed knowledge of the Falklands topography and island community, was limited. Despite the apparent restrictions, including the D-notice system of voluntary restraint, Thatcher was swift to denounce any perceived outbreak of treachery amongst the media. BBC programmes such as *Panorama* were singled out for criticism, as were journalists who attempted to publish photographs of British military losses. As Thatcher noted to the House of Commons, 'I understand that there are occasions when some commentators say that the Argentines did something and then the "British" did something. I can only say, if this is so it gives offence and causes great emotion among many people.'[34]

Later she argued that journalists had published stories speculating on secret military planning: '...that our troops were about to take Goose Green the day before the attack [sic]...Too much talk was giving the Argentinians warning of what we intended, though the fault did not always lie with the media themselves but also with the media management of the MOD.'³⁵ This intense form of news management enabled the British Government in alliance with sympathetic elements of the print media to present the Falklands in a positive manner. The curbs on reporting military losses became significant when an ITV poll commissioned in May 1982 suggested that 55 per cent of respondents agreed that the Falklands was worth the loss of further British lives, as opposed to 38 per cent, who disagreed with the proposition.³⁶

After the sinking of the Argentine cruiser *General Belgrano*, the chance of a peaceful negotiation appeared to recede still further as the Argentine *junta* rejected revised Peruvian peace proposals.³⁷ The loss of HMS *Sheffield* two days later persuaded British military opinion in favour of allowing access to war journalists, provided it did not interfere with the security needs of the task-force. When HMS *Hermes* anchored in San Carlos, the officer-in-charge insisted that the media contingent remained on board for 10 days so as not to interfere with task-force logistical planning. Accusations abounded that the military was actively hindering the transmission of material by simply refusing to transmit or subjecting copy to considerable delay and censorship if it thought 'operational security' was being compromised.³⁸

Patrick Bishop, who worked for the *Observer*, provided one example of how military censors prevented copy being despatched on the grounds of so-called inaccuracies:

> On the day the landing ship, Sir Galahad was sunk we interviewed many of the survivors whose account made it plain that the disaster was at least partly due to bad planning and unnecessary risk taking by the Task Force commanders. I submitted an article to the censors on board HMS *Fearless* quoting the survivors extensively but taking care not to highlight the critical elements of their stories in the hope that they would not be picked up once the despatch reached the Observer. Returning to the ship four days later I checked with the 'minder' to make sure that the article had been sent. 'He had decided against letting that one go,' the minder replied. There had been some 'inaccuracies' which he felt I would have liked to correct for myself before the piece was submitted. The inaccuracies were miniscule and by then the piece was hopelessly out of date.³⁹

To sustain public opinion and the acceptance of British casualties, members of the Conservative Government spoke passionately in the House of Commons of the particular qualities of the Falklands community and their importance to British national identity. As the novelist Jonathan Raban recognised in his recollections of the conflict, the depiction of the Falkland Islanders as 'British in stock and tradition' was not politically or culturally innocent as 'They were visibly, audibly, our kith and kin…they were white'.⁴⁰ However, the policy of 'delaying' stories and images from the battlefront was reversed when they were judged to be 'supportive'. One such example was the photograph taken by Tom Smith of the *Daily Express* in May 1982, depicting a soldier sipping a cup of tea provided by a grateful Falkland Islands family in San Carlos. The *Independent on Sunday*, for example, carried the photograph on its front cover with the caption 'We are so proud of you' and 'A mug of tea for a paratrooper'.⁴¹ Similarly, the *Sunday Mirror* captioned the photograph 'Cuppa for a brave para'.⁴² The picture was used in a blatant attempt to emphasise two issues: first, the common racial and cultural heritage in combination with the reassuring presence of domesticity, and second the welcome extended to the soldiers by the entire community.[43]

Smith's photograph of the paratrooper was clearly judged to be an appropriate image of the conflict and thus was widely released within two days of the San Carlos landing. In its evidence to the House of Commons Defence Committee on media reporting during the conflict, the *Scotsman* later claimed,

> Was it just by chance that the celebrated picture of San Carlos villagers offering a marine [sic] a cup of tea achieved instant currency, whilst others such as one of HMS *Antelope* [Martin Cleaver's famous image was not released until three weeks after the event] exploding suffered considerable delay.[44]

Smith's photograph was adroitly employed to neutralise the political impact of protests against the war in London. Mainstream broadcasters reacted swiftly and ITN broadcast a bulletin which included a reporter questioning Tony Benn (a dissident Labour MP) about the appropriateness of a Falklands peace march given the recent landing of the task-force in San Carlos. Other events, such as a public outburst of patriotic songs at Pier Head in Liverpool on 12 May 1982, received widespread and sympathetic coverage from the television channels.

While the Conservative Government enjoyed close co-operation with most of the national media during the campaign and focused on the need to protect these 'loyal' British subjects, many Falkland Islanders the author interviewed were privately still angry that the crisis had been allowed to happen in the first place. In the absence of Governor Hunt, the Falkland Islanders anxiously awaited the arrival of the British task-force, and subsequently offered invaluable local information and even bravely helped guide the British troops during fierce battles for control over Mount Tumbledown and Mount Longdon. Between late May and mid-June 1982, the land-based contingent of the task-force travelled from the west over the wet and wild landscapes of East Falkland towards the major settlement of Stanley. The fighting was fierce, as the Argentine troops enjoyed the benefits of well-entrenched positions in the hills overlooking Stanley, and British troops had to be mindful of widespread minefields established by Argentine engineers. Considering the exposed terrain and freezing weather, the progress over East Falkland was remarkable, and by 14 June 1982 the British task-force entered Stanley and accepted the surrender of the Argentine forces.

The transformation of the Falklands into a national crusade was dented in places as the soldiers and journalists confronted the grim realities of place and war. David Tinker, who was killed on board HMS *Glamorgan* in the last days of the war, had expressed in his letters to his father that 'I wish the politicians would see sense and stop the war. What is happening here is barbaric and totally unnecessary...All this killing is going on over a flag for a rock with a village population.'[45] Simon Weston, who had been terribly injured in the war, also noted that the 'The Falklands are a god-forsaken place. The islands are empty, bleak, desolate, and inhospitable. I never saw a tree, I never saw one of those famous sheep.'[46] Their geographical disappointment in the Falklands did not ultimately detract from the political significance of the victory. Thatcher noted in the House of Commons that the war 'once again restored Britain's dominance and [has] let every nation know that British sovereign territory will be well and truly defended'.[47] With a speedy conclusion to the conflict and comparatively few British military losses, Thatcher returned to this theme of a resurgent Britain in a speech delivered at Cheltenham on 3 July 1982:

> We have ceased to be a nation in retreat. We have instead a new found confidence – born in economic battles and found true 8,000 miles away…And so today we can rejoice at our success in the Falklands and take pride in the achievement of the men and women of our task force. But we do so, not as some flickering of a flame which must soon be dead. No – we rejoice that Britain has rekindled that spirit which has fired her for generations past and which today begun to burn as brightly as before. Britain found herself in the South Atlantic and will not look back from the victory she has won.[48]

The Falklands was no longer a minor element in the British Empire, and significantly the victory provided further impetus for Thatcher's return to office a year later. If there was a 'Falklands factor', it was most noticeable in her political rhetoric, which was replete with island references and the 'enemy within'.[49] Trade unions and the political left bore the brunt of the Falklands factor, and a new generation of football fans had another country apart from Germany to add to their repertoire of insults. Ironically, both Britain and Argentina performed badly during the 1982 World Cup, with the Argentine football team losing to Belgium on the day before the final surrender. Earlier during the military campaign, the Argentine football manager César Luis Menotti argued that

> Each man has a part in the struggle. In these moments there is a national unity against British colonialism and imperialism. We feel immense pain for the brothers in the battle fleet, but we have been assigned a sports mission and we will try to fulfil it with dignity. We are not going to win or lose sovereignty in a match.[50]

In a post-colonial setting, the 1982 Falklands conflict marked the end of colonial dissolution and British Government policy towards the Falkland Islands sovereignty dispute. Leaseback and sovereignty transfer were no longer political options under Thatcher and, unlike prior administrations, civil servants in the FCO were isolated from her Falklands strategy.

VICTORY PARADE IN THE CITY OF LONDON

In 1901, the Victorian writer Charles Masterman coined the phrase 'heart of empire' to describe London's position within the myriad of trading, political and cultural networks that bound together the imperial centre and the continental and insular hinterlands.[51] Within 10 years of that pronouncement, Britain had embarked on the final chapter of imperial expansion in the previously unclaimed continent of Antarctica. While the frozen continent and the South Atlantic islands may have been one of the most remote and thinly populated parts of the British Empire, London's street names provided daily reminders of the massive geographical extent of this political, cultural and economic enterprise. On any standard map of London, for example, one could find a Falkland Road alongside a Scott Road and even a Shackleton Close. The City of London was literally full of imperial symbols, statues, memorials and shrines attesting to Britain's global empire. Public interest and commercial sponsorship of the 1955–8 CTAE culminated in a public procession to celebrate the return of Fuchs and his team.

When Thatcher decreed that a victory parade would be held in October 1982 to commemorate the achievements of the task-force in re-capturing the Falkland Islands, the City of London appeared politically and culturally most appropriate. Its alleys, lanes and courts play host to the Bank of England, the Guildhall and the stock exchange, and commercial banks bear witness to past Anglo–Argentine commercial relations as sources of credit, financial expertise and major investment projects, such as railway construction. Although financial relations with Argentina changed abruptly on the eve of the Argentine invasion of the Falklands in 1982 when Argentine assets were frozen in retaliation, it had no repercussions for the City of London, which continued uninterrupted as a major financial centre.

According to Jane Jacobs, the City of London remains 'an imperial space in a post-imperial age', and there is much evidence to suggest that the traders downed tools in order to participate in celebrations and processions relating to the reception of positive imperial news.[52] Profit, patriotism and imperialism could always be combined with one another. As the capital city and imperial centre, London was an obvious choice, but as two geographers have noted

> It was surely no coincidence that eighty two years later [after the celebration of the relief of Mafeking] Margaret Thatcher chose to review the Falklands War 'Victory Parade' outside Mansion House; there was presumably no better location in which to resuscitate vestigial memories of imperial power.[53]

The City of London had been at the centre of earlier celebrations, including the 1897 diamond jubilee and the march of the City imperial volunteers on returning from their imperial duties in South Africa. Both processions passed Bank junction, Mansion House, the Guildhall, past memorials to Nelson and Wellington and then St Paul's Cathedral. Large crowds lined the route of the parades, and during the jubilee the hanging of paintings, drapes and the planting of imported trees momentarily transformed the facade of Bank junction.[54]

Following the award of nearly 30,000 South Atlantic Medals, the Falklands victory parade on 12 October 1982 proceeded in armed formation from Armoury House to Guildhall, where Thatcher addressed the lunchtime audience in a reflective mood:

> Military parades and pageantry are part of the distinguished history of the City of London. It is right – and the whole nation will feel that is right – that we gather in the heart of the City to honour all those who took part in the Falklands campaign … I have boundless confidence in the British character. I believe more heroes will spring up in the hour of danger than all the military nations ancient and modern Europe have ever produced [sic]. Today, we know that it is true. But it is not only the people of the Falklands who feel gratitude to the Task Force. Although they are rejoicing with us today and their hearts will be full, we, all the British people, with them are proud of those heroic pages in our island story, proud to be here to salute the Task Force.[55]

Earlier in the morning accompanied by a military band playing 'Rule Britannia' and 'God save the Queen', representatives of the armed forces together with tanks paraded past Mansion House, surrounded by crowds holding aloft banners such as 'The City salutes the Task Force'. As one report by the *Daily Mail* excitedly commented: 'The green berets of the Marines, the red of the Paras, the khaki of the Guards and Gurkhas, the dark blue of the Royal Navy and the light blue of the Royal Air Force – one after the other they came, past the roaring multitudes in a greeting fit for heroes that they are'.[56] The *Financial Times* noted in its discrete article, 'Almost 300,000 people lined the mile-long route to see the 1,250 representatives of the 28,000 Britons who took part in the South Atlantic hostilities and to watch the flypast of helicopters and bombers'.[57]

Some condemned the event as an unnecessary glorification of war, while others highlighted the reluctance of military leaders to include the seriously wounded. As the *Guardian* noted in its reporting, 'Pacifists turned out as well. A group of women turned their backs in protest, 17 people were arrested when a group of anti-militarists tried to chain themselves to nearby lamp posts, and a tall cross holding the message "Jesus Christ was murdered by the military" was erected in the front of a Cheapside church.'[58] Originally, there was a widespread desire among the political and military elite to minimise the very substantial physical and psychological costs of the conflict. As one veteran bitterly noted to the author, the MOD officials 'didn't like to overshadow the Parade with the downside of war'. He later sat in his wheelchair close to the Guildhall.[59] After intense criticism, the MOD relented and the *Daily Mail* led its account of the victory parade with the headline 'The bravest of the brave', and claimed that 'They could not march. But it was their parade as much as anybody's. Six servicemen badly wounded in the Falklands were at the front of the crowd outside the Guildhall today.'[60]

Secrecy at one point prevented virtually all access to information of British casualties sustained by the conflict, which prompted Polly Toynbee to ask in the *Guardian*, 'An itemised list must exist somewhere, and if not why not? How else can we count the cost of war?'[61] Unlike the closely controlled media reporting demanded during the campaign itself, confronting the brutal realities of this conflict, which left more than 250 British dead, 700 injured and countless more suffering from post-traumatic stress disorder, proved more difficult for the military and political establishment.

As a form of ritual or ceremony, the Falklands victory parade provided evidence for assessing the ideological structures of British national identity. Images of the flypast of helicopters and bombers passing over St Paul's Cathedral in a manner reminiscent of World War II symbolising British courage and resilience were widely published. Warming to the theme, the then Lord Mayor of London, Sir Christopher Leaver told the task-force representatives, 'You represent what is best in Britain'.[62] For the political right, the Falklands campaign became synonymous with national pride and resilience. As Thatcher reiterated in her Guildhall lunchtime audience, 'Throughout the land our people were inspired. Doubt and hesitation were replaced by confidence and pride that our generation too could write a glorious chapter in the history of liberty.'[63] As with former parades and ceremonies hosted in the City of London, the victory parade helped to define political and cultural understandings of the Falklands conflict and Britain. Simon Barker has recorded that 'the vessel [the *Mary Rose*] was raised to the surface within hours of the so-called Falklands Victory Parade', and it was claimed that the recovery of a sunken Tudor flagship off the Hampshire coastline epitomised a wider symbolic process of historical and national recovery.[64] The Queen's Commonwealth broadcast on Christmas day 1982 paid tribute to the Falklands task-force and closed with an allusion to the importance of preserving island life.

MEMORIALISING THE FALLEN

Politically, memorial landscapes are seen as intensely moral projects able to garner emotions and foster national mourning while excluding the unwelcome presence of the 'other'. More generally, the involvement of the state in the creation of memorials and monuments can determine the manner in which particular conflicts are remembered. Carefully selected spaces where identities are to be reflected are then further emphasised and solemnised through parades or annual services of commemoration. The 1982 Falklands campaign has been neglected in this respect, and this resultant lacuna is unfortunate as the remembrance of the Falklands fallen still exercises a powerful influence on Falklands society and wider political and moral debate concerning the Falklands question.

Relatives of the British dead who travelled to the Islands in the immediate aftermath of the conflict were, according to the journalist Jean Carr, surprised: 'To many of the passengers on the Cunard Countess, the Islands were nothing like they had expected. Port Stanley had looked like a shanty town from the sea and close up it was not much better.'[65] The main settlement bore the scars of the conflict, military ordinance, overflowing drains and raw sewage engulfed the houses, many of which had been occupied by destructive British and Argentine troops. One nameless bereaved mother from Glasgow exclaimed on landing at Stanley: 'I'm bitter he went through Ireland and then got killed for an island nobody had heard of. They should have blown it out to sea. But I knew he'd like it this way because he was so proud of his country.'[66] For some relatives, the image of the desolate, bleak and windswept Falkland Islands combined with the decay and dilapidation of Stanley compounded their profound sense of loss.

While many had already been buried, there was a break from British military tradition when Thatcher agreed to the repatriation of the servicemen should relatives desire a reburial in Britain. As the official report of the Commonwealth War Graves Commission later concluded:

> In a departure from the policies for the 1914-1918 and 1939-1945 wars but in accordance with precedents, the government agreed that if relatives so wished the bodies of those killed in the Falklands war might be repatriated for permanent burial, therefore of the 255 who died 64 were repatriated to Britain and one to Hong Kong. Of the remaining dead 174 had no grave but the sea and 16 were permanently buried in the Islands.[67]

In an apparent contradiction of the erstwhile symbolic importance of the Falkland Islands, the hallowed fields of battle were judged by many to be too distant from British shores. Yet, while the bodies of British servicemen were being repatriated, the Malvinas War Veterans Group insisted that their fallen were already buried in Argentine soil and therefore flatly rebutted calls from the Falkland Islands community to consider their graves as temporary in nature.

In appreciation of the sacrifice made by the British task-force, the Falkland Islands community helped to construct and maintain a network of memorial sites in the hills and valleys of the Falkland Islands. This has been carried out with great diligence, as a number of the Falkland Islanders bravely assisted the task-force during the conflict. Over the years, plaques and crosses were erected commemorating the sacrifices of individual regiments throughout East Falkland, including one to the Scots Guards on the top of Mount Tumbledown. A memorial to the 13 British servicemen buried on the Falklands sited at San Carlos overlooks the task-force's landing-place. The most spectacular example, however, is to be found in Stanley along Ross Road in front of the secretariat of the Falkland Islands Government. Liberation Monument was funded and built by 'grateful' Falkland Islanders, at an estimated cost of £70,000. Surrounded by a memorial wall containing the names of all those who gave their lives, a large statue designed by Gerald Dixon – composed of a 20-foot polished granite pillar inscribed with the names of the participating military units – dominates the site. At the top of the pillar, an eight-foot tall bronze figure of Britannia commands the view of Stanley Harbour. Local Fox Bay stone paves the area, which is backed by a ten-foot wall, constructed from a variety of stones collected from the battlefields of the campaign. The wall also contains a centrally placed mural depicting fighting scenes, while the front of the monument bears the inscription 'In memory of those who liberated us 14th June 1982'. Since the unveiling of the monument on 14 June 1984, 'Liberation Day' has been celebrated annually. On the tenth anniversary of the conflict, two benches were positioned either side of the monument.

For the overwhelming majority in the Falkland Islands, Liberation Monument pays homage to the British task-force and consolidates a sense of belonging and citizenship. The figure of Britannia remains a reassuring symbol of British national identity and, as Madge Dresser has noted, this icon was linked in the past to Queen Victoria, the British Empire and a British world order.[68] Most Falkland Islanders interviewed by the author equate the monument with the reassuring presence of Britain and Thatcher's determination to maintain the Falklands as a British territory. In recognition of those qualities, the Falkland Islands Government agreed to name the little road running behind Liberation Monument Thatcher Drive, and the 10 January is celebrated as 'Margaret Thatcher Day'.

Exactly one year after the unveiling of Liberation Monument in Stanley, the Queen, whose son Prince Andrew had served as a helicopter pilot during the conflict, unveiled a memorial plaque in St Paul's Cathedral to the South Atlantic task-force. According to the *Sun*,

> The Queen led the nation's homage yesterday to the men who died in the Falklands War...The tearful Queen unveiled a memorial bearing the names of the 255 servicemen and civilians killed. The simple tribute carried the inscription in three-inch gold letters: 'In honour of the South Atlantic Task Force. To the Abiding memory of all those who gave their lives'.[69]

The plaque is located in the crypt of the cathedral close to the tombs of Lord Nelson and the Duke of Wellington. At the same time, 255 trees were planted in the Stanley cemetery for those who lost their lives.

The landscapes of remembrance created in the Falklands have become poignant sites of pilgrimage for the relatives of the dead as well as the growing numbers of tourists – especially the battlefields and the British cemetery in San Carlos. For much of the 1980s, visits by Argentine relatives of the dead were largely limited due to the diplomatic and political impasse between the British and Argentine Governments. While many in the Falkland Islands consider the Argentine cemetery in Darwin to be temporary, Argentines view it as a permanent and appropriate resting-place in a part of the Republic. Throughout the post-conflict era, the Argentine cemetery has been subjected to controversy with fears being expressed that Argentine nationalists might 'exploit' the war dead in order to press home some kind of political advantage regarding the sovereignty question. British flags fluttering over the San Carlos cemetery not only honour the dead but also serve to remind visitors that this is British territory. To allow any Argentine flags to fly over their cemetery could, Falkland Islanders fear, be viewed as a dereliction and only provide further comfort to Argentine nationalists dreaming of reclaiming the Falklands. When the president of Argentina officially opened the monument to the Malvinas fallen in April 1991 in the centre of Buenos Aires, Islanders suspected well-entrenched nationalist sentiments.

Given the enormous symbolic value of the conflict to British national identity, it is perhaps surprising that it was only in November 1999 that a Falkland Islands memorial chapel was dedicated in the UK. The original idea emerged by accident. Pangbourne School in west Berkshire, long associated with the Royal and Merchant navies, desired a chapel for religious and community-based services. After the failure of its original scheme to transport an existing church from Salisbury in Wiltshire, headmaster Anthony Hudson discussed the matter with former pupil Patrick Robinson, an acquaintance of Falklands veteran Admiral Sandy Woodward.[70] In the absence of any form of memorial chapel, they proposed that the school would be a suitable location for such a building. With the support of the Admiral, a team of trustees was appointed to organise an appeal fund in 1995. Controversially, the National Lottery Commission rejected three applications by the trustees for financial support, on the grounds that the commission did not attach sufficient priority to the project. When Lady Thatcher hosted a small party in London, £250,000 was raised in one evening. Other events, including dinners hosted on board HMS *Victory* in Portsmouth, raised over £2.3 million in two years, with 10 individuals responsible for nearly three-quarters of the final total.[71] Students at the school raised £11,000 by organising a 'Tumbledown Ball' and a sponsored walk with members of the British armed forces.

The Royal Fine Arts Commission judged the early designs unsuitable. Under its direction a national competition was organised in 1997, with the winning design for the chapel selected from the 73 entries submitted. Architect Crispin Wride of Reading undertook the project, and construction of the chapel began in October 1998, with completion a year later. According to those involved in the project, the shape of the chapel appealed to senior officers of the Royal Navy because it resembled the hull of a ship, while others praised it for incorporating an information centre about the war, so that visitors could learn about the losses endured. The Royal Fine Arts Commission deemed the proximity of the commemorative garden to the chapel unsuitable but was ignored and the construction went ahead despite its disapproval. The wall, forming a contemplative space, features a geographical depiction of the Falkland Islands. The dedication service in November 1999 was well supported by the relatives of the dead, who praised the value of the chapel as a 'living memorial'. In March 2000, Queen Elizabeth II, accompanied by a Labour Government minister, visited the chapel. Despite the royal patronage, support from the armed forces in the early years of the appeal was lukewarm – but that may well have been due to resentment that the choice of location was Pangbourne rather than Portsmouth or Aldershot. It may not have helped either that in the early 1990s Pangbourne was at the centre of a bullying scandal, as some newspapers were eager to remind their readers.

Monuments, whether located in London, Pangbourne or Stanley, are not just passive reflections of the past, they can invoke power, glory, contemplation and even shame.[72] The inclusion of Falklands veterans in the official Remembrance Sunday Parade made them part of a seamless commemorative tradition which hardly distinguishes between one 'just war' and another.[73] However, it would be wrong to imply that these acts of commemoration were supported by all sections of the population in either the Falklands or the UK. Many people in Britain remain strongly opposed to the 1982 conflict, and were angered by the decision to sacrifice men for a place that few in the FCO cared for. Tragically, many Falklands veterans have taken their own lives, having failed to cope with post-traumatic stress disorder. Similarly, it would also be wrong to conclude that all Falkland Islanders approved of the construction of the Liberation Monument. Some considered that the money raised should have been used in the reconstruction of the shattered infrastructure of the community. Many native-born Islanders and expatriates abroad during the 1982 conflict have complained in private that their absence is frequently invoked effectively to silence, for example, advocates for a more co-operative and forgiving relationship with Argentina. As one native-born Islander noted to the author, 'someone only has to say 'where were you during 1982?' in order to justify at the expense of more moderate views, their own hard-line attitudes about Argentina'.[74] Unfortunately, the articulation of bitter memories relating to the Argentine occupation can still suppress necessary debates about war and its consequences.

SUMMARY

The earliest debates in the House of Commons after that fateful day in April 1982 were filled with ethical condemnation, moral outrage and political fury. This provoked a major shift in the political and cultural awareness of the South Atlantic Empire. From being a place which successive British Governments since 1968 were prepared to hand over, overnight it was transformed into a national crusade. Despite the substantial risks taken by the British Government, the nature of the Argentine regime, the speed of the conflict and the relatively low number of British casualties unquestionably assisted this metamorphosis. Long-standing representations of World War II and stereotypes of Argentina were deployed in order to generate public and parliamentary support for a strong response to the Argentine invasion. Dissent from the political left did not dissuade, and public opinion largely supported the despatch of the task-force and subsequent engagement with Argentine forces. Restrictions on media reporting in combination with formal censorship ensured that no viewer in the UK had to confront, at the time of the fighting, the grim realities of this short military conflict. Labelled by the Argentine media and military 'pirates' and 'imperialists', the task-force completed its mission in June 1982 thus ensuring the survival of Thatcher and her administration.

The victory parade of October 1982 drew 300,000 people to the streets in celebration of national pride and achievement. Even without the architectural legacies, the Falklands conflict will remain an important episode in post-imperial history. However, it is also sobering to remember that on the eleventh anniversary of the Falklands campaign, the IRA detonated a massive bomb close to the London Baltic Exchange, killing three people and causing damage running into millions of pounds.[75] It was another powerful reminder of an unresolved and deeply problematic imperial conflict, one which climaxed in 1984 with the bombing of the Grand Hotel in Brighton and the near death of Thatcher. In their different ways, the IRA and Thatcher recognised the symbolic importance of the City of London, the heart of Britain's imperial domain.

NOTES ON CHAPTER 9

1   J. Raban, *Coasting* (London, Collins Harvill, 1986), pp. 101–2.

2   This was quite strikingly illustrated during a programme shown by BBC Pebble Mill in 1981, when presenter Bob Langley asked people in the streets of Birmingham about the possible geographical location of the Falklands. In the same year, Anglia Television released its film *More British than British*, in an attempt to portray the Falkland Islands community as a loyal if neglected British community. The director of Anglia Television was Lord Buxton, a well-known supporter of the Falkland Islands cause.

3   It should be noted, however, that Argentines were often remarkably ignorant of the cultural qualities of the Falkland Islands. It was not uncommon for many Argentines to believe that the Falkland Islands community was Spanish-speaking rather than predominantly Anglophone.

4   This of course seems in keeping with a crisis, which allegedly witnessed a series of intelligence failures and a lack of ministerial attention. The official inquiry led by Lord Franks into the causes of the 1982 Falklands conflict drew these conclusions, *The Franks Report: Falkland Islands Review* (London, HMSO, 1983).

5   Author interview with Professor David Sugden, 13 September 2001.

6   C. Clapperton and D. Sugden, *Scenery of the South: Falkland Islands, South Georgia, Sub-Antarctic Islands* (Aberdeen, St George's Printing Works, 1975).

7   David Sugden's films of South Georgia during his research visits were used by the BBC in early April 1982, as they also lacked background footage and basic information about the Falklands and the far south.

8   G. Drower, *Britain's Dependent Territories: A Fistful of Islands* (Aldershot, Dartmouth, 1992), p. x.

9   *The Falklands Campaign: A Digest of Debates in the House of Commons 2nd April–15th June 1982* (London, HMSO, 1982). The extract is taken from 3 April 1982. See also M. Thatcher, *The Downing Street Years* (London, HarperCollins, 1993), p. 183.

10   Author interview with Lord Carrington, 22 May 2001.

11   P. Hennessy, *The Prime Minister: The Office and its Holders Since 1945* (London, Allen Lane, 2000), p. 104–6.

12   On the significance of Sir Henry Leach and his belief in British naval capabilities, see M. Hastings and S. Jenkins, *The Battle for the Falklands* (London, Michael Joseph, 1983).

13   *The Falklands Campaign: A Digest of Debates in the House of Commons 2nd April–June 15th 1982*. The extract is taken from a speech on 8 April 1982.

14   *The Falklands Campaign: A Digest of Debates in the House of Commons 2nd April–June 15th 1982*. The extract is taken from a speech on 20 April 1982.

15   *The Falklands Campaign: A Digest of Debates in the House of Commons 2nd April–June 15th 1982*. The extract is taken from a speech on 20 April 1982.

16 *The Falklands Campaign: A Digest of Debates in the House of Commons 2nd April–June 15th 1982*. The extract is taken from a speech on 3 April 1982.

17 When interviewing Islanders about their experiences of the 1982 Occupation it was striking how many of the interviewees cited the Nazi occupation of the Channel Islands during the Second World War in order to argue that people in the UK had little understanding of the impact of such a situation. Islander John Smith published his diary of the occupation under the title *74 Days: Islander's Diary of the Falklands Occupation* (London, Century, 1983).

18 P. Fussell, *Wartime* (Oxford, Clarendon Press, 1989), p. 164.

19 *The Falklands Campaign: A Digest of Debates in the House of Commons 2nd April–June 15th 1982*. The extract is taken from a speech on 3 April 1982.

20 The *Times*, 'We are all Falkland Islanders now', 5 April 1982.

21 *The Falklands Campaign: A Digest of Debates in the House of Commons 2nd April–June 15th 1982*. The extract is taken from a speech on 8 April 1982.

22 Author interview with Lord Carrington, 22 May 1982.

23 Thatcher, *The Downing Street Years*, p. 225.

24 *The Falklands Campaign: A Digest of Debates in the House of Commons 2nd April–June 15th 1982*. The extract is taken from a speech on 29 April 1982.

25 Thatcher, *The Downing Street Years*, p. 173.

26 The role of the then US Defence Secretary, Caspar Weinberger, was critical in persuading President Reagan to support the British task-force after fierce opposition from the US Ambassador to the UN, Jean Kirkpatrick, who warned that relations with the entire Latin American region would suffer as a consequence of that decision.

27 Hastings and Jenkins, *The Battle for the Falkland Islands*.

28 The British Government had no spy satellite and was therefore reliant on a repositioned US satellite for any intelligence material from Argentine diplomatic and military sources.

29 See the analysis by R. Harris, *Gotcha! The Media, the Government and the Falklands Crisis* (London, Unwin, 1983); D. Morrison and H. Tumber, *Journalists at War* (London, Sage, 1988). A useful overview is provided by S. Carruthers, *The Media at War* (London, Macmillan, 2000).

30 B. Ingham, *Kill the Messenger* (London, HarperCollins, 1992). On the relationship between the MOD and journalists, see V. Adams, *The Media and the Falklands Campaign* (London, Macmillan, 1986).

31 Ingham, *Kill the Messenger*, p. 283.

32 Quoted in Carruthers, *The Media at War*, p. 121.

33 P. Knightley, 'Managing the media in wartime', *Index of Censorship* 11 (1982), p. 7.

34 *The Falklands Campaign: A Digest of Debates in the House of Commons 2nd April–June 15th 1982*. The extract is taken from a speech on 6 May 1982.

35 Thatcher, *The Downing Street Years*, pp. 229–30.

36 Glasgow University Media Group, *Industry, Economy, War and Politics* (London, Routledge, 1992), pp. 142–3.

37 For more details on the sinking of the *Belgrano*, see A. Gavshon and D. Rice, *The Sinking of the* Belgrano (London, Secker and Warburg, 1984) and C. Ponting, *The Right to Know* (London, Sphere Books, 1985). The Labour MP Tam Dalyell campaigned in the House of Commons for years in an attempt to force the British Government to publicly account for its decision to sink the ship while it was heading towards its home port in Argentina.

38   See the commentary in Carruthers, *The Media at War*.

39   P. Bishop 'Reporting the Falklands', *Index on Censorship* 11 (1982): p. 7.

40   Raban, *Coasting*, p. 101.

41   *Independent on Sunday*, 'We are so proud of you', 23 May 1982.

42   *Sunday Mirror*, 'A cuppa for a para', 23 May 1982.

43   C. Brothers, *War and Photography* (London, Routledge, 1997), p. 208.

44   Glasgow University Media Group, *Industry, Economy, War and Politics*, p. 136.

45   D. Tinker, *A Message from the Falklands: The Life and Death of David Tinker lieut. RN: From his Letters and Poems* (London, Junction Books, 1982), pp. 180, 190.

46   S. Weston, *Walking Tall* (London, Bloomsbury, 1989), pp. 129–31.

47   *The Falklands Campaign: A Digest of Debates in the House of Commons 2nd April–June 15th 1982*. The extract is taken from a speech on 15 June 1982.

48   Thatcher, *The Downing Street Years*, p. 235.

49   See, for example, the analyses of H. Young, *One of Us* (London, Macmillan, 1990).

50   T. Mason, *Passion of the People? Football in South America* (London, Verso, 1995), p. 164.

51   Cited in F. Driver and D. Gilbert, 'Heart of empire? Landscape, space and performance in imperial London', *Environment and Planning D: Society and Space* 16 (1998): pp. 11–28.

52   J. Jacobs, *Edge of Empire* (London, Routledge, 1996), p. 38.

53   Driver and Gilbert, 'Heart of empire? Landscape, space and performance in imperial London', p. 19.

54   J. Schneer, *London 1900: The Imperial Metropolis* (London, Yale University Press, 1999), pp. 64–92.

55   The *Daily Telegraph* 'Proud Thatcher salutes "the bravest and best", dated 13 October 1982.

56   The *Daily Mail*, 'Tunes of glory…', 13 October 1982.

57   *Financial Times*, 13 October 1982.

58   The *Guardian*, 'Thousands cheer task force reliving its Falkland triumph', 13 October 1982.

59   Telephone interview with Denzil Connick, 15 June 2001. Connick was a former member of the Parachute Regiment who lost his leg as a consequence of the fierce fighting in the Falklands. With the assistance of another Falklands veteran, Dr Rick Jolly, he manages SAMA 82, which provides support to Falklands veterans and their families. See also B. Allen, 'Given the disabled a life (and a ramp), not a year of McDonald's', the *Observer*, 13 June 1999.

60   *Daily Mail*, 'The bravest of the brave', 13 October 1982.

61   P. Toynbee in the *Guardian*, 'Comment', 11 October 1982.

62   The *Guardian*, 'Task force relives triumph', 13 October 1982.

63   The *Daily Express*, 'The Falklands victors cheer their heroine', 13 October 1982.

64   S. Barker 'Images of the sixteenth and seventeenth centuries as a history of the present', in F. Barker, P. Hulme, H. Iversen and D. Loxley (eds), *Politics and Theory* (London, Routledge, 1984), p. 167. See also the *Daily Express*, 'The Mary Rose goes public', 13 October 1982. The men and machines attached to the task-force were later exhibited at the International Boat Show at Earl's Court in London in 1983.

65   J. Carr, *Another Story: Women and the Falklands War* (London, Croom Helm, 1984), p. 144.

66   Glasgow University Media Group, *Industry, Economy, War and Politics*, p. 104.

67 T. Gibson-Edwin and T. Kingsley-Ward, *Courage Remembered* (London, HMSO, 1989), p. 1.

68 M. Dresser, 'Britannia', in R. Samuel (ed.), *Patriotism* (London, Allen and Unwin, 1989), pp. 26–49.

69 The *Sun*, 'Editorial', 15 June 1985.

70 Author interview with Anthony Nelson, 16 July 2001. The analysis that follows of the Falkland Islands Memorial Chapel owes a great deal to Mr Hudson's recollections of events. He is publishing his own account of the construction in 2002 under the title 'Just to see his name: A history of the Falkland Islands Memorial Chapel at Pangbourne School'.

71 One of the major sponsors was Sir Jack Hayward, who had already given a substantial donation to the King Edward VII Memorial Hospital in Stanley. See *Falkland Focus*, 'Battle Day opening for new hospital', November/December 1987.

72 A point made by G. Dijkink 'Geopolitical codes and popular representations', *Geojournal* 46 (1998): pp. 293–9.

73 H. Lefebvre, *The Production of Space* (Oxford, Blackwell, 1998).

74 Author interview with a Falkland Islander, 23 April 2000.

75 J. Jacobs, *Edge of Empire* (London, Routledge, 1992), p. 64.

10

Preserving the South Atlantic Empire

The Falklands conflict directed attention to the Falklands and beyond the Falklands to the Antarctic, and people recognised more than they did before that there is a tenth of the earth's surface beyond the Falklands with potential in a number of areas and that Britain ought to keep its options open.[1]

Gone are the days when the Falkland Islands were a neglected dot in the South Atlantic, known only to FIDS and philatelists. While thankfully no longer at the centre of the world stage, we nevertheless remain the mainstream of international affairs and domestic politics in the United Kingdom. It is essential, therefore, that the Falkland Islanders themselves should state their case at every conceivable opportunity...I would say that Falkland Islanders are as British as Orkney or Shetland Islanders.[2]

INTRODUCTION

Lord Shackleton, the Labour peer and influential author of the 1976 and 1982 reports on the state of the Falkland Islands and the South Atlantic, recognised the interconnection between the different elements of the South Atlantic Empire. As he noted in a discussion on BBC Radio 4 in December 1986,

I have always seen the obvious linkage of the Falklands and the Antarctic as a sort of gateway. Now there is in fact as of this moment no immediate relationship, but if you look at the overlapping claims of Chile, the Argentine and the British, and if you look at the position of southern Chile and the Falklands, quite clearly, especially with the opening of the airfield, Mount Pleasant, there is a potential connection. I don't think that the [Thatcher] government has often put a big enough case forward. And of course the classic argument is the rights of inhabitants and that is what it is based upon. But I think that there are wider interests of a rather more subtle and more sophisticated kind. We simply went to war to repel aggression. I don't think that the Antarctic entered the minds of most people at that time. I happened to feel that it was important. I happen to believe that Mrs Thatcher quickly saw that.[3]

The prevailing geopolitical context of the Antarctic and South Atlantic has changed in the aftermath of the 1982 conflict, as has the political and economic condition of the Falkland Islands. While Anglo–Argentine relations worsened, the Falklands' economy improved markedly through a new source of income. Armed with considerable financial autonomy, the Falkland Islands Government became increasingly confident in its demands to remain a British colony, and in doing so Falkland Islanders enjoyed the explicit support of Thatcher. While the Antarctic was not implicated in the 1982 conflict, Britain and the Antarctic Treaty System (ATS) faced new challenges in the UN General Assembly. As these debates coincided with controversies over polar mining, there were real fears that the ATS could collapse. In order to maintain political and scientific influence in the region it was decided to increase funding for the BAS in 1983. As an FCO memorandum confirmed, 'a continuous display of British sovereignty and activity' would be secured through such a commitment.[4] In the Falklands, the 'wishes' of the Islanders to determine their own future remain paramount in any future discussions on the sovereignty issue.

THE TRANSFORMATION OF THE FALKLAND ISLANDS AND ANGLO–ARGENTINE RAPPROCHEMENT

The new era of colonial permanence began in the aftermath of the 1982 Falklands conflict. The symbolic capital invested in the Falkland Islands by the Thatcher Government was such that no further discussions relating to the sovereignty dispute would be entered into with any Argentine Government regardless of its political leanings or composition. The Falkland Islands had been transformed within political discourse, and the geographical distance from Britain was an irrelevance. As the Prime Minister noted in her Christmas message to the Falkland Islanders in December 1985:

> I know we are separated by 8000 miles and I recall once during the campaign – indeed, it was the day when I was in my constituency and I knew the landings were going to occur – I recall saying that although you were 8000 miles, you were really only a heartbeat away. Today that 8000 miles seems to [sic] shrunk with the building of the new airport at Mount Pleasant when it was opened in May. I was sad not to be able to come ... You in the Falkland Islands were born to freedom, born to democracy, and we must cherish and nurture it. We can never be complacent about it. At the heart of democracy is the right of every man and woman to have his or her say in how he or she is to be governed. That is what the British way of life is all about. You know that we are committed to protecting your right to determine your own future ... you are a very special part of the British family.[5]

The remaining part of the 1980s were characterised by three distinct trends which taken together had the effect of consolidating British resolve with regards to upholding territorial claims to the Antarctic and South Atlantic.

First, no undertaking was given regarding any further political discussions over the sovereignty dispute. For Thatcher, the conflict in 1982 had resolved the crisis in favour of British sovereignty and the outstanding UN resolutions calling upon both parties to continue negotiations over the colonial situation in the South Atlantic were of limited importance.

Second, the Falkland Islands' society and economy was transformed by the introduction of a fishing licensing regime which enabled a raft of new investment in social facilities and infrastructure. With new funds, the Falkland Islands Government emerged as a more confident body, ready to demand increased consultation with the British Government and their London-based office facilitated political lobbying. While the Falklands lobby in London underwent reform, the Falkland Islands Association provided further public support for the Islanders in Britain.

Third, Britain's South Atlantic Empire underwent further constitutional change in 1985, when the Falkland Islands introduced a new constitution at the same time as the remaining parts of the FID were separated so that South Georgia became a distinct dependent territory with its own Government. However, the Governor of the Falkland Islands is also the ex-officio Commissioner of South Georgia.

The rationale for the reorganisation was due to the belief that the outstanding territorial disputes with Argentina would be easier to manage if the Falklands, South Georgia and the South Sandwich Islands were more clearly delineated from one another in a political and legal sense. The influential Shackleton report of 1982 also hinted that 'South Georgia may in the long run be of greater importance to the future development of the potential wealth of the South West Atlantic and the Antarctic than the Falkland Islands'.[6] As if to confirm long-standing Argentine suspicions about Britain's surreptitious interest in resource potential, members of the British armed forces were stationed on both the Falkland Islands and South Georgia for the remaining part of the twentieth century.

For the first eight years or so after the conflict there was little progress on the Falkland Islands question. On the one hand, the British position most famously associated with Thatcher was that the formal sovereignty of the Falklands was non-negotiable. Her personal visit to the Falklands in January 1983 consolidated that basic position of defending the 'wishes' of Islanders, and the 1982 British Nationality (Falkland Islands) Amendment Act was passed to enable all Falkland Islanders to become British citizens. On the other hand, the newly elected President of Argentina, Raul Alfonsín was adamant that no negotiations could be undertaken with Britain regarding the resumption of diplomatic relations unless the sovereignty question was actively addressed and Argentina's territorial integrity respected. As he noted in February 1984, 'In the first place, Argentina will never renounce her legitimate rights on the Malvinas. There can be no doubts about the solution on the islands', and he continued to argue that ultimately the fate of the territory was more important than the 'wishes' of the inhabitants.[7]

Pressure groups such as the Falklands Islands Association in London and the Malvinas War Veterans in Buenos Aires ensured that neither country appeared ready or able to conceive of the dispute in more flexible terms. Both political leaders and their Governments were unprepared either to end the outstanding hostilities (Alfonsín) or plan for a possible resolution of the sovereignty crisis (Thatcher). As a consequence of this intransigence, the British Government declared a 150-mile-wide Falkland Islands protection zone in July 1982, specifically to exclude all Argentine military and merchant ships and planes. Unlike the negotiations with China over Hong Kong, Argentine observers argued that the crude power politics were intended to ensure that Argentina was in no position to exert a dominant force over the Falklands in the wake of defeat. The people of Hong Kong had not been able formally to reject leaseback, and unlike the people of the Falkland Islands, their 'wishes' were not considered to be negotiable.[8]

The diplomatic impasse was most famously exposed in an ill-fated meeting between British and Argentine delegations in Berne, Switzerland, in July 1984.[9] Ostensibly, the meeting was designed to explore the possibility of political progress through the Swiss Government's good offices. According to one retired FCO official present at the meeting, months of negotiations had already been undertaken, and the British had devised the phrase 'not prepared to discuss' the sovereignty question.[10] The Swiss Foreign Ministry had circulated the formal position papers regarding the sovereignty question before the parties arrived in the Swiss capital.

Once both parties had taken up residence, negotiations began after the first night's dinner, with the leaders of the delegations exchanging their formal positions. The chief negotiator of the British delegation, Argentine-born David Thomas, explained in Spanish to the Argentine delegation that Britain was 'not prepared' to discuss sovereignty but was ready to consider other items on the agenda. The Argentine representatives interpreted 'not prepared' as 'not prepared yet', which was unfortunately a complete misreading of the inflexible British position. Almost immediately, diplomatic deadlock ensued, as the Argentine delegation demanded that a mechanism for the discussion of sovereignty be found before the meetings could progress further. The FCO delegation was under strict instructions from Thatcher to avoid any consideration of sovereignty, even though other issues such as the normalisation of cultural, diplomatic, financial and commercial relations could be addressed.

After several days of intense negotiation which led to misleading radio reports from London suggesting that the Argentine delegation had already left Switzerland, both delegations struggled to agree a form of words acceptable for a post-summit communiqué. In the event, the document simply noted that inconclusive talks had been held in Switzerland and that both parties would seek to improve relations with one another. Despite the lack of progress, the Swiss Foreign Ministry had played a crucial role in bringing the two parties together, and diplomatically translated the British position paper and in particular the phrase 'not prepared to discuss' into French rather than Spanish for the benefit of the Argentine delegation. The Swiss had used the French language deliberately to soften the apparently inflexible position (the position paper noted that the British were 'not prepared' rather than 'would never discuss'), which in turn encouraged and placated the Argentine delegation to misinterpret Thomas's opening statement. To the evident surprise of the Argentine delegation, there was no evidence whatsoever that the position articulated by the Prime Minister and the diplomatic team had altered.

The failure of the summit to reach any form of *modus operandi* for post-conflict negotiations set the political tone for subsequent Anglo–Argentine relations in the Alfonsín–Thatcher era. The implication for the Falkland Islands was substantial, as the summit occurred during a period of visible British commitment to the South Atlantic in the fields of military protection and economic development. The creation of Mount Pleasant airbase transformed the dispute, because it enabled a permanent and substantial British military presence, supported by regular flights to Britain via Ascension Island. It was one of the development priorities cited in both economic reports by Shackleton and his team, and was finally implemented in 1984–5 at an initial cost of £400 million to the UK taxpayer.

Located approximately 30 miles west of Stanley, the new base offered the Islanders a clear symbol of Britain's determination to defend the 'wishes' of the Islanders to determine their own political future. The base nonetheless also opened up the possibility of developing logistical links in isolation from South American neighbours. In other words, the trend that had been set in place by the 1971 Joint Communications Agreement was being reversed, because now Islanders were able to leave the Falkland Islands without transiting either Argentina or Chile. In turn this provoked widespread Argentine anger, and Britain was accused of heightening tension in the South Atlantic. Some commentators even alleged that this was part of a secret NATO plot to exert its influence in the region.[11] Notwithstanding the lack of evidence for such a NATO plot, President Sarney of Brazil, with the support of Alfonsín, successfully sought UN support for a South Atlantic zone of peace and co-operation, which called on all parties in the region to reduce their military presence. However, with Argentina's refusal formally to end hostilities with Britain, the Thatcher Government was seemingly presented with a legitimate reason to maintain a military presence in the Falklands.

On account of the changing military context, Thatcher commissioned Shackleton to produce an updated report on the economic potential of the Falkland Islands. Shorter than his original report in 1976, his team's new report of August 1982 reiterated its belief that the community had to undergo some fundamental changes to land-ownership and that new areas for possible development such as fisheries had to be investigated. As had been identified earlier, the high numbers of absentee landlords had stifled investment and agricultural innovation in a depressed wool market. Under the management of the Falkland Islands Development Corporation, farms scattered around East and West Falkland and major settlements such as Port Stephens were sub-divided into five new farming concerns.

Within six years of the 1982 conflict, local land-ownership increased from 24 per cent to a record high of 73 per cent, with the largest change being recorded in West Falkland. While debates raged in the Falklands and elsewhere about the economical effectiveness of the sub-division programme, the most important element of change was arguably cultural. This was widely welcomed by camp-based Islanders who embraced the ending of the quasi-feudal farming conditions employed by the FIC. Under the Department of Agriculture, new efforts were made to diversify the agricultural sector, and the creation of dairy and market-gardening ventures were some of the more successful projects in the Islands. Despite the broadening of land-ownership, many sheep farms continued to suffer at the hands of the declining wool market, compounded by the long distances from the major British market.

Improvements in the economic situation of the Falkland Islands came with fisheries, and especially with the creation of a fishing licensing regime in the South Atlantic. While the Falkland Islands protection zone deterred Argentine ships and planes, it had not been designed to exclude foreign trawlers intent on exploiting squid and fish stocks. The Shackleton reports identified fishing as a major development priority for the Islands, and recommended the creation of a fishing zone. British negotiators were later involved in discussions with Argentina and international bodies such as the Food and Agricultural Organisation to consider the potential for multilateral management of the fishing resources in the southwest

Atlantic. In the absence of a political settlement for the Falklands, these talks were largely preliminary, as Argentina was anxious to avoid any recognition of British *de facto* authority. Following Argentina's unilateral decision to sign bilateral agreements with distant-water fishing nations such as Bulgaria and the Soviet Union to fish in waters close to the Falklands, the British created a 150-mile Falkland Islands Interim Conservation and Management Zone (FICZ) in October 1986.[12]

Despite earlier pressure from the Falklands lobby for such a decision, the declaration of the FICZ was now justified as a response to a unilateral Argentine development, which interfered with British sovereignty in the Falklands and threatened the long-term viability of fish stocks. The FICZ was highly successful, and in the first season over 200 licences were awarded to individual vessels from countries which had previously expressed sympathy for the Argentine claim to the Falkland Islands such as Spain and the Soviet Union.[13] The fishing licensing regime enabled the Falkland Islands Government to generate a source of revenue in excess of £20 million per year, but this new-found financial autonomy alarmed Argentina as it lessened the prospect for a sovereignty transfer.[14] By the second year of the FICZ, £25 million pounds was raised, which financed a state-of-the-art secondary school, hospital, road expansion and additional social services (see figure 10.1). Rapid improvement in the urban fabric of the major settlement was widely welcomed by Islanders, especially where the impact of war was still obvious namely damaged housing and inadequate public services. New employment opportunities were created by private-sector businesses such as Seafish (Falklands) Limited, which evolved from the implementation of the fisheries regime. As a former Governor of the Falkland Islands, Gordon Jewkes, recognised in 1986, 'The Falkland Islands, probably for the first time in its history, has a source of income, which should provide a sizeable surplus of income over expenditure for investment in development'.[15] Politically, the fishing regime allowed the Government not only to invest in new community projects but also enabled the Overseas Development Administration to announce that British assistance would cease in the late 1980s.[16] The final tranche of aid was spent in 1992, and since then no further aid has been provided.

For the Islanders, the political and constitutional condition of the Falklands changed noticeably in the post-war period as a new constitution, similar to the one in Gibraltar, was introduced and the principle of self-determination was cited as the major determining factor in the Islands' future. The 1985 constitution stated that all Councillors to the FIG would be directly elected (rather than some being nominated), thereby diminishing the office of the Governor of the Falkland Islands to one of a more advisory role. The longevity of the Thatcher Government was critical for future prospects because the then leader of the Labour Party, Neil Kinnock committed his party to discussing the disputed sovereignty of the Islands with Argentina (as did David Steel of the Liberal Party).[17] In an interview with the British journalist John Simpson, President Alfonsín acknowledged that 'They [Kinnock and Steel] were understanding enough to lead us to think that we'll be able to start a really constructive dialogue including all those subjects separating us from Great Britain'.[18] However, with Thatcher's third electoral victory in 1987, followed by another Conservative victory in 1992, the prospect for change lessened, and by the time a Labour Government was returned to office in 1997 the argument concerning the protection of the 'wishes' of the Falkland Islands was political orthodoxy.

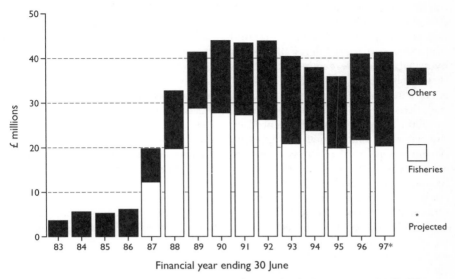

Figure 10.1: Fishing licensing income for the Falkland Islands Government (1987–97)

Accusations have nonetheless abounded that the residents of Stanley have benefited more from the licensing money than the small and scattered farming communities in West Falkland. In contrast, some farmers on East Falkland have been able to secure alternative employment in Stanley thanks to the improved road conditions in the camp. The continuing decline in farming exposed the lack of opportunities available for camp-based residents and created a population movement to Stanley. In one of the smallest democracies in the world, these differences appear more immediate because of the face-to-face nature of decision-making and the proximity of Falkland Islands Councillors to the majority of citizens living in Stanley. Many Islanders have noted that they have gained a greater collective confidence regarding the public expression of issues, while some interviewees confided to the author that the memories of the 1982 occupation were powerful symbolic resources which were employed to restrain the views of others. Some Islanders and expatriate residents resent these particular claims to 'divine wisdom' and argue that political debate in the Falklands remains constrained by periodic outbursts invoking the 1982 conflict. Nonetheless, these intellectual restrictions are seen as a small sacrifice in return for minimal contact with Argentina.

Argentina's reluctance formally to end hostilities, and its traditional understanding of the conflict as exclusively bilateral, further alienated an increasingly confident Falkland Islands Government supported by over 94 per cent of the Falklands' population, according to local opinion polls, who favoured maintaining British sovereignty.[19] As importantly, British public opinion too, apart from the Labour Party and informal organisations such as the South Atlantic Council, was reluctant to endorse a new territorial solution. Created in November 1983 and composed of academics, political figures and business people, the South Atlantic Council attempted to promote contact with Argentine counterparts and pursued discussions with regard to the sovereignty dispute, citing the damage done to Anglo–Argentine relations and the ongoing defence costs shouldered by the British taxpayer. The cost of the British garrison was relatively small, at £257 million, compared to a total defence budget of £18 billion for the financial year 1987–8. The Labour Party leadership also argued that Falkland Islanders should not enjoy an effective 'veto' over any future sovereignty discussions. Despite a veritable cottage industry in conflict resolution, the opponents of Thatcher's position vis-à-vis the Falklands were never able to shift the political balance in the UK, and the sizeable parliamentary majorities enjoyed by her Governments unquestionably endorsed her stance.[20]

With the election of President Carlos Menem in 1989, it was recognised that the failure to end formal hostilities with the UK would have ramifications for Argentina's political relationship with the EU. As an FCO brief in March 1990 acknowledged, 'Recognising the need to restore relations with Britain, especially if Argentina is to develop a satisfactory relationship with the European Community (EC), he proposed direct talks, with sovereignty put to one side ("under an umbrella")'.[21] Despite Menem's fiery rhetoric relating to the need for the 'recovery' of the Falklands by the year 2000, he noted that the disputed Islands were 'a matter we will never give up, and, I think, neither will the United Kingdom. Meanwhile we can have a civilised dialogue.'[22] Notwithstanding the diplomatic support of Italy and Spain, the lack of rapprochement with Britain was considered harmful to Argentina's trading negotiations and wider political reputation. New bilateral talks were held in Madrid in October 1989 and later in February 1990 for the purpose of mending diplomatic fences and exploring the potential for political, logistical and economic co-operation.[23]

The British and Argentine Governments agreed to implement a so-called 'sovereignty umbrella' in order to initiate new talks over the Falklands and to restore consular and trade relations. Similar in nature to Article IV of the 1959 Antarctic Treaty, the 'sovereignty umbrella' allowed both parties to concentrate on fostering co-operation especially in areas where bilateral contact made good sense in political and practical terms. Issues such as communication and fishing in the southwest Atlantic were identified as central to this co-operative spirit and ultimately beneficial to both parties.

The South Atlantic Fisheries Commission, created to improve resource conservation and management in the southwest Atlantic owes a great deal to the supportive intervention of Argentine Foreign Minister Dr Guido Di Tella. Unlike his predecessor Domingo Cavallo, who was more interested in improving Argentina's international financial relations, Di Tella was instrumental in persuading Menem that the Falklands question could only be resolved by confidence-building and patient diplomacy. Both parties agreed to consult further on the development of regional relations between the Falklands and Argentina against a background of the British military presence in the Islands. By the mid-1990s, a new air link with South America via Chile had been established and was routed with Argentina's approval through their air space. Simultaneously, Di Tella was deeply involved in a highly personal campaign to establish cordial relations with the Falklands community, which involved the despatch of presents to the Islanders. Other approaches included personal telephone calls to Islanders, the despatch of Christmas presents and repeated offers of generous financial compensation if the Islanders agreed to a transfer of sovereignty. While not entirely welcomed, it was at a least a change from previous Argentine foreign ministers and their refusal to recognise the attitudes of the local community in any bilateral negotiations with Britain. The Argentine Foreign Ministry would have preferred an exclusively bilateral approach to the dispute but Di Tella, as a fluent English speaker, acknowledged and even solicited contact with the Falkland Islands community. However, all these overtures were carried out against a backdrop of the 1994 Argentine constitution, which committed all future Governments to the eventual recovery of the Malvinas for Argentina.

In the same year as the Argentine constitution was amended, the Conservative Government re-branded the remaining islands and enclaves 'dependent territories' in a further attempt to remove the last remaining traces of colonialism. The then Foreign Secretary, Douglas Hurd, travelled to the Falkland Islands in 1994 to reassure the community that the British Government remained committed to the Falklands. In his recollections to the author, Hurd noted that the Falklands question was rarely a ministerial matter during the Major Government (1990–7), even though he remained interested in the Islands because his father had been a director of the FIC. The political consensus within the Conservative Party reflected Thatcher's doctrine that the Falklands was an issue that united all in their commitment to defend the dependent territory against any form of Argentine aggression or opportunism. The Falkland Islanders were, in the words of Hurd, 'Thatcher's children', and no-one dared upset that basic commitment to secure their political future.[24]

In terms of domestic politics, Thatcher's legacy to the Falkland Islands ensured that when Labour was elected in May 1997, it did not revert to the earlier policy of conducting sovereignty negotiations with Argentina. Unlike Neil Kinnock's inclination as leader of the opposition to discuss formally the sovereignty issue with Argentina, Tony Blair's Government continued the Conservative policy of respecting the 'wishes' of the Falkland Islanders, much to the disappointment of Argentine observers hoping for a change in British foreign policy. The new Government oversaw the first round of oil exploration in the Falklands in 1998 and agreed to support further hydrocarbon development in the South Atlantic. While it also dealt with post-colonial matters in Hong Kong, Fiji, Belize, Sierra Leone and Zimbabwe, the Falklands, along with the other remaining parts of the British Empire, were now re-classified as 'Overseas Territories'. According to Robin Cook, the then Foreign Secretary, the new term was intended to convey a sense of 'partnership on which we want to build our relationship'.[25] A white paper on 'Britain and the Overseas Territories' argued that the Labour Government was anxious to promote self-government for the Overseas Territories while avoiding the difficult questions raised by the Falklands and Gibraltar, which, unlike the other overseas territories are legally challenged by neighbouring states.[26] Notwithstanding the vagaries of the white paper, Falkland Islanders who read the document were swift to recognise that this transformation nonetheless endorsed the right of the community to shape, where possible, its own political future.

BRITAIN, THE 'FALKLANDS FACTOR' AND THE 'QUESTION OF ANTARCTICA'

In the aftermath of the Falklands campaign, attention inevitably turned towards Britain's future role in the Antarctic and the dependencies of South Georgia and South Sandwich. Notwithstanding the reassuring backdrop of the Antarctic Treaty,

Britain's presence in this region had been assured by the scientific endeavours of the BAS and the function of Royal Navy ships such as HMS *Endurance*. Stung by political criticism that the Thatcher Government had been inattentive to the symbolic importance of these activities, civil servants attached to the Polar Region Section of the FCO were asked to review for ministers the political, resource and scientific importance of the South Atlantic and Antarctic region. While Shackleton's report pointed to the strategic significance of South Georgia, it presented a less detailed commentary on British Antarctic territory. To maintain Britain's influence in the Antarctic, it was judged necessary to increase the funding for the BAS in order to allow for major investment in logistical support and base maintenance. It was noted that

> we see threats to the future peace of Antarctica arising from competition for its resources and from opposition by the Third World to the Antarctic Treaty System as the basis for dealing with the future of Antarctica. We have for many years expected that the international community would eventually focus on the Antarctic and were not surprised when the question of Antarctica was raised for debate in the last UN General Assembly'.[27]

FCO officials anticipated a growing political interest in the Antarctic, but Roberts, as one of the major architects of the Antarctic Treaty, never envisaged a substantial role for the UN. His ideal model was a small club of Antarctic nations managing the continent for the benefit of all humankind. In the late 1950s, large parts of the so-called Third World were still under colonialism and thus unable to participate in any of the formative discussions relating to the future management of the polar continent. This position was hardly surprising, as involvement in the Antarctic programmes relating to the 1957–8 IGY had been the benchmark for participation at the Washington Conference. When post-colonial states such as India tried to raise the issue of the management of Antarctica in the UN General Assembly, they were urged to drop such proposals by members of the Antarctic Treaty club. By jealously guarding the political and legal authority of signatories, the Antarctic Treaty established the membership rules. New states could accede to the ATS, but in return for full club membership they first had to carry out 'substantial scientific research' within the Antarctic Treaty region.[28] Unfortunately, the treaty itself never defined the qualification and it was unclear how a state would meet the requirement. Would a permanent base count as unambiguous evidence of 'substantial scientific research'? Did scientists from a prospective member state have to submit a certain number of reputable scientific publications, and did networking with major bodies such as the Scientific Committee for Antarctic Research help? Until the 1980s, the balance between the seven claimant states and the non-claimant states hardly shifted, as very few states, notably West Germany, were admitted to full club membership.

Impressive scientific achievements, the creation of various resource and environmental conventions and agreed measures could not disguise the fact the ATS was a secret club. Conversely, it could be argued that scientific co-operation in a zone of peace only succeeded because of the limited number of interested parties involved. Roberts supported this basic view, and his successor, Dr John Heap, sought to uphold this tradition of secret consultations in the ATS with limited reference to other interested international bodies such as the UN and non-governmental organisations. As the international political attention intensified following increased resource speculation, the clandestine nature of the ATS was subject to fierce debates within the UN, as was the continued membership of the international pariah, South Africa. However, the immediate catalyst was probably the ending of the Law of the Sea negotiations in December 1982, which encouraged states such as Malaysia to focus global attention on the status of the uninhabited polar continent. In particular, the question was raised whether the principles of common heritage could be applied to the Antarctic if they were to be applied to the ocean floors.

The ATS found itself exposed to a decade-long intensive form of political scrutiny in the UN after the Secretary General invited information and opinions from all interested parties in the 'Question of Antarctica'. Antarctica became caught up in a global rhetoric which disrupted the dominant political geographies of administration and control. The fate of Antarctic resources and later its ice caps evoked powerful expressions of the impact of global environmental and political processes. Three major themes emerged from the eventual report issued in the name of the Secretary-General, and these concentrated on the workings of the ATS, the ownership of mineral resources and the continued participation of apartheid South Africa.

First, the post-colonial states of Malaysia and Antigua raised the issue of whether a select group of nations should be allowed to determine the political future of Antarctica via a treaty system created during a period when many states were still under the control of imperial powers such as Britain. As Lloyd Jacobs, the then UN representative of Antigua, argued,

> To add to all of this, the world has vastly changed since the Antarctic Treaty was signed in 1959. There are now 169 member-states of the United Nations, most of which are developing countries. In 1959, they had neither the opportunity nor the sovereign competence to participate in Antarctica. It is not only unfair, it is unjust to suggest that we should abide by decisions made without our involvement. Indeed, we warned the world that if the status quo in Antarctica is maintained and further institutionalised a confrontation is bound to develop between the consultative parties and the rest of the world.[29]

Second, Malaysia in particular raised the issue of living and non-living resource ownership in Antarctica and quoted a well-known US Geological Survey estimate from 1974, which suggested the possibility of high yields of oil and natural gas.[30] While the ATS was negotiating a Convention on the Regulation of Antarctic Mineral Resources Activities (CRAMRA), other UN members demanded that non-ATS member states should be allowed to determine the political and economic future of the Antarctic. As a common space of humankind, Malaysia argued that the ATS should be dismantled in favour of a new regime regulated by the UN so that industrialised nations would be prevented from exploiting Antarctica for their own benefit. This was a position supported by members of the Non-Aligned Movement, who had urged in 1983 that 'The inherent logic of the new international economic order demands that the resources of Antarctica be available for the benefit of Mankind. It is only the United Nations that can play a role representing as it does the interests of all member states.'[31]

Third, members of the UN General Assembly pointed to the continued membership of South Africa and questioned whether the ATS should tolerate the presence of a racist regime. In 1985, African states, notably Kenya and Zaire, introduced a resolution noting, 'with regret the racist apartheid regime of South Africa, which has been suspended from participation in the General Assembly of the United Nations, is a Consultative Party to the Antarctic Treaty'.[32] While UN resolution 140/156C, calling for the immediate expulsion of South Africa was passed by the General Assembly, ATS members such as Britain declined to participate in the vote.

It would be wrong to imply that there was a Third-World consensus on Antarctica, but there was agreement that the ATS was exclusive, undemocratic and illegitimate. According to the then British permanent representative to the UN, Sir Anthony Parsons, the question of South African membership had the potential to undermine the 'united front', and while Britain deplored the nature of the Government in Pretoria it was not prepared to expel South Africa from the ATS. Indeed, the Antarctic Treaty makes no mention of whether fascist or racist regimes would ever be excluded in favour of democratic states committed to upholding the principles of peace and scientific co-operation. More alarming to the experienced British scientist Fuchs was the demand for greater UN involvement. As the former director of the BAS noted,

> To expect 150, or whatever it is, nations to be able to agree, sensibly, on what you do in a region where they do not understand the conditions – very few of them, that is – doesn't seem to me very sensible. The Treaty itself is one course open to any nation to join. The original signatories were twelve, and today there is a total of 32 nations who have adhered to the Treaty. So it's only up to the others, if they have got an interest, to say they will sign on.[33]

This view was widely shared within the British Antarctic community at the time, as was opposition to further UN involvement, because most of the states demanding change had no experience of the actual physical environment. Malaysia was described as simply not 'qualified' to comment, let alone administer a region of which they had no record. Moreover, the membership of the ATS had expanded to include the Third-World states India, Brazil and China, and as a consequence the charge of 'exclusiveness' and 'northern hemispheric bias' was no longer quite so appropriate.

Malaysia and Antigua, as former colonies, also raised issues relating to the geopolitics of knowledge and the political hegemony of international regimes such as the ATS. When British delegates in New York resisted calls for greater UN involvement in the management of Antarctica, British scientists urged for more vigorous research in Antarctica, given the potential to influence global environmental systems. The discovery of the 'ozone hole' by the BAS in 1986 was profound in Antarctica's political and environmental transformation and helped to consolidate the BAS's financial position. Since 1983, under Thatcher's direct intervention, funding for the BAS improved, but only after she had clashed with officials who sought to direct scientific funding elsewhere.

The significance of her intervention belies the fact that support for the BAS became embedded in a confused form of political rhetoric, which drew on territorial, resource and scientific factors to justify the British presence. Her comments of March 1989 further added to Argentine suspicions that the major reason underlying the British presence in the Falklands and the Antarctic was due to the unknown potential of mineral resources:

> I have always been interested in Antarctica. There is some marvellous wildlife there. There is quite a good deal of mineral deposits there. And you never quite

know what's going on in those fantastic, remarkable icy lands. They are not wastelands. Scientists said that it was not really sufficiently scientifically important to put more money into the Antarctic Survey. And I said that I did not know whether it was scientifically important. But I did think that it was very, very important for Britain. We have lands there. It was a fascinating place. We wanted to know more about the seas there. It was a fascinating place. And I did actually over-ride them and say the Antarctic Survey must have more money. And it was they who discovered the depletion of the ozone layer.[34]

Ironically, this observation occurred amid complaints by the British National Audit Office that funding for the BAS was poorly managed and that a number of projects, including the replacement of a new supply and science ship, were over budget.[35]

Apart from concerns over the financial management of the BAS, the political debate on Antarctica came to a head in 1988–9, when the Antarctic Treaty consultative parties announced that CRAMRA was available for formal signing in May 1988. After six years of considerable criticism within the UN and environmental campaigns by Greenpeace, the British Government was willing to ratify the convention in 1988, despite opposition from environmental critics fearing a scramble for mineral resources in the region. Britain – along with other major Antarctic parties – was charged with double standards, given that on the one hand it was concerned about global environmental change and yet on the other hand was prepared to sign an agreement which would allow mineral exploitation in the Antarctic. As Catherine Wallace of the pressure group, Antarctic and Southern Ocean Coalition contended, 'The Antarctic needs much tighter controls. When we disturb that, we disturb the regulatory effect it has on the global climate, and we jeopardise its unique life forms.'[36]

Malaysia condemned CRAMRA for allowing the Antarctic Treaty consultative parties to establish regulations which would allow for the eventual exploitation of the region's mineral resources. On this issue Britain and Argentina were agreed that Third-World pressure should not be allowed to weaken the ATS because that would jeopardise the two countries' positions within the Antarctic. While British officials responsible for negotiations regarding CRAMRA argued that the convention was intended to put in place regulations before any such activity took place, it only heightened speculation elsewhere that Britain and the US were intent on exploiting those resources contrary to official denials.

The initial expressions of public support for CRAMRA were effectively derailed by the decision of two claimant states, Australia and France, in 1989 to reject the provisions on the basis that Antarctica should be protected from mining indefinitely. Pressurised by environmental movements, Prime Ministers Hawke of Australia and Rocard of France were no longer willing to ratify the convention despite the attempts by Argentina, Britain and the US to prevent a schism on mineral resources. British officials charged with maintaining relations with ATS parties were angered by this public rejection, but noted in more diplomatic terms that:

The Australian case rests on an insubstantial assertion that Antarctic mineral activity is now suddenly environmentally unacceptable. The idea of maintaining the Antarctic as an unsullied paradise free of environmentally damaging mining activities is attractive. But the purpose of the convention [CRAMRA] is precisely to avoid environmental damage from mining in Antarctica. Instead of such prospecting being carried out openly within Antarctica and subject to proper control, as laid down in the convention, it would be done covertly under the guise of scientific research.[37]

Without the political support of these two parties, the convention was not going to be ratified, and the ATS was faced with its greatest crisis since the ratification of the 1959 Antarctic Treaty. Criticised by UN member states and environmental groups, the ATS's working culture of consensus was exposed as hollow, and furthermore the cosy workings of the correspondents group composed of Australia, New Zealand, Britain, and the US were shattered. Unsurprisingly, given the importance attached by the British to the ATS in protecting their claims and influence, the FCO began frantic negotiations with other claimant states such as Chile and Norway in an attempt to rescue negotiations over the future management of Antarctica.

By November 1989, a meeting of the Antarctic Treaty consultative parties was held in Vina del Mar in Chile, for the purpose of exploring possible areas of compromise between the supporters and critics of CRAMRA. After heated discussions, it was agreed that the environmental protection of the Antarctic would have to be the central element of any new convention, and that mining in the Antarctic would have to be banned for at least 50 years after the ratification process was completed. The eventual emergence of a Protocol on Environmental Protection (Protocol) helped to ease fears that the question of mineral resources would tear the ATS apart as claimant and non-claimant states argued over the regulation. The British Government hailed the emergence of the protocol as a diplomatic triumph, notwithstanding earlier support for CRAMRA. As an FCO briefing noted, 'HMG delighted that Protocol is to be opened for signature in Madrid today'.[38]

It is interesting to note that the UN challenge evaporated once the Protocol was signed.[39] While it was abundantly clear that the long-term issue of mineral resources was not resolved, the ATS committed itself to the environmental protection of Antarctica instead. Just as science had been extolled in the late 1950s as a unifying factor, so environmental protection was now claimed as a cause for common concern in the late 1980s.[40] For Britain, the survival of the ATS was paramount as it not only continued to protect territorial and political interests but also provided a mechanism for dealing with issues in a region that was considered a global problem. Within the General Assembly, the debates surrounding the 'question of Antarctica' changed noticeably as the high profile Malaysian Government toned down its criticism of the regime and acknowledged the Protocol's commitment to prohibit mining in the Antarctic Treaty region. Once the immediacy of the minerals issue receded, the BAS no longer enjoyed the generous levels of funding granted by Thatcher after the Falklands conflict. The formal ending of apartheid in South Africa in 1994 also helped to restore diplomatic stability to the international politics of Antarctica.

The Antarctica Act of 1994 enabled the ratification of the Protocol by the British Government and was finally adopted by all parties in January 1998. A considerable amount of work is still required with regard to implementation, monitoring and regulation of activities within the region: the Protocol managed to defuse some of the immediate intensity of the minerals debate. Other activities, such as tourism, which brings over 10,000 annual visitors to the Antarctic, will have to be monitored by all interested parties. As long as territorial sovereignty in the Antarctic remains unresolved, the Protocol, much as the 1959 Antarctic Treaty did before, reaffirms the significance of the sovereignty umbrella in facilitating peace and co-operation.

Notwithstanding pressures on funding, the BAS remains an important symbol of continued British commitment to the Antarctic Treaty and even the wider South Atlantic region. In March 2001, the British troops stationed on South Georgia since the 1982 South Atlantic conflict were replaced by a new BAS research station committed to research in polar biology and fish-stock monitoring around the island.[41] As revenue from fishing licences remains the major source of income for the South Georgia Government, forthcoming research is expected to concentrate on the consequences of illegal, unregulated and unreported fishing. The justification for the troop withdrawal is based on the ability to summon aid from the military base on the Falkland Islands in case of any security threat in the future.

LEARNING TO LIVE WITH NEIGHBOURS

One of the most important post-1982 agreements to affect the Falkland Islands was in part provoked by the arrest in London of the former president of Chile, General Augusto Pinochet in October 1998. As is well-known, his military regime provided invaluable if covert political and military support to Britain during the 1982 conflict as well as indirectly enabling the Falkland Islands to enjoy a post-war economic transformation.[42] Chile, in combination with Brazil and Uruguay, helped to end the Falkland Islands' isolation from the wider world by providing permission for British aircraft and shipping to use their logistical facilities. In the case of the RAF flights from Ascension Island, for instance, the availability of emergency and diversion landing facilities in Uruguay and Brazil are considered vital given the unpredictable nature of the South Atlantic weather.[43] When an air service was established by the Chilean airline DAP and later replaced by a jet service provided by LanChile, the Falklands community enjoyed a direct air link with South America which effectively bypassed Argentina. New economic relations were created between the Islands and the Chilean town of Punta Arenas and the Falkland Islands' tourist and hotel sector benefited accordingly. More importantly, the benign political support of Chile and to a lesser extent Brazil and Uruguay helped facilitate Thatcher's position of no concessions to Argentina over the sovereignty of the Falkland Islands. In the light of the fact that Chile was nearly invaded by Argentina in 1978 because of their dispute over the Beagle Channel, many Chileans – including Pinochet – were reportedly relieved that Argentina was defeated in the Falklands, therefore forestalling a new attack on its near neighbour.

The arrest of Pinochet in London provoked angry reactions in Santiago de Chile, where many observers complained that the fate of the former dictator was a matter for the Chilean judiciary. However, the public culture surrounding international law and human-rights protection had changed a great deal since the end of the Cold War, and the British Government was faced with a Spanish petition requesting Pinochet's arrest to stand trial for human-rights violations. The arrest of Pinochet consolidated an important precedent that former heads of state should not be immune from prosecution on the basis that it might interfere with national jurisdiction. Over the months that followed the General's detention in a house close to Royal Holloway College, the then Chilean Government responded by suspending the air service between the Falklands and southern Chile. For several months during 1999, the loss of the air link with Chile caused economic hardship not only to Falklands businesses but also to the economically depressed Punta Arenas. More damagingly, Argentina placed pressure on Brazil and Uruguay to withhold emergency landing facilities to the RAF flights operating between Ascension and the Falkland Islands. The prospect of total isolation loomed large for the Falkland Islands in March 1999.

The Pinochet crisis coincided with expressions of concern raised by eight Falkland Islands Councillors that illegal fishing in the South Atlantic was under-mining the long-term economic position of the islands. The currency crisis in East Asia had depressed the sale of fishing licences in the Falklands, as the vessels of the major customers, South Korea and Japan, looked for cheaper licensing options in Argentina.[44] One Councillor, Mike Summers, held a private conversation in December 1998 with Di Tella about the importance of improving co-operation on fisheries management and air transport.[45] Falkland Islands Councillors realised that both issues depended upon Argentine co-operation, or at the very least goodwill as, for example, the Chilean air link with the Falklands required their permission to enter Argentine air space. Moreover, in the management of fishing the co-operation of coastal states was essential if a multilateral framework for the conservation of fish stocks was to be established and maintained. The South Atlantic Fisheries Commission was designed to enhance co-ordination between the interested parties, but there had been private complaints from the Falkland Islands Government that Argentina was not totally committed to ensuring effective regulation of fishing in the South Atlantic.

Given the dependency on fisheries revenue, the Councillors were eager for the British Government to enter into negotiations with Argentina in April–May 1999 even if it meant that the Government ban on Argentine passport-holders entering the Falklands would have to be part of any diplomatic discussions or concessions. Deeply resented by successive Argentine Governments, the ban on entry was considered one of the most effective displays of *de facto* authority available to the Government, and many Islanders were reluctant to see the ending of such a restriction. Talks between the two states continued in the aftermath of the annual UN meeting of the Special Committee on Decolonisation (C24) in July 1999. Encouraged by the FCO to secure some kind of agreement with Argentina before the forthcoming October 1999 presidential elections in Argentina, the Councillors were prepared to abandon shibboleths such as the ban on Argentine passport-holders.

After some intense discussion, British and Argentine representatives agreed a Joint Statement, signed on 14 July 1999. The Joint Statement contained a commit-ment to improve co-operation in fisheries management in the South Atlantic as well as the ending of the Falkland Islands Government ban on entry of Argentine passport-holders and the early resumption of the Chile–Falkland Islands air route. Other elements related to the land-mine clearance on the Falklands, a proposal for a new memorial at the Argentine cemetery in the Falklands and a review of Argentine place names for the Falklands, such as Puerto Argentino, imposed by the military regime in 1982. The Joint Statement was significant for the Falkland Islanders because it consolidated Argentina's public commitment to co-operate with fisheries management and facilitated the return of an air link with the South American mainland with the lifting of emergency landing restrictions. The price of the agreement was that the Falkland Islands Government would have to end its ban on Argentine passport-holders. In addition, it was also agreed that the renewed air link with Chile would have to include a monthly stop-over at the Argentine town of Rio Gallegos. For the first time since 2 April 1982, Argentina would be included in an air link with the Falklands by granting permission for the Chilean service to enter Argentine air space.

In its last few months in office, the Menem Government was eager to gain recognition for its decade-long rapprochement with Britain and indirectly with the Falkland Islands community. The elimination of the ban on Argentine passport-holders was considered desirable by the FCO, as was the decision to allow another memorial to be constructed at the Argentine cemetery in Darwin prior to the signing of the Joint Statement. The provision for possible clearance of land mines left over from the 1982 occupation relates to wider international obligations under the 1997 Ottawa Convention for the removal of unexploded mines.

The Falkland Islands community benefited most from the Joint Statement, as it ended the damaging period of isolation from the South American mainland. The period between March and July 1999 also demonstrated that the small community could no longer rely on the support of Chile and Uruguay. As the Falkland Islands Government remains dependent on fishing licensing, the clampdown on illegal fishing is in its immediate and long-term interest. A decline in fishing revenue would curtail public spending in the Falklands, particularly as public expenditure rose sharply from £5 million in 1985–6 to £27 million in 1996–7. For the Menem Government, the Joint Statement reaffirmed its public commitment to the sovereignty umbrella, which for the present can only benefit the Falkland Islands and British Governments. Moreover, the Argentine delegation allowed two Falkland Islands Councillors to witness the signing of the Joint Statement, and later agreed to recognise the authority of the Building and Planning Committee of the Falkland Islands Government to review any Argentine plans for a new memorial in Darwin. Finally, Argentine passport-holders will have to accept that their passports will be stamped by the immigration authorities of the Falkland Islands Government which, in keeping with all disputed territories, easily fills a standard page of an Argentine or British passport.

Notwithstanding these elements of concession and benefits, the implementation of the Joint Statement was not a panacea. The reaction in the Falkland Islands was mixed, as many Islanders complained that all bar one of the Councillors (Norma Edwards) had reneged on their 1997 election pledges not to alter the existing ban on Argentine passport-holders. Many Islanders who supported the need for the Joint Statement protested that the Councillors should have consulted with the electorate before agreeing to honour these provisions. Numbering several hundred, they took to the streets of Stanley to protest against the provisions and bemoaned the lack of political consultation as an 'act of betrayal'. In a micro-democracy where everybody knows the elected Councillors well, this demand for consultation – while understandable – underestimated, so the majority of Councillors believed, the need for an agreement with Argentina. It was repeatedly argued that a new Argentine Government might not have been so sympathetic to their community, particularly once the stalwart Di Tella left political office.

Despite the protests, the least problematic aspect of the Joint Statement appears to have been the entry of Argentine passport-holders into the Islands. After an initial flurry of interest from journalists and public personalities, many would-be Argentine visitors were deterred from visiting the Islands by the relatively high costs of flights and hotel accommodation. At present it is necessary to spend at least one week in the Islands because of the weekly flight schedules from Chile. It is most likely that the only regular visitors from Argentina will be relatives of the war dead rather than tourists eager to explore a stark environment reminiscent of southern Patagonia. Far more important are the regular summer-season visitors from Antarctic-bound cruise ships and the crew from vessels licensed to fish around Falkland Islands waters. Islanders' complaints that they no longer recognise everybody walking down the streets of Stanley are outweighed by the economic opportunities provided by fishing and tourism.

The design for an Argentine memorial near the small settlement of Darwin continues to be highly contentious. While most Islanders living in Stanley rarely see the Argentine cemetery because it is located over 50 miles away, its presence remains highly sensitive because of its symbolic importance as a final resting-place for Argentine servicemen killed during the conflict. At present the cemetery is surrounded by a white fence and is composed of a number of rows of white crosses and plaques. Initial proposals for the memorial depicted a tall white cross and a small chapel, but the Malvinas War Veterans Group wanted to include the image of the patron saint, La Virgen del Rosario, who is traditionally clad in the blue and white colours of the Argentine flag.[46] Disagreement within the Falklands community over the final design turned to anger when the possibility of the Argentine flag fluttering over the cemetery was envisaged. As in Northern Ireland and Israel/Palestine, symbols of nationalism such as national flags have the capacity rapidly to inflame local opinion, and virtually every Islander would oppose the spectre of an Argentine flag, albeit in the cemetery. In July 2001, it was reported that the Building and Planning Committee of the Falkland Islands Government rejected the Argentine design on the grounds that the proposed memorial, including a white cross, was inappropriate. According to local media reports, some of the residents of Darwin and Goose Green complained that they did not want to be confronted by the sight of a large white cross. The Argentine architects were requested to submit a new design, which would then be presented again for public comment in the Falkland Islands. As a symbol of Falkland Islands Government authority, there is a danger that an element of the Falklands community prolongs the debacle over the memorial beyond the bounds of acceptable deliberation.

The final element of the Joint Statement that raises difficulties for all interested parties is the question of the buried land-mines in East Falkland. Due to poor record-keeping during the 1982 campaign, it is estimated that around 18,000 Argentine mines remain unaccounted for. A limited number of mines were destroyed after the end of hostilities, and British engineers identified the general whereabouts of other minefields, which they fenced off and declared out-of-bounds to residents and visitors. Most Islanders, while bitter about this imposition, recognise that this precaution has protected human life from serious injury and unintentionally created conservation areas where wildlife can flourish without interference. However, under the terms of the 1997 Ottawa Convention, all signatories, including Argentina and Britain, have an obligation to explore the possibility of removing all mines from the physical environment. Article 5 of the convention states that 'Each State Party undertakes to destroy or ensure the destruction of all anti-personnel mines in mined areas under its jurisdiction or control, as soon as possible but not later than ten years after the entry into force of this Convention for that State Party'.[47] In the case of disputed territories, the identification of the state party is inevitably controversial given the implication for formal sovereignty. While Britain enjoys *de facto* sovereignty over the Falklands, Argentina would not wish recognition of Britain as a state party for the purposes of Article 5 of the convention. Unlike in Angola and Cambodia, the land-mines on the Falklands have not resulted in the deaths of innocent civilians, and most Islanders interviewed by this author were not convinced by the need for such action, as no guarantee could be offered of total clearance.

However, as part of the Labour Government's much-vaunted 'ethical dimension' to British foreign policy, it was argued that local 'wishes' should not prevent Britain from meeting its international obligations and in particular the Ottawa Convention. With the difficulties involved in formally identifying a state party, it might be that a joint Anglo–Argentine task-force could be mustered to explore the feasibility of land mine clearance. In October 2001, the British and Argentine Governments agreed to conduct a feasibility study for the de-mining of the Falkland Islands; this will be carried out by a joint British–Argentine working party. The sovereignty umbrella will continue to protect both sides' legal positions and thus the land-mine clearance, regardless of whether it is finally implemented, would avoid the immediate difficulties raised by the convention.

There has been limited public discussion of the symbolic significance in the local community of the buried land-mines. Arguably, the issue contributes to a prevailing culture of militarism as, for example, the British army briefs all visitors to Mount Pleasant airbase on the dangers posed by the mines. Throughout East Falkland, travellers routinely encounter minefields sectioned off with signs warning of hidden dangers. Local artist James Peck conveys through his paintings the lingering anxieties and bitterness of the 1982 conflict. His work frequently depicts the Falklands as being composed of dirty and muddy landscapes filled with vague images of Argentine soldiers. In an interview with the author, he argued that the land-mines might provide a curious source of reassurance to some Islanders because they offer a constant and at times daily reminder of the Falklands campaign and the pain inflicted by the Argentine occupation.[48] By removing the land-mines, Peck argued that the local community might have to think of Argentina as a neighbour rather than as a perpetual enemy.

The long-term implication of the Joint Statement is harder to assess, despite its renewal of the existing *modus operandi* of the sovereignty umbrella for Anglo–Argentine co-operation over the Falklands and the southwest Atlantic. The former Argentine Government, under President de la Rua (1999–2001), supported rapprochement even if Foreign Minister Giavarini reportedly took less interest in the Islands than his predecessor Di Tella. Argentine media sources note that the Foreign Ministry will promote a return to the traditional legal approach and thus direct contact with the Falkland Islands community will be kept to a minimum.[49] The events surrounding the arrest of General Pinochet and the suspension of the Chilean air service to the Falklands in 1999 serve as poignant reminders that the long-term well-being of the Islanders remains dependent on the political goodwill of South American neighbours.

The RAF service via Ascension Island, while providing a so-called lifeline, was shown to be vulnerable to collective South American diplomatic pressure. Notwithstanding the explosion of telephone and fax lines in the Falklands, the geographical proximity of Argentina and Chile cannot be ignored when discussing matters such as fisheries management, hydrocarbon exploration, environmental protection and communication networks. As Argentine reports have noted, the territorial claim of Argentina will not evaporate, and the provisions of the Joint Statement do not jeopardise any claims to the disputed Islands.[50]

SUMMARY

The South Atlantic and Antarctic elements of the British Empire have undergone considerable change since the 1982 Falklands campaign. Few commentators fail to cite the so-called 'Falklands factor' in their analyses of contemporary developments: the political and geographical impact of the conflict was considerable and long-lasting. A remote and poorly understood corner of the South Atlantic transformed British political life and sped the demise of the Argentine military regime in 1983. For the Falkland Islanders, the invasion, as one remarked to the author, was a 'godsend' because it acted as a catalyst for renewed British commitment. The following eight years under Thatcher transformed the military and economic condition of the Falklands, despite Argentine protests. British activity in the Antarctic and South Georgia expanded, as the armed forces remained on South Georgia and the BAS received increased funding for its research in the Antarctic Treaty area. The British territorial claim and wider political influence survived the intense criticism of the ATS directed at it by the UN General Assembly and environmental movements. In a manner once urged by Shackleton, the Thatcher Government appreciated that the South Atlantic and Antarctic are symbolically connected, whereas the legal disputes with Argentina over the Falklands, South Georgia and Antarctica are distinct.

By the time the Labour Party returned to political power in 1997, the new Government was not inclined to question the orthodoxy of the political right that the 'wishes' of the Falkland Islanders in this ongoing dispute were paramount. Although the Anglo–Argentine polar dispute remains protected by the provisions of the 1959 Antarctic Treaty, Britain agreed in July 2001 to drop its long-standing opposition to Argentina's proposal for a new ATS secretariat based in Buenos Aires. As the Argentines have had to accept, these gestures of goodwill do not compromise the legal positions of protagonists, even if the apparent symbolic importance of the secretariat in consolidating Argentina's position as a major Antarctic power appears significant.

The outstanding sovereignty dispute with Argentina over the Falklands remains politically sensitive, and the Joint Statement does not alter this basic position. As democracies, the challenge for Britain and Argentina remains not only the consolidation of confidence-building but also the strengthening of democratic modes for dealing with issues such as living resources and air transport. The South Atlantic is not immune from a wider recognition that states will have to learn to co-operate with one another over issues and problems that spill over national boundaries. Both parties recognise this trend and have sought to manage cross-border bodies such as the South Atlantic Fisheries Commission, which in turn actively create 'South Atlantic issues'. Over time, all interested parties will have to continue to share political power in overlapping spheres of interest and retain a flexible attitude towards the Falklands question.

NOTES ON CHAPTER 10

1   Dr Richard Laws, the then Director of the BAS, on Radio 4 *File on Four* broadcast on 2 December 1986.

2   Sir Rex Hunt, Chairman's address to Legislative Council, delivered on 22 November 1983.

3   Lord Shackleton on Radio 4 *File on Four* broadcast on 2 December 1986.

4   FCO memorandum dated 10 November 1982, cited in P. Beck, *Who owns Antarctica? Governing and Managing the Last Continent Boundary and Territory Briefing* (International Boundaries Research Unit, University of Durham, 1994), p. 43.

5   Message from Thatcher, to the Falkland Islanders, Christmas 1985.

6   Lord Shackleton (Chairman) and the Falkland Island Economic Study of 1982 (London, HMSO), p. 3.

7   Official Communiqué of the Secretary of State for Public Information on President Alfonsín's answers to the press on the Malvinas question in Caracas on 1 February 1984.

8   P. Beck, 'The future of the Falklands: a solution made in Hong Kong?' *International Affairs* 61 (1985): pp. 650–1.

9   Switzerland acted for the UK as a diplomatic intermediary during the period 1982–1989, when diplomatic relations with Argentina were strained.

10 Interview with a retired FCO official, 15 February 2001.

11 See, for example, R. de Hoyos, 'Malvinas/Falklands, 1982–1988: The new Gibraltar in the South Atlantic?' in P. Kelly and J. Child (eds), *Geopolitics of the Southern Cone and Antarctica* (Boulder CO, Lynne Rienner, 1988), pp. 237–49. For a more sober analysis of the post-war developments in the South Atlantic, see L. Hepple, 'The geopolitics of the Falklands/Malvinas and the South Atlantic: British and Argentine perceptions, misperceptions and rivalries', in the same volume.

12 Proclamation Number 4 1986, 'Interim Fishery Conservation and Management Zone' issued by the Governor of the Falkland Islands, Gordon Jewkes.

13 *Falkland Focus*, 'Falkland Islands Fishing Zone operational' (Falkland Islands Government office, February–March 1987). Two-hundred-and-fifteen licences were issued for the 1987 season, and the list of national vessels included Chile, Japan, Poland, Soviet Union, Spain, Taiwan and the UK.

14 An economically weak Falkland Islands was more likely to be persuaded that a sovereignty transfer in favour of Argentina was beneficial. The introduction of a fisheries regime provided a pathway towards greater autonomy. Unsurprisingly, the Argentine Government was fiercely critical of the declaration of a FICZ in 1986 and sought wider Latin American support for their cause. See, for example, the resolution adopted by the Organisation of American States on the Fisheries Question in the Western South Atlantic, dated 11 November 1986, and the declaration by the Foreign Ministers of the Group of Eight, dated 25 February 1988.

15 Statement cited in Falkland Islands Development Corporation's Report and Accounts (Stanley, Falkland Islands Government, 1986), p. 1.

16 Y-H. Song, 'The British 150-mile fishery conservation and management zone around the Falkland (Malvinas) Islands', *Political Geography Quarterly* 7 (1988): pp. 183–96.

17 Press statement relating to the meeting of Neil Kinnock, leader of the opposition with President Raul Alfonsín at Paris on 18 September 1985. Significantly, the

press statement talked of the 'interests' of the Falkland Islanders rather than their 'wishes' being respected.

18   *Newsnight* BBC 2 John Simpson interview with President Alfonsín of Argentina. The interview was shown on 9 October 1985.

19   UKFIC/MARPLAN Falkland Islands Sovereignty Survey carried in March 1986, which showed that out of a poll of over 900 Falkland Islands electors, 94 per cent favoured the legal status quo and only 1.6 per cent favoured independence. Virtually no-one advocated a transfer to Argentina.

20   The Falkland Islands continued to be embroiled in the wider politics of the UN which, in November 1986, passed a resolution calling for the British and Argentine Governments to initiate new negotiations; this was passed by 116 votes to 4 against (the UK, Oman, Belize and Sri Lanka). Some of Britain's EEC partners such as Spain, France and Italy supported the resolution calling for an end to the sovereignty dispute, while the US abstained from the vote.

21   FCO, 'Britain and Argentina: Restoring Relations' background brief, March 1990.

22   The *Guardian*, 'Menem says Falklands are Argentine', 19 July 1989.

23   The UK and Argentina Joint Statement dated 16 February 1990. The Joint Statement was agreed by British and Argentine delegations at Madrid on 15 February 1990, and contained four annexes covering information exchange, safety measures for naval and air units, maritime and air search and rescue and finally, safety of navigation. The first Joint Statement had been signed on 19 October 1989 in Madrid.

24   Interview with Lord Hurd of Westwell, 22 February 2001.

25   Keynote speech by UK Foreign Secretary Robin Cook to the House of Commons on 17 March 1999.

26   *Partnership for Progress and Prosperity: Britain and the Overseas Territories* (London, HMSO, 1999).

27   A commentary on Dr Peter J. Beck's memorandum, 'Britain's Future Policy in Antarctica', contained in a letter from Foreign Secretary Sir Geoffrey Howe to Julian Amery, dated 19 June 1984. I owe thanks to Professor Beck for sharing with me his correspondence with the FCO.

28   See P. Beck, 'Britain's Antarctic dimension', *International Affairs* 59 (1983): pp. 429–44.

29   Lloyd Jacobs on Radio 4 *The World Today* broadcast on 9 January 1985.

30   The 1974 US Geological Survey estimated that there might be a possible yield of 45 billion barrels of oil and 115 trillion cubic feet of natural gas. In 1986 the American Association of Petroleum Geologists estimated that the figure could be over 200 billion barrels of oil. This, however, is based on speculation rather than detailed scientific investigation of Antarctica, but nonetheless the 1974 survey was important in raising interest in the Falklands and the Antarctic.

31   Cited in K. Dodds, *Geopolitics in Antarctica: Views from the Southern Oceanic Rim* (London, John Wiley, 1997), p. 203.

32   Cited in Dodds, *Geopolitics in Antarctica*, p. 204.

33   Sir Vivian Fuchs on Radio 4 *The World Today* broadcast on 9 January 1985.

34   The comments of Thatcher recorded on BBC 2 *Nature* broadcast on 2 March 1989.

35   Report by the National Audit Office, *The British Antarctic Survey: Management of Major Capital Projects and Scientific Programmes* (London, HMSO, 1989).

36   Cited in *New Scientist*, 'Miners vote to plunder the treasures of Antarctica', 28 January 1988, p. 28.

37   Cited in Dodds, *Geopolitics in Antarctica*, p. 103.

38   FCO News Department briefing, dated 4 October 1991.

39   For critical assessments of the Protocol, see L. Elliot, 'Environmental protection in the Antarctic: Problems and prospects', *Environmental Politics* 3 (1994): pp. 247–72 and D. Lyons, 'Environmental impact assessment in Antarctica under the Protocol of Environmental Protection', *Polar Record* 29 (1993): pp. 111–20.

40   See 'Chilean funeral for Antarctic minerals pact', *Nature* 348 (1990): p. 269.

41   *Financial Times*, 'War-torn shore returns to its natives', 10–11 March 2001.

42   For some interesting recollections of the incident, see A. Gurr, *A Little Piece of England* (London, Blake Publishing, 2001). Andrew Gurr was the Chief Executive of the Falkland Islands between 1994 and 1999.

43   There was some concern that the logistical resources of the RAF was also overstretched because of growing humanitarian commitments in South East Europe and Africa.

44   Interview with John Barton, Director of Fisheries in the Falkland Islands, 15 December 1999. In 1998–9, a fishing licence for Ilex squid cost approximately £120,000 for a four-month season. The Falkland Islands Government hoped to sell around 90–5 licences for the entire season.

45   Interview with Mike Summers OBE, 20 December 1999.

46   The military codename for the Argentine occupation of the Islas Malvinas was Operación Rosario.

47   The text of the 1997 Ottawa Convention can be accessed on http://www.mines.gc.ca/english/documents/index.html (accessed on 8 June 2000).

48   Interview with James Peck, 18 December 1999.

49   *Clarín*, 'Malvinas: quieren volver a hablar de la soberanía', 12 July 2000.

50   For example, see *Clarín*, 'El Canciller la reclamará hoy en la ONU', 11 July 2000.

CONCLUSIONS

The basis for our partnership remains the same as it has for generations – the deep bond of affection and respect that exists between the people of Britain and the peoples of the Overseas Territories. Our partnership must be founded on self-determination. Our overseas territories are British as long as they wish to remain British.[1]

INTRODUCTION

There has been an extraordinary renaissance of interest in nineteenth- and twentieth-century polar exploration.[2] Some have sardonically referred to this as a 'new ice age', but the Antarctic and Southern Ocean have long been a source of fascination for Europeans as well as a place for expressions of individual bravery and endurance. Antarctica continues to exert an irresistible attraction, which surely must explain the return to popularity of well-known Edwardian explorers like Apsley Cherry-Gerrard, Ernest Shackleton and Robert Falcon Scott, who were immortalised in the British public imagination via art, books, public monuments and films such as *Scott of the Antarctic* (1948).[3] The resurrection of the Anglo-Irish explorer Shackleton and his 1914–17 Imperial Trans-Antarctic Expedition is all the more remarkable when one remembers that his feats were largely unrecognised at the time of his return to a country in the grip of the First World War. By the end of 1918, a poverty-stricken Shackleton was paying off his debts through writing and extensive lecturing.[4]

A revival of interest in the polar world is to be generally welcomed, but it is important to recognise that exploratory and scientific activities did not occur within a geopolitical or imperial vacuum. Shackleton and his team's exploits coincided with a political desire to administer the Antarctic Peninsula and South Atlantic. Over the following two decades the Colonial Office, in conjunction with the FO, developed new political networks and refined established scientific techniques such as surveying in order to consolidate British imperial claims. Without the reassuring foothold in the northerly islands of the Falkland Islands and South Georgia, the Colonial Office as administrator would have been reluctant to pursue additional claims to the polar continent. As a gateway, the Falkland Islands were essential to the logistical and political organisation of the South Atlantic Empire. Strategic shipping lanes, in combination with whaling activity in the FID, provided a powerful impetus for territorial claims and aggrandisement. It was only later that the Colonial Office established a research and development fund, which supported the scientific and political activities of the FIDS.[5] After the Second World War, privately organised explorations finally gave way to large-scale Government-funded operations with an established network of permanently occupied research stations and the services of the Royal Navy (and parties of Royal Marines) to defend these distant possessions.

After 1945, Britain's regional role was increasingly conditioned by the rival claimant states of Argentina and Chile, international parties and global processes associated with scientific endeavour, multilateral co-operation and the formal ending of colonialism. Despite trying to engineer a sovereignty transfer of the Falkland Islands in the 1960s and 1970s, the South Atlantic was seen as a resource-rich region with considerable oil and natural-gas potential. Ultimately, successive ministers decreed that the resource potential of the Falklands region was not sufficiently important to prevent a possible territorial settlement with Argentina. The 1982 invasion of the Falklands by the Argentine military transformed this strategic assessment, and Thatcher reasserted Britain's determination to maintain an advantage in this remote region, regardless of prevailing international pressure to resolve the colonial situation.

Pink Ice has charted Britain's relationship with Argentina, the US and Chile, and the effects of this co-ordination on scientific, commercial, political and military activities in the South Atlantic and Antarctic. Persistent territorial disputes such as those over the Falkland Islands were never isolated from these wider currents, and there is ample evidence to illustrate how sport, the arms and meat trades, and even film, infiltrated the Anglo–Argentine diplomatic arena. This concluding chapter does not seek to summarise the earlier material, rather it highlights two important themes which will shape Britain's future role in the Falklands, South Georgia and Antarctic region. The first involves the preservation of the 1959 Antarctic Treaty, which provides the legal and geopolitical bedrock to the South Atlantic Empire; the second concerns the contemporary challenges facing the Falkland Islanders and wider Anglo–Argentine relations over the Falklands question.

ENDURING CONNECTIONS: BRITAIN AND ANTARCTICA

Over the last 40 years, the 1959 Antarctic Treaty has been the foundation for Britain's South Atlantic Empire. Ratified by Macmillan's Conservative Government in May 1960, Article IV of the treaty has effectively preserved an imperial claim to the Antarctic Peninsula, despite the great distances between Antarctica and the shores of the British Isles. Successive Governments recognised that Britain enjoys an influential role in this extraordinary international regime (the ATS), which enabled territorial strife to be replaced by international co-operation throughout the Cold War. Current policy acknowledges not only that the overseas portfolio will continue to contain British Antarctic territory but also that the BAS will remain the most potent symbol of Britain's involvement. As the 1999 White Paper on Overseas Territories recalled, 'While the BAT [British Antarctic Territory] has no indigenous population, the UK's presence in the territory is provided primarily by the BAS'. In terms of justifying the continued British presence, the Overseas Territories Department of the FCO continues to promote the value of scientific activity rather than resource or geopolitical value of Antarctica.[6]

With a budget of £27 million per year, the BAS operates four major research stations in the Antarctic region: Halley, Rothera, Signy Island and Bird Island.

Significant research is carried out on ocean ecosystem dynamics, global interactions with the Antarctic ice-sheet, the management of marine ecosystems and upper atmospheric research studies. A major effort is underway to enhance public awareness of Britain's role in Antarctica, with new funding for humanities and arts-based projects, in addition to providing all schools and colleges with Antarctic learning resources.[7] Brian Roberts would have been gratified that Britain remains actively involved in the Antarctic arena even though the remit has changed greatly from an earlier period of intense territorial competition. The Antarctic Peninsula hosts not only the scientific stations of other countries but also a significant number multinational tour operators who operate out of the South American gateway ports. King George Island in the South Shetland is now home to an excessive number of research stations huddled together for the explicit purpose of conducting scientific research. In doing so, they fulfil the requirements of the 1959 Antarctic Treaty which stipulated that all parties must conduct 'substantial scientific research' in order to qualify for the status of consultative party. As Brian Roberts recognised, the price of joining the 'Antarctic club' is scientific endeavour.

With the ratification of the Protocol on Environmental Protection in January 1998, the Antarctic Treaty regime entered into a new political and environmental phase as parties turned their attention to the implementation of its provisions. The Protocol is a supplement and thus neither modifies nor amends the treaty. It adopted a comprehensive rather than issue-specific approach to environmental protection. The political storms of the 1980s have now abated as the explosive issue of mining in the Antarctic was banned. Article 7 of the Protocol states unambiguously that 'any activity relating to mineral resources, other than scientific research, shall be prohibited'. This effectively silenced the critics in the UN and improved a greater flow of information from the ATS to other interested parties. The UN adopted a consensus resolution in 1994, which expressly acknowledged the merits of the ATS in the governance of Antarctica.

The implementation of the Protocol will continue to demand careful management, as it will have to co-exist with a range of global and regional legal agreements and mechanisms, namely the International Maritime Organisation, Law of the Sea Convention and the UN Environment Programme. The legal and environmental provisions relating to the Protocol are complex and the Committee for Environmental Protection will have the task of ensuring comprehensive implementation. The rhetorical flourishes of comprehensiveness aside, legal and geographical ambiguities remain, as it is not clear from the Protocol whether its provisions apply to the entire area south of 60 degrees latitude. Does Article 7 on mining prohibition, for example, apply to the continental shelf of Antarctica but south of 60 degrees latitude or to the continental shelf extending beyond 60 degrees? Antarctica is thus embedded in a number of international legal regimes involving the seabed and Southern Ocean, and to compound matters still further, the domestic legislation of consultative parties such as Britain, South Africa and the US fail to concur with one another.[8] There are also other legal and practical problems to resolve relating to the management of tourism, the regulation of an environmental liability regime and the alarming expansion in illegal, unregulated and unreported fishing in the Southern Ocean. The new and emotive game of living resource geopolitics involves fishing vessels, the geographically proximate states of New Zealand, South Africa, Australia and Namibia as well as pressure groups and intergovernmental organisations. Given the contested sovereignty of Antarctica, compliance with the Protocol is difficult to enforce when so many fishing vessels and even cruise ships fly the flags of third parties or simply 'flags of convenience'.

Britain's claim to Antarctica is preserved by Article IV of the treaty, but the implementation of sovereign control has always been conditioned by the very geography of the polar environment with its vast expanses of ocean, difficult sea conditions and great distances from centres of population. Issues of jurisdiction, control and enforcement have become more complicated in the 40 years since the 1959 Washington Conference. In terms of formal membership of the ATS,the claimant states are now a minority group. National claims co-exist with a bewildering mixture of authorities with jurisdiction or interest in the immense Southern Ocean and Antarctic continent. Notwithstanding the legal complexities, the presence of the British Antarctic Territory has been very convenient, and without it active scientific and political involvement in the region might have ended with the ratification of the Antarctic Treaty in 1961. As the White Paper on Overseas Territories readily acknowledges, the British Antarctic territory also generates reasonable sums of money in terms of postage stamp sales and tourist visits to the restored research station Port Lockroy.

LEARNING TO LIVE WITH THE FUTURE: BRITAIN AND THE FALKLAND ISLANDS

The Falklands question remains unresolved. A British victory in 1982 did not alter this basic position. With the political backing of the major British parties, the Falkland Islanders have been resolute in their determination to resist any legal change, and many Islanders would even deny, with good reason, that there is a 'sovereignty dispute'. The White Paper on Overseas Territories was also emphatic on the question of sovereignty:

> Argentina asserts a claim to sovereignty over the Falklands. But the British government has no doubt about British sovereignty over them and does not regard this as negotiable. The British government remains committed to defend the Islanders' right to self-determination. In exercise of this right the Islanders have repeatedly made known their wish to remain British.[9]

As part of a broader repertoire of public performances, Falkland Islands events such as Liberation Day on 14 June, celebrate deliverance from an unwanted Argentine occupation. Many Islanders feel quite strongly that any gestures of goodwill towards Argentina might be wrongly interpreted as a sign of diminishing gratitude to those British forces.

Over the last decade, Britain and Argentina have sought to rebuild diplomatic, economic and political relations, even if for many Islanders it is still too early to embrace rapprochement with Argentina. The exchange of cordiality and renewed co-operation between the two protagonists has been impressive, yet the Falklands question remains as divisive as ever. All parties are nonetheless learning that they cannot live and negotiate in splendid isolation. Moreover, the very place names of the Falklands/Malvinas provide a powerful reminder of cultural and political interdependence. For instance, Spanish topographical names such as *rincon* (corner) are freely acknowledged on British and Argentine maps of the Islands. Past episodes of French settlement in the eighteenth century are commemorated in places such as Port Louis, and the contribution of the English-speaking community is richly acknowledged from names of past settlers (Chartres) to British naval vessels (Ajax Bay).[10] As Richard Munro notes, 'The history and culture of the Islands are inextricably linked to the names of its topographical features, settlements, streets and houses'.[11]

If place names provide evidence for multiple occupancy, they do not provide a ready answer to the prevailing sovereignty dispute. From the perspective of the Falkland Islanders, co-operation and trust are still not the norm in Argentine–Anglo–Falkland relations. This will take time, and Argentina and Britain must recognise that the power-geometry of place is skewed in favour of a large continental neighbour. When a small community is still struggling to deal with the legacies of war and territorial counter-claims, the call to develop a closer relationship with Argentina can make little political or cultural sense – especially when Britain continues to offer the promise of military protection. Unlike the unionist community in Northern Ireland, the Falklands are neither incorporated into Britain's Westminster-based Government nor located about an hour's plane flight away from London's major airports.

As improvements in Anglo–Argentine relations have gathered pace, so bilateral negotiations over fishing, oil licensing, transport and tourism have progressed. Cordiality has led to the gradual recognition of a shared loss resulting from the 1982 conflict. The decision to allow Argentine relatives of the war dead to visit the Falklands in 1991 was courageous given the enduring bitterness about the Argentine occupation. In the last few years, representatives from the Malvinas War Veterans Federation and the British-based South Atlantic Medal Association (SAMA 82) have held high-profile reunions in an attempt to promote a view of the conflict that acknowledges a shared loss. These kinds of gestures, sometimes on a small and informal scale, are significant in terms of releasing all interested parties from slavish devotion to the assumed memories of the war dead. This active recognition of shared loss and responsibility was epitomised most clearly when the then Argentine President Carlos Menem laid a wreath in St Paul's Cathedral in London in October 1998, and Prince Charles reciprocated at the memorial to the Malvinas dead in Buenos Aires in March 1999. SAMA 82, under the leadership of two veterans, Dr Rick Jolly and Denzil Connick, has been at the forefront of promoting reconciliation and understanding. This organisation (with over 1000 UK veteran members) has advised the FCO and the royal family over contact with Argentine veterans and visits to Argentina.[12] SAMA 82 organised large-scale reunion visits of British veterans in 2002, and the Falkland Islands Government hosted a series of memorial services on the twentieth anniversary of the conflict.

The controversies surrounding the Islands have considerable relevance for both the Falklands and Britain, seeking to come to terms with the fact that the British Isles does not have (and never had) a singular identity or history. Devolution in Scotland, Northern Ireland and Wales will not only alter the constitutional status of the UK but also disrupt claims to stable national identities. Any future analysis of the Falklands problem will have to engage actively in the deconstruction of the image of the island. As Di Tella noted, 'Now, the problem with islands in general is that they have sex appeal. We lose our minds, but you also lose your mind...And you love to collect islands of all sorts around the world'.[13] As Gillian Beer reflects, the idea of the island is associated with values such as 'defensive, secure, compact, even paradisal [sic] – a safe place too from which to launch the building of an empire. Even now remote islands – the Falklands or Fiji – are claimed as peculiarly part of empire history.'[14] All parties should actively question discourses and practices invoking defensive responses to political change and exclusive forms of national identity. Any new sense of place for the Falklands/Malvinas would involve an active recognition that these Islands have been shaped by a range of cultural, economic and political flows and interconnections. This does not mean, therefore, that a firmly held commitment to place and a particular tradition is tantamount to reactionary politics. Falkland Islanders are, for example, often eager to acknowledge that their earlier forms of rural existence have many similarities with nineteenth-century Patagonian sheep farmers and gauchos. More recently, Argentine writers have at least acknowledged that there is an Anglophone community in the Falklands even if they are less willing to examine Argentina's obsession with the recovery of these Islands.[15] Routine attempts to promote either a sentimental heritage based on a few favoured anniversaries or selective cultural influences are unlikely to be able to deal with the aftermath of conflict and competing territorial claims.[16]

All parties will have to develop a shared sense of interconnection, interdependence and human loss resulting from the 1982 conflict. Generating a new sense of place and belonging remains a tentative project even if it is recognised that a commitment to place and tradition does not have to lead to a retrogressive and defensive politics. As with other insular communities, free-flowing transformations and new economic opportunities in fishing, commerce and tourism will alter the future profile of the population. Communities can negotiate these cross-boundary flows, and in the Falklands' case benefit from them, as the revenue raised from fishing licensing has amply demonstrated. The Falkland Islands is not a poor and oppressed colony, and perhaps in the future Britain and Argentina will acknowledge a truly independent Falkland Islands. For the time being, however, the territorial dispute remains unresolved, and as such Britain's South Atlantic Empire endures.

NOTES ON CONCLUSIONS

1   *Partnership for Progress and Prosperity: Britain and the Overseas Territories* (London, HMSO, 1999).

2   For example, F. Fleming, *Ninety Degrees North: The Quest for the North Pole* (London, Granta, 2001) and S. Soloman, *The Coldest March: Scott's Fatal Antarctic Expedition* (New Haven CT, Yale University Press, 2001).

3   M. Jones, 'Our king on his knees: The public commemoration of Captain Scott's last Antarctic expedition', in G. Cubitt and A. Warren (eds), *Heroic Reputations and Exemplary Lives* (Manchester, Manchester University Press, 2000), pp. 105–22.

4   See the excellent review by R. Huntsford, *Shackleton* (London, Abacus, 2000), especially pp. 626–48.

5   The 1934–7 British Grahamland Expedition was supported by a Colonial Office grant of £10,000. See the official account of the expedition in J. Rymill, *Southern Lights* (London, Chatto and Windus, 1938).

6   *Focus International Britain and Antarctica* (London, FCO, March 2000).

7   See *Antarctic Science in the Global Context 2000–2005* (Cambridge, NERC–BAS, 2000).

8   See D. Vidas (ed.), *Implementing the Environmental Protection Regime for the Antarctic* (Dordrecht, Kluwer Academic Publishers, 2001).

9   *Partnership for Progress and Prosperity: Britain and the Overseas Territories*, p. 57.

10   These arguments are developed further in K. Dodds and L. Manovil, 'A common space? The Falklands/Malvinas and a new geopolitics of the South Atlantic', *Geopolitics* 6 (2001): pp. 99–126.

11   R. Munro, *Place Names of the Falkland Islands* (London, Shackleton Trust Fund, 1999), p. 3.

12   Telephone interview with Denzil Connick of SAMA 82 on 1 February 2000.

13   This intellectual process should not be seen as a task for British and Falkland Islands commentators alone. It is striking that few Argentine scholars have actively sought to explore the cultural and ideological significance of islands not only within the British cultural imagination but also to think about how it relates to Argentina's continental development.

14   G. Beer, 'The island and the aeroplane: The case of Virginia Woolf', in H. Bhabha (ed.), *Nation and Narration* (London, Routledge, 1991), p. 269.

15   C. Bullrich, *Falklands or Malvinas?* (Buenos Aires, Nuevohacer Grupo Editor Latinamerciano, 2000).

16   One example was the celebration of '1992' as a major year of 'Falkland Islands heritage' because it coincided with among other things the hundredth anniversary of the creation of Stanley Cathedral and the tenth anniversary of the Falklands campaign. The purpose of the celebration was to bolster the British identity of the Falklands, but little reflection was apparent as to how this process was contributing to the 'invention of tradition'. See E. Hobsbawm and T. Ranger (eds). *The Invention of Tradition* (Cambridge, Cambridge University Press, 1983).

APPENDIX

A basic chronology of the 1982 Falklands conflict

April 2   The Argentine task-force invades the Falkland Islands and, after a short but fierce battle, overwhelms the small contingent of British Royal Marines. Governor Rex Hunt is transported by the Argentines to Montevideo, Uruguay.

April 3   Argentine forces seize the island of South Georgia. UN Resolution 502 is passed, calling on the Argentines to withdraw and cease hostilities in the region.

April 8   Secretary of State Alexander Haig begins his 'shuttle diplomacy' with a visit to London.

April 10   Haig travels to Buenos Aires and the EEC agrees to impose trade sanctions against Argentina.

April 17   Haig travels again to Buenos Aires and on 19 April returns to the US after failure to make further diplomatic progress.

April 25   British forces recapture the island of South Georgia after a short battle in which an Argentine submarine is disabled. The British task-force leaves from Portsmouth destined for the South Atlantic. The British declare a war exclusion zone.

April 30   Haig's mission officially ends and President Reagan of the US declares his support for Britain and approves economic sanctions against Argentina.

May 1   British planes attack Stanley airfield.

May 2   President Belaunde Terry of Peru presents a peace proposal to General Leopoldo Galtieri. The initial reaction of Argentina is supportive to the proposal. The British nuclear-powered submarine HMS *Conqueror* sinks the Argentine cruiser *General Belgrani* outside the war zone with the loss of nearly 400 men. After hearing the news the Argentine Junta rejects the proposal.

May 4   The British frigate HMS *Sheffield* is hit by an Argentine air-to-surface missile and one British harrier plane is destroyed.

May 7   The UN enters into peace negotiations.

May 9–14   Argentine and British airforces engage in combat, and British special forces destroy 11 Argentine aircraft on Pebble Island.

May 18   A peace proposal supported by UN Secretary-General Perez de Cuellar is rejected by the British Government.

May 21   The British task-force lands at Port San Carlos and British forces advance eastwards to Stanley after conflict in Darwin and Goose Green. The British ship HMS *Ardent* is sunk by an Argentine air attack.

May 23   The British frigate HMS *Antelope* is attacked and destroyed. The Argentines lose a further 10 planes.

May 25   HMS *Coventry is* hit by Argentine aircraft and sinks three days later with the loss of 12 men.

May 28   British 2nd Battalion of the Parachute Regiment engage in fierce fighting for Goose Green. Despite being outnumbered, the British troops prevail but lose Colonel Jones, who is posthumously awarded the Victoria Cross for gallantry.

May 29   There are further attacks on Argentine positions in East Falkland by British aircraft.

May 30   The British Commando forces secure Douglas settlement and the Parachute Regiment recaptures Teal Inlet.

May 31   British troops encircle Stanley after fighting in the mountains. Additional British troops move into position.

June 8   An Argentine air attack on the British landing crafts HMS *Sir Galahad* and HMS *Sir Tristram* near Bluff Cove results in 50 deaths.

June 12   British Parachute Regiment (3 Para) launches an assault on Mount Longdon. Some of the fiercest fighting occurs during this battle, in which nearly 30 men die. One of the casualties is Sergeant Ian John McKay, who is posthumously awarded the Victoria Cross. The Argentines lose over 50 men, and many more are injured.

      British 45 Commando takes Two Sisters and 42 Commando takes Mount Harriet, while the Scots Guards seize Mount Tumbledown in another costly encounter.

      HMS *Glamorgan* is hit by an Argentine air-to-surface missile as Royal Navy ships contribute to the land-based battles.

June 14   The Argentine garrison in Stanley is defeated, and the Argentine commander General Mario Mendez agrees to a ceasefire. Approximately 10,000 Argentine troops surrender to the British authorities. The Falkland Islands is restored to British Sovereignty.

June 20   Britain re-occupies the South Sandwich Islands and formally ends hostilities. A 150-mile Falkland Islands Protection Zone is established.

This undeclared war lasted 74 days, and cost 255 British lives and over 655 Argentine lives.

BIBLIOGRAPHY

ARCHIVES

Australian Archives (AA)
British Antarctic Survey (BAS)
Economic Survey of the Falkland Islands
Falkland Islands Development Corporation's Report and Accounts
National Archives of Canada (NAC)
New Zealand Archives (NZA)
Public Record Office (PRO)
Scott Polar Research Institute (SPRI)
South African Archives (SAA)
United States Archives (Telegrams)

NEWSPAPERS

Auckland Star, Clarín, Daily Sketch, Des Moines Register, Evening News, Evening Advertiser, Falkland Focus, Falkland Islands Gazette Supplement, Falkland Islands Monthly Review, Falkland Islands Weekly News, Financial Times, Independent on Sunday, Kinematograph Weekly, New York Times, News of the World, Paris Match, Penguin News, Southland Daily News, Sun-Herald, Sunday Dispatch, The Birmingham Post, The Canberra Times, The Christchurch Press, Daily Express, Daily Mail, Daily Telegraph, Dominion, Evening Post, Evening Star, Guardian, Listener, Observer, Scotsman, Star (Johannesburg), Sun, Sunday Telegraph, Times, Variety, Waikato Times.

SECONDARY REFERENCES

Adams, V., *The Media and the Falklands Campaign* (London, Macmillan, 1986).
Adamthwaite, A., 'Britain and the world 1945–1949: The view from the Foreign Office', *International Affairs* 62 (1985): pp. 223–35.
Adie, R., '25 years of Antarctic exploration', *University of Birmingham Gazette* 20 (1968): pp. 127–9.
Africa Confidential 17/22 (5 November 1976).
Alzerreca, C., *Historia de la Antartida* (Buenos Aires, Editorial Hemisferio, 1949).
'Antarctic Crossing', *Monthly Film Bulletin* 26/300 (1959).
'Antarctic Science in the Global Context 2000–2005', Cambridge NERC–BAS (2000).

Arbena, J., 'Generals and goals: Assessing the connection between the military and soccer in Argentina', *International Journal of the History of Sport* 7 (1990): pp. 120–30.

— 'Nationalism and sport in Latin America, 1850–1990: The paradox of promoting and performing', *International Journal of the History of Sport* 12 (1995): pp. 220–38.

Archetti, E., 'Argentinian football: A ritual of violence?', *The International Journal of the History of Sport* 9 (1992): pp. 209–35.

— *Masculinities: Football, Polo and Tango in Argentina* (London, Berg, 1999).

Assef, A., *Proyeccion Continental de la Argentina* (Buenos Aires, Editorial Pleamar, 1980).

Aulich, J., (ed.), *Framing the Falklands War: Nationhood, Culture and Identity* (Milton Keynes, Open University Press, 1992).

'Australia's all-out bid to develop her Antarctic territories', *BP Magazine New Series* 1 (1961): pp. 10–15.

Balcon, M., 'The technical problems of *Scott of the Antarctic*', *Sight and Sound* 17 (1948–9): pp. 153–5.

— *Michael Balcon Presents...A Lifetime of Films* (London, Hutchinson, 1969).

Barber, N., *White Desert* (London, Hodder and Stoughton, 1958).

Barker, S., 'Images of the sixteenth and seventeenth centuries as a history of the present', in F. Barker, P. Hulme, H. Iversen and D. Loxley (eds), *Politics and Theory* (London, Routledge, 1984).

Beck, P., 'Britain's Antarctic dimension', *International Affairs* 59 (1983): pp. 429–44.

— 'The future of the Falklands: A solution made in Hong Kong?', *International Affairs* 61 (1985): pp. 650–1.

— *The International Politics of Antarctica* (London, Croom Helm, 1986).

— *The Falkland Islands as an International Problem* (London, Routledge, 1988).

— 'Who owns Antarctica? Governing and Managing the Last Continent', *Boundary and Territory Briefing* (International Boundaries Research Unit, University of Durham, 1994).

— 'Argentina and Britain: the Antarctic dimension', in A. Hennessy and J. King (eds), *The Land that England Lost* (London, British Academic Press, 1992).

— *Scoring for Britain: International Football and International Politics 1900–1939* (London, Frank Cass, 1999)

Beer, G., 'The island and the aeroplane: The case of Virginia Woolf', in H. Bhabha (ed.), *Nation and Narration* (London, Routledge, 1991).

Beeves, B., 'Work of the FIDS', *The Crown Colonist* 18 (1948): pp. 613–15.

Biermann, H., 'The Republic of South Africa and the Southern Hemisphere', Occasional Paper (Centre for International Politics, University of Potchefstroom, 1973).

Bingham, E. W., 'Recent British activity in the Antarctic', *United Empire* 39 (1948): pp. 31–5.

Bishop, P., 'Reporting the Falklands', *Index on Censorship* 11 (1982): pp. 7–8.

Blanksten, G., *Perón's Argentina* (Chicago IL, University of Chicago Press, 1974).

Bloom, L., *Gender on the Ice: American Ideologies of Polar Exploration* (Minneapolis MN, University of Minnesota Press, 1994).

Bowen, E., 'The Welsh Colony in Patagonia 1865–1885', *Geographical Journal* 132 (1966): pp. 16–32.

Bowler, D., *Winning isn't Everything: A Biography of Sir Alf Ramsey* (London, Victor Gollancz, 1998).

Bowman, G., *From Scott to Fuchs* (London, Cox and Wyman, 1960).

'Britain and Argentina: Restoring Relations' (FCO background brief, March 1990).

Brothers, C., *War and Photography* (London, Routledge, 1997).

Brunt, D., 'The Halley Bay Expedition and the IGY', *The Royal Society IGY Antarctic Expedition Halley Bay, Coats Land, Falkland Islands Dependencies 1955–1959* (London, Royal Society, 1960), pp. 1–7.

Bullrich, C., *Falklands or Malvinas?* (Buenos Aires, Nuevohacer Grupo Editor Latinamerciano, 2000).

Callaghan, J., *Time and Chance* (London, HarperCollins, 1987).

Calvert, P., 'British relations with Southern Cone states', in M. Morris (ed.), *Great Power Relations in Argentina, Chile and Antarctica* (New York, St Martins Press, 1990).

Carr, J., *Another Story: Women and the Falklands War* (London, Croom Helm, 1984).

Carruthers, S., *The Media at War* (London, Macmillan, 2000).

Carse, D., 'The survey of South Georgia 1951–1957', *Geographical Journal* 125 (1959): pp. 20–37.

Casey, R., *Friends and Neighbours* (Sydney, Cheshire, 1954).

Charlton, M., *The Little Platoon: Diplomacy and the Falklands Dispute* (Oxford, Blackwell, 1989).

Chaturvedi, S., *The Polar Regions: A Political Geography* (Chichester, John Wiley, 1996).

'Chilean funeral for Antarctic minerals pact', *Nature* 348 (1990): p. 269.

Churchill, W., *A History of English Speaking Peoples* (London, Cassell, 1956).

Clapperton, C. and D. Sugden, *Scenery of the South: Falkland Islands, South Georgia, Sub-Antarctic Islands* (Aberdeen, St. George's Printing Works, 1975).

Clifford, M., 'FIDS', *Corona* 1 (1950): pp. 10–13.

Conil Paz, A. and G. Ferrari, *Argentina's Foreign Policy 1930–1962* (London, University of Notre Dame Press, 1966).

Cosentino, B., 'El valor estrategico de las Islas Malvinas', *Estrategia* 6 (1970): pp. 76–87.

Cosgrove, D. (ed.), 'Nuclear engineering and geography', *Ecumene* 5 (1998): pp. 263–322.

— *Apollo's Eye: A Cartographic Genealogy of the Earth in the Western Imagination* (Baltimore MD, John Hopkins University Press, 2001).

Coutau-Begarie, H., *Geostrategie de l'Atlantique Sud* (Paris, University of Paris Press, 1985).

Cromley, R., 'We're losing the Antarctic', *American Mercury* 87 (1958): pp. 5–11.

Cutts-Dougherty, K., M. Eisenhart and P. Webley, 'The role of social representations and national identities in the development of territorial knowledge: A study of political socialization in Argentina and England', *American Educational Research Journal* 29 (1992): pp. 809–32.

Dalglish, D., '2 years in the Antarctic', *St Thomas' Hospital Gazette* 2 (1952): pp. 62–5, 111–17.

Darwin, J., *Britain and Decolonization* (London, Macmillan, 1988).

Daus, F., *Geografia y Unidad Argentina* (Buenos Aires, El Ateneo, 1957).

Dawson, G., *Soldier Heroes: British Adventure, Empire and the Imagining of Masculinities* (London, Routledge, 1994).

de Hoyos, R., 'Malvinas/Falklands, 1982–1988: The new Gibraltar in the South Atlantic?', in P. Kelly and J. Child (eds), *Geopolitics of the Southern Cone and Antarctica* (Boulder CO, Lynne Rienner, 1988).

Debenham, F., '*Scott of the Antarctic*: A personal opinion', *Polar Record* 5 (1949): pp. 311–16.

— *Antarctica* (London, Herbert Jenkins, 1959).

Dijkink, G., 'Geopolitical codes and popular representations', *Geojournal* 46 (1998): pp. 293–9.

di Tella, G. and C. Watt (eds), *Argentina Between the Great Powers 1939–1946* (Pittsburgh PA, University of Pittsburgh Press, 1990).

Dockrill, M., *British Defence Since 1945* (Oxford, Blackwell, 1989).

Dodd, P., *The Battle over Britain* (London, Demos, 1995).

Dodds, K., 'Geopolitics in the Foreign Office: British representations of Argentina 1945–1962', *Transactions of the Institute of British Geographers* 19 (1994): pp. 273–91.

— 'The end of a Polar empire? The Falkland Islands Dependencies and Commonwealth reactions to British Polar policy 1945–1962', *Journal of Imperial and Commonwealth History* 24 (1996): pp. 392–421.

— *Geopolitics in Antarctica: Views from the Southern Oceanic Rim* (London, John Wiley, 1997).

— 'Enframing the Falklands: Identity, landscape and the 1982 South Atlantic War', *Environment and Planning D: Society and Space* 16 (1998): pp. 733–56.

— 'Screening Antarctica: Britain, the Falkland Islands Dependencies Survey and *Scott of the Antarctic* (1948)', *Polar Record* 34 (2002): pp. 1–10.

Dodds, K. and D. Atkinson (eds), *Geopolitical Traditions* (London, Routledge, 2000).

Dodds, K. and L. Manovil, 'A common space? The Falklands/Malvinas and a new geopolitics of the South Atlantic', *Geopolitics* 6 (2001): pp. 99–126.

Dresser, M., 'Britannia', in R. Samuel (ed.), *Patriotism* (London, Allen and Unwin, 1989).

Driver, F. and D. Gilbert, 'Heart of Empire? Landscape, space and performance in imperial London', *Environment and Planning D: Society and Space* 16 (1998): pp. 11–28.

Drower, G., *Britain's Dependent Territories: A Fistful of Islands* (Aldershot, Dartmouth, 1992).

Economic Survey of the Falkland Islands (London, Economist Intelligence Unit, 1976).

Edney, M., *Mapping an Empire: The Geographical Construction of British India 1765–1843* (Chicago IL, University of Chicago Press, 1997).

Ellerby, C., *British Interests in the Falkland Islands: Economic Development, the Falklands Lobby and the Sovereignty Dispute 1945–1989* (Unpublished DPhil thesis, University of Oxford, 1990).

Ellerby, C., 'The role of the Falklands lobby 1968–1990', in A. Danchev (ed.), *A Matter of Life and Death* (Oxford, Oxford University Press, 1992).

Elliot, L., 'Environmental protection in the Antarctic: problems and prospects', *Environmental Politics* 3 (1994): pp. 247–72.

Escolar, M., Quintero S. Palacios and C. Reboratti, 'Geographical identity and patriotic representation in Argentina', in D. Hooson (ed.), *Geography and National Identity* (Oxford, Blackwell, 1994).

Escude, C., 'Argentine territorial nationalism', *Journal of Latin American Studies* 20 (1988): pp. 139–65.

— *El Fracaso del Proyecto Argentino* (Buenos Aires, Instituto de Torcuato Di Tella, 1990).

— 'Education, public culture and foreign policy: The case of Argentina', Working Paper (Latin American Studies Program, Duke University, 1992).

Ferns, H., 'Britain's informal empire in Argentina', *Past and Present* 4 (1954): pp. 60–75.

— *Argentina* (London, Ernest Benn, 1969).

— 'Argentina: Part of an informal empire?', in A. Hennessy and J. King (eds), *The Land that England Lost* (London, British Academic Press, 1992).

Fleming, F., *Ninety Degrees North: The Quest for the North Pole* (London, Granta, 2001).

Focus International Britain and Antarctica (London, FCO, March 2000).

Fogg, C., *A History of Antarctic Science* (Cambridge, Cambridge University Press, 1992).

Forrest, T., 'Brazil and Africa: geopolitics, trade and technology in the South Atlantic', *African Affairs* 81 (1982): pp. 3–21.

Freedman, L., *Britain and the Falklands War* (Oxford, Blackwell, 1988).

Freedman, L. and V. Gamba-Stonehouse, *Signals of War* (London, Faber and Faber, 1990).

Fuchs, V., 'The FIDS 1948–1950', *Journal of the Royal Society of Arts* 4866 (1951): pp. 193–211.

— *Scientific Reports No 1: Organization and Methods* (London, HMSO, 1953).

— 'The Crossing of Antarctica', *National Geographic* CXV (1959): pp. 25–47.

— *Of Ice and Men* (Oswestry, Anthony Nelson, 1982).

— *A Time to Speak* (Oswestry, Anthony Nelson, 1990).

Fuchs, V. and E. Hillary, *The Crossing of Antarctica* (London, Cassell, 1958).

Fussell, P., *Wartime* (Oxford, Clarendon Press, 1989).

Gavshon, A. and D. Rice, *The Sinking of the Belgrano* (London, Secker and Warburg, 1984).

Gibson-Edwin, T. and T. Kingsley-Ward, *Courage Remembered* (London, HMSO, 1989).

Gilroy, P., *There ain't no Black in the Union Jack* (London, Hutchinson, 1987).

Girouard, M., *The Return of Camelot* (London, Yale University Press, 1981).

Glasgow University Media Group, *Industry, Economy, War and Politics* (London, Routledge, 1992).

Graham-Yooll, A., *Goodbye Buenos Aires* (Nottingham, Shoestring Press, 1999).

Gravil, R., *The Anglo–Argentine Connection 1900–1939* (Boulder CO, Westview, 1985).

Guglialmelli, J., *Geopolitica del Cono Sur* (Buenos Aires, El Cid, 1983, 3rd ed.).

— 'La crisis Argentina: una perspectiva geopolitica', *Estrategia* 73/74 (1983): pp. 9–30.

Gurr, A., *A Little Piece of England* (London, Blake Publishing, 2001).

Hansen, P., 'Confetti of empire: The conquest of Everest in Nepal, India, Britain and New Zealand', *Comparative Study of Society and History* XX (2000): pp. 307–32.

Harper, S. and V. Porter, 'Cinema, audience tastes in 1950s Britain', *Journal of Popular British Cinema* 2 (1999): pp. 66–82.

Harris, R., *Gotcha! The Media, the Government and the Falklands* (London, Unwin, 1988).

Hastings, M. and S. Jenkins, *The Battle for the Falklands* (London, Michael Joseph, 1983).

Hattersley-Smith, G., 'King George Island', *Alpine Journal*, 58 (1951): pp. 67–75.

Heap, J., 'Dr Brian Roberts CMG', in H. King and A. Savours (eds), *Polar Pundit: Reminiscences about Brian Birley Roberts* (Cambridge, Cambridge University Press, 1995).

— 'The Treaty and the Protocol', in G. Mudge (ed.), *Antarctica: The Environment and Future* (Geneva, International Academy of the Environment and International Peace Research Institute, 1998).

Hennessy, A., *The Frontier in Latin American History* (London, Edward Arnold, 1978).

Hennessy, P., *The Prime Minister: The Office and its Holders Since 1945* (London, Allen Lane, 2000).

Hepple, L., 'The geopolitics of the Falklands/Malvinas and the South Atlantic: British and Argentine perceptions, misperceptions and rivalries', in P. Kelly and

J.Child (eds), *Geopolitics of the Southern Cone and Antarctica* (Boulder CO, Lynne Rienner, 1988).

Hernandez, P. and H.Chitarroni, *Malvinas: Clave Geopolitica* (Buenos Aires, Castaneda, 1977).

Hickey, J. 'Keep the Falklands British? The principle of self-determination of dependent territories', *Inter-American Economic Affairs* 31 (1977): pp.77–88.

Hobsbawm, E. and T.Ranger (eds), *The Invention of Tradition* (Cambridge, Cambridge University Press, 1983).

Howells, G., 'The British press and the Peróns', in A.Hennessy and J.King (eds), *The Land that England Lost* (London, British Academic Press, 1992).

Hunt, R., *My Falkland Days* (Exeter, David and Charles, 1992).

Hunter Christie, W., *The Antarctic Problem* (London, George Unwin, 1951).

Huntsford, R., *Shackleton* (London, Abacus, 2000).

Hutchinson, R., *It Is Now! The Real Story of England's 1966 World Cup Triumph* (London, Mainstream Publishing, 1993).

Illingworth, F., 'Scramble for Antarctica', *New Commonwealth* (23 November 1953).

Ingham, B., *Kill the Messenger* (London, HarperCollins, 1992).

Jacobs, J., *Edge of Empire* (London, Routledge, 1996).

James, D., Scott of the Antarctic: *The Film and its Production* (London, Convoy Productions, 1948).

Jones, M., 'Our king upon his knees: The public commemoration of Captain Scott's last Antarctic expedition', in G.Cubitt and A.Warren (eds), *Heroic Reputations and Exemplary Lives* (Manchester, Manchester University Press, 2000).

Keogh, D., 'Argentina and the Falklands: The Irish connection', in A.Hennessy and J.King (eds), *The Land that England Lost* (London, British Academic Press, 1992).

King, H. and S.Savours (eds), *Polar Pundit* (Cambridge, Cambridge University Press, 1995).

Kirwan, L., 'Polar exploration in the last twenty years', *Geographical Magazine* 32 (1959): pp.355–64.

Klotz, F., *America on the Ice: American Policy Issues* (Washington DC, National Defense University Press, 1990).

Knape, J., 'Anglo–American rivalry in post-war Latin America: The question of arms sales', *Ibero-Amerikanisches Archiv* 15 (1989): pp.318–50.

Knightley, P., 'Managing the media in wartime', *Index of Censorship* 11 (1982): p.7.

Labra, O., *Chilenos en la Antartida* (Santiago, Direccion General de Informaciones y Cultura, 1947).

Law, P., *Antarctic Odyssey* (Melbourne, Heinemann, 1983).

Lefebvre, H., *The Production of Space* (Oxford, Blackwell, 1998).

Lewis, C., 'Anglo–Argentine trade 1945–1965', in D.Rock (ed.), *Argentina in the Twentieth Century* (London, Duckworth, 1975).

Lewis, C., *British Railways in Argentina 1857–1914* (London, Athlone Press, 1983).

Low, D., *The Eclipse of Empire* (Cambridge, Cambridge University Press, 1991).

Lyons, D., 'Environmental impact assessment in Antarctica under the protocol of environmental protection', *Polar Record* 29 (1993): pp.111–20.

MacDonald, C., 'End of empire: The decline of the Anglo–Argentine connection 1918–1951', in A.Hennessy and J.King (eds), *The Land that England Lost* (London, British Academic Press, 1992).

Macintosh, N., 'The fifth commission of the RRS *Discovery II*', *Geographical Journal* XCVII (1941): pp. 201–16.

McCannon, J., 'To storm the Arctic: Soviet polar exploration and public visions of nature in the USSR 1932–1939', *Ecumene* 2 (1995): pp. 15–31.

McIlvanney, H. (ed.), *World Cup '66* (London, Eyre and Spottiswoode, 1966).

Madeley, J., *Diego Garcia: A contrast to the Falklands* (London, Minority Rights Group Report, 1985).

Manzo, K., *Creating Boundaries: The Politics of Race and Nation* (London, Lynne Rienner, 1996).

Marquis, M., *Anatomy of a Football Manager: Sir Alf Ramsey* (London, Arthur Barker, 1970).

Marwick, A., *A History of the Modern British Isles* (Oxford, Blackwell, 2000).

Mason, D., 'The FIDS: Explorations of 1947–1948', *Geographical Journal* CXV (1950): pp. 145–60.

Mason, T., *Passion of the People? Football in Latin America* (London, Verso, 1995).

Mawby, S., 'Britain's last imperial frontier: The Aden Protectorates 1952–1959', *Journal of Imperial and Commonwealth History* 29 (2001): pp.75–100.

Mayes, H., *The Football Association's World Cup Report 1966* (London, William Heinemann, 1967).

Milia, F. (ed.), *La Atlantartida: Un Espacio Geopolitico* (Buenos Aires, Editorial Pleamar, 1978).

'Miners vote to plunder the treasures of Antarctica', *New Scientist* (28 January 1988), p. 28.

Morgan, K., *Callaghan: A Life* (Oxford, Oxford University Press, 1997).

Mott, P., 'Airborne surveying in the Antarctic', *Geographical Journal* CXXIV (1958): pp. 1–17.

— *Wings Over Ice* (Exeter, Wheaton, 1986).

Munro, R., *Place Names and the Falkland Islands* (London, Shackleton Trust Fund, 1999).

Murray, W., *Football: A History of the World Game* (Aldershot, Scolar Press, 1994).

Myhre, J., *The Antarctic Treaty System: Politics, Law and Diplomacy* (Boulder CO, Westview, 1986).

The British Antarctic Survey: Management of Major Capital Projects and Scientific Programmes (National Audit Office, London, HMSO, 1989).

Ommanney, F., *South Latitude* (London, Longman, 1938).

Ó Tuathail, G., *Critical Geopolitics* (London, Routledge, 1996).

Ó Tuathail, G. and S. Dalby (eds), *Rethinking Geopolitics* (London, Routledge, 1998).

Owen, D., *Human Rights* (London, Jonathan Cape, 1977).

— *A Time to Declare* (London, Michael Joseph, 1991).

Partnership for Progress and Prosperity: Britain and the Overseas Territories (London, HMSO, 1999).

Paul, K., *Whitewashing Britain: Race and Citizenship in the Post-War Era* (London, Cornell University Press, 1994).

Phythian, M., *The Politics of British Arms Sales Since 1964* (Manchester, Manchester University Press, 2000).

Pion-Berlin, D., *The Ideology of State Terror* (Boulder CO, Lynne Rienner, 1989).

Platt, D. (ed.), *Business Imperialism 1840–1930* (Oxford, Oxford University Press, 1977).

Ponting, C., *The Right to Know* (London, Sphere Books, 1985).

Pyne, S., *The Ice: A Journey to Antarctica* (Seattle WA, University of Washington Press, 1992).

Raban, J., *Coasting* (London, Collins Harvill, 1986).

Richards, J., *Films and British National Identity* (Manchester, Manchester University Press, 1997).

Roberts, J., 'The FIDS', *British Medical Journal* 15 (1949): pp. 863–4.

Roger Louis, W. and R. Robinson, 'The imperialism of decolonization', *Journal of Imperial and Commonwealth History* 22 (1994): pp. 462–511.

Ronne, F., *Antarctic Conquest* (New York, G.P. Putnam and Sons, 1949).

Rymill, J., *Southern Lights* (London, Chatto and Windus, 1938).

Scalabrini Ortiz, R., *Historia de los Ferrocarriles Argentina* (Buenos Aires, Reconquista, 1940).

— *Politica Britanica en el Rio de la Plata* (Buenos Aires, Reconquista, 1940).

Schneer, J., *London 1900: The Imperial Metropolis* (London, Yale University Press, 1999).

Shaw, T., *British Cinema and the Cold War* (London, I.B. Tauris, 2001).

Shipman, D., *The Story of Cinema Volume 2* (London, Hodder and Stoughton, 1984).

Smith, A.M., *New Right Discourse on Race and Sexuality 1968–1990* (Minneapolis MN, University of Minnesota Press, 1994).

Smith, J., *74 Days: Islander's Diary of the Falklands Occupation* (London, Century, 1984).

Soloman, S., *The Coldest March: Scott's Fatal Antarctic Expedition* (New Haven CT, Yale University Press, 2001).

Solomos, J., *Race and Racism in Contemporary Britain* (London, Macmillan, 1989).

Song, Y-H., 'The British 150-mile fishery conservation and management zone around the Falkland (Malvinas) Islands', *Political Geography Quarterly* 7 (1988): pp. 183–96.

Spufford, F., *'I may be some time': Ice and the English Imagination* (London, Faber and Faber, 1996).

Sullivan, W., *Quest for a Continent* (New York, McGraw-Hill, 1957).

Taylor, P,. *Britain and the Cold War: 1945 as Geopolitical Transition* (London, Pinter, 1990).

Templeton, M., *A Wise Adventure: New Zealand and the Antarctic 1923–1960* (Wellington, Victoria University Press, 2001).

Thatcher, M., *The Downing Street Years* (London, HarperCollins, 1993).

The Falklands Campaign: A Digest of Debates in the House of Commons 2nd April–15th June 1982 (London, HMSO, 1982).

The Franks Report: Falkland Island Review (London, HMSO, 1983).

Tinker, D., *A Message from the Falklands: The Life and Death of David Tinker Lieut. RN: From his Letters and Poems* (London, Junction Books, 1982).

'Trans Antarctic epic', *BP Magazine* 34 (1958): pp. 22–3.

Tulchin, J., *Argentina and the United States: A Conflicted Relationship* (Boston MA, Twayne Publishers, 1990).

Vansittart, P., *In the Fifties* (London, John Murray, 1995).

Vaughan-Williams, U., *RVW* (Oxford, Oxford University Press, 1964).

Verrier, A., *Through the Looking Glass* (London, Jonathan Cape, 1983).

— 'The quarter in Britain', *Sight and Sound* 18 (1949): pp. 49–50.

Vidas, D. (ed.), *Implementing the Environmental Protection Regime for the Antarctic* (Dordrecht, Kluwer Academic Publishers, 2001).

Wall, P. (ed.), *The Indian Ocean and the Threat to the West* (London, Stacey International, 1975).

Wallace, W., 'Foreign policy and national identity in the UK', *International Affairs* 67 (1991): pp. 65–80.

Walton, D. (ed.), *Antarctic Science* (Cambridge, Cambridge University Press, 1987).

Weston, S., *Walking Tall* (London, Bloomsbury, 1989).

Williams, G., *The Desert and the Dream: A study of Welsh colonization of Chubut 1865–1915* (Cardiff, University of Wales Press, 1965).

— 'Welsh settler and native Americans in Patagonia', *Journal of Latin American Studies* 11 (1979): pp. 41–66.

Wordie, J., 'The FIDS 1943–1946', *Polar Record* 32 (1946): pp. 372–84.

Young, H., *One of Us* (London, Macmillan, 1990).

Ziegler, P., *Wilson* (London, Weidenfeld and Nicholson, 1993).

INDEX